Inventing
Philosophy's
Other

Inventing Philosophy's Other

Phenomenology in America

Jonathan Strassfeld

The University of Chicago Press
Chicago and London

The University of Chicago Press, Chicago 60637
The University of Chicago Press, Ltd., London
© 2022 by The University of Chicago

Published 2022
Printed in the United States of America

31 30 29 28 27 26 25 24 23 22   1 2 3 4 5

ISBN-13: 978-0-226-82157-3 (cloth)
ISBN-13: 978-0-226-82159-7 (paper)
ISBN-13: 978-0-226-82158-0 (e-book)
DOI: https://doi.org/10.7208/chicago/9780226821580.001.0001

Library of Congress Cataloging-in-Publication Data

Names: Strassfeld, Jonathan, author.
Title: Inventing philosophy's other : phenomenology in America /
    Jonathan Strassfeld.
Description: Chicago : University of Chicago Press, 2022. |
    Includes bibliographical references and index.
Identifiers: LCCN 2022008945 | ISBN 9780226821573 (cloth) |
    ISBN 9780226821597 (paperback) | ISBN 9780226821580 (ebook)
Subjects: LCSH: Phenomenology—Study and teaching—
    United States.
Classification: LCC B829.5 .S754 2022 | DDC 142/.7—dc23/
    eng/20220307
LC record available at https://lccn.loc.gov/2022008945

♾ This paper meets the requirements of ANSI/NISO Z39.48-1992
(Permanence of Paper).

Contents

Introduction

The schism of professional philosophy into distinct discourses—analytic and Continental philosophy—was a defining event in twentieth-century intellectual history. Even in a discipline prone to stark division, the analytic-Continental divide was an exceptional case. Philosophical disagreements typically lead to dispute and debate—tracts and tomes of savage critique and rebuttal. By comparison, the analytic-Continental divide was a gulf of neglect across which most philosophers ignored one another, breaking their silence only occasionally to shout invective into the chasm.

The "Continental" side of this landscape was occupied by followers of various nineteenth- and twentieth-century philosophical schools, methods, and traditions, ranging from Hegelianism to poststructuralism and the Frankfurt School. At the center of this constellation of ideas was phenomenology—a philosophy of experience first described by Edmund Husserl and subsequently developed by others such as Martin Heidegger, Jean-Paul Sartre, and Maurice Merleau-Ponty. Phenomenology explores the domain of *human* life, denying its objectification while resisting subjectivistic relativism by starting from what is immediately given in experience and disallowing all metaphysical constructions and presuppositions. From its modest origins in Göttingen at the dawn of the twentieth century, the phenomenological movement spread from Germany and Austria to France, Italy, and Spain. By midcentury, it had become one of continental Europe's most fecund wellsprings of novel humanistic thought, flowing into both secular and religious discourse, and a growing influence on philosophers in Latin America and parts of Asia.

In postwar America, however, analytic philosophy dominated university philosophy departments. As advances in symbolic logic made it possible to formalize procedures for determining an argument's validity, analysts attempted to liberate philosophy from the pseudoproblems and paradoxes that arose from linguistic ambiguity. While high hopes that philosophy could eliminate disagreement simply by providing tools for clarifying language quickly faded, the techniques and methods that analytic philosophers developed were successful at articulating a shared space of problems within which a community of philosophers could conduct research. Here, the implications of fundamental questions such as the relation of linguistic propositions to the entities they described and the meaning of terms like *possibility* and *necessity* captured the interest of American philosophers. Through a commitment to clarity and respect for the methods and evidence of empirical sciences, American philosophers secured acceptance of their ancient discipline within the modern research university. Continental philosophy, by contrast, was dismissed by its critics as inimical to American sensibilities and the empiricist ethos of modern scientific understanding.

During the second half of the twentieth century, phenomenologists were scantly represented in most American philosophy departments. At some institutions, American undergraduates remain more likely to encounter Continental philosophy as "theory" in disciplines such as anthropology and comparative literature than as "philosophy" in a setting where it is taught by philosophers. However, the postwar marginalization of this tradition belies a richer and more complex history of the phenomenological movement in the United States. Phenomenology had an important and attentive American audience nearly from its inception. The phenomenological movement was the subject of sustained interest at Harvard University during the first half of the twentieth century, and the immigration of refugee philosophers to the United States during the 1930s and 1940s brought some of its foremost figures to American shores. Given this background, Continental philosophy's striking absence from American philosophy departments is a puzzle that demands explanation.

This work traces the phenomenological movement's development in the United States, charting the patterns of its reception and evaluating the experiences of those who embraced it. Going further, it examines the movement's postwar struggles, showing how the emergence of "Continental philosophy"—a category that stipulated phenomenology's otherness—reflected the dynamics of institutional hierarchies, a new understanding of America's relationship to Europe, and the causally distant repercussions of structural changes to American academia. Finally, in recovering the overlooked history of American phenomenology, it offers a corrective to Whiggish and triumphalist narratives that claim, simply, that analytic philosophy won out because it was better philosophy practiced by the better philosophers. In this, I take particular inspiration from historians of science such as Peter Galison, whose study of the material culture of laboratories demonstrates the site-specific logics of disciplinary development. By applying these critical tools to the history of phenomenology in America, my work explores how everyday administrative needs and institutional structures are inscribed in regimes of knowledge, even in a field as seemingly detached from the material and quotidian as philosophy.

∗   ∗   ∗

Although mine is the first systematic historical study of phenomenology in the United States, the new ground it charts sits within a significant and growing historiography. The pioneering work of historical scholarship on the professionalization of philosophy in the twentieth century is Bruce Kuklick's *Rise of American Philosophy*.[1] I owe a tremendous intellectual debt to this monograph on Harvard's Philosophy Department, which demonstrates that the logic of formal thought's development in America implicates the relationship of philosophers to the institutions through which philosophy was practiced and shows that quantitative techniques can be used effectively by intellectual historians. *Converts to the Real* (2019) by Edward Baring is another important companion to my work, providing a revealing counterpoint to my study of phenomenology's development in America by charting its spread in Europe through the institutional and intellectual networks of the Catholic Church.[2] Several other historical monographs have also been written on aspects of phenomenology's reception in the United States: George Cotkin's *Existential America* (2003), Ann Fulton's *Apostles of Sartre* (1999), and Martin Woessner's *Heidegger in America* (2011).[3] However, the American reception of Husserlian phenomenology during the first half of the twentieth century has gone virtually unnoticed by historians. Recovering the lost early history and foundational activities of the phenomenological movement in the United States, this work invites a reevaluation of its subsequent development, trajectory, and potential.

Invariably, a history of phenomenology in America must situate its reception within the broader history of the division between analytic and Continental philosophies. Here, too, I am able to build on the admirable work of Peter Gordon's *Continental Divide* (2010) and Michael Friedman's *A Parting of the Ways* (2000), which challenge the often-presupposed incommensurability of these philosophical traditions by stressing their common origins.[4] My research reveals the persistence of opportunities for philosophical engagement between these traditions, particularly on the American shores to which a significant number of Husserl and Heidegger's followers fled between 1933 and 1941. Reconsidering the story of the analytic-Continental divide from this side of the Atlantic, I show how the institutional structure of academic philosophy in the United States limited representation of phenomenologists during the second half of the twentieth century and gave new meaning to the concept of "Continental" philosophy.

This work is also a response to the challenge, raised at the 1977 Wingspread Conference, that intellectual historians ground their interpretations of thought in rigorous social analysis of its production and reception.[5] The subject of this study presents a peculiar evidentiary and explanatory challenge because my story is, in important respects, the history of an absence: the story of why certain texts and ideas failed to interest most American philosophers. The methods I have developed to explain what *did not happen* shape this work. Historians employ various techniques for understanding the reception of works and ideas. We may, for instance, look for their imprint on the writing of others, examine the process of their publication, and trace their transmission in the catalogs of libraries and private collections. Yet, such evidence is unavailable when we study works that were largely ignored and attempt to understand why they did not receive attention.

Conventional wisdom tells us that the Continental tradition occupied a marginal position within American academic philosophy during most of the twentieth century. Although this judgment largely withstands scrutiny, the ease with which it is asserted belies ambiguities that become apparent when the phenomenological movement is made the subject of historical inquiry. For instance, before we begin looking for evidence of marginalization, we must clarify whether marginality is intended as the predicate of a set of ideas or a group of scholars. In the first formulation, the question asks why many American philosophers ignored a body of contemporary German and French works that their peers on the European continent considered to be of premier importance. This story combines aspects of absence and presence. While phenomenology and Continental philosophy were ignored or shunned by most mainstream American philosophers, their influence within other disciplines of the American academy was significant. As phenomenologically influenced "theory" (such as deconstruction and poststructuralism) came into vogue outside the discipline of philosophy during the 1960s and 1970s, phenomenology became an absent presence within philosophy, marking the limits of the discipline.

In the question's second formulation, it asks us to consider the experience and position of scholars in America who *did* emphasize these topics.

Here, marginality is expressed in the limited representation of Continental philosophy on the faculties of mainstream American philosophy departments and the growth of alternative communities dedicated to phenomenology and Continental philosophy that were largely disconnected from the discipline's elite institutions. To be clear, the categories of "elite" and "marginal," which I will use throughout this work, do not signify the virtues of either group; they refer to relations of power, access, exclusivity, and prestige within a concrete historical situation. Unsurprisingly, the marginality of phenomenological ideas and phenomenological philosophers are inextricably interlinked. I will argue generally for the priority of social factors, situating the ideology of the divide's success within the stratified institutional dynamics of professional philosophy in America. However, it is ultimately by understanding the interchange and elective affinities between these levels of explanation that we achieve the greatest historical insight.

Although it is normally a small portion of their curricula, most philosophy departments do offer some course or courses on the thought of Heidegger, Sartre, and other Continental philosophers. Likewise, although they are a minority within the profession, a significant number of American philosophers work within the Continental tradition; moreover, there are a significant number of departments in which Continental philosophy is a primary research focus. The marginality of these ideas and thinkers, therefore, reflects a relationship different from outright exclusion. It is an expression of the gradients of power and influence among scholars and ideas respectively that exist along the malleable topography of a discourse. To chart this topography, I have turned to tools honed by social historians and, particularly, the methods of community studies. Classic works in the field, such as Paul Johnson's *A Shopkeeper's Millennium,* used quantitative analysis to examine the demography and experiences of groups whose membership was defined by shared locality. Because local archives provided rich and comprehensive information on these communities, historians were able to rigorously analyze and explain relationships between society, culture, and experience. However, the easy mobility of persons and ideas during the twentieth century allowed for the formation of communities that were socially and intellectually cohesive despite being geographically disparate. Because technology now permits distant access to archival and human sources, the study of these communities has become possible. Using quantitative techniques to analyze hiring and promotion, this works draws on demographic data from an elite stratum of American philosophical institutions to identify the sources of their cohesiveness and explain how analysis emerged as their de facto program during the second half of the twentieth century.

Marx's exhortation to substitute action for philosophy aside, the professional philosopher is a worker whose productive labor is objectified in the texts she publishes. The logic of philosophical discourse is, of course, different from the logic of capitalist production in several respects. Most important, an approximation of precapitalist apprenticeship replaces the division between labor and capital within the humanistic departments of the academy. It is also worth considering that the form of activity that defines the capitalist mode of production, M-C-M—the expenditure of capital for the purpose of selling a purchased commodity at a higher price—does not occur in a "marketplace of ideas."[6] Unlike the money form of value, which the capitalist cyclically reinvests to improve production, the scholar cannot use the recognition of her peers to think more or better ideas. Rather, hierarchies among academic institutions organize the discipline to provide professional benefits to those who are deemed successful by their peers. A work's success is coin that buys its author access to larger markets and conditions of employment that favor research and scholarship. However, like the fetishized commodity, the *social relations* between philosophers that circumscribe the production of philosophical works are obscured by the meritocratic value ascribed to their discursive success, which appears as an *intellectual* relation. Demystifying the practice of philosophy therefore requires a critique of the relationship between the social organization of philosophers—between one another and within the university—and the intellectual history of their ideas. Yet, a system of social relations does not persist by simple inertia, but must instead be continually *reproduced*, renewing both the material capacities it requires and a framework of beliefs and practices that legitimates its organization and distribution. Therefore, this work focuses particularly on the sites dedicated to the reproduction of philosophy and philosophers, seeking an understand of how these engender, in Louis Althusser's words, the "reproduction of [their] submission to the rules of the established order."[7]

* * *

This work is structured by two distinct organizational schemata: a sequence of narrative chapters and a set of exegetical and biographical chapters. The narrative chapters proceed chronologically, broadly exploring the structure and development of philosophy as a discipline in the United States and examining the reception of phenomenology within it. Beginning from phenomenology's reception at Harvard during the first decades of the twentieth century (chapter 2), these chapters chart the phenomenological movement's American trajectory through the immigration of European refugees to the United States during the 1930s and 1940s (chapter 3), the postwar institutional transformation of American universities (chapter 4), the emergence of "Continental philosophy" as a concept that organized the intellectual landscape of the postwar era (chapter 5), and its development within a network of heterodox institutions outside the mainstream American philosophical establishment (chapter 6). Although it is primarily exegetical in content, chapter 1, which introduces the philosophy of Edmund Husserl, Martin Heidegger, Jean-Paul Sartre, and Maurice Merleau-Ponty, is included in the narrative scheme because it provides background that nonspecialists may require to understand phenomenology's philosophical significance and continuing development in America. The exegetical and biographical chapters each examine a significant figure within the American phenomenological movement: Marjorie Glicksman Grene, Alfred Schütz, Hubert Dreyfus, and Iris Marion Young. These interludes are branches from the narrative trunk, which focus on ideas and experiences that may be obscured by the logic of social history. They highlight the remarkable originality of phenomenologists as unremitting and persuasive dissenters in a period of American intellectual history dominated by mechanistic scientism. Considering the movement's development as both a discourse with its own internal logic and a shared project that philosophers undertook out of various personal commitments, these chapters rebut those who would dismiss them as thinkers of little intellectual interest and show what phenomenology meant to its American practitioners.

I see the marginalization of phenomenology in postwar American philosophy as a lost opportunity. During the second half of the twentieth century, unparalleled power and prestige were granted to technocratic experts who believed that models and measurements could provide objective answers to all meaningful questions about human life and society. From systems analysis and neoliberal reform to public choice theory and Rawlsian justice, Western discourse was dominated by reductive theories that derived authority from their claim to distill away the impurities of subjective experience from the grist of objective analysis.[8] Against this, phenomenology provided the foundation for humanistic methodologies that allowed scholars in a range of fields to challenge the nearly irresistible clout of epistemic regimes patterned on the practices and style of natural science. Its neglect by American philosophers was a significant retreat from their discipline's traditional, and once vital, role as a mediator between different regimes of knowledge.

Although I am critical of the attitudes of condescension or contempt some mainstream American philosophers effected toward their Continental counterparts, I do not believe that the analytic tradition, which remains dominant in the United States, is an unworthy or inferior philosophical program. Neither do I claim that the most important works of twentieth-century American philosophy were written by the relatively small group of phenomenologists who situated their careers in the United States. Quite clearly, most of the most brilliant philosophical writings from postwar America are exemplars of the analytic tradition, many of them flavored by pragmatism's subsumed influence. However, across the Atlantic, the opposite was true. Because I have attempted to explain the American side of this dynamic, those with the greatest agency in my story are members of the analytic mainstream. It follows that many of the institutions and individuals that contributed to American philosophy's disciplinary division most significantly were as well. However, I want to preemptively admonish against inferring that analytic philosophy is, per se, narrow or flawed, or that Continental philosophy exhibits virtues opposite these vices. Left to another historian is the project of examining the history of analytic philosophy in postwar Europe. This scholar will, I expect, find many occasions to fault the practices of Continental philosophers and European academic institutions. After all, the enmity across the analytic-Continental divide was mutual and, in my view, detrimental to both traditions. Indeed, until it can be considered alongside the history of analytic philosophy in Europe, the history of phenomenology in America will remain unfinished. Nevertheless, it is my hope that, incomplete as it is, this effort to show the initial promise of phenomenology in the United States and the historical contingency of the events that effected its marginalization will further the cause of reconciliation and establish phenomenology's vital salience to the American intellectual tradition.

1

Understanding
Phenomenology

Phenomenology in general may be characterized as a philosophy which
has learned to wonder again and to respect wonders for what they are in
themselves, where others see only trivialities or occasions to employ the
cleaning brush.
—Herbert Spiegelberg

To Edmund Husserl, phenomenology was a rigorous science that returned
"to the 'things themselves.'" Raymond Aron explained to Jean-Paul Sartre
that a phenomenologist "can talk about [a] cocktail and make philosophy
out of it." In Martin Heidegger's words, phenomenology aims to "let that
which shows itself be seen from itself in the very way in which it shows
itself from itself."[1] Those who are satisfied with the clarity and sufficiency
of these remarks may skip to the next chapter. To all others, perhaps confused and increasingly skeptical of phenomenology, I am pleased to report
that you have attained a personal familiarity with the affective register in
which most American philosophers engaged this mouthful of a movement
during the latter half of the twentieth century. To many, phenomenology
was at once banal and esoteric; both a glib eschewal of philosophical rigor
and a jargon-filled obscurity, likely born of obscurantism. Such prejudices, which both shaped and reflected the problem of phenomenology's
reception, are an important element of the story that will follow. For this
chapter's duration, however, I will set aside the American theme and ask
you to suspend your presuppositions so that I can clarify what, exactly,
phenomenology is.

What follows is a brief introduction to the phenomenological writings of Edmund Husserl, Martin Heidegger, Jeal-Paul Sartre, and Maurice
Merleau-Ponty. Of course, the scope and diversity of the phenomenological tradition cannot be captured by discussing four of its canonical
figures. Even if it could, this brief survey leaves most of their own work
untouched, focusing on organizing principles and basics of methodology.

Nevertheless, I am presenting phenomenology in this way because Husserl, Heidegger, Sartre, and Merleau-Ponty became the four cardinal poles of phenomenological discourse: transcendental phenomenology, hermeneutic phenomenology, existential phenomenology, and embodied phenomenology. While there are significant divisions within these traditions as well as overlapping spheres of influence among their constituencies, nearly every twentieth-century phenomenologist located his or her work within the methodological and thematic projects these poles organized. Thus, this introduction serves both as a general map of the phenomenological movement's intellectual geography and an introduction to the problems and techniques that American phenomenologists brought to diverse environments throughout the United States. More than this, however, I hope this technical preamble engenders an appreciation of the phenomenological movement's distinctiveness, fecundity, and urgent sense of purpose, setting the stakes of the struggle to establish it in the United States both historically and for its adherents.

* * *

There is no common credo, list of propositions, or methodological device that, if accepted, identifies a philosopher as a phenomenologist. Yet, as a way of doing philosophy, phenomenology has a distinctive character that makes its adherents recognizable. In this way, the corpus of phenomenological philosophy finds, if not unity, a coherent theme in its focus on life as it is lived as a source of philosophical knowledge, its archaeological approach to identifying and describing what makes experience what it is, and the application of this inquiry's results in grounding the various branches of philosophy and extraphilosophical disciplines of knowledge.

Although the term *phenomenology* has been used differently in various contexts, the term *phenomenological movement* designates a distinct philosophical tradition, originating in the work of Edmund Husserl. Born in 1859, the same year as the American philosopher John Dewey, Husserl's earliest phenomenological writings were published during 1900/01 in a two-volume treatise he titled *Logische Untersuchungen* (*Logical Investigations*). The work is a rebuttal to the doctrine of "psychologism," an influential German philosophy that holds "psychological processes," such as abstraction and combination, to be the foundation of logic.[2] Contingent facts of psychology, Husserl argued, could not guarantee the certainty of logical truth; only a pure *a priori* logic of formal concepts would be sufficient to ground mathematics and, ultimately, the broader domain of apodictic knowledge Husserl sought.[3] The pure logic of Husserl's early phenomenological investigations was a theory of theories: a foundational framework from which all theoretical knowledge might be derived. Disciplines such as ethics, chemistry, and sociology, in this schema, describe "regional ontologies," bound by the laws of pure logic but differentiated by the subject matter that defines the objects and rules of their domain. The task of identifying and rigorously describing the entities of a particular domain fell to disciplinary specialists. However, phenomenology would fulfill the special role of a "first philosophy," investigating the ideal concepts of pure logic that dictate the form of and relations between all possible legitimate theories and disciplines.[4]

To become a "first philosophy" or "rigorous science," the phenomenological project could not begin, as other sciences might, on a foundation of abstractions, mediated intuitions, or any theoretical assumptions from which doubt might arise. Phenomenology would have to go back, as became Husserl's motto, "to the 'things themselves.'" All "presuppositions"—Husserl's term for concepts that lacked "adequate phenomenological justification"—would need to be eliminated. As such, no theoretical premises could be accepted in advance, and all entities "not permitting of a comprehensive phenomenological realization" would be set aside by the phenomenologist. However, Husserl realized that the philosopher cannot arrive at a presuppositionless theory except by way of those realms to which she has direct access. Therefore, Husserl's phenomenological investigations began from what is given in our various modes of experience.[5]

While the early phenomenology of the *Logical Investigations* suggested a realist metaphysics to many of its readers, Husserl abandoned any vestige of realism in his 1913 *Ideen* (Ideas), which limits the realm of phenomenological analysis to the "region of pure experience."[6] As Husserl's ideas developed, his followers organized into several groups with different metaphysical commitments. The earlier Munich and "Göttingen" Circles, whose members included Max Scheler, Adolf Reinach, Moritz Geiger, Dietrich von Hildebrand, Alexandre Koyré, and Edith Stein, drew primarily from the methods and framework of the *Logical Investigations*.[7] The Freiburg Circle, by contrast, was composed of Husserl's later followers who encountered Husserl during his idealist phase. These philosophers were engaged, either constructively or critically, with the techniques of Husserl's "transcendental phenomenology," working in a wide range of fields including ontology (Martin Heidegger), physics (Oskar Becker), aesthetics (Fritz Kaufmann), gestalt psychology (Aron Gurwitsch), ethics (Herbert

Spiegelberg), and the philosophy of science (Wilhelm Szilasi).[8] Both realist and idealist schools of Husserlian phenomenology continued to attract followers throughout the twentieth century.

Even during his "realist" period, Husserl understood that our everyday orientation toward the world, what he called the "natural attitude," was laden with unexamined beliefs and theoretical commitments. However, he held that experience *as such* requires a foundational act of intuition that is prior to any theory or mental construction. This intuition apprehends ideal essences, ranging hierarchically from the singular and ontologically regional (e.g., the color red) to the universal (e.g., the category "substance").[9] Subsequent mental construction, Husserl insisted, could not account for the apprehension of these "pure essences," which are perceived immediately and directly. Calling this the "principle of all principles," Husserl wrote that "whatever presents itself in 'intuition' in primordial form (as it were in its bodily reality), is simply to be accepted as it gives itself out to be." Phenomenology begins, therefore, with those "distinctions which are directly given to us in *intuition* . . . exactly as they are present themselves, without any admixture of hypothesis or interpretation."[10]

From what is initially given by intuition, the phenomenologist must ensure every subsequent act of description and analysis remains uncontaminated by presuppositions. Recognizing the challenge this presented, Husserl introduced techniques called "reductions" to assist phenomenological analysis. In the "phenomenological reduction," the philosopher adopts a stance called *epoché*, withholding any positive or negative judgment on "the theoretical content of all previous philosophy" and abandoning all concepts that objectify the contents of experience. Husserl described this technique, which even prohibits raising the question of the external world's existence, as "bracketing." The bracketed belief, he explained, is left "*as it were 'out of action.'* . . . [It] still remains there like the bracketed in the bracket . . . *but we make 'no use' of it.*"[11] The purpose of the *epoché* is not merely to step back from the certainties of everyday experience but, in Eugen Fink's words, to return to a state of "'wonder' before the world."[12]

What remains when one withholds all presuppositions about the world, "including ourselves and all our thinking," is a "stream of experience."[13] Within this stream, Husserl differentiated two modes of consciousness: consciousness of experience and consciousness of a thing. Consciousness of experience (e.g., memory, imagination, symbolic representation) is *immanent*: it is immediately given just as it is. There is nothing of the immanent experience that is not in its intuition. By contrast, consciousness of a "thing," what the natural attitude accepts as external reality, is *transcendent*. Here, Husserl required a novel definition of transcendence to avoid invoking the concept of an "external world," which would commit him to the presupposition of its reality. Considering the experience of circumambulating a table, Husserl noted that his perception was "constantly in flux; the perceptual now is ever passing over into the adjacent consciousness of the just-past." Yet, these different perspectives—none of which nor any continuum of which can ever fully determine their object—were perceived as "one identical thing derived through the confluence into one *unity of apprehension*." By contrast, an immanent experience of memory or imagination had "no perspectives" and was given over in its entirely. Thus, Husserl concluded, the essential characteristic of transcendent experience, or "thing-perception," was that it "remain forever incomplete."[14]

Husserl's prohibition against taking up the existence of entities effected a radical break, even from prior idealist epistemologies. Without being able to invoke a substantial *mind*, Husserl could not ask, for instance, what attributes a mind must have to do things like represent objects of experience or have abstract thoughts. Indeed, all accounts of mental activity that divide cognition into "thinker" and "thought," or perception into "perceiver" and "perceived" are foreclosed within the phenomenological reduction, since their existences cannot be presupposed.[15] Without any such objects to which attributes or faculties can adhere, the locus of identity remains an active process, about which the phenomenologist must ask not *what* consciousness and the world are but *how* conscious acts about the world occur. For example, a phenomenological account of perceiving a tree might begin by bracketing its existence. However, within brackets, the tree does not disappear or become unreal. Indeed, even the recognition of the tree as a material object external to one's own mind survives the phenomenological reduction, as the perception of material reality "belongs essentially to the phenomenon" and is ineliminable from the experience as such. However, the phenomenologist does not "co-operate" with this aspect of the experience by refusing to acknowledge it as a judgment about reality that can be affirmed or denied. Instead, the experience of the tree's reality is treated *as a phenomenon*; it is made an object of analysis, taken as a mode of experience that an adequate account of consciousness must explain.[16]

Despite any differences, Husserl noted, all mental acts, including perceiving, judging, remembering, and hallucinating, share common features. Each act—*I want, I think, I see*—"proceeds" from some self. Although that being's existence is bracketed within the phenomenological reduction, the aspect of belonging to a subject is ineliminable from conscious acts.[17] Further, all conscious acts are consciousness *of something*. Whether the objects "intended" in a mental act exist is of no interest from the phenomenological perspective. Even if one considers an *a priori* impossibility, such as a round square, the act of positing it retains ineliminable aspects of "aboutness" and direction, which flow from an ego pole to an object pole. The directed character of these acts, their "intentionality," is, Husserl concluded, "the essential property of Consciousness in its general form."[18] Perception, in this account, is not a process of representation, synthesis, or construction that the mind performs on a manifold or complex of sensations to imbue it with significance. Rather, when Husserl sees a blossoming tree, he engages in a conscious act whose intentional object is a tree and which has that intention fulfilled through experience. Even while Husserl's tree undergoes changes—growing apples or shedding its leaves—the intentional object, the "perceived tree as such," endures untouched, so that "the tree plain and simple can burn away . . . [but] the meaning of *this* perception, something that belongs necessarily to its essence—cannot."[19]

In his later phenomenology, Husserl described intentionality as a two-fold structure in which experience is constituted from its *hyletic* and *noetic* aspects. Hyletic data encompasses the full range of nonintentional elements of experience, including sensations, impulses, and feelings. *Noesis*, therefore, identifies the intentionally directed aspects of consciousness.[20] This new formulation gave Husserl a framework to explore the relation between intention and intentional content, an ideal entity he now called its *noema* (in the plural, *noemata*). The noema is the meaning of a noetic act in a "pregnant" sense, encompassing all aspects of meaningfulness as they are given through it: "the whole fullness of realization which marks our awareness of it in the experience."[21] The essential unity of noesis and its correlate noema implies that the noemata of different kinds of noetic acts are not identical, even if they concern the same object. For example, conceiving a work of art, viewing a work of art, and valuing that same work share noematic elements, but not a full noema. In the latter act, the work of art is given, not merely simpliciter, but also such that having value is essential to it as it is given.[22] However, Husserl affirmed the work of art's identity through these different intentional acts. We experience the object as identical throughout, he explained, because these acts share a *noematic nucleus*: "the pure X in abstraction from all predicates."[23]

Following the publication of *Ideas*, Husserl's research turned to the problem of intersubjectivity, exploring how the experience of a shared world is given in the transcendentally constituted consciousness of individual egos.

Husserl described a period of epistemological rupture in which "objective truth" was elevated over and above the pragmatic knowledge of natural existence. As Enlightenment rationality recast nature to the measure of the ruler and the scale, he argued, existence was pre-predicatively mathematized and geometrized, so that our consciousness now presupposes the reality of the world as given to the scientist: "The visible measuring scales, scale markings, etc., are used as actually existing things, not as illusions." This understanding must be grounded outside individual consciousness "within the horizon of our fellow men," which Husserl called the *Lebenswelt*, or "lifeworld," pregiven in experience as the "world common to us all."[24] Not merely science but all human activity, including transcendental subjectivity, occurs within this pregiven lifeworld. Thus, Husserl realized, explicating the lifeworld's structure and role in intentional activity remained a fundamental challenge for phenomenology.[25]

Husserl could not account for the lifeworld's role in intentional activity unless he explained how background and contextual knowledge inform positing activity. Although, according to Husserl, every act must have a "thetic," or positing, component that intends a noema, he concluded that a nonthetic "horizon" surrounds the noematic "core of determinate quiddity" as the indeterminate realm of the intended object's various possibilities. For example, when new characteristics of an intended object are perceived, they emerge, without a new act of judgment, within this horizon of potentialities so that they have "the precise sense of elements" implicit in the object's structure. However, the horizon is always apprehended indeterminately, bounded only by the logical and commonsense limits of our expectations. The moment we bring the horizon into focus, it ceases to be a horizon, becoming an object that is explicitly determined by the positing activity of thetic consciousness. Thus, the horizon is "passively apprehended," structuring perceptions and informing behavior without explication.[26]

* * *

In 1929 Husserl formally retired from his professorship at Freiburg. Although he continued to present lectures and compose new material, his primary mode of influence from this point onward was through those devoted disciples who had committed themselves to preserving his conception of phenomenology. However, Martin Heidegger, seen by many as Husserl's successor, advanced a new vision of philosophy, described as "existential" or "hermeneutic" phenomenology. The break between Husserl and Heidegger echoed in tensions between their followers, who have, sometimes sharply, disputed each other's claim to represent the phenomenological tradition. To his supporters, Heidegger carried the project of phenomenology forward, surpassing Husserl and supplanting him as its authoritative interpreter. To his detractors he was "merely a corruptor of, or even a deserter from, 'orthodox' phenomenology."[27] Indeed, after 1930 Heidegger made few explicit references to phenomenology in his writings, providing fodder to those who wished to exile part or all of the Heideggerian corpus from the phenomenological canon.[28]

No matter how else he is categorized, Martin Heidegger was a brilliant philosopher, whose erudition and creativity were as apparent in his novel interpretations of classic texts as his radical reinterpretation of being. He was also a German chauvinist, an anti-Semite who embraced, in varying degrees, the racial ideologies of 1930s Germany, and a servile opportunist who ingratiated himself to the Nazi party in the hope of advancing his career. Heidegger's sins have been adjudicated elsewhere, and his legacy does not require new appraisal in this work.[29] However, they must be noted, not merely because some stains should not be washed away, but because of the long shadow they would cast over the phenomenological movement after the conclusion of World War II. Normal philosophical territoriality, anger over Heidegger's treatment of Husserl, and a belief that Heidegger's philosophy was tainted by Nazi ideology all contributed to tensions within the phenomenological movement.

There are, nonetheless, strong continuities between Husserlian and Heideggerian phenomenology, both of which begin from experience, suspending our everyday understanding of its contents to uncover the foundational structures through which it is constituted. The gulf that separated Husserl and Heidegger is, above all else, a disjuncture in their fundamental conceptions of philosophy's purposes and possibilities. Heidegger's interpretation of phenomenology as the "hermeneutics of Being" is a significant departure from Husserl's program of "rigorous science." Heidegger did not simply reject the techniques of transcendental phenomenology, such as Husserl's reductions, but the goal of apodictic certainty entirely. Instead, Heidegger's major systematic work, *Sein und Zeit* (1927; *Being and Time*), reoriented phenomenology toward a different, fundamental problem: "what we really mean by this expression 'Being.'"[30] Heidegger's existential phenomenology raised the question of Being, not hoping to gain purchase on some Olympian vantage above existence, but as an always incomplete project of overcoming the naïve misapprehensions and theoretical dogmas that obscure our understanding of and "authentic" relation to our own existence.

Many philosophers invent terminology or repurpose language; it is, so to speak, how the game is played. Yet, few have ever taken that game as far as Heidegger, whose corpus of verbal inventions could fill a dictionary if his manner of using language did not rage against stasis, eschewing confinement by a definition that would pose it, like a taxidermized animal, in a display that could only gesture at its dynamism.[31] "Language," Heidegger wrote, "is the house of Being. In its home man dwells." By establishing the similarity or difference of entities and adjudicating what is sensible or ludicrous through its everyday use, language erects the limits on what we can think and do. More fundamentally, even, language is the form in which man's relation to Being is given. Heidegger contended, however, that this original relation has been occluded by the elevation of reflective activity and theoretical knowledge above other modes of experience and forms of truth.[32] Thus, Heidegger's disorienting language is not a purposeless monument to opacity but, in his conception, a necessary bulwark against the presuppositions embedded within modern philosophy. His phenomenological campaign against unfounded theory is waged not through technical devices like Husserl's reductions, but through the *Destruktion* of Western metaphysics, a tradition he believed was too contaminated by metaphysical presuppositions and pseudoproblems of its own creation to allow it to speak of Being.[33]

To provide an ontological account of Being from the phenomenological material of experience, Heidegger invoked a new concept of human being: Dasein. The word is an amalgamation of the preposition *da* ("there") and the infinitive verb *sein* ("to be"). While Dasein may appear as an "I" in everyday experience, it is not a subject, a cabinet of consciousness, or a locus of individual identity apart from the world. To the contrary, Heidegger argued, by misapprehending consciousness as an essence or a thing, philosophers since Descartes had been caught in a thicket of seemingly intractable problems relating to the mind's transcendence into the world. Likewise, Heidegger indicted Husserl for not following the phenomenological method to its conclusions in his account of "pure" consciousness. By positing the ego as disembodied transcendence—the structure of consciousness reified—Husserl made an ideal construct, not lived experience, his subject. This, Heidegger argued, led Husserl to mistake the structures of intentionality for essences, lapsing into the errors of traditional metaphysics by determining the Being of consciousness before it could be phenomenologically considered.[34]

Heidegger's alternative to Cartesian subjectivity charted a route around its pitfalls by radically decentering the subject; it is one of his most significant accomplishments. A theory of knowledge that admits the existence of some *res cogitans* ("thinking thing") must explain how entities like ideas escape their mental confines to become "about" things in the world. Dasein, however, is not a *res*—a thing or entity—nor would Heidegger have accepted *cogitans* as a phenomenologically grounded description of its activity. *Sein* is a verb: be-ing. As Dasein, this mode of be-ing is ontologically characterized by its engagement with the situation of its existence. This circumvents the problem of explaining transcendence because Dasein is always already in the world—it is, literally, "being-there." To be clear, Being-in-the-world does not signify Dasein's mere physical presence alongside other entities and beings. The world is, rather, a realm of significance in which Dasein dwells, constituted in public meanings, practices, and relationships with others. In fact, Dasein and the world are not distinct entities, with the former "in" the latter. Being-in-the-world is a "unitary phenomenon" that, despite its different constitutive elements, is meaningless except as a whole. Thus, there is no gulf between subject and object to be overcome in our pre-theoretical experience. Transcendence is a pseudoproblem that arises only when philosophers mistake our existence for an essence or entity that can be ontologically characterized prior to its existing.[35]

What instead distinguishes Dasein from other entities is, as Heidegger wrote, that "in its very Being, that Being is an *issue* for it." That Dasein always already has an understanding of its own existence as meaningful is not incidental, but the "constitutive state of [its] Being."[36] Dasein's intrinsic grasp of its own Being is also central to Heidegger's conception of philosophy as "a mode of knowing . . . in which Dasein is ruthlessly dragged back to itself, and relentlessly thrown back upon itself."[37] The term Heidegger adopted for this was hermeneutics. The object of hermeneutical analysis, our own Being, is not merely interpretable, but demands interpretation so that it is always encountered "in some state of having-been-interpreted."[38] The hermeneutics of Dasein, in other words, is the investigation of our faculty for investigation by means of that same faculty. This does not lead to an ultimate grounding outside of existence but back to Being itself, which is understood anew, awake to features concealed in the natural attitude. Therefore, rather than progressing, as Husserl did, in a line from conscious experience through the phenomenological reductions to its "pure" ground, Heidegger's methodology follows the path of a circle, developing "a possibility of [Dasein's] becoming and being for itself in the manner of an *understanding* of itself." Such understanding is "fundamentally labile."[39] It is not an end point but an invitation, calling Dasein's hermeneutical gaze back on itself—not to where it was before, but having been interpreted anew.[40] In Heidegger's words, this hermeneutics "speaks *from out of* interpretation and for the sake of it."[41] One might fairly ask the purpose of following the voice of interpretation, speaking to itself of itself, down a winding path that promises no final truth or certain knowledge. On this question Heidegger was frustratingly quiet.

Heidegger's analysis of existence proceeds from the fact that for each of us, our Being, Dasein, is "*in each case mine.*" This mineness is not a predicative property. It is not like the coloration or size of a material object—what Heidegger called *ontic* features—which are the factual characteristics an entity might or might not possess. Dasein's mineness is *ontological*—a structure of human Being. It is the "how" or mode of be-ing of the Being whose existence is an issue for it. From this beginning, Heidegger's phenomenological hermeneutics repeatedly returns to our experience to uncover its deeper ontological structures. In this, Heidegger cautioned, our customary understanding of our own existence—the narrative we recount when asked, "What did you do?"—is constructed from precisely the experiences in which our own Being is most obscured by theoretical presuppositions. "That which is ontically closest and well known," he explained, "is ontologically the farthest and not known at all." The reflexive self-portrait of our lives that predetermines Dasein as a "concrete" entity with "the differentiated character of some definite way of existing," is not ground on which phenomenological analysis can begin. Thus, Heidegger sought to recover a primordial understanding of Being by investigating the moment of prereflexive engagement with the world during which one's own existence withdraws from one's attention.[42]

"Proximally and for the most part," Heidegger argued, Dasein is "not 'I' in the sense of my own Self" but a way of being he called *das Man*. Translated as "the One" or "the They," the term *das Man* captures the essences of a phrase like "it is what one does" or the legal concept of a "reasonable person," which conceives of a fictional individual whose imagined response to a situation stands for the whole genus of persons whose behavior comport with the norms of "publicness." "One," for instance, shakes with the right hand, chews with one's mouth closed, and avoids toppling fellow pedestrians. For most of us, our life is lived, without our own recognition, as this "*they-self*," speaking how "one speaks" and doing what "one does," as though by some law of nature. Indeed, the public world's structure of significances—identifying what entities are and who or what they are for—is constituted for this "they," not for any concrete individual.[43] In Heidegger's prose:

In this averageness with which it prescribes what can and may be ventured, it keeps watch over everything exceptional that thrusts itself to the fore. Every kind of priority gets noiselessly suppressed. Overnight, everything that is primordial gets glossed over as something that has long been well known. Everything gained by struggle becomes just something to be manipulated.[44]

It is only in a mode of being Heidegger called "authenticity" that Dasein fully grasps the freedom to choose those possibilities given to it ontologically as its own. For the most part, Dasein's Being is "inauthentic." It forgets or turns away from its ownmost potentialities, mistaking the ontic determinants of language, custom, and everyday self-understanding for facts of ontological necessity. In this mode, Dasein "falls" or becomes "absorbed" in "the groundlessness and nullity of inauthentic everydayness," accepting uncritically the judgments of preontological experience: that one's essence is that of a materially constituted individual subject; that one exists in a physical world that has an essential reality over and above one's own experience; that this world is imbued with meanings and significances that make demands of it by the power of their objective truth. Yet, while Heidegger's hermeneutical phenomenology endeavors to overcome the ontic misapprehensions of everyday experience, Heidegger insisted that he gave no moral or valuative significance to inauthenticity. Authenticity is not a path to spiritual liberation, means of personal uplift, or consciousness of the natural or some superior social order. Authenticity and inauthenticity are both and equally primordial modes of Dasein's Being.[45]

* * *

In the second half of the twentieth century, as the phenomenological movement spread across the European continent, its center shifted from Freiburg to Paris, where phenomenology grew in concert with existentialism. It was, first and foremost, the philosophers Jean-Paul Sartre and Maurice Merleau-Ponty who adapted the phenomenology of Husserl and Heidegger to the milieu of midcentury France. Sartre's existentialism, encapsulated in the maxim "Existence precedes essence," is an atheistic philosophy that disaffirms the validity of any essential "human nature," whether conceived as the reflection of a divine image, a universal kernel of shared humanity, a historical or cultural identity, or the biological characteristics of individuals, families, or races. With no preordained destiny or innate character, one is born as nothing but freedom.[46] "Man is nothing other than his own project," Sartre wrote. "He exists only to the extent that he realizes himself, therefore he is nothing more than the sum of his actions, nothing more than his life."[47] In barbarism there is no neglected humanity. In resignation there is no unrealized potential. Behind callousness there is no "true" inner self. We are, and we are only, what we choose to do. Thus, Sartre delivered a call to take ownership of existence by acknowledging our freedom to act in accordance with our own purported principles and refusing bad faith representations that misplace responsibility for our choices beyond each of ourselves on some external duty or perceived necessity.[48]

Sartre published his philosophical magnum opus, *L'Être et le néant* (*Being and Nothingness*) in 1943. Despite its superficial similarity to Heidegger's *Being and Time*, however, *Being and Nothingness* is no mere adaptation: it is a philosophical chimera, in which the phenomenologies of Heidegger and Husserl are fused by means of a solder that each would have considered *treyf*. This Hegelian ethos of dialectical negation and synthesis runs throughout *Being and Nothingness* beginning with its title, which is an obvious allusion to, and critical reversal of, Heidegger's *Being and Time*.[49] Yet, while Sartre attributed his formulation "Existence precedes essence" to Heidegger, the relevant passage from *Being and Time*—"the 'essence' of Dasein lies in its existence"—is subtly but importantly different. Heidegger deliberately avoided the metaphysical categories of "essentia" and "existentia" because, he explained, "the opposition between *existential* and *essential* is not under consideration, because neither of these metaphysical determinations of Being, let alone their relationship, is yet in question."[50] Thus, Heidegger's formulation implies only that *Existenz* is the mode of being *unique* to Dasein. Sartre's humanistic existentialism, by contrast, takes a being that is already determined *as a human being* for its subject. By giving being this "what," he reintroduced the inherited metaphysical concepts of existence and essence, simply reversing their traditional priority.[51]

Sartre's phenomenological writings adopted Husserl's general framework of consciousness as an intentional structure but reintroduced a Cartesian distinction between the mind and the world that Husserl and Heidegger would have rejected. "The type of existence of consciousness," Sartre wrote, "is to be consciousness of itself. And consciousness is aware of itself *in so far as it is consciousness of a transcendent object*."[52] Yet, Sartre held, the inward experience of one's own consciousness is "lucid," perfectly clear as "purely and simply consciousness of being conscious of [an] object."[53] This was a contradiction, since, as Husserl described, a transcendent object was "a center of opacity," revealed only ever incompletely in perspectives. "If one introduces this opacity into consciousness," Sartre wrote, "one congeals consciousness, one darkens it."[54] Thus, he concluded that the lucidity of self-knowledge is foreclosed to the transcendental ego. Such a being as Husserl's transcendental ego could not exist, for "if it existed it would tear consciousness from itself; it would divide consciousness; it would slide into every consciousness like an opaque blade."[55] Consciousness, therefore, is merely a sequence of intentional acts, not an enduring metaphysical entity.[56] Indeed, Sartre noted, in our normal mode of unreflecting consciousness, there is often no "I" to be found: "When I run after a streetcar, when I look at the time, when I am absorbed in contemplating a portrait, there is no I. There is consciousness *of the streetcar-having-to-be-overtaken.*"[57] The *I* is present, therefore, only in the self-reflection of consciousness.[58] Yet, while denying the existence of a transcendental ego, Sartre affirmed the existential primordiality of subjectivity, rejecting Heidegger's *Destruktion* of the cogito. This produced an account of consciousness that is at once ontologically profligate, paradoxical, and insightful.

"Nothingness," Sartre declared, "lies coiled at the heart of being—like a worm." Everywhere that there is consciousness there is negation, destruction, separation, and absence. Both one's past and future are held at a remove by a chasm of nothingness. While a person is free to be what she makes of herself, past actions hold no power over her present. The nothingness of not-being one's past self, for instance, is revealed in the anguish that past promises, even earnestly made, cannot define the existentially free cogito. This negation, Sartre argued, is not merely an abstract logical connective. It is fundamental and cannot be conceived "outside of Being." It is not *a* being and yet it appears, active everywhere as nihilation.[59] The point is subtle and best made through illustration, such as Sartre's phenomenological description of searching for his missing friend Pierre:

> We must observe that in perception there is always the construction of a figure on a ground. No one object, no group of objects is especially designed to be organized as specifically either ground or figure; all depends on the direction of my attention. When I enter this café to search for Pierre, there is formed a synthetic organization of all the objects in the café, on the ground of which Pierre is given as about to appear. This organization of the café as the ground is an original nihilation. Each element of the setting, a person, a table, a chair, attempts to isolate itself, to lift itself on the ground constituted by the totality of the other objects, only to fall back once more into the undifferentiation of the ground; it melts into the ground. . . . Thus the original nihilation of all the figures which appear and are swallowed up in the neutrality of a *ground* is the necessary condition for the appearance

of the principle figure, which is here the person of Pierre. This nihilation is given to my intuition; I am witness to the successive disappearance of the objects which I look at—in particular the faces, which detain me for an instant (Could this be Pierre?) and which as quickly decompose precisely because they "are not" the face of Pierre. . . . This figure which slips constantly between my look and the solid, real objects of the café is precisely a perpetual disappearance; it is Pierre raising himself as nothingness on the ground of the nihilation of the café.[60]

The simple abstract judgment "Pierre is not here" lacks the fecundity to vivify the experience described above. Nothing and negation are not merely judgments about presence. At their core is "a refusal of existence. By means of [them] a being (or a way of being) is posited, then thrown back into nothingness." They nihilate, occasioning a break from the world in which one becomes conscious of "the not."[61]

Consciousness brings nothingness into the world, Sartre held, from a "fissure" at its heart. This fissure could not be spatial, temporal, or material—it could not be a being—since the introduction of any external element to the cogito would "shatter its unity [and] destroy its translucency." It must be, Sartre wrote, "the pure negative . . . the nothingness of being and the nihilating power both together." Indeed, conscious entities are distinctive precisely because they can *not-be*. A material object is itself and nothing else. This does not mean that it cannot be altered, broken, or put to a new use. However, there is no aspect of being within it that is not fully determined as exactly what it is. In one sense, a person is also a material entity with no being over and above its physical existence and past. In this respect, the person who has trained and works as a carpenter *is* a carpenter. Yet, she also *is not* a carpenter because, unlike the mere object, she is free. At any moment she might decide *I am no longer a carpenter*, setting down her tools forever. Consciousness is a sliver of nothingness within being, Sartre concluded, that divides it—not into two separate beings, but as a being that is whole only by being at once what it is and what it is not. Nothingness is, thus, the foundation of consciousness. Only by being what he is not can a man be both experience and experiencer, believe what he knows is in doubt, and be at once his present and the past and future selves he is not. It's pretty. It's clever. It is, perhaps, even human. But is it phenomenology?

At least to a degree, the answer is yes. Though lacking Husserl's rigor, Sartre's descriptions are generally phenomenological and often exemplary accounts of how phenomena are given in experience. Yet, where Sartre supplanted Heideggerian hermeneutics with his own methods, his existential phenomenology fell back into the realm of metaphysics. Heidegger kept metaphysics at bay by preserving Being as a question. When, for instance, Heidegger identified "care" as an ontological structure of Dasein, he granted care no existence beyond the modes of being it characterized. No determinations of being can be derived from care or excluded by it as, for instance, logic dictates there can be no square circle. The terms of Heidegger's phenomenological hermeneutics are beyond entailment. Being is disclosed solely and directly in experience. Sartre, by contrast, began with a metaphysics of being, and attempted to reach, by a sort of logical analysis, an ontological characterization of consciousness that could support the varieties of experience he described. Thus, Sartre proceeded at once descriptively, backward from experience, and metaphysically, forward by deduction, reaching a point in the middle. In this, Sartre gained the tools to construct a systematic theory of consciousness that is particularly attuned to its peculiarly human, psychological dimensions, but abandoned phenomenology's claim to withhold presuppositions.

* * *

While Maurice Merleau-Ponty did not attain the fame of Jean-Paul Sartre during his lifetime, his contributions to the phenomenological movement match if not surpass those of his better-known contemporary, collaborator, and sometimes friend. Like Husserl, Merleau-Ponty understood phenomenology as descriptive philosophy and was committed to a methodology that proceeded through the meticulous analysis of intentional acts. However, he was not a dogmatic Husserlian, following Husserl's fragmentary analysis of the perceptual fringe, intersubjectivity, and historicity to what he considered their natural conclusions. Husserl had failed, Merleau-Ponty believed, to understand that his own work provided "the formula for an existential philosophy."[62] Thus, he turned Husserlian methodological rigor to the Heideggerian task of existential phenomenology, generating fundamental insights about the importance of embodiment.

Merleau-Ponty argued that the abstracted cogito described by Husserl and Sartre could not provide sufficient grounds for phenomenological analysis of real human consciousness. Drawing from the Gestalt theory of psychology, he concluded that perception could be reduced neither physiologically to a collection of stimuli and reflexes, nor psychologically to a set of discreet acts; it is an irreducible whole comprising the mutually constituting pair of figure and background.[63] Throughout his 1945 work,

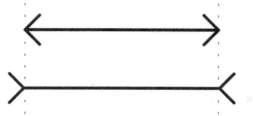

FIGURE 1.1 The Müller–Lyer Illusion.

Phénoménologie de la perception (*Phenomenology of Perception*), Merleau-Ponty highlighted the failure of both empiricism and idealism to ground the gestalt of lived experience. Though traditionally treated as antipodal, he held that these philosophical standpoints share a common, fundamental dogma: whether real or ideal, each adhered to "an unquestioned belief in a universe perfectly explicit in itself."[64] Through a litany of examples, Merleau-Ponty illustrated how this principle is contradicted in experience. For example, the perception of a line cannot consistently be reduced to the apprehension of its qualities, like length or curvature, since, as in optical illusions, our mental representations may exhibit qualities different from those of the object perceived. Unlike the objective domain of science, perception tolerates ambiguities—"a certain 'shifting' or 'haziness'"—as, for instance, in the Müller-Lyer illusion, in which two line segments appear at once equal and different.

Qualities of objects, such as the length of two lines or the mathematical formulae governing the properties of circle, are made definite in thetic consciousness. One may measure the Müller-Lyer lines and will always find them equal. However, the nonthetic consciousness that takes up the whole gestalt of lines, arrows, and the space between eludes the logician's demand of noncontradiction and, Merleau-Ponty argued, is the originary mode of perception on which reflective experience and objective thought are grounded.[65]

Merleau-Ponty's most significant contributions to phenomenology are his investigations of experiences not encompassed in the realm of thetic, cognitive acts. His phenomenology is a philosophy of action and feeling. The agent of these actions is not a cogito but a body that, he argued, cannot be adequately understood by deconstructing it into its parts or faculties. It is only by "taking up for [one's self] the drama that moves through [the body] and merging with it" that the body becomes known. A correlate to consciousness, the body and its modes of being can be understood only as a unity that is "always implicit and confused."[66] One's body, Merleau-Ponty continued, "is in the world just as the heart is in the organism: it continuously breathes life into the visible spectacle, animates it and nourishes it from within, and forms a system with it."[67] At the same time, however, the embodied subject is not pure subjectivity because a language of significance, in which the body is literate, is encoded into the structure of the world. The object, Merleau-Ponty wrote, is "the correlate of my body . . . constituted in the hold my body has upon it; it is not first a signification for the understanding, but rather a structure available for inspection by the body."[68] The surface of a painting, for instance, solicits our gaze to the perception of a color. However, it is the unity of sensation in embodied experience that allows its structure to be encountered as a realm of significance. The body is not passively attuned to significations by some mystical faculty. Rather, these significations are disclosed through the unity of experience in the coexistence of consciousness, body, and the world. Thus, the object is pre-reflectively grasped, imbued with meaning within a "field of existence" in which "each phenomenon that appears polarizes my entire body, as a system of perpetual powers, toward it."[69]

Merleau-Ponty devoted significant attention to individuals who had experienced traumatic brain injuries, such as a patient called Schneider whose condition had been described by the psychologists Kurt Goldstein and Adhémar Gelb. While Schneider was fully capable of performing habitual tasks, such as grasping his nose, he could not fulfill abstract commands (e.g., "raise your right arm" or "point to your nose") except by watching himself as he performed a series of experimental motions. Merleau-Ponty concluded that grasping and pointing exemplify different modes of being, not reducible to their physiological or psychological components. "From its very beginnings," he wrote, "the grasping movement is magically complete; it only gets under way by anticipating its goal, since the ban on grasping is enough to inhibit the movement." Schneider was "conscious of bodily space as the envelope of his habitual action." However, he did not understand it as an "objective milieu."[70] He could, for instance, follow the well-learned path to an acquaintance's house. Yet, if he passed the same building on an unrelated trip, it was unrecognizable to him "because he [had] not gone out with the intention of going there." Thus, Schneider could never simply go "out for a walk," since he had lost the mode of Being-in-the-world that gave him access to the meanings of entities outside of the specific context in which they are encountered.[71] Schneider could grasp his nose because he understood its mechanics as a completed action. Yet, although Schneider understood the existence of his arm and nose intellectually, he lacked a relation to his arm as a nexus of possibilities of engagement with the world around it.[72]

Merleau-Ponty inferred from this analysis that motricity is not a founded mode of experience, but an original mode of being that is passed over by Cartesian metaphysics. Our lived spaces are not an "inert mass at the foundation of our consciousness." To be familiar with a room is to "hold" it in one's hands and legs, so that it can be navigated without reflection or consideration. The room is, thus, reached by "a multitude of intentional threads [that] run out toward it from [one's] body."[73] As such, consciousness is "originally not an 'I think that,' but rather an 'I can.'" In other words, "movement is not a movement in thought, and bodily space is not a space that is conceived or represented."[74] Rather, the world is disclosed presymbolically through our bodies as a "praktognosia." Merleau-Ponty explained:

> The gesture of reaching one's hand out toward an object contains a reference to the object, not as a representation, but as this highly determinate thing toward which we are thrown, next to which we are through anticipation, and which we haunt. Consciousness is being toward the thing through the intermediary of the body. A movement is learned when the body has understood it, that is, when it has incorporated it into its "world," and to move one's body is to aim at the things through it, or to allow one's body to respond to their solicitation, which is exerted upon the body without any representation.[75]

After the act, space and external objects are conceptualized objectively in reflection. However, this is only possible on the basis of their prior significance in the sphere of motricity. Thus, to follow Husserl's credo back "to the things themselves," Merleau-Ponty argued, we must return to the original experience of the bodily acts in which they are given. This takes phenomenology beyond the "constituting consciousness" of Husserl's transcendental idealism, and into the realm of Heidegger's existential analysis of Being-in-the-world.[76]

While Merleau-Ponty affirmed the intentional structure of consciousness, the sort of intentional projection involved in motricity refuses reduction to the noematic structures of meaning expounded by Husserl. Rather, Merleau-Ponty explained, consciousness follows an "intentional arc" through our bodies and the world that "projects around us our past, our future, our human milieu, our physical situation, our ideological situation, and our moral situation, or rather, that ensures that we are situated within all of these relationships."[77] A simple example of this is binocular vision. Physiologically understood, we perceive depth because the mind merges the monocular images cast on the retina of each eye into a single image. However, this description portrays vision as a neutral process accomplished by an "epistemological subject," mistaking the mechanism of binocular vision for its cause. Proceeding via phenomenological description rather than theoretical explanation, Merleau-Ponty noted that the images from each eye are not passively synthesized. For example, a nearby object will appear doubled when one looks into the distance. It is only when both eyes collaborate to focus on a particular point in space that the gaze succeeds in grasping its object. This synthesis occurs because the subject engages in the "prospective activity" of looking for an intentional object it must anticipate in advance. When the nearby object appears doubled and out of focus, the subject experiences a sort of "disequilibrium," intimating that the perception has not reached the world and compelling the eyes to focus. This disequilibrium is a bodily experience that signals the failure of the eyes to function as a "single organ" and calls on the "latent knowledge that [the] body has of itself" so that, without conscious thought, the gaze reaches the intentional object via this arc through the body.[78] Thus, in perception, Merleau-Ponty wrote, "we do not think the object and we do not think the thinking." Rather, "we are directed toward the object and we merge with this body that knows more than we do about the world, about motives, and about the means available for accomplishing synthesis."[79]

Unlike Sartre's perfectly lucid ego, Merleau-Ponty's embodied subject must reach itself "through the thickness of the world." I experience feelings, he wrote, "to which I do not give a name" and "false joys to which I am not entirely committed." Likewise, I encounter objects as physically determinable without being determined. For instance, looking into the distance, I may perceive a large flat stone that, on closer inspection, is revealed instead to be a patch of sunlight. Despite the haziness of this vision, the belief in this initial illusory perception commits one's whole being to it. "I see the illusory stone," Merleau-Ponty argued, "in the sense that my entire perceptual and motor field gives to the light patch the sense of a 'stone on the lane.' And I already prepare to sense this smooth and solid surface beneath my foot." This illusion is not, in other words, merely a visual representation that is contradicted by later perception. Illusion is discovered in the totality of experience and is possible only because the structure of the world permits misperception and correction. "To perceive," Merleau-Ponty held, "is to believe in a world." It is "suddenly to commit to an entire future of experiences in a present that never, strictly speaking, guarantees that future." That to which one commits, however, is not the validity of any particular appearance, but of the world *as a whole*. Thus, when one's foot fails to find the smooth surface of the stone, signaling a break from the anticipated future, one does not abandon one's perceptions as fantasy. Instead, the world offers an explanation that was always held, implicitly, as the possibility of any perception: one suffered an illusion because of the limitations of embodied perception necessitated by the world's underlying natural structure, such as the difficulty of seeing clearly at a distance.[80]

Thus, Merleau-Ponty preserved the distinction between true perceptions and illusion without appeal to a correspondence between reality and a mental representation. In this accomplishment, however, he rejected the possibility of a consciousness fully possessed of itself in immanent experience and gave up Husserl's goal of apodicticity. As Merleau-Ponty wrote, "I only know myself in ambiguity." Yet, this concession does not mean that the perceived is merely the skeptic's "permanent possibility of perception." "Possibility and probability," he explained, "presuppose the prior experience of error, and they correspond to the situation of doubt." Belief in the world remains anterior to doubt, as the ground for the possibility of doubting. The child and the scientist both see the sun "rise" as a real phenomenon in the world of experience. The scientist may, of course, "cross out" this perception as an illusion. However, she does this by replacing it with another, scientific perception, already given as a possibility in her world. This is possible only because she affirms the world's existence over and above any particular perception as an "inexhaustible reservoir from which things are drawn."[81]

2

First Encounters

Harvard has prepared me for Germany—in Germany I prepare again for
Harvard.
—Marvin Farber

In the first decade of the twentieth century, phenomenology was a nascent
German movement whose shadow touched American shores only in passing. Little published discussion of phenomenology appears in English-
language journals before the 1920s, where Husserl's movement received
occasional mention in reviews or surveys of philosophical developments
in Europe.[1] However, despite the geographic specificity of phenomenology's early history, it is important to avoid essentializing phenomenology
as a "European" philosophy, which risks imposing an ideological divide
between continental European and Anglo-American philosophers on an
era in which it did not yet exist. During the second half of the twentieth
century, it would become necessary for American phenomenologists to
convince their often-skeptical compatriots that phenomenological analysis
was relevant to philosophers in the United States. However, at the century's beginning the boundary between America and Europe was permeable,
allowing for both physical and intellectual exchanges between the con-
tinents. Indeed, America's engagement with phenomenology had begun
years before the first English publications on the movement appeared in
print, while Husserl himself was still relatively unknown, even in Germany.
This story is, therefore, different than most histories of the reception of
European texts and ideas in the United States. In the first half of the twentieth century, phenomenology was not, for the most part, passively received
by Americans as an established doctrine. Rather, it was *encountered as a
work in progress* by American men and women who studied with the movement's founders and alongside its growing coterie of followers in Germany.

The first American to encounter Husserl was William Ernest Hocking, then a graduate student under Josiah Royce at Harvard. Royce himself was familiar with Husserl's work, which he praised in his 1902 address to the American Psychological Association.[2] However, it was the Marburg Kant scholar Paul Natorp, then also lecturing at Harvard, who suggested to Hocking that he seek out Husserl in Göttingen during his 1902 tour of Germany.[3] A report to Hugo Münsterberg, who chaired the Harvard committee that granted Hocking's travel stipend, opened with this proviso: "Philosophy cannot be said to flourish in Göttingen. A philosophical desert in Germany is a contradiction in terms, but this is about as thin a spot as one could have picked out." Nevertheless, Hocking continued, "I have found exceptional advantages here, so that my choice may have been the best available." Hocking enrolled in courses on logic and epistemology with Husserl and attended his seminar on Hume. Indeed, Hocking wrote, "it would be more accurate to say that this study is under the guidance of Professor Husserl himself, for he has been kind enough to take a personal interest in my work, and has given me every opportunity to converse with him and bring him my questions."[4] Münsterberg, however, was unimpressed, replying to Hocking: "I should never have moved your fellowship if it had been for Göttingen. . . . You have only one winter in Germany and the idea is that the fellowship holder spends it in a large city. . . . Göttingen was the last place to choose." Thus, after less than three months with Husserl, Hocking was compelled to leave for Berlin. However, the philosophers remained correspondents and friends for the rest of Husserl's life. Despite its brevity, the reverberations of this first encounter would establish the trajectory of phenomenology's development in America.[5]

The second American to enter Husserl's orbit was Walter Pitkin, a future professor at Columbia and cofounder of the "new realist" movement. Pitkin visited Göttingen a year after Hocking, intent on discussing Husserl's "monumental" *Logical Investigations* with its author. His journey was well rewarded:

> [Husserl] kept me in his home for a long time and put in part of every day explaining to me various problems in his new logic. His ability as a teacher was amazing. He put everything so clearly and repeated the key propositions at such well timed intervals that, even if I had not been keenly interested, I could not have failed to understand his philosophy.[6]

In 1905 Pitkin received Husserl's permission to translate *Logical Investigations*, but the project did not come to fruition. By Pitkin's account, it was scuttled by William James, who advised the publisher Houghton Mifflin that "nobody in America would be interested in a new and strange German work on Logic."[7] If the story is true, it flavors later efforts to connect the philosophies of Husserl and James with a hint of irony. Regardless of the reason, however, *Logical Investigations* did not appear in English until 1970.

Harvard was not the only point of contact between America and the phenomenological movement. Michigan's Charles Bruce Vibbert visited Husserl in 1908.[8] Henry Lanz, a Russian expatriate who had studied with Husserl, immigrated to America and joined Stanford's faculty of philosophy in 1918.[9] Andrew D. Osborn, a graduate student in philosophy at Columbia, also studied with Husserl under the auspices of a fellowship from the American Council of Learned Societies.[10] Nonetheless, in this age of Atlantic crossings, the central hub for the transmission of German thought into the United States was Cambridge, Massachusetts. At the start of the nineteenth century, Harvard had split from Princeton and Yale by rejecting the leadership of Calvinist theologians and aligning itself with the Unitarian movement. Because of Unitarian interest in German "higher criticism," Harvard students soon began visiting German universities to study biblical exegesis, forging connections between Harvard and continental Europe. The philosophers George Herbert Palmer, George Santayana, and William James all spent time in Germany, and Hugo Münsterberg was himself a German. When Harvard established its program of graduate education in the 1870s, doctoral students commonly took time to study in Germany before beginning work on a dissertation.[11] This exchange was not entirely unidirectional; in addition to Paul Natorp, Moritz Geiger, a student of Husserl, visited Harvard in the winter of 1907, staying for three months and working with Royce, Santayana, and James.[12] Harvard formalized its support for these foreign intellectual tours in 1908, when Amey Richmond Sheldon gave the university a bequest of more than $300,000 to establish a permanent fund for travel abroad by "exceptional cases . . . of men who appear to have the capacity for really original work." These Frederick Sheldon Traveling Fellowships were awarded to the university's ablest graduate students, nominated by their departments and selected by a special committee. Over the next three decades, Sheldon fellows from Harvard's Philosophy Department would be perennial visitors to Germany.[13]

In 1891 Harvard's faculty had been formally split into academic divisions by its president, Charles Eliot. The philosophers Eliot had recruited to Harvard, including George Herbert Palmer, William James, Josiah Royce, George Santayana, and Hugo Münsterberg, were organized as the Division of Philosophy and Psychology.[14] The historian Laurence Veysey described

this unit as "the supreme philosophy department." Its faculty "formed a striking ensemble, one which in its smooth functioning amid diversity of talent
became the envy of most other academic departments, then and later. The
diversity was not so much tolerated as positively courted."[15] Palmer called it
"the first well-rounded staff for teaching philosophy organized in this country."[16] The entire department was engaged in teaching survey courses, and
the introductory course in philosophy was taught by a team of three professors, ensuring students were exposed to a variety of viewpoints.[17]

By today's standards, Harvard's early pluralism may appear feeble,
marked by a clear preference for philosophers whose work followed empiricist and naturalist lines.[18] Moreover, Harvard philosophers believed few to
be as talented as Harvard graduates who, accordingly, made up a supermajority of its faculty. However, against the backdrop of a nineteenth-century
tradition in which philosophy instruction served to instill in its students a
university's particular doctrine of correct belief, the diversity of opinion
represented at Harvard was novel, as Hocking described in his essay "What
Does Philosophy Say?":

> I came hoping to find the truth at Harvard. Needless to say, I did not find the
> finished product. I found Royce and James, Palmer and Santayana, Munster-
> berg and Dickinson Miller, engaged in high debate, and rejoicing in the pres-
> ence of their colleagues as thinkers with whom they might happily differ.[19]

By R. B. Perry's description, Harvard "directly aimed at diversity in our
staff. When a new member was proposed we at once asked whether he
had the same mental attitude as someone we had already. If so, we did
not want him. There is therefore no Harvard 'school' of philosophy."[20]
Indeed, when asked whether the department's practices reflected a "conscious desire to attain . . . a diversity of views and methods" in a 1937 survey of Harvard's departments, the Philosophy Department's reply was
"definitely affirmative."[21] Whatever its limitations in practice, the idea of
pluralism was important to the self-conception of Harvard's Philosophy
Department. This ethos was also recognized at Harvard's peer institutions,
as highlighted in a 1927 report from Columbia's Philosophy Department:

> One of [our convictions] is that the organization of the Department should
> include men working in all the major fields and problems of philosophic
> interest, and representing opinions and viewpoints that are determined
> by the nature of their subject-matter. Of the other two major graduate

departments of Philosophy in the country, Chicago, closely united by many ties to Columbia, shares this aim, while Harvard prefers to include representatives of differing philosophic positions.[22]

Thus, because of its institutional links to Europe and philosophical heritage of pluralism, Harvard was uniquely positioned to introduce new philosophical ideas, including phenomenology, to the United States at the start of the twentieth century.

At the same time, however, some philosophers grew concerned with the implications of pluralism, fearing that it threatened philosophy's vitality and place in the university. Intellectual progress, they argued, required agreement on basic principles and methods of inquiry. Union Theological Seminary's William Adams Brown voiced these misgivings in a 1921 letter to R. B. Perry, writing that this "pluralistic and specializing tendency has gone so far as to threaten complete sterility and barrenness" in philosophy.[23] Indeed, even those who held pluralism as an ideal had some qualms. In a 1903 letter to Sarah Wyman Whitman, William James expressed his reservations about Harvard's approach, comparing it to philosophy at Chicago under John Dewey. "The result [in Chicago]," he wrote, "is wonderful—a *real School*, and *real Thought*. Important thought too! Did you ever hear of such a City or such a University? Here we have thought, but no school."[24] When religious education had been a core function of the college, "their libraries were inadequate, their education mediocre, and the literary culture in which they lived sentimental and unsophisticated."[25] However, philosophy's role within the university curriculum and the relationship of the philosopher to the community he served had been well defined. The transformation of the university into a space for professional training dislodged the philosopher from his central place as mediator of institutional norms and values. As R. B. Perry described in his 1931 tract, *A Defense of Philosophy*:

> Once in effective occupation of the whole empire of knowledge, the province of philosophy has been subdivided among its scientific progeny until there is no parental domain left. Philosophy thus becomes an empty title to the whole, a sort of Holy Roman Empire. Or, to change the figure, the philosopher becomes a sort of intellectual hobo wandering through ancestral estates, where he is tolerated as a concession to the past, but where he must be content to sleep in barns, and eat scraps at the back doors, of the scientific landed gentry.[26]

In their inability to settle on a common set of accepted methodologies for answering philosophical questions, philosophers stood in growing contrast to scholars in the physical sciences and emerging social scientific fields such as psychology, sociology, and economics. Thus, against the perception that philosophy was becoming outmoded by positivistic disciplines, some American philosophers began to reassess their role in the academy, adopting a *wissenschaftlich* view of their discipline meant to facilitate the development of a common formal framework. In the words of Arthur Lovejoy, philosophers should not esteem "diversity among men . . . so precious a thing that it were better that many men should to the end remain in error about some of the greatest matters of human concernment, than that, by knowing the truth, they should fall into a drab unanimity."[27]

The most influential American realist movements of the early twentieth-century, neorealism and critical realism, exemplified the effort to win scientific standing for philosophy. In 1910, a group of six philosophers, including Perry and Pitkin, published an article titled "The Program and First Platform of Six Realists," which opens: "Philosophy is famous for its disagreements, which have contributed not a little towards bringing it into disrepute as being unscientific, subjective, or temperamental." In the six essays that follow, the "Platform" provides a list of propositions conferred on and accepted by the group as a whole: a set of "axioms, methods, hypotheses and facts" that could serve as the common basis for a program of realist philosophy.[28] Finding consensus, they believed, was critical for the discipline. Indeed, as Pitkin wrote in a subsequent essay, titled "Is Agreement Desirable?," the question of its possibility amounts to "whether there are any fundamental philosophical issues or not."[29]

Pitkin and Perry were initially drawn to phenomenology by Husserl's analysis of logical entities in *Logical Investigations*, which had important parallels in their own work. Commonalities between their movements were also noted by phenomenologists. Aron Gurwitsch reported in 1940:

> To my surprise I have seen how close these American things can come to phenomenology when a couple of things are eliminated which are themselves intrinsically indefensible. Then it is almost child's play to translate neo-realism into the phenomenological, and both parties gain infinitely with this translation.[30]

Beyond these similarities, however, the American realists' search for a common method that could ensure a certain ground for philosophy shared important aims with Husserl's phenomenological "first philosophy." As

Marvin Farber wrote in 1928, "[Husserl] holds it to be a scandal that the philosophers disagree, whereas the experts in other fields come to agreement readily enough."[31] While the different intellectual genealogies and historical aims of these movements should not be understated, this transatlantic convergence on common ideas provided hospitable soil for the reception of Husserl's thought in America.

* * *

As R. B. Perry took a leading role in Harvard's Philosophy Department during the 1910s, interest in phenomenology at Harvard grew. Harry Costello's notes from Royce's fall 1913 seminar, "Scientific Methods," show the author's familiarity with Husserl and suggest phenomenology's inclusion in the course.[32] Harvard students also returned to Germany, studying under Husserl for the first time since Hocking's 1902 visit. Albert Chandler attended Husserl's lectures in 1912 while visiting Germany under the auspices of Harvard's Parker Fellowship. His dissertation, completed in 1913, was a study of Husserl and Plato.[33] The following year, another student in Harvard's Philosophy Department, R. L. M. Underhill, traveled to Germany with the support of a Henry Bromfield Rogers Memorial Fellowship. Although Underhill had planned to study phenomenology in Göttingen, he remained in Berlin after learning that Husserl was not offering his advanced course that fall.[34]

In 1914 Harvard's Philosophy Department also offered an assistantship appointment to Winthrop Pickard Bell, a philosopher from Halifax, Nova Scotia, who had received a master's degree in philosophy from Harvard in 1909. Bell began his subsequent doctoral work in Germany at Leipzig but transferred to Göttingen in 1911 to study phenomenology under Husserl.[35] With Bell on the verge of finishing his doctorate in 1914, Perry was excited by the prospect of his returning to Harvard to "help to fructify us with your knowledge of Husserl."[36] Writing the dean of the Graduate School, Perry explained that Bell's work on Husserl held "great promise," and that "he would bring to us a conversance with certain tendencies in German thought which we are very anxious to have represented."[37] Bell was guaranteed a teaching load that would leave at least half of his time for work on a book-length, English-language introduction to phenomenology.[38] Perry was also enthusiastic about Bell's proposal to teach a course on German philosophy in its original language. Urging him to accept Harvard's offer, Perry wrote: "I think that there is a strong probability that there would be more work open to you when you come," noting that the assistantship allowed the "opportunity to establish yourself more firmly for the following year." Perry continued: "There is a genuine opportunity for one or more younger men, and the one who is on the ground will always have considerable advantages over others."[39]

World events intervened to hinder Perry's plans. The completion of Bell's dissertation in 1914 coincided with the outbreak of war on the Continent and Bell's internment as a foreign national. Bell became the first Anglo-American to receive a doctorate from Husserl after defending his thesis from inside of detention facility. "The professors with whom I was to have my examination enquired and found that there was no actual rule that a candidate must be examined in the Aula," Bell recalled, "so they together with the distinguished man who was to be chairman of the affair, came to the place of my 'Haft' [detention] . . . and examined me there."[40] With doctorate in hand, Bell remained a prisoner. Despite Harvard's entreaties to the American State Department to secure his release, Bell was detained in Germany for the duration of the war.[41]

While Bell's detention thwarted Perry's effort to add a phenomenologist to Harvard's faculty, the university did appoint W. E. Hocking, Husserl's first American student, as an assistant professor in 1914. In the following decades, Hocking served as an important link between Harvard and Germany's growing phenomenological movement.[42] Although Harvard's Philosophy Department became fiercely antagonistic toward German thought during the First World War, the rift was short lived.[43] Repatriated at its conclusion, Bell was hired by Harvard as an instructor in 1922, a position then recommended only "when there is some expectation that the appointee may develop in such a way that the Department will be prepared to recommended appointment as assistant professor at a suitable later date, or that he will at least be a good candidate for similar openings elsewhere."[44] That same year, another PhD candidate at Harvard, Marvin Farber, departed to study in Germany under the auspices of a Sheldon Fellowship. Farber initially landed in Berlin, where he studied Kant and Hegel with Heinrich Maier and F. J. Schmidt, but he traveled to Freiberg in February of 1923 to meet Husserl, carrying a letter of introduction from Hocking.[45]

Husserl's influence and reputation in Germany had grown significantly since Hocking's 1902 visit, and phenomenology was a thriving philosophical movement, with circles of followers in Freiburg, Munich, Berlin, and Marburg. Between 1923 and 1937, at least ten Harvard students attended lectures by and, in some cases, studied directly under Husserl and Heidegger. Some were convinced by what they heard; others, of course, were not. Those who were drawn to phenomenology would be among the movement's early American promoters and contributors. However, among those who did not become phenomenologists themselves were philosophers such as Paul Weiss and Charles Hartshorne, who made important intellectual and institutional contributions to American metaphysics in the second half of the twentieth century, creating space for speculative philosophies like phenomenology that had few sympathetic venues in a philosophical landscape dominated by linguistic analysis.[46]

From Freiburg, Farber wrote to Hocking that he was so impressed by Husserl that he quickly "formed a resolution to sit at the feet of this sage." Husserl's *Logical Investigations* and *Ideas* became Farber's "daily companions" as he remained at Freiberg for the 1923/24 university term with a second year's funding as one of Harvard's Parker fellows.[47] Farber returned to America in 1924 and received his PhD from Harvard in 1925. His dissertation, *Phenomenology as a Method and as a Philosophical Discipline*, which was published in 1928, placed Husserl in dialogue with contemporary American philosophy, calling for a return to a common method of inquiry. As the first systematic treatment of Husserl's thought in the English language, it also gave most American philosophers their first opportunity to assess the movement that was making such a stir at Harvard. Susanne Langer, then a tutor at Radcliffe, expressed her appreciation to Farber in a 1929 letter, thanking him for a copy of his work. "It is," she wrote, "the first clear and straightforward account I have seen of what Phenomenology really is supposed to be. So far I have always thought of it as 'that which everybody goes to Germany to study and nobody will ever expound.'"[48]

The institutional transformations within Harvard University and American higher education that allowed American philosophers to encounter phenomenology in Germany simultaneously created a crisis for a growing community of thinkers who yearned for philosophical certainty through agreement on a common program. Yet, this crisis also fueled American interest in Husserl's phenomenological program, and Farber's dissertation provides valuable evidence of the role some American philosophers envisioned for it. Almost half a century after Farber traveled to Freiburg to study with Husserl, John Wild would argue in *The Radical Empiricism of William James* that James's psychology was a species of phenomenology "in the broader sense." Like Heidegger and Merleau-Ponty, James had enunciated an antireductive philosophy of existence. He treated experience as irreducible, identified its ground in preconceptual feeling that carried with it a fringe of meaning, and challenged Cartesian distinctions without yet knowing "how to escape from the use of dualistic language."[49] It is, therefore, ironic that for Farber and many of phenomenology's early adherents at Harvard, its allure reflected precisely the aspect of Husserl's project—its foundationalism—that contrasts most with Jamesian pragmatism.

Husserl's phenomenology, Farber explained, was a "first philosophy" in the tradition of Descartes and Socrates. Socrates advocated rigorous method, arguing that reason could pursue objective truth against the Sophist claim that "one can find theoretical grounds in support of every proposition, and at the same time just as strong grounds to refute them." Descartes had established the ideal of certain knowledge as the starting point of philosophy.[50] Husserl's phenomenology realized these objectives, providing "a sheerly descriptive method, setting up descriptions in the place of theory, and avoiding all constructions." The result was a new mode of discourse in which "in place of propositions and assertions, 'seeing' becomes our organon."[51] Husserl, Farber wrote, had restored the certain beginning of Descartes's *Meditations* and brought it to "an infinitely extended domain that is equally certain."[52]

> Descartes gave the title "Ego cogito" to the region of pure subjectivity. That is absolutely closed within itself, is immediately given, indubitable, and cannot be "crossed out." Husserl speaks of *one* universal science of subjectivity itself. There thus arises a science which is absolutely independent of all others: it does not presuppose any knowledge which is not derived from its field. . . . All transcendental disciplines and all sciences which are transcendentally founded arise out of it.[53]

From this indubitable beginning, Farber promised, phenomenology would provide the first concepts upon which the sciences of mathematics, space and motion, consciousness, and even society could be constructed.[54]

Starting with the first sentence of his dissertation, "The problem of a beginning in science (and a fortiori in philosophy) is a very difficult one," Farber presented Husserl's program as a mode of scientific inquiry. "Transcendental phenomenology," he wrote, "is the source of all possible methods and sciences. It is a thoroughly radical science, and its elaboration constitutes an infinite task for mankind to perform."[55] In characterizing the philosopher's task as a scientific endeavor, Farber was in the company of many leading American realists. Arthur Lovejoy, using similar language, called for philosophy to become a "science among sciences," and the new realists sought "a common technique, a common terminology, and so finally a common doctrine which will enjoy some measure of that authority which the natural sciences possess."[56] Farber, however, stipulated that philosophy is unique among sciences.

> It is a science of a decidedly new type and is of infinite extension. It has such methodological rigor, that none of the modern sciences can approach it in that respect. All philosophical disciplines are rooted in it, and it is only upon its elaboration that they receive their first force. It makes philosophy possible as a strict science.[57]

In other fields, the scientist would be free "to take some [terms] for granted from another discipline, which may be regarded as being the more fundamental *in this respect*." Psychology, for example, relies on physics to explain mechanical processes, while physics remains silent on the properties of mind. Thus, rather than reach an ultimate ground, Farber argued, "science as a whole moves in this circle of terms and their definitions."[58] Husserl's phenomenology promised an escape from this circle by providing a language that could serve as a common foundation for all sciences. Identifying another point of comparison with American philosophy, Farber invoked the concept of a "system-function-function," proposed by the Harvard logician Henry Sheffer, explaining that this language would "be that in which one [system-function-function] were the fundamental invariant, and from which ultimately all systems could be deduced."[59]

Farber worked to demonstrate the relevance of phenomenology to contemporary American philosophy throughout his dissertation. The genesis of its fifth chapter, "The Perceptual Object," illustrates the ease with which this was accomplished at Harvard during the 1920s. Slightly more than half of the chapter is taken verbatim from a paper Farber wrote for Alfred North Whitehead's seminar "Philosophical Presuppositions of Science." The most obvious differences between the seminar essay and dissertation chapter are the addition of entire sections, including "The Phenomenological Description of Perception."[60] However, the more elucidating changes are the systematic insertions of references to phenomenology into sentences and paragraphs that already existed in the seminar paper. In its original form, the following passage from the beginning of "The Perceptual Object" reads:

> It might be argued that if one is to speak of existence at all it is in the original and absolute sense subjective in character, a predicate, and that "objective"

existence is derived from it. To adhere for the moment to the schematism of an act-content-object, contents would have a first form of *derived* existence, objects a second form.[61]

In Farber's dissertation, the same passage reads:

> **It is argued in phenomenology** that if one is to speak of existence at all it is in the original and absolute sense subjective in character, a predicate, and that "objective" existence is derived from it. **The phenomenologist, having eliminated "I" existence, asks how we come to posit existence, and so seeks to determine its original meaning.** To adhere for the moment to the schematism of an act-content-object, contents would have a first form of *derived* existence, objects a second form.[62] [Additions shown in boldface.]

Similar insertions were made at least five times in the sections from the seminar paper, and a number of footnotes were added that address or include text from Husserl's *Ideas*. While the original paper takes explicitly phenomenological positions, arguing that a philosophy of "pure consciousness" provides a "presuppositionless beginning," it makes no mention of phenomenology and does not even name Husserl until its final pages.[63] Phenomenology is not, here, part of a separate Continental discourse that needs to be reconciled with American philosophy. Its name does not even need to be invoked for it to be understood.

* * *

To consider Farber's engagement with Husserlian phenomenology historically, it is useful to consider the environment in which he encountered it. Few details of Farber's subjective impressions of Germany have been preserved beyond his report that Freiberg was "a veritable hot-bed of Phenomenology" and his account of Husserl "an eminently fine teacher" whose "personal guidance and instruction" he was "fortunate" to have.[64] However, the diary of the British philosopher W. R. Boyce Gibson, who spent four months of 1928 in Freiburg, provides valuable evidence of the unique conditions that shaped the reception of phenomenology by the foreign philosophers who studied the movement on its native soil. Husserl fostered an ethos devoted to collaboration that called on his students "to take his ideas and work them for all they can." It was like, Gibson wrote, being conscripted as "privates in the great *Wissenschafts-armee*" in which "each of us disinterestedly [contributed] his quota."[65] Husserl himself was revered as a sage by this phalanx of philosophers, illustrated in Gibson's description of the frenzy that accompanied his lectures:

> Attended Husserl's first lecture on Phenomenological Psychology. Arrived in Hörsaal 2 at 5.5. Got seat on front bench. Room then became crowded out, students sitting on window ledges, standing against walls, thronging the doors. Beadle comes and shouts "Hörsaal 6," and there is a great stampede. Got a good seat in middle of room. The 168 places soon filled up and students left standing.[66]

Despite the image this scene evokes, Husserl was not a natural celebrity. His lectures were not fiery or prophetic but slow and deliberate, usually delivered from a prepared text. Neither did Husserl cultivate personal deference. Far from aloof or pretentious, he was uncommonly informal by the standards of German academia. Husserl shared long walks with students, invited them to dine at his house, and asked Gibson to address him as Herr Kollege. Indeed, Gibson noted, "I wish to set on record here how immensely I am impressed with Husserl's personality. He is wonderfully good to his students, takes endless trouble to make things clear to them." The reverence in which Husserl was held appears to have derived from his genuine conviction of phenomenology's epochal importance. Husserl was "full of the significance of his work, but with nothing petty about him."[67] It was, Gibson concluded, the "union of passion and intellectual power that makes the greatness of Husserl."[68] This passion was infectious, and, for those outsiders drawn into Husserl's orbit, Freiburg promised not only the chance to study phenomenology but the opportunity to become Husserl's collaborators in his great work.

In Farber's second year in Europe, he was joined by Charles Hartshorne, a future professor at the University of Chicago and significant contributor to American discourse on the philosophy of religion. Hartshorne was, like Farber, a graduate student in the Philosophy Department at Harvard and a beneficiary of a Sheldon Fellowship. Recommending Hartshorne for the fellowship, James Woods had explained that he planned "to study in the severest German schools of philosophy either at Marburg or at Göttingen," continuing: "We should be glad to add Hartshorne to our staff after he returns."[69] Hartshorne began the 1923 academic term in Britain, meeting professors at Oxford and St. Andrews. From there, he traveled to Holland, Belgium, and France in August, and attended the International Summer School at the University of Vienna in September. He remained in Vienna for October and November to work with the university's philosophy faculty. In December he traveled to Munich and finally joined Farber in Freiburg, where he met Husserl. Hartshorne remained with Husserl for six weeks before traveling to Marburg, where he became the first American to study with Martin Heidegger.[70] While Hartshorne's subsequent philosophical development was influenced more by Whitehead than Heidegger, he reviewed Heidegger's *Being and Time* for the *Philosophical Review* in 1929—the first analysis of the work in an American journal. The review was mixed. Hartshorne was critical of Heidegger for his reliance on "abstract" and "indefinite" categories like "consciousness of," but praised Heidegger as "the most subtle and painstaking, perhaps the most original and profound, of all contemporary German philosophers known to the present writer."[71]

> Not since Hegel has such use—for good and perhaps ill—been made of this plastic and flexible power [of the German language]. . . . As for the technical import of the new Phenomenology, a really adequate study of it, at least by a non-German, would call for more heroic labors than the foregoing review can pretend to represent, possibly than any student will find it altogether worth his while to attempt. Yet there is more than philosophical brilliance to reward him; there is, I think, genius.[72]

Nonetheless, Hartshorne was also forced to wonder "if much of his originality is not rather oddness, a new manner of speech, than novelty in fundamental conceptions," and confessed himself unable to make sense of the work's second division.[73]

While Farber was in Europe and Hartshorne readying his departure, Winthrop Pickard Bell was teaching the course "Philosophy of Value" at Harvard, which emphasized phenomenological analysis. Among his students was another future Sheldon fellow, Dorion Cairns. Of all Harvard's itinerant students, Cairns's experiences may best represent the transformative power of these young American philosophers' intellectual encounters in Germany. In support of Cairns's fellowship application, C. I. Lewis testified: "He is undoubtedly one of our best students and, when his age is considered, probably the most promising of all."[74] Hocking added, "His mind is subtle and inventive and capable of great steadiness in examining a difficult matter, and of unusual clearness in explaining it."[75] With letters of introduction from Hocking and Bell and an uncertain command of German, Cairns arrived on Husserl's doorstep in September 1924.[76] In their first meeting, Cairns wrote, Husserl "turned around in his desk chair, took down the first part of the second volume of [*Logical Investigations*], and said: 'Study this.

Study it pen in hand. If you don't understand or if you object, write down your question or objection. Come to me next week with what you have done and we shall discuss it together.'"[77] At first Cairns struggled to make sense of Husserl's teachings. Cairns's knowledge of phenomenology was limited to what he had learned from Bell, and his poor understanding of German "discouraged" him from attempting to read *Logical Investigations* on his own.[78] Thus, as he reported to James Woods, he "had to begin at the beginning":

> We would expound on the ABCs [of phenomenology] once, twice, many times again. This was getting nowhere, but at last I hit upon a better method. Instead of telling my troubles I would display (not too crudely) my understanding of some point related to that which bothered me. This worked excellently. One never discusses with Husserl; rather one suggests themes whereon he may hold forth. My new method of suggestion ensured that the ensuing disquisition would be an enlargement rather than a repetition of views already familiar. My questions, moreover, by remaining silent generally found their answers.[79]

It was, Cairns wrote, as if Husserl would "lay his mind alongside that of the student" to work through philosophical problems with them together. "I feel when leaving his study," he remarked, "that I have been listening to one of the great philosophers. And it is a beneficial experience, that of occupying oneself almost entirely in thinking the thoughts of a true philosopher after him, and seeing thereby the coherence of a system of ideas." With Husserl's help, Cairns wrote that he was making progress toward developing a theory of judgment informed by phenomenology.[80] Ultimately, Cairns concluded: "The guy [Husserl] is right! And nobody else. He's right . . . and I'm going to stick with him. Who cares about a grand tour?"[81]

The following year, Harvard's Philosophy Department nominated Vivian J. McGill for a Sheldon Fellowship. McGill's application indicates that he intended to study with G. E. Moore, C. D. Broad, and J. M. E. McTaggart in England.[82] However, after spending the fall in Cambridge, McGill left for Freiburg and Husserl in 1925.[83] There, McGill joined Cairns, whose Sheldon Fellowship had been renewed to facilitate his continuing studies with Husserl. Indeed, when Cairns returned to Harvard in 1926, James Woods petitioned the Sheldon Committee to extend Cairns's fellowship for an unprecedented third year. "The man whom I recommend," he wrote, "has just completed a term as Sheldon Fellow. His record was an exceedingly high one when he was recommended . . . but during the past month we have had an opportunity to see how greatly he has increased his powers under the influence of Husserl."[84]

Cairns did not receive a second fellowship renewal and, so, returned to Harvard in 1926. Despite his teachers' high estimation of his abilities, Cairns struggled to complete his dissertation.[85] In the fall of 1931, with his thesis still unfinished, Cairns returned to Germany to resume work with Husserl. Husserl believed Cairns to be one of his most promising disciples, describing him to Aron Gurwitsch as "the future of phenomenology in the New World" and writing that Cairns was "among the very rare ones who have penetrated into the deepest sense of my phenomenology."[86] During his second visit to Freiburg, Cairns was given access to Husserl's unpublished manuscripts and kept records of his 150 meetings with the professor.[87] In the spring of 1932 he wrote to R. B. Perry at Harvard:

> I have been working with Husserl since last June, preparing a book on his philosophy. I intend to offer it as a thesis at Harvard a year from now and if possible to publish it thereafter. . . . [Husserl] has taken great interest in my work and thinks that for its sake I should stay a year longer than I can on my own means. I agree but on the other hand I feel that my friends at Harvard probably think that by the fall of 1933 it will be time that I took a position and showed I can fill it. . . . But Husserl is seventy-three and may very well lose his mind or die before then. I could still work on his MSS but would lose the great advantage of personal discussion. This consideration moved me to come here as soon as I could instead of staying in America for a degree and a job. It makes me want to stay here now. . . . I am increasingly convinced of Husserl's tremendous importance not only for German but also for American philosophy. Indeed, I feel there is nothing else quite so important.[88]

Ultimately, Cairns did return to America, and in 1933 he submitted his dissertation, titled "The Philosophy of Edmund Husserl." It represented the most sophisticated analysis of the ultimate stage of Husserl's program that had thus far been written in the English language.[89]

After 1926, three years passed before Harvard students returned to Germany to study phenomenology. However, interest in the movement did not wane in Emerson Hall. The same year that McGill returned to Harvard, Ralph Monroe Eaton, a logician who had been appointed as an assistant professor at Harvard, received a Guggenheim Fellowship to conduct research in Freiburg for a work on Husserl's phenomenology. A 1926 letter from Eaton to Harvard's Dean Clifford Moore reported that his work with Husserl had made him "sure he is the greatest of present-day German philosophers."[90] The following year, in the spring of 1927, Winthrop Bell taught the first course on phenomenology offered at Harvard or in the United States: "Philosophy 29: Husserl and the 'Phenomenological' Movement." Bell's notes from the seminar's first session observed that Harvard students seemed "drawn to Freiburg." However, for those who could not visit Husserl to study phenomenology, "Well, why not read it?" With no published translations of Husserl's writings in existence, enrollment in the course, required German proficiency. Close readings of Husserl's *Logical Investigations* were the seminar's principal focus, supplemented by Bell's notes from his studies with Husserl and discussion of other phenomenologists, such as Max Scheler and Alexander Pfänder. Although his main focus was Husserl's Göttingen period, Bell also assigned selections from Husserl's *Ideas* and included a question about *epoché* on the course's final exam.[91] While Bell's seminar demonstrates the possibility of phenomenological education in America during the interwar era, it was offered only once. Bell left Harvard at its conclusion, turning down reappointment and returning to Canada to care for his wife's health.[92] The next seminar on Husserl offered in America would be taught by Alward Embury Brown, another Harvard PhD, at Indiana University in 1934.[93] However, phenomenology endured at Harvard despite Bell's departure. In 1930 R. B. Perry visited Husserl in Freiburg, and the Harvard Philosophy Department's qualifying exam in Logic included a question about Husserl. In 1932, W. E. Hocking reported to his former teacher in Germany that "Philosophy flourishes vigorously at Harvard, and the interest in Phenomenology is keen."[94]

* * *

In the subsequent decade, American engagement with phenomenology shifted toward Husserl's apparent heir, Martin Heidegger. The next Americans to study phenomenology in Germany were Paul Weiss, then an instructor at Harvard, who made the journey to Freiburg under the auspices of a Sears Fellowship, and Everett John Nelson, a recipient of Harvard's Sheldon Fellowship. Weiss reported that Heidegger "is very popular here—he reads to 400 students four times a week." However, Weiss did not count himself among the converted. "So far as I have been able to discover," he continued, "Heidegger is the best man they have. It has proved well worth being here, but it begins to look as if phenomenology is soon going to show terrible gaps."[95] Weiss's disillusionment with phenomenology appeared to be complete by the fall of 1931, when he wrote to R. B. Perry that Husserl's *Ideas* was "about as bad a philosophic work I have ever read."[96] Nelson also attended Heidegger's lectures, which he found "very hard to understand." Although Husserl did not offer courses during Nelson's time in Freiburg, he reported that they had become personally acquainted. Nelson found Husserl to be "a very amiable old man, though quite absorbed in his own doctrines, and having undoubting faith in the future importance of his work."[97]

Following Weiss and Nelson, John Wild visited Heidegger during 1930–1931. Wild had served as an instructor in Harvard's Philosophy Department since 1927 and, like Eaton, received a Guggenheim Fellowship to conduct philosophical studies in Europe. The stated purpose of Wild's fellowship was "a study in England and in Ireland of the philosophical works of George Berkeley; and for research in other European libraries, and consultation with authorities."[98] However, Wild also journeyed to Freiburg, where he participated in Heidegger's seminar on Aristotle.[99] His correspondence with Perry described his impressions of Heidegger: "One can understand from his really extraordinary command of the texts why the students flock to hear him as they do. His clear cut demand for sharp and exact thought is extremely necessary here, as the Germans are so apt to go off in a blurge [*sic*] of mystical Schwärmerei."[100] The paucity of archival records from this period in Wild's life makes it difficult to know more about his experience with Heidegger in Germany. That more than two decades would elapse before phenomenology became a major focus of Wild's writings further impedes efforts to discern the impact of this encounter on his thought. However, correspondence with Dorion Cairns shows that Wild remained intellectually engaged with phenomenology during the 1930s.[101] After a promotion to assistant professor at Harvard in 1933, Wild expressed interest in teaching a new course titled "Time and Existence," focusing on Henri Bergson, Husserl, and Heidegger. He also offered to take over instruction of "Contemporary Philosophy" from J. W. Miller, noting that he would include units on Bergson and Heidegger. Instead, the department elected for Wild to teach a course on Augustine and an advanced seminar in ethics during the 1935/36 term.[102] However, it appears that Wild did incorporate Heidegger's philosophy into his regular course instruction. A 1940 letter from W. E. Hocking, recommending Wild for promotion to associate professor, praised Wild's "vitality" and "continued growth," citing the breadth of his teaching, which included "courses in ancient philosophy, using Greek texts, English empiricism, Kierkegaard and the contemporary German philosophy of Existenz as exemplified by Heidegger."[103]

Wild also contributed to phenomenology's development during the 1930s by overseeing dissertations that took phenomenological themes.

Wild was a member of the committee for Dorian Cairns's dissertation, "The Philosophy of Edmund Husserl," Charles Malik's "The Metaphysics of Time in the Philosophies of A. N. Whitehead and M. Heidegger," and Erminie Huntress's "The Phenomenology of Conscience." Unfortunately, little information is available on Huntress, who received her PhD from Radcliffe in 1937. Her dissertation, which offers an account of moral intuition grounded in Heideggerian analysis of being, is intriguing, placing Heidegger in dialogue with such thinkers as John Dewey and Sigmund Freud. Huntress also summarized substantial sections of both divisions I and II of *Being and Time*, predating later efforts to faithfully paraphrase Heidegger's seminal work in English by more than a decade.[104]

After a brief lull, four more Harvard students traveled to Germany to study with Heidegger between 1935 and 1938: Henry Veatch, William Frankena, Charles Malik, and Robert Trayhern.[105] Their experiences varied significantly, as did the effect of their encounters. For instance, Frankena visited Freiburg at the end of a term that included studies at Oxford and Cambridge. After attending Heidegger's lectures, Frankena reported:

> Thus far I have not been impressed by anything I have heard here, though I am glad to have opportunity [*sic*] to observe Heidegger's method of conducting a seminar . . . but Cambridge has, I fear, penetrated too far under my skin for me to follow suit, at least in the short time I have to spend here.

Even still, phenomenology was not without interest to Frankena. "I am now reading Scheler," he continued, which "makes me wish I knew Husserl and the other phenomenologists."[106] In the years that followed, Frankena established himself as an important contributor to analytic philosophy. However, he remained convinced of phenomenology's importance, and of the value of pluralism at Harvard. Frankena was among those whom Harvard's Philosophy Department consulted in 1961 while considering the appointment of John Rawls to a position vacated by John Wild. "I hope the recommendation to appoint Rawls," Frankena wrote, "does not mean that Harvard is departing from its tradition of having representatives of the most various interests and points of view, e.g.[,] of continental European philosophy."[107]

Charles Malik, whose studies under Heidegger were concurrent with Frankena's, was more immediately affected by his encounter with phenomenology:

> I began to understand clearly what Heidegger talked about, and this understanding thrilled me immensely. I suddenly realized I was miles and miles

behind the scholarship of the Germans, and it was plain that it was hopeless for me ever to catch up with them. I do not know whether you can really appreciate the sting of the terrible feeling of complete existential hopelessness. Will you be kind enough to make an effort to believe me as I say that I now sincerely believe that I know absolutely nothing. This is no sentimentalism; this is an expression of what I literally believe.[108]

For Malik, who would later oversee the drafting and passage of the 1948 UN Universal Declaration of Human Rights, the discovery of Heidegger's phenomenology was a profound personal event. Using language that mirrors Heidegger's description of *anxiety* as a technical term, Malik wrote that his own previous work "took on an immediate air of unreality and childishness" in the wake of this encounter.[109] However, as a Lebanese national in Germany during 1936, Malik's experience was also marked by personal difficulties. Nazi racial ideology pervaded the German intellectual society Malik so admired. As he recounted in a letter to Hocking:

It is brought home to me on every side and in diverse and subtle ways that I belong to a defeated race; that individual goodness anywhere is complete nonsense; that there are as many truths as there are "races," if not "peoples"; that because I belong to a country which cannot boast of an immediate brilliant history, I am rightly to be accounted nothing; that good-will and innocence and well-meaning questioning are sin; that because my blood does not trace itself to Nordic origins I possess throughout all eternity a distinctly inferior soul.

The tone of Malik's letter is alternatingly tortured and mocking, presenting in the same list the ludicrous ("That Plato and Aristotle were great because they had a preponderance of Nordic blood in them") and the terrifying ("that the highest virtues of the noblest 'races' can manifest themselves only in war; that these virtues should so manifest themselves; that no nobleness can arise in these noblest 'races' except on a basis of some systematic hatred"). Living in Germany, Malik wrote, "I had to feel and face these things," and, he admitted, "it is impossible for me to pretend that I am, or can be, 'above' these things." Most of all, Malik was tormented by his own conviction of Germany's philosophical superiority. As he wrote:

The anguish of my being arises not from the fact that I <u>know</u> that the above doctrines are false, and that I cannot proclaim their falsehood there. This anguish arises from the fact that I definitely do <u>not know</u> that these doctrines are false, and that they may all be true. My anguish is the following question which many a time stares me with all seriousness, and which I sometimes half-believe: May not all these doctrines be true?[110]

Malik's experience in Germany signaled the end of a unique period in transatlantic history. During the late nineteenth and early twentieth centuries, barring the interruption of the First World War, advances in transportation and political stability in Europe allowed a certain class of Americans unprecedented ability to experience European culture both widely and intimately. In this grand age of the Wanderjahr, American students encountered European intellectual life, not as the passive readers of foreign imports, evaluated for their suitability to American discourse, but as active participants in the great philosophical debates of old Europe. As subsequent chapters will explore, the rise of Nazism and fascism radically changed this dynamic, reversing the flow of intellectual migration between Europe and America and permanently altering the vision of continental Europe in the American mind.

A

Marjorie Glicksman Grene

Marjorie Glicksman Grene, born in 1910, was one of the very few women of her generation to attain professional success as a philosopher in America. As one of the country's first interpreters of Heidegger and Sartre's work, she was also an important mediator of existential phenomenology's reception in the United States. For more than a decade, before the Macquarrie and Robinson translation rendered *Being and Time* into English, Grene's books were among the rare scholarly works on Heidegger's philosophy available to Americans. However, as a pioneer along multiple axes, her career and intellectual trajectory followed a winding path, unique even among the figures profiled in this work. During a period of philosophical productivity that lasted almost seventy years, Grene's writings touched on many of the twentieth century's important philosophical traditions, including deconstruction, existentialism, linguistic analysis, logical positivism, phenomenology, and pragmatism. At the same time, Grene was an insightful interpreter of historical figures such as Plato, Aristotle, Descartes, Hume, and Kant. "Since we are histories, and Western philosophy is a history," Grene explained, "locating our own concerns judiciously within that history illuminates and enriches our own beliefs and our own arguments."[1]

Phenomenology was part of Grene's personal history, built into the foundational layer of a philosophical life, both long and fractured, in which she repeatedly returned to the phenomenological tradition as an interpreter, as a critic, and as an original philosopher enriched by its insights. Yet, despite her importance within the American phenomenological movement, Grene explicitly rejected identification as a "phenomenologist." This was, in part, a matter of terminology. Grene did not, for instance, consider Merleau-Ponty to be a phenomenologist, applying a narrow definition of phenomenology that emphasized technical features of Husserl's *Ideas* such as the phenomenological reduction.[2] Still, even under a broader definition of the phenomenological movement, Grene is more accurately classified as a fellow traveler than as a member. Grene insisted that she was not an admirer of Heidegger, and her earliest writings on him were scathing. Indeed, she wrote, "I have been angry with Heidegger ever since I heard the Heidelberg version of his *Rektoratsrede*," in which he embraced the Nazi Party. Grene consistently dismissed Heidegger's later writings as "pretentious nonsense," deplored "his deep and fanatical German nationalism," and regarded even *Being and Time* as a deeply flawed work.[3] Yet, she also praised Heidegger as "the first great philosopher of this century systematically to evade the Cartesian alternative," writing in 1974 that "for this reason if for no other it is fair to say that any contemporary philosophy ought to proceed from the foundation established once and for all in *Being and Time*."[4]

While Grene's relationship with phenomenology was complicated by both personal and philosophical reservations, her original work incorporated important ideas from the phenomenological tradition that were largely ignored by mainstream American philosophers. Thus, against the polarization of the analytic-Continental divide, Grene's ambivalent relationship with Heidegger and the broader phenomenological movement adds depth to the story of its reception in the United States. Her novel contributions to epistemology and the philosophy of science show how engagement with phenomenology might have contributed to mainstream American philosophy, even if its methods and style did not win unqualified acceptance.

* * *

Grene's intellectual and professional life were defined by the dynamics of her search for alternatives to the constraints of tradition and society. Her writings drew widely on ideas from across traditions and time, soldered into a systematic philosophy by the admixture of her unique perspective on the production of scientific knowledge and her ability to identify commonalities in diverse philosophical approaches. In her analysis of philosophy's perennial problems, Grene eschewed established poles of debate, rejecting dichotomies such as the opposition of subjectivity and objectivity, knowledge and belief, material and mind, and the human and natural worlds, while refusing to collapse them entirely. Instead, Grene charted a path that retained these distinctions even as she asserted the impossibility of explicitly defining them, arguing for a realism marked by ineluctable ambiguity. Personally and professionally, Grene lived within the narrow constraints afforded an American woman born in 1910. Her struggle within and against her historical situation shaped not only the context but the content of her work. In the age of professionalization, Grene's distance from the academy might have foreclosed participation in philosophical discourse altogether. Yet, although Grene could not escape the mark of her outsider status within the profession, she discovered that her position permitted an alternative: working as an interpreter of a philosophical tradition that the American mainstream also had not assimilated.

Working under the auspices of Harvard's Philosophy Department, Grene received a PhD from Radcliffe in 1935. Given her proximity to the currents that directed so many of Harvard's graduate students to study philosophy in Germany, it is surprising that Harvard played no role in Grene's encounter with phenomenology. For this reason, Grene's experiences also provide an illuminating perspective on the phenomenological movement and professional American philosophy from outside the restrictive worlds of Harvard men and European émigrés who dominate this narrative. Grene had traveled to Freiburg in 1931 as a German American research fellow from Wellesley, where she had studied as an undergraduate. There, she attended Heidegger's lectures and "participated (silently!)" in Heidegger's seminar on *Phaedrus*.[5] Her account of this experience, written several years later during a phase of engagement with positivism, is reminiscent of a captivity narrative.

> It should be added, perhaps, that the forcefulness of Heidegger's "aristocratic" arguments depends in large part on the personality of the lecturer. One is caught as in a political rally by the slow intensity of his speech. The contemptuous epigrams with which he dismisses the protest of logic or good sense sting the listener's ears with their acidity; and his prophetic solemnity when he invokes the quest for Being ties one as spellbound as if one were a novice taking his first step into the rituals of the Eleusinian mysteries. One sits on the edge of one's chair and agrees breathlessly: no point-of-viewlessness, only courage of point of view—and oh, were one but among the blessed few to have it.[6]

In Grene's case, Heidegger's enchantments did not survive outside of Freiburg. After returning to America, Grene gradually concluded that her enthusiasm for membership in Heidegger's philosophical aristocracy had been misplaced. Her 1938 "Confessions of a Young Positivist" represent the nadir in a dynamic relationship with Heidegger's work, during which she claimed to find no insight in it. "A close examination seems rather to expose," she wrote, "within the ponderous sentences of essay and lecture, a very insubstantial basis for a flimsy superstructure. Heidegger's philosophy is unique only in its rampant misuse of language and its own emphatic claim to uniqueness."[7]

By skipping from 1931 to 1938, however, I have bypassed several important events in Grene's life and intellectual development. While Grene later claimed that her initial reading of *Being and Time* showed "minimal understanding—certainly no grasp of the great question of Being," she admitted that Heidegger's seminar on *Phaedrus* had been "not only an excellent exercise in reading a philosophical text; it was also the start of my life under the guidance of the *Phaedrus* and the *Symposium*."[8] Heidegger's approach to textual analysis, which sought both to recover a work's original meaning and to interpret it as a historical event in the genealogy of metaphysics, left an indelible mark on Grene. However, her engagement with the history of philosophy lacks the egocentric edge of Heidegger's *Destruktion*. Where Heidegger cast himself as the first thinker to see through millennia of mistaken philosophical edifice back to the question of Being, Grene tended toward self-effacing modesty.

After returning to Germany to study with Karl Jaspers in 1932, Grene began her doctoral studies at Radcliffe. Impressively, she completed the degree in only two years, working with David Prall, Alfred North Whitehead, and C. I. Lewis. Grene's dissertation, "The Concept of *Existenz* in Contemporary German Philosophy," attempted to render the philosophy of Heidegger and Jaspers into the epistemological framework of Lewis's "conceptual pragmatism," which transplanted a quasi-Kantian epistemology into a pragmatic framework that eschewed the poles of idealism and realism. Lewis's philosophy shared important features with Heidegger's existential phenomenology: it privileged everyday experience, made a problem of the subject-object distinction, emphasized action, and rejected efforts to render truth in terms of correspondence. Of course, the work of assimilating existentialist thought required some elements of Lewis's epistemology to be radicalized; Grene's dissertation, following Heidegger, goes much further than Lewis in rejecting the Cartesian ego's "closet of consciousness," which is ontologically distinct from the world. However, this approach allowed Grene to translate Heideggerian concepts into a framework that was familiar and accessible to many American philosophers. For instance, Grene interpreted Heidegger's dichotomy of the ontic and ontological in terms of Lewis's distinction between extension and intension.[9] Likewise, Heidegger's critique of Cartesian subjectivity was rendered as: "When the category of motion or possibility is made prior to the category of substance, there is no need to ask how a subject-substance reaches out to an object substance. The process of empirical cognition can be examined <u>as</u> a process."[10] This interpretation of Heidegger's ontology does considerable violence to the text, rendering existential phenomenology epistemologically and evading the "question of Being," which Heidegger considered its objective. Yet, while the language of Lewis's conceptual pragmatism is a variously deficient framework for the interpretation of *Being and Time*, this approach did not, at least, parse Heidegger's prose as meaningless pseudophilosophy as had Carnap's demonstration of its translation into a "logically correct" extensional language.[11]

Grene later wrote that the topic of her dissertation had held no particular interest for her. Rather, she explained, she "thought foolishly if I did something quickly I could get out and get a teaching position." Grene described her dissertation as "hasty and atrocious," adding her hope that its home in Radcliffe's library was "very deep and inaccessible."[12] However, a devastatingly self-critical register is not atypical of Grene's writing. A Heideggerian sensitivity to the historicity of existence not only motivated Grene's engagement with the Western philosophical canon, but also seems to have instilled a recognition of being-her-own-history that accounts for Grene's unusual relationship with her own writings. In a career marked by its thematic and methodological variations, Grene came to regard much of her work as flawed or outdated. Rarely did she praise old arguments or articles. Plentiful, by contrast, were regrets over a "defective" work or a "book I should have left unwritten."[13] However, like Dasein "relentlessly thrown back upon itself" to ask "the question of Being," Grene's mode of philosophy was characterized by a sort of hermeneutical motion. Philosophy is a response to one's situation that, by taking up new possibilities of knowing and being, perpetually constitutes the philosopher's world. Grappling with this historicity, as I believe Grene did, requires the philosopher, again and again, to return to her work, not as the permanent foundation for future constructions, but as an element of a holistic composition-in-process.[14]

On the subject of philosophical criticism, I hasten to add that Grene possessed a formidable wit, which peppers her works with razor-sharp barbs and clever asides. To give one example, after rebutting Descartes's argument for distinguishing thinking humans from "brute" animals, Grene joked, "Of course, attacking poor Descartes for his brutism is beating a very dead horse."[15] For philosophers, such verbal agility is often considered a virtue, which helped elevate masters of quips like Sidney Morgenbesser to mythic stature. From a woman speaking of and to men in the 1930s, however, a cutting remark was hardly guaranteed to earn approval. The minimal extant record of Grene's experience outside her life as a writer leaves one to wonder how the presence of such a woman registered in the professional spaces she occupied. In this context, however, Grene's silence in Heidegger's seminar takes on another possible meaning.

Perhaps it was not "foolish" for a talented student such as Grene to believe that completion of a dissertation at Radcliffe would provide entry to the world of American professional philosophy. After all, it should have. Certainly, however, her belief was misinformed. As the next chapter will highlight, academic hiring was at a virtual standstill in 1935. However, even before the Great Depression, there had been little space for American women in the profession of philosophy. As subsequent chapters will detail, the "old boy's network" was not merely a component of philosophy's professional organization but the mechanism of appointments in its entirety. When a department received permission to make a junior appointment, its chair would send letters to leading graduate programs in philosophy that described the opening and solicited recommendations of potential candidates from among the program's recent students. While these appointment requests rarely specified gender exclusions explicitly—one exception is a 1961 letter from the University of Maine, which reads, "Basically, we are interested in a good <u>man</u>" [emphasis in the original][16]—the mechanism of departmental nominations was usually a reliable patriarchal barrier.

The most successful woman in early twentieth-century American philosophy was Susanne Langer, a talented student of Alfred North Whitehead whose work earned her an appointment as a tutor at Radcliffe from 1927 to 1942. Despite significant publications, Langer did not receive a tenured appointment until 1954.[17] Grene did not receive a tenured appointment until 1965, when she was hired by the University of California, Davis.[18] Indeed, no woman was appointed as an assistant professor, associate professor, or professor of philosophy in any of the discipline's leading departments before 1949, when Elizabeth Flower was appointed as an assistant professor by the University of Pennsylvania. In this group of leading departments, consisting of Berkeley, Chicago, Columbia, Cornell, Harvard, Michigan, Pennsylvania, Princeton, Stanford, UCLA, and Yale, only one other woman—Mary Mothersill (Chicago)—was hired before 1960. During the 1960s, the group hired only three other women: Isabel Hungerland (Berkeley), Patricia Ann James (Yale), and Margaret D. Wilson (Princeton).[19] Outside the stratum of elite departments, the situation was not much better. According to a survey of 827 degree-granting institutions, of the 891 individuals employed as full-time faculty in philosophy during the 1955/56 collegiate year, only forty-four (4.9%) were women. In a separate survey of 727 institutions of higher education, only four reported that "qualified women might be employed in larger numbers" within their philosophy departments.[20]

Despite Grene's accomplishments, the only professional spaces open to her in American philosophy were marginal or peripheral. However, using her knowledge of phenomenology (itself an inhabitant of American philosophy's periphery), she created opportunities for herself. After completing her dissertation, Grene was awarded a fellowship to study Kierkegaard in Denmark and, the following year, an appointment as the assistant director of residence at Monticello College, a women's junior college. As Grene recounted, the posting at Monticello was her return on a job search in which she inquired after positions at 129 colleges and universities. A formal offer of employment at Monticello was made only after an interview by a Bostonian friend of the college's president, dispatched to ensure that Grene, then still Glicksman, was not a Jew. In 1937, Grene's situation improved when she was hired as a teaching assistant for Rudolf Carnap at the University of Chicago. It was in this context that Grene wrote her "Confessions" on Heidegger. However, her dalliance with logical positivism was brief, as she quickly concluded that a science such as biology was not explicable through extensional logic.[21]

Grene returned to this topic decades later, in her paper "Philosophy of Medicine: Prolegomena to a Philosophy of Science," which offers an account of science that takes medicine rather than physics as its model—"if instead of with Copernicus and Galileo, we began with Vesalius, if we concentrated on the physic, not the physics, of Padua." Using John F. Murray's *The Normal Lung* as a case study, Grene derived fundamental principles of science at odds with the reductionist tendencies of physics. These include a presupposition of the existence of "natural kinds," the irreducibility of processes from real-world organic systems, a continuity between "perception and quantification" as well as "belief and knowledge," and the character of science as a cognitive and technical "art." Medical science, Grene argued, also relies on a concept of "normality" that is neither reducible to statistical frequency nor a measure of health. Thus, she held, a philosophy of science applicable to medicine would need to admit normative judgment as an ineliminable element of empirical observation, "rooted in the perception-mediated understanding of what goes on in the real natural world."[22]

Although Grene considered leaving philosophy to study law, her appointment by Chicago as an instructor in philosophy kept her in the profession and provided the opportunity to teach courses on the history of philosophy. Grene continued as an instructor at Chicago until 1944, publishing an anthology titled *From Descartes to Kant* in 1940, as well as several articles. However, with enrollments diminished by the war and without the protection of tenure, she was dismissed, told that her "services were no longer wanted."[23] Grene described what followed as a fifteen-year "exile" from philosophy, during which time she lived in Illinois and Ireland with her husband, the classicist and farmer David Grene. Marjorie Grene said little about this period of her life, during which she raised her children while working on the family's farm. However, it seems that exile was not entirely without its pleasures. Her daughter, Ruth Grene, recalled, "My mother always said that she enjoyed being 'Mrs. Grene of Clash,'" the small village outside Dublin in which they lived.[24] Her unconventional trajectory also provided intellectual benefits. Later, Marjorie Grene attributed her insights about Descartes's and Hobbes's analyses of human and animal minds in "On Some Distinctions between Men and Brutes" to her experience as a mother and a farmer.[25] Moreover, she continued to make significant contributions to the philosophy of the English-speaking world despite her distance from the academy. Her 1948 *Dreadful Freedom: A Critique of Existentialism* was among the first scholarly works on existentialism published in the English language, and the first to provide an extended examination of Heidegger's thought. Her monograph *Martin Heidegger* followed in 1957.[26]

In a 2002 autobiographical essay, Grene wrote that she had been skeptical of the enclosed subjectivity of the Cartesian cogito even during her limited encounter with philosophy in her undergraduate years at Wellesley. Her search for an alternative to Cartesian dualism that recognized the holistic unity of the self and its environment was, in her account, "one persistent strand implicit or explicit in much of my work."[27] However, *Dreadful Freedom* veers off this purportedly straight trajectory, focusing on Sartre's subjectivistic existentialism and discussing Heidegger primarily through the lens of Sartre's interpretation of him as an existentialist. *Dreadful Freedom* also eschews Heidegger's critical distinction between the ontic and ontological modes of analysis, which Grene had discussed in her dissertation, stating that on matters of ontology "I must humbly confess, I simply cannot follow them unless in the spirit in which one follows Alice down the rabbit-hole."[28] As such, the work's scope is restricted, focusing on the examination of existentialism as an ethical and psychological alternative to the dominant traditions in Western thought. Existentialism's novelty, Grene wrote, lay in its efforts to "reinterpret human nature in terms of human subjectivity itself, not through superhuman religious or subhuman material categories." By showing the derivation of human values from their "desperately human" situation, the work of Sartre and Heidegger is "if not valid, at least terribly relevant to the dilemma of those who can find comfort in no creed of God or science."[29]

The search for alternatives is, of course, a well-represented theme in American philosophy. James Kloppenberg, for instance, has argued that late nineteenth- and early twentieth-century pragmatism sought a via media between the era's philosophical and social absolutes.[30] However, Grene's perspective on American society was foundationally different from that of James or Dewey. Grene found that pragmatism had little to offer an American woman in the 1930s. Reminiscing on her life from the dawn of the twenty-first century, Grene wrote that "when my colleagues mention James or Dewey, I simply scream or gnash my teeth."[31] From Grene's position, America appeared beset by injustice and despair, masked only by a cultural imperative "to forget all unpleasantnesses and therefore most realities." Against this context, she believed, pragmatism cultivated "the 'adjusted' individual, the stereotyped individual, the individual who has forgotten how to be an individual." As an ethics guided by the "comfort" of the social body, she wrote, pragmatism was "afraid to face evil" and, therefore, of little use to a woman maladjusted to a patriarchal academy and effectively excluded from the ranks of professional philosophy.[32] Existentialism, however, denied the transcendent validity of any social or biological standard, leaving each individual alone and responsible for her choices. "This is, one may say, a terrible doctrine," Grene wrote. "And, in fact, the realization of my responsibility to make of my world what it, and with it I, can be brings inescapably, when it is genuine, terror before the full meaning of that responsibility."[33]

Despite its terrible virtues, Grene also rejected existentialism's sufficiency as a ground for ethical philosophy. To its credit, existentialism extols authenticity and provides an account of guilt that does not reduce it to feelings of pain or displeasure. Yet, the solitary existentialist, responsible only to her own freedom and alone in facing death, is a poor guide to the shared world in which we dwell.[34] Heidegger's account of Being-with-others, Grene noted, does not appear to support authentic modes of social relations such as friendship or family.[35] As Grene wrote, "Like Heidegger, to view the existence of others only as a means to my freedom is worse than not good enough—it is positively evil. Yet it is difficult, in existential language, to say why."[36] Grene diagnosed a similar blindness to relations with others in Sartre's ethics, critiquing his famous advice to a young man deciding between joining the Free French resistance and caring for his mother. She rejected Sartre's conclusion that he was left alone to make the choice:

True, the boy's choice is this very concrete particular choice which no pre-existent values can determine. But he does not therefore choose as if, suddenly and out of all relation to the freedom of any other person, he alone had to decide. . . . It is the history of two people together that is at issue. Yet, existentially seen, the son chooses not only in his situation but alone in it.[37]

Relationships are not, in other words, incidental to an existence that is essentially solitary and free. They constitute the shared world of human life. One's possibilities for freedom are ways of being within this mutually constituted lifeworld, not projections into material objectivities. A philosophy that fails to recognize one's intersubjective and historical situation as the ground of one's freedom could not theorize an ethics that takes anything but the individual as its subject. Thus, despite its insights, Grene concluded that "existentialism provides . . . no adequate means of elevating the individual's search for freedom to the status of a universal principal."[38] In this respect, despite its countercultural status, existentialism is more of a parallel than an alternative to dominant atomistic social sciences, like rational choice theory, which constrains individual freedom only by the criterion that preferences be ordinally consistent.

In her next work, *Martin Heidegger* (1957), Grene cast the titular philosopher as the central figure of the existentialist tradition, writing, "There *is* an existentialist Heidegger: a Heidegger whose existence Heidegger himself denies, but who is, nevertheless, the Heidegger that matters most, whose place in intellectual history is assured."[39] The first half of Grene's work addresses this aspect of Heidegger's philosophy, focusing on *Being and Time* and, in particular, the topics of fallenness (translated by Grene as "forfeiture"), authenticity, and death. There are several shortcomings of her exegesis. Most problematic is Grene's translation of the term *Dasein* as "human being," which renders Heidegger's ontological analysis psychologically in an existentialist register.[40] However, although the anthropomorphization of Dasein distorts important aspects of *Being and Time*, it allows Grene to show both that Heidegger's work is part of a continuous examination of problems within the Western philosophical tradition and that his novel approach provides a framework that clarifies or supersedes the analysis of his predecessors:

Man is determined, yet free, free yet enslaved. If I am here, now, what heredity and environment have made me, so are these conversely, what *I* make of them. . . . Spinoza, Leibniz, Kant all have described man as bound yet free. But it is the double nature of this bondage which Heidegger has shown us.[41]

Indeed, one of the book's strengths—particularly as one of the first texts to introduce Heidegger's philosophy to a wider American audience—is its ability to identify Heidegger's kinship to other thinkers. For instance, Heidegger argued that the entities of the world are originally disclosed to Dasein as equipment "ready-to-hand" for its use, not as material entities. The hammer is encountered as a means of hammering. The keyboard is encountered as a means of typing. This readiness-to-hand is a structure of significance—the equipment's "in-order-to"—which includes a context of meanings, uses, and relations that constitute Dasein's possible ways of being along with it. Indeed, Heidegger argued that a tool's existence as a "present-at-hand" physical object is founded on its ontologically primordial readiness-to-hand, revealed only when our absorption in the world is broken because equipment fails to perform its function and becomes "obtrusive."[42] Grene identified in this analysis a kinship with Dewey and Bergson, whom Heidegger joined as "participants in a twentieth-century revolt against the simple word-picture of Descartes or Newton." However, this comparison obscured as well as illuminated, portraying Heidegger's analysis epistemologically rather than ontologically.[43]

While Grene did not ignore Heidegger's ontological analysis, she attempted to quarantine it, confining it to the second half of her book. This was, from her perspective, a matter of separating wheat from chaff, saving Heidegger's valuable psychological insights from an infection of metaphysical nonsense. "The trouble with Heidegger's ontology," she wrote, "is not that it is ontology, but that it is spurious ontology."[44] First and foremost, Grene rejected Heidegger's starting point, writing, "Man *is*, certainly, and man thinks about Being, certainly; but to think about man is not to think about Being as such."[45] This again suggests that Grene had not yet fully apprehended Heidegger's rejection of subject-object dualism, even in 1957. Similarly, Grene still associated Heidegger's concept of ontic and ontological phenomena with the Kantian *a posteriori* and *a priori*.[46] However, this was a category mistake. The Kantian *a priori* and *a posteriori* identify classes of knowledge, whereas the ontic and ontological refer to phenomena and the structures of being that make phenomena as such possible. The root of these oversights in Grene's *Martin Heidegger* was a failure to comprehend Heidegger's hermeneutical method, which began from the being whose existence is an issue for it because its *way of being* could be interrogated from the contents of experience without the need for metaphysical constructions. As one of the first English works on him, interpretive shortcomings were inevitable and hardly diminish Grene's accomplishment. However, unless Heidegger's method is understood, the circular movement that characterizes the argument of *Being and Time* is mystifying. As Grene wrote, "The text reads like a series of blows with a sledge-hammer. Each blow says, *now* the post is driven home—and the next and the next and the next hammer the same post with the same vigour and definiteness—only to be succeeded by still another."[47]

Like Grene's doctoral thesis on *Existenz*, her midcentury works on Sartre and Heidegger were the product of professional necessity rather than passion:

> After I lost my job, I thought I should do anything more or less respectable I was given a chance to do. I loathed existentialism, but since I'd studied with two of the supposed representatives of that "school," I was asked to write about it when it came into fashion after the war and did so, for the first time, with little understanding. Every decade or so I was asked to do something in that field and every time I finished by declaring: "Never again!"[48]

However, beginning in the 1960s, the focus of Grene's scholarship and the role of phenomenology within it changed. The biggest differences in Grene's circumstance were her divorce and return from exile, finally appointed as a full professor at UC Davis in 1965 after working as a lecturer in philosophy at Belfast from 1960 to 1965.[49] Another important event in Grene's development was her collaboration during the 1950s with Michael Polanyi, for whom she worked as a research assistant, editor, and "advisor on the history of philosophy." Polanyi's 1958 *Personal Knowledge* argues that knowing relies on "tacit" and personal background that cannot be explicitly formalized. Although Polanyi's influences and methods were distinct from the phenomenological tradition, his argument echoes Maurice Merleau-Ponty's analysis in *Phenomenology of Perception*. For Grene, this similarity prompted a return to phenomenological analysis. Finally, she wrote, after encountering *Phenomenology of Perception* in 1961, "I realized I *had* learned something from that tradition."[50]

In Merleau-Ponty, Grene found an exposition of Heidegger's Being-in-the-world that appeared "the best concept available for the rethinking of philosophical questions about human beings as responsible agents and in particular as knowers."[51] Compared to Heidegger, Grene spent little ink analyzing Merleau-Ponty's work—likely, as she remarked, because "I have always found it easier to expound a philosophical position I disagree with then to state clearly the chief points of a position I do accept."[52] Although Grene continued to refuse the title of phenomenologist, associating it with

Husserlian "bracketing mumbo-jumbo," the language of existential phenomenology gave Grene a "voice."[53] From this point forward, as Grene developed her own philosophy of knowledge and biology, her writings bore the imprint of Heideggerian existential phenomenology, mediated through Merleau-Ponty and influenced by the work of Husserl's student Helmuth Plessner. Among Grene's principal themes were the rejection of Cartesian subjectivity and scientific objectivity, the irreducible reality of a lived world of human being, and the primacy of futurity in human existence. Indeed, she took "all knowledge is orientation" as her "slogan," emphasizing that it is impossible to know without being always already of and within the world.[54]

Grene's major work of systematic philosophy, *The Knower and the Known* (1966) is an extended reflection on the possibility of knowledge about the world. From Plato's *Meno* to Kant's *Critique of Pure Reason*, it surveys the concept of mind's development as it was variously conceived as the apprehending partner of forms, substance, Newtonian machinery, and noumena. These efforts equated the possibility of knowledge with the apprehension of exact, explicit, and necessary or universal truth. Now, Grene argued, the dominant position of scientific discourse in modern culture has fostered a dogmatic commitment to a metaphysics in which living nature is unreal. To be modern is to accept that reality consists of atoms and molecules, elements and chemicals. Society, culture, and living organisms are mere aggregates of these *real* building blocks of nature.[55] At the same time, however, biological science relies on concepts, such as the identification of types and the relation between parts and wholes, that resist exact definition. If one accepts the Newtonian ideal of science as mechanistic and objective, biology is a deficient science. Grene, however, maintained that biology's unformalizable elements are an accurate reflection of the world's real structure. Providing a secure footing for scientific knowledge, therefore, would require that we "put finally to rest our Newtonian delusions, to renew our conception of nature as *living*, and so to see ourselves once more as living beings in a world of living beings."[56]

Admitting the existence of ambiguous entities like natural kinds, Grene concluded, requires an ontology that "allows life its due place in the natural world."[57] Yet, while seeking to preserve life from mechanical reductionism, Grene remained committed to naturalistic realism. To reconcile these seemingly contradictory impulses, Grene drew on Polanyi, arguing that existence is not a single reality but a spectrum of copresent "*grades* of reality." Their structure is described by a rule Grene called the "principle of ordinal complementarity":

What the higher level of organization does is in some sense to *control* the lower. Parts become the parts they are in relation to the whole, organs are organs *as* their function dictates, embryos develop toward their specific norm. . . . In every case the lower level specifies conditions, while the higher principles of organization, ends or reasons. The conditions are indeed necessary, but while it is possible to understand the principles without reference to the detailed conditions, it is *not* possible to understand the conditions *except* as conditions of the whole.[58]

The relationship between higher and lower levels is "asymmetric and normative." For instance, DNA carries a genetic "message" that can be deciphered through in vivo experimentation. However, without its relation to an organism, a strand of DNA is just biochemical noise, a string of base pairs without meaning or function. As Grene explained: "A message may be analysed into its particular constituents, but it cannot be reduced to them, let alone explained by them. The particulars, on the other hand, though physically *caused*, are *explained* by their role in the message."[59] The frameworks of physics, biology, and psychology are not merely tools for answering different types of questions about reality. Rather, Grene held, a naturalistic ontology must recognize each of these grades of existence as both real and *"just different one from another."*[60] This, she continued, "is as true of our world as of ourselves. Indeed it is true of ourselves because it is in relation to our world, as a concretion in and of the world, that we have our being."[61]

In affirming the unity of the world and ourselves, Grene rejected any ontological pluralism that, like Cartesian dualism, splits the universe into distinct realms, instead maintaining "the existence of a rich variety of realities, not all of which need exist in identifiable, spatio-temporal separateness."[62] These levels of reality are nested, but their elements cannot be reductively described in terms available at a more "inclusive" level. The "natural world" of purely mechanical physical systems is the most inclusive level of reality. Within the natural world, a subset of entities occupies the "living world." Beings within the living world are composed of physical matter that is "so ordered as to generate systems that function in some new and interesting fashion . . . [that] constitute higher levels of organization within the physical system in question." A further subset of these living beings is "learners," which are "not wholly dependent throughout their lives on their packet of genetic information, but able to increase and alter information through experience." Moving from the level of living beings to learning animals, we should note, requires the introduction a nonmechanistic concept: "experience." An animal is not merely a physical body but an entity that *has* a body. As Grene explained, "It lives as center of perceiving and acting, in and out of its given biological endowment and into and out of its given biological environment." Although learners are physical entities, the animal environment is a level of reality ontologically distinguished from the natural world by the existence of relationships between beings and their environment, manifested in perception, experience, and habitation.[63]

Finally, within the class of learning entities exists the distinct subclass of human beings. It is the human world's *ambivalence*, Grene claimed, that distinguishes it from the animal environment of learners. For example, both humans and animals use sticks as tools. Only for the human, however, does the stick retain its identity as the branch of a tree while it is used as a tool. It is, Grene wrote, "this *equivocal* relation to things that underlies our ability to produce full tools—to take things as appropriate for a *possible* use. . . . It is the transcendence of the immediate milieu, the immediate need, that characterizes human work as human." A human orientation toward the world therefore requires the experience of *objectivity*. In contrast to the animal environment, entities in an objective world have properties, relations, and a history not revealed in the "natural perception" of their immediate context.[64]

Grene's objectivity was not, to be clear, value neutral. To the contrary, she wrote, objectification is possible only because the world is shaped "under the guidance of a 'system of values'":

> Objectification, evaluation and freedom are inseparable. Through submitting to certain rules of judgment, and imposing them on what confronts him, the human person makes himself with a part of himself into an impartial observer. But *he* makes himself so by imposing on himself the detached spectator, and accepts the responsibility for living his part. He legislates into existence the *value* of detachment. Far from preventing impartiality, the "intrusion" of "judgements of value" is essential to its existence.[65]

It is precisely this capacity for objectification that distinguishes humans from other animals. Thus, Grene concluded, personhood is not a characteristic or "kind of thing" that humans possess. Rather, *being a person* is an achievement that human organisms alone *accomplish*. This, Grene explained, takes the first year of life in particular, what Adolf Portmann calls the year of the social uterus ... the year in which the human infant learns to stand upright, to speak and to perform responsible actions. And that's also where [the human world] comes in, or has always already come in: for human infants become persons by participation in a culture or a social world. And by that I mean not just the world of knowledge, but the whole human world. This world is indeed objective in the sense that it is what the human beginner finds himself in; it surrounds him as surely and necessarily as the natural environment surrounds any organism. But it is also conventional in that it is man-made.[66]

As the human organism becomes a person, it learns to take, in Plessner's terminology, an "eccentric" position toward the world: one that can stand apart from the organism's "biological and physical being and consider [itself] in relation to them." This uniquely human orientation requires neither a soul nor homunculus mind, but "the social world of a culture."[67]

Merleau-Ponty argued that social reality is an originary dimension of experience, irreducible to the sum of external phenomena or of the thoughts, beliefs, and practices of an individual consciousness. Born into an unfamiliar landscape, a child adopts a cultural habitus through its embodied resemblance and relations to others. Before these traditions and mores can be enunciated systematically or explicitly, they must be "lived concretely," announcing their cultural logic "silently and as a solicitation."[68] This social world is not, Grene explained, a realm apart from nature but a modification of it, accessible only to human animals and, at the same time, our initiation into human being:

> The sphere of culture in which we find ourselves is itself contained in nature: not so much a screen between ourselves and nature as a variant of it: a variant that we have made and that at the same time makes us—and that serves us as a glass, now telescope, now microscope, through which we grasp the realities around us, both cultural and natural.[69]

It is only because the cultural world is both real and defies reduction to explicit terms or mechanical rules, Grene concluded, that persons can stand at once within and apart from nature to objectify it. Whereas the animal environment exists only within its immediate context, the cultural world is constituted holistically as the concretion of a history of human practices and relationships that instills each moment with a modality of ways of being, not merely within the natural world but as a person inhabiting an intersubjective realm of human relationships.

3

Philosophy in Conflict

Things here are going the way they can go in these days in which the riders of the apocalypse are again on the loose. All of the terrors of the past years repeat themselves again and again, but in steadily increasing extent and on an always broader basis. It is a dreadful consciousness to experience the end of a world and to live through the final stages again and again. We belong to a generation—as you once said—that never got its chance; it seems to me that we, fleeing from our fate, fled into it.
—Aron Gurwitsch

The phenomenological movement was formed in an age of conflict. Even as Harvard's students studied phenomenology in Germany, the gradient of intellectual migration that had brought Americans such as them to Europe was reversing. At first as a trickle and then as a torrent, European scholars fled west to an American continent that was itself grappling with economic crisis. As the phenomenological movement, fragmented by war, was refounded in the United States, it organized to adapt Husserl's vision of a collaborative enterprise to the unique social landscape of American society, creating space for a novel synthesis of cultures and traditions. However, Depression–era scarcity allowed few opportunities for humanistic endeavors, and phenomenology was not the only novel philosophy to reach American shores through the robust network of early twentieth-century transnational exchanges. In another international import, the nascent movement known as analytic philosophy, Husserl's followers found a rival in the contest to provide new grounds for certainty and agreement among philosophers.

In general terms, analytic philosophers are concerned with clarity and the formal validity of arguments, frequently employing symbolic logic to avoid ambiguity and assure rigor. Analytic philosophers take science seriously. The study of language is central to analytic philosophy, which roots its method in the analysis of propositions, sentences, and meaning. By the second half of the twentieth century, the term *analytic philosophy* had become fixed in the philosophical lexicon, identifying a specific group of philosophers and their works. However, nineteenth- and early twentieth-century literature is littered with references to "analysis" and "analytic philosophy" that bear no relation to its contemporary meaning, obscuring efforts to trace the development of analytic discourse *as such*. One approach to understanding the history of philosophical analysis identifies the analytic movement with "a trail of influence" leading to particular philosophers—usually a subset of Gottlob Frege, Bertrand Russell, G. E. Moore, Rudolf Carnap, and Ludwig Wittgenstein.[1] However, even identifying Frege or Russell as an "analytic philosopher" is itself somewhat misleading, invoking a discourse that had not yet constituted itself. When Bertrand Russell wrote *Principia Mathematica*, he understood himself to be investigating the logical basis of mathematics, not "doing analytic philosophy." When his book was published in 1910, he was engaged in a broad and diverse project that included mathematicians and philosophers from Germany, Great Britain, Austria, Italy, and the United States, the contours of which did not always correspond with our contemporary categorization of analytic and nonanalytic philosophers. To clarify, I do not mean that the existence of an analytic movement was contingent on its members' prior understanding of "analytic philosophy" as an idea or identity. Analytic philosophy was a name applied to an intellectual formation that philosophers discovered through their shared participation in it.[2] The idea of *an* analytic philosophy—a distinct philosophical method—gained currency because it was useful for understanding and describing a material discursive network and set of intellectual practices that already existed. A logician may, of course, object that a definition of "analytic philosopher" that appeals to membership in analytic discourse is impredicative. Yet, if such "vicious" circles are closed to mathematicians, the historian may explore them in search of their virtues.

The style, methods, and professional networks of early analytic philosophy were rooted in an expansive late nineteenth- and early twentieth-century discourse on the nature of mathematics, logic, and language. During the nineteenth century, innovators such as George Boole and Giuseppe Peano realized that logic might be developed into a general calculus of propositions: an instrument for uncovering and eliminating the ambiguities of everyday language like "a microscope which is appropriate for observing the smallest difference of ideas." This new logic was not merely a catalog of the forms of valid inference like that created by Aristotle. It was a system of rules for determining the validity of complex arguments by reconstructing them as a sentence of primitive variables and operators in a symbolic language that could be evaluated algebraically.[3]

While the mathematization of logic was a powerful analytical tool, it made apparent the fact that certain, fundamental concepts remained ill understood. By the nineteenth century, mathematics had become a highly abstract field whose techniques invoked entities such as sets, infinities, and spaces of functions, which did not exist as the objects of empirical experience. Troublingly, the tools of logical analysis discovered that accepted definitions gave rise to paradoxes. Motivated by a desire to resolve the paradoxes of mathematical logic, logicians and philosophers turned to a new project: deciphering the underlying logic of mathematics to understand the meaning of mathematical expressions and determine whether novel proofs and techniques could be credited.[4]

The project of deciphering the logical underpinnings of mathematics was not restricted to analytic philosophers. Phenomenology was associated with the "intuitionist" position in the philosophy of mathematics, whose advocates argued that mathematical objects are ideal, existing only in the minds of mathematicians. This limited the range of possible mathematical entities to those that could be constructed in a finite number of steps, which might, at least in theory, be performed by a mathematician. The Husserlian phenomenologist Felix Kaufmann, for instance, was a significant contributor to the debate over construction in proofs and, like contemporary analysts, saw clarification as "the central problem of philosophy."[5]

Participants in this discourse understood that the domain of algebraic logic was not merely mathematical objects but any entity that could be described using symbolic notation. In other words, any language that followed certain rules could become the subject of logical analysis.[6] However, the task of preserving the meaning of ordinary-language sentences while translating them into a form suitable to logical analysis proved fraught. Gottlob Frege was the first to give this problem serious attention in a modern context. In his seminal essay, "Über Sinn und Bedeutung" ("Sense and Reference"), Frege investigated the identity relation (=), exploring how meaning is produced in complex linguistic statements. Take, for instance, the mathematical equivalence $e^{i\pi} = -1$. Although not intuitively true to nonmathematicians, the terms $e^{i\pi}$ and -1 *refer* to the same object and may, therefore, be substituted for one another in mathematical expressions. Yet, one unfamiliar with this equivalence may well believe a statement such as $-1 < 0$ without believing that $e^{i\pi} < 0$. Frege concluded that, in addition to a reference, names have a *sense* "wherein the mode of presentation is contained." This sense would change depending on how a referent is identified and might vary between interpreting individuals, even when the same name was used. A declarative sentence such as $e^{i\pi} = -1$ refers only to a truth value (in this case, "true"), determined solely by its logical structure and the referents of its individual terms. Nevertheless, the sentence expresses a sense with cognitive value beyond mere truth or falsity. By contrast, a statement about attitudes like beliefs does not refer to a truth value but expresses a thought determined by the senses of its terms.[7]

Although groundbreaking, Frege's semantics left much in dispute about the relation of language, meaning, and truth. For example, Bertrand Russell argued in his 1905 essay "On Denoting" that Frege's system resolves the truth values of phrases that refer to nonexistent objects "inexactly," giving rise to logical contradictions. Dispelling ambiguities in the relationship between language, thought, meaning, and truth was a matter of supreme importance for philosophers who hoped to set empirical knowledge on a secure basis, since most knowledge, Russell held, is attained through linguistic description, not by direct experience.[8] These linguistic investigations inaugurated fruitful discourses not only on semantics and meaning but how philosophical disputes in fields like epistemology and ethics might be resolved by rigorously restating them in clear terms. The logicization of language was also an essential tool for philosophers who hoped to clarify developments in modern physics, such as relativity and quantum mechanics, which seemed at odds with traditional philosophical accounts of space, time, and causality.[9] Centered in Berlin and Vienna, the "logical empiricists" or "logical positivists" led a campaign against metaphysics, holding the only valid sources of knowledge to be empirical observation and statements of logical equivalence. If the concepts expressed in science and everyday language were properly clarified, it would be possible to employ algebraic logic to determine whether a conclusion is merited by its premises. If a language that eliminated all ambiguities were then constructed, it would be possible to definitively identify statements that are, in principle, verifiable through empirical experimentation. All others, they held, are meaningless. This was a radically deflationary epistemology that left to the philosopher only the tasks of clarification, translation, and coordination among different fields of empirical study.[10]

The idea of *an* analytic philosophy—a separate species of *homo philosophicus* split off from other branches of the family tree encompassing these discourses—was only beginning to emerge in the 1930s, decades after the analytic movement's first canonical texts were published. This change was less the result of conscious effort to identify or create a philosophical school than a linguistic response to the material reality of a broad discursive community that formed through the practical and professional activities of logicians and philosophers of language. Whereas *analytic* had previously functioned adjectivally, *analytic philosophy* became a compound noun. No particular moment, decision, or text brought this new idea of "analytic philosophy" into being. Rather, it gradually concretized as institutions prescribed norms and created a canon of texts. For instance, in 1933, British philosophers founded a new journal, *Analysis*, "devoted to short discussions of questions of detail in philosophy, or of precisely defined aspects of philosophical questions." The first issue's "Statement of Policy" describes the journal's purpose as "supplementing, and perhaps connecting, the oral discussions which go on where philosophy is studied systematically, or by groups of people, and ... supply those who are out of reach of these discussions with a substitute for them."[11]

The phrase analytic philosophy also proved useful for discussing the transnational crosscurrents in which philosophers and the philosophy of logic and language moved in the twentieth century. One of the earliest instances in which analytic philosophy is clearly used as a name is Ernest Nagel's 1936 article "Impressions and Appraisals of Analytic Philosophy in Europe," which describes the philosophies its author encountered during a year's travel in England, Austria, and Poland.[12] These did not constitute, Nagel held, a distinct philosophical school, but "there is much they have in common, methodologically and doctrinally," first and foremost a "preoccupation ... with philosophy as analysis."[13] However, Nagel continued, "I am very conscious that in this paper I am reporting less what certain European schools of philosophy profess, and more what I got out of a year's study abroad," and "any Weltanschauung such as the one I am indicating would never be asserted by these men as a formal part of their philosophy."[14] Thus, analytic philosophy was a community first imagined not by its canonical originators, but by those whose geographic and intellectual mobility gave them access to its various constituent discourses. Once the term was in play, however, it became a powerful tool in establishing just such a community, by creating a framework for these works to be viewed together in publications, organizations, and classrooms. Thus, analytic philosophers were only beginning to identify themselves as participants in a shared tradition when the rise of Nazism in Europe drove the Continent's leading logicians and logical positivists to seek refuge in the United States. As a consequence, American universities became the principal sites for the construction of analytic philosophy in subsequent decades, at a moment when new geolinguistic unity both facilitated the creation of an identifiable body of analytic texts and linked together the community that the framework of analytic philosophy had begun to imagine.

* * *

During the first three decades of the twentieth century, logic and the philosophy of language also garnered attention from American philosophers, particularly those at Harvard. Just as Harvard's generous fellowships allowed graduate students to travel to Germany for studies with Husserl and Heidegger, they provided a steady stream of students to Cambridge, Vienna, and Prague, where philosophers such as Henry Sheffer and W. V. O. Quine studied with Europe's leading figures in logical analysis.[15] Harvard also boasted a native tradition in the study of formal logic, the legacy of Josiah Royce, and by the 1920s logic had become a significant component of Harvard's curriculum.[16] It is necessary to stress, however, that American college instruction in logic was, in this era, a field of study split between modern and mediaeval traditions, touching many points in between. What Harvard philosophers identified as logic constituted a broad discourse on rules of argumentation and the justification of beliefs. For instance, the "Seminary in Logic" offered by Josiah Royce in 1915 was described as "A Comparative Study of Various Types of Scientific Method."[17] As modern formal logic appeared with increasing frequency in the Harvard curriculum, it supplemented, rather than replaced, other conceptions of the field. Rudolf Hoernlé's 1918 course "Logical Theory," for example, was described as "a comparative study of Logical and Epistemological Theories, with special attention to [F. H.] Bradley and [Bernard] Bosanquet, and references to Russell, Husserl, and [Alexius] Meinong."[18] Indeed, no problems requiring the use of logical calculus appear on the logic section of Harvard's preliminary examination for the PhD in 1929. Rather, questions included: "Mill asserts that both the method of Agreement and of Difference are 'methods of elimination.' Elucidate this statement"; "Compare 'material,' 'formal,' and 'strict' implication"; and "Does the syllogism, and deduction in general, commit the fallacy of petition principii?"[19]

Nevertheless, European logical analysis exerted growing influence on young American philosophers during the interwar period, and the problems and methods of logical analysis earned followers among many of that generation's greatest philosophers, including W. V. O. Quine, Ernest Nagel, and William Frankena. Indeed, by 1930, logicians and men with ties to the centers of linguistic philosophy in Europe held four of nine positions in

Harvard's department: two of seven senior positions and both junior positions.[20] However, for most American philosophers, logic remained part of a broader discourse on the nature of inquiry that aimed to understand science and restore to philosophy some of the authority the sciences had captured. Thus, the future dominance of analysis in America was by no means a fait accompli in the 1930s. In fact, positivism's deflationary commitment to making philosophy a project of logical clarification was antithetical to the vision of philosophers like Harvard's R. B. Perry, who wrote in his 1931 pamphlet, *A Defense of Philosophy*:

> Philosophy is that branch of knowledge which seeks to be both profound
> and comprehensive, even at the risk of abstractness and inexactness. . . .
> Philosophy, then, is that branch of knowledge which attempts to get to the
> bottom of things, and embrace the whole of things.[21]

When asked in 1934 to recommend "the most eminent scholars in [their] field" who might be honored and invited to lecture at Harvard's tercentenary, its Philosophy Department's overwhelming first choice was Étienne Gilson, in their words "the most eminent of living French philosophers, and the most eminent living scholar in the field of medieval philosophy." Behind Gilson came John Dewey in second, and Rudolf Carnap in third. That Carnap ranked only third is particularly striking given Perry's assertion that their recommendations reflected "present productivity and distinction rather than past eminence or seniority."[22]

More surprising, however, was the department's fourth choice, Martin Heidegger, who ranked ahead of the analytic eminences Bertrand Russell (5) and G. E. Moore (6). Perry described Heidegger in a letter to Jerome Greene, the secretary of the Harvard Corporation, as "the leader of the most vigorous and promising of the more recent movements in German thought" and reported that he was "generally regarded as the most interested and original of the younger men in German philosophy." The letter also offered a maximally generous interpretation of Heidegger's association with Nazism, later shown to be false: "It might be of interest to you to know that he was for a time a member of the Nazi party, but having become disillusioned, resigned from the party under circumstances that were peculiarly painful to himself. I cite this as evidence of his extreme moral sincerity."[23] A subsequent letter to the corporation registered Perry's "disappointment" at learning that the committee was considering only Gilson from his department's list, substituting Benedetto Croce and Joseph Bidez, whom the department had not nominated. Perry explained that "the Department deliberately omitted the name of Croce on the ground that his philosophical eminence belonged to the past rather than to the present. On that ground, of course, he deserves to be honored, but he does not count as significant in current philosophical thinking as do Carnap and Heidegger."[24] With Greene agreeing to give the department's recommendations "fresh consideration,"[25] Perry added:

> [Heidegger] is generally regarded as the most influential contemporary philosopher in German, and is beginning to make his influence felt in other countries including America and in particular [at] Harvard.... As representing the metaphysical and mystical tradition, he presents a most interesting contrast to the teachings and influence of Carnap.[26]

The Tercentenary Committee appears to have rejected the philosophy department's request, as Heidegger was not included among those invited. However, these interactions show that, despite significant interest in logical analysis, Harvard's Philosophy Department was not hostile to other, decidedly nonanalytic modes of thought. Indeed, it sought to create a forum for dialogue between analysis and phenomenology.

Further, although American interest in analytic philosophy continued to grow, it would not be possible for any new method of philosophy to become institutionally dominant in the United States during the 1930s. With university hiring stagnant because of the Great Depression, any transformation of philosophy department faculties was severely inhibited. However, financial pressures also acted as a catalyst for changes initiated by the professionalization and departmentalization of universities, and as philosophy departments were asked to demonstrate their value to university administrators, a subterranean transformation of philosophy's nature and purpose began to take place. A 1938 report by the American Philosophical Association (APA) on "conditions affecting employment" summarizes the effects of the Depression on philosophy, describing what it stipulates were interrelated trends:

1. Depression conditions have made administrations susceptible to questions of numbers of students enrolled in departments of philosophy. Decrease of enrollment seriously affects junior positions. . . .
5. The teaching of philosophy is adversely affected by the fallacy of thinking that the College of Liberal Arts is an aggregation of specialties.
6. Depression conditions fostered the demand for vocational courses and programs of study; this fact, and the conviction that philosophy is

remote from matters of livelihood, tended to reduce demand for work in philosophy.

7. In academic circles philosophy is either regarded amiably, but as inessential, or else it is viewed with actual hostility. . . .

9. There exists a growing tendency for other departments to provide, so to speak, their own philosophy courses, quite independently of the department of philosophy and its instructors. This seems to be especially noticeable with respect to the social sciences.[27]

At many colleges and universities, the APA found, philosophy had been dropped as a requirement for a baccalaureate degree, resulting in severely diminished enrollments. Moreover, many respondents reported that the recent growth of the social sciences drew students away from philosophy. Particularly in "institutions less stable in financial condition," diminishing enrollments meant not only a halt to the opening of new positions in philosophy, but the "indefinite postponement of replacements" when philosophers retired. Instead, funds were reallocated to open new lines in the social sciences. Nevertheless, some respondents reported that colleagues in other departments showed "a growing tendency to regard philosophy as peculiarly integrative" in an era of increasing specialization and a valuable area of "collateral study." The report's authors thus remained optimistic that the demand for courses in philosophy would continue to grow in "areas that seem allied to social science." In particular, they wrote, there was "even a striking tendency to offer logic for freshmen, and to require an elementary course in philosophy as prerequisite for admission to professional schools." Thus, the primary contribution of the university philosophy department began to shift from instruction in philosophy for its own sake to the teaching of logic, rigor, and clarity to students from other departments to use in their own specialties.[28]

On balance, however, philosophers faced dismal job prospects in the late 1920s and early 1930s. As R. B. Perry reported to one job seeker in 1932, "The fact is that we are having a great deal of difficulty in providing for [Harvard's] annual crop of Ph.D.'s."[29] As the crisis deepened, the APA formed a committee, led by Henry Bradford Smith and including Harvard's Perry, "to provide a means of bringing together prospective vacancies and candidates for positions in philosophy."[30] Plans for publicizing vacancies in the *Journal of Philosophy* did not come to fruition. However, it was decided that the committee itself would serve as an appointment bureau that would "keep a file of names and qualification of persons seeking employment in philosophy and to transmit this information to institutions willing to make use of it in filling vacancies."[31] For his part, Perry was skeptical that this "new machinery" would have much effect on the job situation. However, he endorsed the plan because of a belief "that nothing should be left undone that could possibly be of service in the present crisis."[32] Indeed, whatever effect the APA's efforts to coordinate job seeking might have had, they simply could not create opportunities where none existed. America's ten leading philosophy departments, as ranked in a 1925 assessment, made only thirty-six appointments of assistant, associate, or full professors between 1930 and 1944: on average, only once every 4.2 years.[33]

The struggles of Alward E. Brown, who received his PhD from Harvard in 1927, demonstrate the difficulties that even well-credentialed philosophers faced. Brown was highly regarded by his department, garnering praise from R. B. Perry as "the best man from this year's crop, and a distinctly strong man, with an acute, independent mind, and considerable constructive power."[34] In 1937, W. E. Hocking wrote to Duke that Brown "wrote one of the most extraordinary theses we ever had—one to which we should like to have given a mark of special honor if there were such marks to give."[35] Brown held term-limited positions in philosophy at Minneapolis and Seattle from 1927 to 1930.[36] However, an August 1930 letter to Harvard reported that Brown had not "heard from any possible teaching positions for this fall."[37] A reply from James Haughton Woods affirmed Brown's impression that the economy had made positions scarce, and, after a year of disappointments, Woods again wrote to him: "I am very sorry that you too have had the experience of the depression. . . . At present the situation everywhere seems unfavorable for appointments."[38] After two more years without success in his field, Brown secured "temporary part-time" employment as an assistant at Indiana University in the winter of 1933, where he taught a seminar on Husserl and assisted in courses on logic and Whitehead. However, in 1934, Brown was once again searching for employment through "teachers' agencies and the government educational program," supporting himself by working in an insurance office.[39] While Brown continued revising the manuscript of his dissertation for publication, he reported that he remained "without gainful employment" in 1935.[40] Brown was still seeking a teaching position in 1937.[41]

In this context, the careers of Husserl's and Heidegger's itinerant American disciples can be considered successful. Some had secured positions before the start of the Depression. Charles Hartshorne was hired by the University of Chicago in 1928, remaining on its faculty until 1955. John Wild, who had served as an instructor at Harvard since 1927, received a tenure-track appointment in 1934 on the strength of his work on Berkeley, which R. B. Perry called "perhaps the best which has been done in the field of the history of philosophy in America."[42] However, Wild and Hartshorne were alone among Husserl and Heidegger's former students in America in obtaining appointments at what, as we will see, was an exclusive and influential group of elite institutions in the United States. The rest were employed at the periphery of the profession, where they had limited influence and few opportunities to train graduate students in phenomenology during the interwar era. Marvin Farber received an appointment in philosophy from the University at Buffalo in 1927, where he remained for most of his career. After serving in temporary positions at St. John's College and Columbia University, V. J. McGill secured an assistant professorship at Hunter College in 1929. McGill remained at Hunter until 1954, when he was dismissed after refusing to testify for the McCarthyite Rapp–Coudert Committee.[43] Those who entered the job market in the 1930s fared similarly. Everett Nelson was hired as an assistant professor by the University of Washington in 1930. Paul Weiss secured a position at Bryn Mawr in 1931. Dorion Cairns was hired by Rockford College in 1933. Robert Trayhern was appointed an assistant professor of philosophy at the University of Rochester in 1935.[44]

* * *

The rise of fascism initiated one of history's most significant intellectual migrations, as Jews and those with Jewish ancestry, political radicals, members of other persecuted groups, and scholars who could not tolerate the political regimes of their home countries fled Europe for refuge abroad. This movement of minds and bodies, which included such figures as Albert Einstein, Kurt Gödel, and Thomas Mann, also changed the world configuration of philosophical discourse, bringing eminent logical positivists to the United States, where their work influenced a generation of American philosophers. However, the philosophical migration of the 1930s was not wholly, or even primarily, analytic. Between 1933 and 1941, fourteen phenomenologists and three other students of Husserl and Heidegger immigrated to the United States, many using the connections Husserl had fostered over the previous three decades to secure their own rescue and navigate professional world of American academia. The contours of this network would leave a lasting imprint on phenomenology's development in the United States.

Economic depression was a serious impediment to placing émigré scholars in America, with universities making few appointments and

TABLE 3.1 Émigré Phenomenologists and Students of Phenomenology

Name	Year of immigration to US	Field of philosophy	Academic appointments through 1945
Herbert Marcuse	1933	Critical theory	Institute for Social Research, 1933–1942
Moritz Geiger	1934	Aesthetics, philosophy of mathematics, philosophy of psychology	Vassar, 1933–1937
Günther Anders	1936	Philosophy of art, social philosophy	None
Gerhart Husserl	1936	Philosophy of law	UVA Law School, 1937–1939; University of Washington, 1940–
Fritz Kaufmann	1937	History of philosophy, philosophy of art, social philosophy	Northwestern, 1938–
Maximilian Beck	1938	Philosophy of psychology	International Institute of Social Research, 1939–1940; Yale, 1942–1944; Wilson College, 1944–1945
Felix Kaufmann	1938	Logic, philosophy of law, philosophy of mathematics, philosophy of social science	New School, 1939–
Herbert Spiegelberg	1938	History of philosophy, philosophy of law, ethics, aesthetics	Swarthmore (German), 1938–1941; Swarthmore, 1940–1941; Lawrence College, 1941–
Alfred Schütz	1939	Philosophy of social science	New School, 1943–
Aron Gurwitsch	1940	History of philosophy, philosophy of psychology, philosophy of social science	Johns Hopkins, 1940–1942; Harvard (physics), 1943–
Alexandre Koyré	1940	History of philosophy, philosophy of science	New School, 1942–
Dietrich von Hildebrand	1940	Catholic philosophy	Fordham, 1941–
E. Hans Freund	1940	Philosophy of mathematics	Pendle Hill School, 1941–1943
Hannah Arendt	1941	Social philosophy	None
Karl Löwith	1941	History of philosophy, philosophy of history	Hartford Theological Seminary, 1941–
Arnold Metzger	1941	Ethics, history of philosophy	None
Jean Wahl	1942	Existential philosophy	Mount Holyoke College, 1942–1945

facing pressure to provide opportunities for recent American graduates. The most successful philosopher-émigrés were those like the positivists Rudolf Carnap, Carl Hempel, and Hans Reichenbach, whose international reputations made them choice targets for universities. The deliberations of Harvard's Philosophy Department on the university's tercentenary suggest that Husserl or Heidegger might have attained a similar position had they immigrated to the United States. Indeed, the University of Southern California attempted to lure Husserl to Los Angeles in 1933 on either a visiting or permanent basis.[45] Husserl replied that he was enticed by the timely offer, which guaranteed refuge in "the Californian Paradise on the Pacific ocean" where "the political waves do not so powerfully and turbulently surge as here."

> Again and again young philosophers come to me from over there to Freiburg. . . . It would be a beautiful thought to establish within the walls of a School of Philosophy a school of phenomenology as a scientifically workable organization. Surely very soon gifted philosophers would come from other universities to the country in order to acquire thru personal instruction that which has not completely been possible to attain thru publications.

However, Husserl would accept an appointment only if Dorion Cairns were hired as an assistant to help with his English and aid in seminar instruction.[46] The issue of Cairns's role proved a sticking point for USC as well. As the chair of its Philosophy Department, Ralph Tyler Flewelling, explained, the university already required outside funds for Husserl's appointment and had others who could aid him on its staff.[47] With both parties still expressing interest, negotiations stalled, and Husserl remained in Germany.[48]

Already near the end of his life when discussions of his immigration to the United States began, Husserl would have had little opportunity to influence American philosophy even if he had left Germany in 1933. However, the failure of negotiations with USC had other ramifications. Although Cairns obtained an appointment at Rockford College, he struggled with the demands of academic life without Husserl's oversight. Cairns's work as a section instructor at Radcliffe had been marred by reports of lapses, such as occasional unannounced absences and the submission of high grades for students who were not in his section.[49] To be sure, these negative portrayals are balanced by testimony from later students who recall Cairns as "a superb scholar but also a compelling teacher . . . [who] came meticulously prepared" for lectures. However, likely due to the combination of health problems and drinking, Cairns was unreliable and at times deficient in his professional responsibilities. During his seventeen years at Rockford, Cairns published only four articles. While his productivity improved after his appointment at the New School in 1950, where he translated Husserl's *Cartesian Meditations* and *Formal and Transcendental Logic*, Cairns published few original works and "missed many classes for health reasons." Despite these shortcomings, Cairns retained the respect of Husserl's followers. The nineteen posthumous articles that have been published from materials in Cairns's *Nachlaß*, which contains more than five thousand pages of work, testify to his insight as a phenomenologist. However, his unrealized potential was a loss to the movement that Husserl believed Cairns was uniquely qualified to bring to America.[50]

Despite their reputations in Europe, few members of the phenomenological movement were known to most Americans. Scholars in their situation had to depend on personal connections and an ad hoc employment system established by charitable organizations to underwrite temporary appointments for refugees. The most important émigré organization was the Emergency Committee in Aid of Displaced Foreign Scholars, which was founded in the summer of 1933 by Stephen Duggan, a historian and scholar of education at the Institute of International Education. The committee served both logistical and financial functions. In the former role, it identified American universities willing to offer positions to foreign scholars. In the latter, the committee raised money and organized funds from larger organizations, such as the Rockefeller Foundation and Oberlaender Trust, to provide grants to cash-strapped and often-skeptical American universities to subsidize the employment of foreign scholars.[51] However, this decentralized system could leave scholars in tenuous circumstances, employed at a university but reliant upon outside agencies for remuneration. A 1939 letter from Fritz Kaufmann, who was scheduled to teach at Northwestern the following day, explained that he remained in "imminent danger" of becoming destitute and did not know who would pay him at the month's end.[52]

Practical restrictions also circumscribed the organization's activities. First and foremost, as its secretary, Betty Drury, explained, the committee could not provide aid to displaced scholars until "some American university or college [made] us a formal request for his services." This was "the inevitable result of public opinion regarding the unemployment of American teachers." Moreover, there were simply more scholars in need of aid than the committee could possibly support. As such, it was decided that grants would be awarded "only in cases where a reasonable assurance of permanent faculty appointment for the scholar in question [was] offered by the university making application."[53] In practice, this was an ideal rather than a rule, and one that was frequently abandoned. However, it meant that, in general, younger faculty who had already established their careers in Europe had the greatest chance of receiving aid.

The program for placing refugee scholars was a boon for universities, which hosted new faculty whose salaries were paid, in part or in whole, by outside organizations. Nevertheless, there was often significant resistance to hiring émigrés. Much of this was simple xenophobia. Overt expressions of hostility toward refugees were well within the mainstream of American discourse. The House Committee on Un-American Activities, formed in 1938, stoked the fires of anti-immigrant hysteria, and Breckinridge Long, leader of the State Department division responsible for granting visas to refugees, instructed American consulates to engage in "delaying tactics," creating bureaucratic red tape, scrutinizing credentials, and holding inquiries into political affiliations of potential immigrants. Indeed, during the 1930s, opinion polls consistently showed a supermajority of the American public opposed to relaxing quota restrictions on immigration. Not all objections to hiring foreign scholars—such as concerns about their ability to provide instruction in English—were entirely illegitimate. However, xenophobia often colored the reception of refugees within the academy.[54]

Elite universities might also discount the talents of refugee scholars, most of whom were relatively unknown in America. For instance, Harvard's Dean Kenneth Murdock informed members of the university's Psychology Department in 1933 that its president had "decided that Harvard would do nothing formally in connections to place Jewish professors who have lost their positions in Germany." Murdock continued: "The feeling seemed to be, and I think rightly, that we should confine our appointments, as in the past, to men whose ability, entirely apart from other circumstances, recommended them to us."[55] General skepticism is also on display in Brand Blanshard's recommendation of the German philosopher Robert Hartman: "He seems to me a clever and attractive fellow; and it is so unusual for such people to be anything but rather pitiable flotsam."[56] In fact, philosophers appear to have faced particular suspicion, as one correspondent with the committee noted: "There are always questions about these displaced foreign scholars and nowhere more than in philosophy positions."[57]

Despite these obstacles, most refugee phenomenologists found a professional home in America through the aid of benevolent organizations, universities, friends, colleagues, family relations, and heroes who devoted themselves to securing employment for threatened scholars. The first phenomenologist to seek refuge in the United States was Moritz Geiger, a Jewish student of Edmund Husserl and Theodor Lipps, who lost his position as a professor at Göttingen in 1933. Geiger had visited America twice before, lecturing at Stanford in 1926, and before that, in 1907, spending three months at Harvard, where he had "an almost daily discourse with William James," described as "one of the deepest impressions on his life."[58] Thus, Geiger was well connected within America's philosophical community, counting as references Columbia's Frederick Woodbridge and Horace Friess, Harvard's R. B. Perry, and Stanford's Henry Waldgrave Stuart. In less than two months, Woodbridge arranged for a grant from the Rockefeller Foundation to cover Geiger's salary and, through the committee for refugee scholars, secured for him an appointment as chair of Vassar's Philosophy Department.[59]

Geiger understood his fortune in finding such amenable circumstances, writing: "It is a special privilege to get this chair at a time where so many scholars of your own country are out of positions."[60] It was more than just a professional opportunity—Geiger and his wife were made a part of the Vassar community. "All members of the faculty and all students," Geiger wrote, "have welcomed us like old friends, and the atmosphere is so full of humanity that we dare to think that the cause of liberty is not entirely lost."[61] Vassar's class of 1937 awarded Geiger the annual "Vassarion" prize, lauding him for his "unfailing enthusiasm, imagination, and keen perception" as a teacher and "the breadth of humanity and understanding which such a fund of knowledge, coupled with sympathy and insight, can bring."[62] Several months later, however, Geiger died, tragically and unexpectedly. In the wake of his passing, Vassar informed the committee that "in spite of the very fine impressions that Geiger made," a faction of their faculty was opposed to appointing another German in philosophy. Vassar accepted no more refugee philosophers.[63]

In general, scholars whose work could contribute to the war effort had a professional advantage over others.[64] Particularly after America's entry into the war, there was such demand for instructors of mathematics and sciences that proficient émigrés whose expertise lay elsewhere were recruited to teach courses in these fields. This was the case for Aron Gurwitsch, a phenomenologist specializing in the philosophy of psychology and the social sciences who sustained himself through the war as an instructor in physics. Gurwitsch immigrated to America in 1940, serving as a visiting lecturer in philosophy at Johns Hopkins University.[65] He was acutely aware of both his fortune in escaping Europe and his status as an outsider in the

United States, sentiments expressed in his extensive correspondence with his fellow émigré, phenomenologist, and friend, Alfred Schütz:

> We are very comfortable in my aunt's house. It is actually a rather fantastic story: we were intended for the concentration camp and then for everything that the Nazi invasion brought with it, and instead of that one finds oneself in this roomy house, one sits on the porch and works on Sartre's theory of the ego. One has to "realize" all that. And where might Sartre be? At times I have the feeling that I am working on nothing other than obituary notices.[66]

In this letter, otherwise written in German, the word *realize* is in English, as though signifying the effort of translation between these two worlds, coexistent but so mutually foreign that one can only be made real within the other by an act of will. As Gurwitsch explained in another letter, "We are quite lonely here. And that not merely in the sense that we see so few people here. But even among those whom we see, we feel very alone, since we are still rooted in another world."[67]

Gurwitsch, who had been among the first rank of Husserl's students, made a considerable impression on his colleagues at Johns Hopkins. The philologist Leo Spitzer wrote that Gurwitsch was "one of the scholars who really live for scholarship," praising him as "the picture of a scholar and teacher whom any university or college ought be proud to have on its staff." However, the university would not provide the funds to retain him.[68] Gurwitsch wrote to Schütz:

> I am running the Graduate School practically alone. . . . But what does that, as well as the fact that I use up the publication budget of our department all by myself, have to say when compared to my disqualifications: foreigner, Jew, unbaptized, Jewish wife, etc. *That* is too much. They could tolerate it if someone would buy me a *chair* for $150,000. Then they would take me in the hope, as one of the professors . . . told me today, that I wouldn't live all too long, such that the successor would be more acceptable in the social sense.[69]

Gurwitsch was unable to find another position in philosophy in 1942, but he was sustained by a research grant from the American Philosophical Society and a "fellowship by courtesy" at Harvard, secured for him by R. B. Perry.[70] Here, Gurwitsch again found a measure of community among the European intellectuals drawn to the university.[71] Still without prospects for a permanent position in philosophy, Gurwitsch was able to retain his connection to Harvard by accepting a position as an instructor in physics the following year. He remained at Harvard from 1943 to 1946, teaching courses for army recruits.[72]

As Gurwitsch's account suggests, antisemitism complicated the transmission of phenomenology to the United States. Particularly given the stain Heidegger's Nazism would leave on phenomenology in the postwar era, it is important to note that the movement was overwhelmingly Jewish. In total, ten of the phenomenological refugees who came to America were Jews, and four others had Jewish ancestry that left them subject to Nazi race laws. It is impossible to say with certainty what effect prejudice in America had on the careers of these philosophers. However, philosophers who faced antisemitism in Germany had seen their careers stalled or foreclosed. This mark followed them to the United States, where it was, intentionally or not, reduplicated by administrators who looked to CVs to evaluate the candidates competing for all too scarce American positions. America's domestic antisemitism also should not be underestimated, and the academy was no haven from bias. Beyond Gurwitsch's account, the only *direct* evidence that émigrés associated with phenomenology were denied employment because of their Jewish heritage is a letter from Louisiana State Law School, stating they would not hire Gerhart Husserl, the son of Edmund Husserl, because the "combination of Jewish ancestry and undoubtedly broken English would place him at such a handicap with our somewhat provincial student body that it would be almost impossible for him to do the type of work that we want."[73] Thus, it is difficult to point to particular positions or advantages that might have been denied phenomenologists because of their Jewish heritage. However, prejudice often operates through silences that archives are unable to preserve. It is only when universities actually responded to the call to hire refugee scholars that records of deliberations, negotiations, and contracts exist. Given the pervasiveness of antisemitism within the American academy, it is difficult to imagine that opportunities were not foreclosed.[74] Indeed, antisemitism was so normal that even those expressing overtly antisemitic views might deny holding any bias. For instance, Cornell's efforts to place one of their Jewish students in 1940 elicited the reply from Dartmouth: "We should not at present, however, appoint a Jew, not because we have any racial prejudice, but because we already have one full Jew and another man whose fractional status is anywhere from 1/8 to 8/8 in our Department."[75]

The most significant migration of phenomenologists to America occurred between 1937 and 1939, bringing Felix Kaufmann, Fritz Kaufmann, Alfred Schütz, and Herbert Spiegelberg to the United States. Fritz Kaufmann was the first to arrive. In Germany, Kaufmann had served at Freiburg as *Privatdozent* and Husserl's assistant. However, as a Jew, he was denied promotion despite his faculty's recommendation and, in 1936, was officially removed from his position. From 1933 to 1936, Kaufmann had also offered *Volkshochschulkursen* to Jewish students who had been denied entry to universities because of Nazi race laws. Yet, the combination of political and financial pressures on the one hand, and the plight of Germany's Jewish youth on the other, left Kaufmann feeling "like a candle lit at both ends" and in search of means with which to provide for his family.[76] A grant from the Society for the Protection of Science and Learning in London allowed Kaufmann to leave Germany for England in September 1936.[77] There, he came to the attention of the Emergency Committee both because of his scholarly credentials and his relief work within the Jewish community in Germany, which had caused him to forfeit "the chances of positions outside Germany which he might have had had he left Germany earlier."[78] Kaufmann's recommenders for an American position included Gilbert Ryle and R. G. Collingwood, with whom he shared an interest in the philosophy of history. Indeed, Collingwood wrote, "I feel quite confident judging by what he has already done and by the way in which he discussed his subject with me, that if he can go on with his research the results will be of real value."[79] Kaufmann immigrated to the United States in November 1937 and, with the help of the committee, secured a series of temporary appointments in philosophy at Northwestern University.[80]

Herbert Spiegelberg arrived in America at the beginning of 1938. Born in 1904, Spiegelberg was one of Husserl's younger students. As such, he was at the beginning of his career, focusing on ethics and the philosophy of law, when the Nazis assumed power in Germany. Although Spiegelberg had been raised a Protestant in Alsace-Lorraine, his Jewish ancestry left him unable to find university work in Germany. Possessing a solid command of English, a strong recommendation from the legal philosopher Morris Raphael Cohen, and references that included R. B. Perry, Alfred North Whitehead, Horace Friess, and Arthur Lovejoy, Spiegelberg was a good prospect for a position in America.[81] Nevertheless, at the end of 1937 he was still without a stable appointment, living in Cambridge, England. After receiving news of the death of Moritz Geiger, who was his former teacher, Spiegelberg traveled from England to the United States, hoping to fill his position at Vassar.[82] Spiegelberg was interviewed in February 1938, but with Vassar having already determined not to hire another refugee, it was a charade. The notes from this interview read in their entirety: "Called. A nice, polite person. Straight, brushed up hair cut (Prussian). Glasses. Bows from waist. A little angular. Nice."[83]

While Vassar was a dead end, Spiegelberg succeeded in obtaining an appointment as a German instructor at Swarthmore College. His letters report that he was "perfectly delighted with the place and with the people" and that Swarthmore's president, Frank Aydelotte, was happy to renew his appointment despite the poor chances of a permanent position in philosophy becoming available.[84] At the year's end, Spiegelberg traveled to England to visit family, intending to return to Swarthmore for the start of the fall semester. However, Spiegelberg booked return passage on the SS *Athenia*, fated to become the first British passenger ship sunk by Germany during World War II. Fortunately, Spiegelberg was not among those killed in the disaster. Indeed, he reported that he was "almost ashamed to say that, apart from the loss of our belongings on board, we escaped without injuries." However, as the holder of a German passport, Spiegelberg was detained until his identity could be verified. Throughout the ordeal, Spiegelberg maintained his good humor, reflecting that detention was "quite an experience for somebody who has an inveterate interest in penology."[85]

Spiegelberg eventually returned to Swarthmore and another successful year of teaching German. The following year, President Aydelotte and Brand Blanshard arranged for Spiegelberg to receive a part-time appointment at the college as a research associate in philosophy, which would allow him to teach an honors seminar for upper-level philosophy students.[86] However, both Swarthmore and the committee continued to search for an opportunity that would allow Spiegelberg to devote himself solely to philosophy. Aydelotte was effusive in his praise of Spiegelberg, writing that he was "such a fine scholar and is so attractive on the personal side that I feel sure a place can eventually be found for him in the subject in which he is best prepared." He continued: "I may say that one of the finest things about him is the courage and cheerfulness with which he faces the future and the interest which he takes in all the activities of the college. He is the type of man whom it is a pleasure to help."[87] In 1941, an opening at Lawrence College allowed Spiegelberg to assume a position in philosophy.[88] Although Spiegelberg found the "general scholastic atmosphere" at Lawrence lacking by comparison to Swarthmore, he discovered other important virtues for a refugee in Appleton, Wisconsin:

> I wish I could think, however, that what applies to Lawrence would also hold for other communities: a spirit of warm and unreserved hospitality, which I would even hesitate to call hospitality because very soon I felt no longer as a mere guest, and no trace of xenophobia, at least not on the side of the faculty.[89]

Spiegelberg would remain at Lawrence until 1963.[90]

Felix Kaufmann (unrelated to Fritz Kaufmann) also immigrated to the United States in 1938. In a memorial of Kaufmann, Alfred Schütz noted the breadth of his interests, which included logic and the philosophy of mathematics, the methodology of social sciences, and the philosophy of criminal law, all of which made "a consistent whole . . . in spite of their astonishing diversity."[91] Kaufmann had been in Switzerland at the time of Austria's invasion by the Nazis and, as both a Jew and an associate of Austria's socialist party, was warned not to return.[92] A grant for $3,000 was quickly obtained from the Rockefeller Foundation to cover the majority of Kaufmann's salary at the recently created Graduate Faculty of Political and Social Science at the New School for Social Research, where Kaufmann remained until his death in 1949.[93] Kaufmann was a significant contributor to early twentieth-century debates over logic, the foundations of mathematics, and construction in proofs. Like the early analysts, Kaufmann saw clarification as "the central problem of philosophy."[94] His most substantial work, in this respect, was his 1930 *Das Unendliche in der Mathematik und seine Ausschaltung* (The infinite in mathematics and its elimination), which attempted a logical construction of mathematics with a finitist ontology that did not admit the existence of sets or infinitesimals. Kaufmann's book was translated into English and published in 1978 with an introduction written by the analytic philosopher Ernest Nagel. The translated volume also included an unpublished 1931 work that eschewed emerging methodological divisions, drawing on Husserl's description of intentionality and theory of generalizations from *Logical Investigations* to rebut Wittgenstein's claim that propositions represent reality and to critique Russell's resolution of logical paradoxes through his theory of types.[95]

In 1943, another phenomenologist, Alfred Schütz, joined Kaufmann at the New School. Schütz, who will be profiled in the next chapter, was a respected philosopher of the social sciences who immigrated to the United States in 1939. With a faculty that included Kaufmann, Schütz, and Husserl's former student Alexandre Koyré, the New School for Social Research quickly became one of the world's preeminent centers of phenomenological expertise. The school's existence dated back only to 1919, when it was founded as an institution for adult education by a group of progressive intellectuals that included Charles Beard and James Harvey Robinson. In this form, the New School was a unique venue in America, which provided the broader public exposure to academic discourse on economics, politics, sociology, history, and philosophy. Indeed, Dorion Cairns taught a course on phenomenology at the New School in 1933, open to all at the cost of $1 per lecture. That same year, the New School's director, Alvin Johnson, initiated a campaign to fund the creation of the University in Exile: a graduate program at the New School that would fill its faculty with scholars who had lost their positions under the Nazi regime. By concentrating European scholars in a single institution, Johnson hoped to preserve European academic traditions that were being suppressed within Europe itself. Because the Graduate Faculty of Political and Social Science, which had grown to twenty-six members by 1941, enjoyed significant autonomy within the New School, refugee scholars were able to make the University in Exile a sort of "European scholarly enclave in the American scene" while gaining recognition as an American academic institution.[96]

Notably, at a time of growing specialization and departmentalization, the New School stood apart with a uniquely interdisciplinary focus and distinctive traditions, such as the "general seminar," in which faculty presented papers of interest to the entire university.[97] This unique model of graduate education reflected necessities imposed by the Graduate Faculty's limited size and resources. However, it was also the product of faculty discussions that affirmed philosophy's role as the "generative center" of a humanistic education that stressed the "essential unity" of the social sciences in "the aspiration to liberty and justice." As a 1941 report by the university's Coordinating Committee to the Graduate Faculty stated:

> The Faculty emphasizes the organic unity of the social sciences and strives to realize cooperation between the social sciences. The organic unity of the social sciences is not a goal in itself, but in their focusing on the doctrine of man, on the doctrine of society, in the light of the requirements of truth, of justice, of the dignity of man ... instead of accepting it as the purpose of our teaching to make of our pupils mere specialists, we must aspire to educate them as veritable "university men."[98]

The New School's distinctive organization and decidedly foreign ethos also marked it as something different from and potentially inimical to American academe, as illustrated in deliberations over whether the philosopher Eric Gutkind should be invited to offer a course at Harvard's summer school. W. E. Hocking wrote to Kinley Mather, who was serving as the summer school's director in 1936, that "[Gutkind's] position at the New School for Social Research is certainly the foundation of a recommendation. On the other hand, things have been known to come out of that School which might alarm a conservative Harvard audience."[99] Mather provocatively replied: "I should hope that he might do precisely that."[100]

* * *

By the late 1930s, the currents of world events had brought a critical mass of phenomenological talent to the United States. Reliant on an informal network of American acquaintances and European peers already established in America, émigré phenomenologists retained a semblance of shared community through their diaspora. However, it was far from guaranteed that these tenuous links would be sufficient to reconstitute phenomenology as a movement on American shores. Even the desirability of such a goal could hardly be taken as a given. Many refugee intellectuals, though grateful to their adoptive countries, never came to think of these new places as their own; instead, their eyes were set on a return to Europe. Even those who established roots on American shores confronted choices about whether to focus on an audience of their expatriated peers or to attempt to engage with broader American philosophical discourse. Among the group of émigré phenomenologists were scholars particularly committed to the latter course. Still, it is doubtful that phenomenology would have been restored as cooperative project in the United States if not for two factors: the death of Edmund Husserl in 1938 and the organizational efforts of Marvin Farber.

In the decade after his encounter with Husserl in Freiburg, Farber maintained only occasional contact with his former teacher. However, Farber was drawn back into Husserl's orbit in 1936 as Edmund and his wife, Malvine, sought assistance in securing a position in America for their son Gerhart, a philosopher and legal theorist.[101] In continuing correspondence with Farber, Husserl also discussed phenomenology's prospects in America. He was particularly encouraged by the news that Farber had recently met with Dorian Cairns, urging his American followers to pursue phenomenological συμφιλοσοφειν, a term that might be translated as "philosophizing together" or, more literally, "sharing a love of knowledge." Husserl had always conceived of phenomenology as a "cooperative task." As Farber's colleague Kah Kyung Cho explained, "In a grand patriarchal fashion, [Husserl] envisioned the future of phenomenology as a collective and cumulative undertaking in whose process a dedicated community of scholars would participate." Grateful for the help Farber provided his son, Husserl also encouraged his American disciples to take up the project that was his intellectual progeny. "There is nothing more beautiful in this woeful world," he wrote to Farber, "than a free συμφιλοσοφειν on the same ground, in sharing the same fundamental methodological beliefs!"[102]

Afflicted by pleurisy, Edmund Husserl died on April 27, 1938. Barred from the academy because of his Jewish ancestry, Husserl worked in relative isolation in his final years, attended to primarily by his devoted assistant Eugen Fink, who alternately played the roles of sounding board, devil's advocate, and editor as Husserl attempted a final, radical revision of his philosophy.[103] After Husserl's passing, it quickly became clear that his vast collection of unpublished manuscripts—an important resource for future students of phenomenology—would be lost if it were not taken beyond the Nazis' reach. In a matter of months, Herman Leo Van Breda, a Franciscan priest who had written a thesis on Husserl, executed a plan to evacuate Husserl's *Nachlaß* to the Catholic University of Louvain in Belgium. Husserl's papers, "a few hundred kilograms of texts," were transported first to Konstanz by a Benedictine nun, then to Berlin where they were delivered to the Belgian embassy by Van Breda. By the end of November 1938, Husserl's papers had arrived in Louvain, sent via a diplomatic pouch to prevent their discovery and destruction by Nazi authorities. Louvain's administration had been unaware of Van Breda's machinations and had made no prior commitment to take ownership of Husserl's manuscripts. However, faced with this fait accompli, they consented to establishing the Husserl Archives at Louvain, hiring both Eugen Fink and Husserl's former assistant Ludwig Landgrebe to organize and oversee the collection. Thus, Louvain emerged almost immediately as a natural successor to Freiburg as the seat of the Husserlian movement.[104]

Husserl's passing also reunited his disciples, both American and European, in the project of paying tribute to their former teacher. The idea for a volume dedicated to Husserl seems to have originated with Farber. By mid-May, he had begun to discuss compiling a collection of essays by Husserl's "friends and pupils" with Fritz Kaufmann, who pledged that "for such a work you can count on my contribution as well as on my cooperation in every respect."[105] Over the following months, Farber and Kaufmann compiled a veritable directory of Husserl's former students and acquaintances, phenomenologists, and fellow travelers residing in America. Kaufmann also brought Farber's plans to the attention of Malvine Husserl, who recommended consulting Fink and Landgrebe.[106] Fink offered to contribute an article to the volume on the efforts in Louvain to preserve and publish the "unknown real philosophy" of Husserl's later manuscripts, and Farber suggested that a selection from the manuscripts be included in the volume.[107] This first collaboration with Louvain was only a partial success. Fearing publicity could imperil the archive, Fink and Landgrebe withdrew their offer to contribute an essay about the archives and requested that Farber not mention the situation of Husserl's *Nachlaß*.[108] However, the memorial volume did include an essay from Husserl's unpublished manuscripts, provided by Louvain.[109]

Philosophical Essays in Memory of Edmund Husserl was published by Harvard University Press in 1940 and includes articles by Dorion Cairns, John Wild, W. E. Hocking, Aron Gurwitsch, Herbert Spiegelberg, Felix Kaufmann, Fritz Kaufmann, and Alfred Schütz, among others.[110] The long work of commissioning and obtaining manuscripts renewed ties between those in America who had been touched by Husserl, defining the outline of a new Husserl circle with Farber at its center. However, the process of compiling and editing the collection also revealed host of obstacles to importing Husserl to America. For instance, clarity required the creation of a common lexicon of English translations for Husserl's technical vocabulary.[111] Further, even in Germany, Husserl's reticence to publish meant that his later philosophy was not widely understood. In America, many of those who had studied with Husserl in the 1920s or earlier remained entirely ignorant of these developments. This problem was highlighted by the first draft of Hartshorne's contribution, of which Fritz Kaufmann remarked: "God forgive him as he does not know what he is talking about."[112] Reluctant to refuse a paper already written by an invited contributor, Farber wrote to Kaufmann: "If we are to hope to introduce [phenomenology] to the American scene, we cannot afford to alienate friends or potential friends. Unanimity was never achieved in Germany; and it cannot be expected here."[113]

Farber understood that his editorial decisions could affect the contours of the phenomenological movement in America. A product of Harvard's pluralist ethos, he adopted an attitude of tolerance toward those who broadly shared Husserl's aims. However, Farber also gave significant weight to the opinions of his principal collaborators: Fritz Kaufmann, Dorion Cairns, and Gerhart Husserl. It is impossible to know how different choices might have changed the history of phenomenology in the United States. Nevertheless, it is interesting to consider what might have come from Kaufmann's proposal to solicit materials from Max Horkheimer and Herbert Marcuse, who had studied with Husserl in Freiburg.[114] Had this plan been realized, Farber might have brought the Frankfurt School in closer contact with American philosophers and allied the phenomenological movement with this influential group of European émigrés. However, Gerhart Husserl regarded Horkheimer and Marcuse as unqualified, and, in deference to Husserl's son, the matter was dropped.[115]

It was against the backdrop of these deliberations that Farber conceived of a new phenomenological organization based in America, far from the reach of the Nazi Reich. The first reference in Farber's correspondence appears in a July 1939 letter to Fritz Kaufmann:

> I have in mind the formation of a philosophical society with the ideal of [philosophy as a rigorous science] and also a publication. For the latter, there is one problem, the financial one of course, which I hope will be met; for the former I am selecting the names of all interested, and have already learned of or met quite a number. If possible, we can have a luncheon meeting of all interested at the Christmas meeting of the [philosophical association] in New York. I shall initially wish to work in close connection with you in all these matters.[116]

Five months later, on December 26, the core members of the nascent International Phenomenological Society (IPS) met at the New School, adopting a constitution and electing officers, including Marvin Farber as its president. The following day, just before the start of the annual meeting of the American Philosophical Association, the IPS reassembled to address a wider group of potential members about the society's activities and aims.[117] The next year, in an article titled "New Science Unit Centers in Buffalo," the *New York Times* announced: "As a result of the upheaval in world affairs the University of Buffalo has become the center of one of the major philosophical movements of the modern day—phenomenology."[118] With so much accomplished so quickly, Farber's hopes for the organization were high. "If our undertaking succeeds," he wrote to Eugen Fink, "we shall have instated phenomenology as a major philosophical tendency in the United States."[119]

In the five months before the IPS's first meeting, Farber and his collaborators undertook the enormous work of organizing a new society, securing its funding, and planning the first issue of its journal, *Philosophy and Phenomenological Research*. This journal was the IPS's principal expense, subsidized by an annual subvention of $1,000 from the University at Buffalo.[120] Its other major financer was Harvard University's Philosophy Department, which gifted the journal $300 in 1940, $200 per year from 1941 to 1943, and subventions of $100 in 1944, 1946, and 1947.[121] The name *Philosophy and Phenomenological Research* (hereafter *PPR*), as various observers noted, was quite a mouthful. George Boas wrote to Farber, "You were most kind to send me a copy of the June number of P. and Ph.R (wouldn't it be wonderful to dream up a shorter title?)." The editors had considered alternatives that might, as Farber put it, mitigate "the fright experienced by librarians when confronted with the present title." Indeed, a Buffalo librarian had written to the journal, complaining that phenomenology is "a formidable word and is another example that causes we poor ordinary individuals to wonder just why it is that the intellectuals must hide their thoughts in verbiage that most of us cannot understand."[122] To phenomenologists, however, the title *Philosophy and Phenomenological Research* had a particular and powerful connotation: it drew a direct line between Farber's journal and Husserl's periodical, the *Jahrbuch für Philosophie und phänomenologische Forschung* (Almanac for philosophy and phenomenological research), in which many of the movement's most significant texts had first appeared. Indeed, a draft announcement explicitly refers to *PPR* as the "successor to Husserl's *Jahrbuch*."[123]

The rapid organization of IPS and *PPR* was possible only because of the network that had been established by the Husserl memorial, whose contributors composed the nucleus of the new group. Farber's principal collaborators were Fritz Kaufmann, Dorion Cairns, Gerhart Husserl, Felix Kaufmann, and Alfred Schütz, on whom he relied for both advice and organizational labor.[124] Farber also sought the aid of Eugen Fink and Ludwig Landgrebe in Louvain, to whom he wrote: "It will be very encouraging, if not absolutely indispensable, to have your collaboration on the regular publication."[125] At times, the labor was overwhelming. "I have given up everything in the interest of this undertaking," Farber wrote to Schütz, "so much so that I have had no rest whatsoever. All day—and most evenings—I am at work on it—answering letters, reading and editing papers, and directing the campaign. . . . I am wondering whether I have done well to be so involved."[126] However, as Farber noted, the "experience gained in connection with [the Husserl] memorial volume" had helped prepare the group for their new endeavor: "We should know how to avoid errors."[127]

One challenge suggested by the memorial project was the difficulty of cultivating a quantity of high-quality material sufficient for regular publication from the modest group of American phenomenologists. Farber hoped to overcome these limitations by organizing the phenomenological society internationally and tailoring *PPR* for a global audience. In early discussions of the journal, Farber advocated accepting works from scholars around the globe and publishing abstracts for each with translations in three languages. Farber also made the Argentine philosopher Francisco Romero an ex officio member of the IPS council and asked Fink and Landgrebe to identify candidates among Husserl's far-flung disciples to represent Italy, Great Britain, Latin America, and Japan on the journal's editorial board.[128] Schütz, who lived in Paris before immigrating to the United States, offered to make contacts with French phenomenologists.[129] Farber never abandoned his aspiration to lead a truly international phenomenological organization. However, his vision changed as he struggled to realize it. The growing worldwide conflagration was a major impediment to international cooperation. Indeed, a note at the end of *PPR*'s first issue explained with a tone of dark understatement that "due to world conditions the list of foreign members of the editorial staff must be incomplete for the present."[130]

Farber's most important foreign collaborators were Fink and Landgrebe, who could provide him with selections from Husserl's manuscripts. While the manuscripts in Husserl's *Nachlaß* were, in Schütz's words, a kind of "scrapbook of his thought" that "should not be considered as papers . . . [or] even as rough drafts of future literary works," few other windows into the final stage of Husserl's thought existed. Many who studied with him during his Freiburg years believed that these late works held his most important discoveries and were the key to phenomenology's future progress. However, the project of publishing Husserl's papers in *PPR* faced significant obstacles. Husserl's notes were fragmentary and written using "symbols of a strange German shorthand known only by Husserl himself and by very few of his closest assistants." What was more, Louvain both possessed Husserl's papers and held the rights to their publication.[131] It was significant news, therefore, when Marvin Farber received a letter from Malvine Husserl informing him that Louvain had decided to "cooperate actively" with *PPR* by providing the journal a manuscript to be published in every other issue. While she could not yet provide specifics about the collaboration, Husserl explained, she was determined to send notice before "the enemy of the world" could reach them. In fact, the letter had been sent on May 10, 1940, the date Hitler's invasion of Belgium began.[132] A long period of silence followed, during which those in America struggled against despair. Kaufmann lamented:

> No word about the unspeakable misery of these days and its consequences not to be foreseen. Perhaps finally vision and imagination will not always be the monopoly of the devil! Poor Mrs. Husserl!!—And what about the archives? But what use have these papers anyway in a world turned an inferno?[133]

It was not until September that those in America even verified that the Louvain contingent had survived.[134] Clearly, collaboration had become impossible. The only works of Husserl that would be published by *PPR* during the war were the essay mentioned above and a 1931 lecture titled "Phänomenologie und Anthropologie."[135]

The first issue of *PPR* was published in September 1940, containing articles by Farber, Landgrebe, Felix Kaufmann, John Wild, Fritz Kaufmann, and Edmund Husserl himself. Although each of these men was connected with the phenomenological movement, a note at the issue's conclusion explains that the journal was committed to fostering broad philosophical discourse:

> While the philosophy of Edmund Husserl is the point of departure for the publication, it represents no special school or sect. Its aim is to maintain philosophy in the ancient sense, as an exact, descriptive discipline, at the same time bringing it to bear on the modern world.[136]

These words are clearly Farber's, mirroring remarks he had written in an August 1939 letter to Schütz and reflecting the values he learned both from Husserl and at Harvard. In the letter, Farber had argued that, taking Husserl's idea of a rigorous science as its beginning, their society should "perform the *epoché* with regard to all standpoints and preferences," emphasizing the "cumulative progress of philosophical research" across traditions:

> It would indeed be sufficient to dedicate a new society to the study and propagation of E. H.'s work. But I would rather use that as a point of departure—as an honor—and attempt to foster international cooperation among scholars on a broader basis of methodology, the value of which E. H. never denied, but on the contrary accomplished.[137]

At times, Farber's policy of tolerance drew him into conflict with phenomenologists who favored a more focused emphasis. However, his broad outlook won the approval of the group's most important collaborators. A December 1 letter from Fink, for instance, cautioned Farber not to form a school or *Pietätsverein* (brotherhood of the devout) and encouraged him to organize a community of philosophers who would work on the questions Husserl raised in their own way. Its members would thus share a "common heritage" in Husserl's phenomenology but avoid dogmatism. This advice, Fink made clear, was his own. However, the letter also stressed that the administration of Louvain, which had legally assumed ownership of Husserl's corpus, was protective of its prerogatives. Thus, Fink's advice doubled as a warning against organizing a Husserl society that Louvain might see as a competitor.[138]

As *PPR*'s second largest financial contributor, Harvard's Philosophy Department also had the power to influence *PPR*'s governance and editorial policies. For instance, one letter from Wild stated:

> In the opinion of this Department . . . success will depend upon our interesting a wider group of young American philosophers obviously untrained in Husserlian technicalities. In the course of discussion I was able to state that an attempt at least was being made to free the policy from sectarian limitations, and to make the Journal into an organ for descriptive philosophy.[139]

In the next few years, *PPR* would feature articles by prominent American philosophers such as Ernest Nagel, Richard Brandt, Roy Wood Sellars, and Harold R. Smart, as well as European positivists and logicians including Alfred Tarski, Rudolf Carnap, and Hans Reichenbach.[140] This did not meet universal approval among *PPR*'s supporters in the American phenomenological community, as will be discussed in chapter 5. However, Farber's work succeeded in establishing *PPR* as a publication of significance that earned plaudits from figures across the broad American philosophical community. Despite the journal's troublesome name, it had, in the words of the New School's Horace Kallen, "taken an important place in the philosophical enterprise of the United States . . . [as] one of the liveliest and one of the best-written and edited of the periodicals in the field."[141] Indeed, *PPR* even won the acknowledgment of W. V. O. Quine, who wrote to Farber in 1945: "I have watched the progress of your journal with much admiration, and heartily congratulate you."[142]

B

Alfred Schütz

The phenomenological movement that formed in the United States during the 1930s and 1940s was not transplanted from Europe intact or reassembled unaltered, as a building from a blueprint. American-born phenomenologists played a critical role in renewing connections among Husserl's followers and orienting their efforts into new American discourses and institutions, different from those in which phenomenology had first developed. However, this does not diminish the importance of émigré phenomenologists to the nascent American movement. This generation of philosophers carried phenomenology to the United States as an ongoing project, continued through their own investigations, and provided the students whom they mentored a living connection to the ideas, practices, and heritage of a world removed by time and violence. While no single figure can represent the diverse experiences and commitments of this group, Alfred Schütz's efforts to develop American phenomenological institutions, original philosophical insights, and interdisciplinary influence exemplify the group's essential contributions to phenomenology in America.

Alfred Schütz was born to a middle-class Austrian family during the last year of the nineteenth century. While his early life was shaped by a caring family that encouraged his interest in creative pursuits such as poetry and music, Schütz came of age during a time of war. He enlisted in the Austrian army at the age of seventeen, serving in an artillery unit on the Italian front during the last years of World War I. When Schütz returned home, he had difficulty reintegrating into Viennese society as he struggled to find personal meaning in the routines and requirements of everyday life. According to his former student and biographer Helmut Wagner, this crisis contributed to Schütz's growing intellectual interest in the social world's construction and structure. Schütz studied law at the University of Vienna, conducting research in sociology, philosophy, and economics with Hans Kelsen and Ludwig von Mises. With Mises's assistance, Schütz begin a career as a banker, working for the Association of Austrian Middle Banks from 1921 to 1927 before becoming an executive officer at the firm Reitler and Company. Schütz also joined the Mises circle—an interdisciplinary group that hosted regular meetings featuring presentations by its members and discussions of their work. Thus, Schütz was inaugurated into the company of pioneering young European intellectuals, including noted economists such as Friedrich Hayek and Fritz Machlup, the sociologist Eric Voegelin, and the Husserlian philosopher of mathematics Felix Kaufmann.[1]

From early in his intellectual development, Schütz was drawn to the *verstehen*, or "interpretive," sociology introduced by Max Weber as a methodological alternative to the positivist paradigms of Comte and Durkheim. The task of the interpretive sociologist, in Schütz's words, was "to interpret the actions of individuals in the social world and the ways in which individuals give meaning to social phenomenon." Indeed, Weber held, it was the conferral of meaning on activity that distinguished human "action" from mere animal "behavior." Thus, the primitive element in Weber's sociology was not Durkheim's personally anonymous "social fact" but the "meaningful act of the individual."[2] Particularly important to Weber was "social action": the subset of meaningful acts that take "account of the behavior of others."[3] These others might be directly involved in the social action, as are one's partners in a conversation, or remote strangers, as when one accepts money as payment, understanding that its value will be recognized in future transactions with unmet and unknown partners. In either case, one confers meaning on one's own action through an understanding of the other's behavior.[4] As Schütz explained, "Weber reduces all kinds of social relationships and structures, all cultural objectifications, all realms of objective mind, to the most elementary forms of individual behavior."[5] Weber, then, bridged the gap between personal meaning and general behavior through the description of "ideal types": abstract concepts such as a "handicraft economy" or "capitalist production," both of which, "although found nowhere in reality" (at least in pure form), are able to "make the *characteristic* features of [a] relationship pragmatically *clear* and *understandable*" through "an accentuation of [its] essential tendencies." Ideal types thus served as tools "to analyze historically unique configurations or their individual components by means of genetic concepts."[6]

Weber also conceived of sociology as a *wertfrei* discipline, committed to understanding social phenomena without making value judgments about them or allowing preconceived theories to determine the interpretation of empirical particulars.[7] Schütz accepted this ideal, which paralleled important phenomenological themes, but he perceived gaps in Weber's theory where philosophically difficult problems had not been addressed. Most important, in his view, Weber failed to specify how an "actor attaches a meaning to his action" or is able to "understand the behavior of others."[8] Schütz wrote:

> I became convinced that while Weber's approach was correct and that he had determined conclusively the proper starting point of the philosophy of the social sciences, nevertheless his analyses did not go deeply enough to lay the foundations on which alone many important problems of the human sciences could be solved. Above all, Weber's central concept of subjective meaning calls for thoroughgoing analysis.[9]

By eschewing the task of rigorously defining meaningfulness, Weber introduced ambiguities into important sociological concepts. His classification of types of behavior as rational, affective, and traditional, for instance, presupposed that "the meaning of an action is identical with the motive of an action." Without a rigorous theory of meaning to ground this claim, its implications were unexplored, and a secure foundation for humanistic sociology remained out of reach.[10]

Schütz searched for a philosophical framework that could clarify interpretive sociology's study of meaning, identifying Henri Bergson's account of temporal experience as a promising first candidate.[11] However, Husserl had also addressed the problem of time consciousness in his later work, arguing that the experienced present could not be reduced to a punctiform now. "Every temporal being 'appears,'" Husserl wrote, "in one or another continuously changing mode of running off." Thus, the perception of an object is marked by perpetual change. Through this flux, the object remains unitary only because past impressions are "held" with it in what Husserl called "retention." This retention is not a memory; it is not, therefore, reached via an intentional act of reflection and representation. Rather, although it is different from the ongoing primary sensation, the retention remains immanent in experience *as part of the present*, albeit inexplicitly, fading through continual modification in the temporal flux into the "distant past" of "diminishing clarity." At the limit of clarity, the experience falls wholly into the remembered past, reachable only through reflective acts. Thus, both the experience of duration and the apprehension of objects as "constituted unities in the primordial temporal flux" are given through the faculty of retention.[12] Indeed, Husserl wrote, "immanent contents are what they are only so far as during their 'actual' duration they refer ahead to something futural and back to something past." These retentions and forward-projecting protentions have "an obscure horizon" that flows into the "past and future running-off" of consciousness. Through them, Husserl concluded, "the actual content of the stream is joined together."[13]

It was Felix Kaufmann who first introduced Schütz to Husserl's phenomenology. During his years in the Mises circle, Kaufmann became both Schütz's friend and a mentor who guided his intellectual development. Another link from Schütz to Husserl was Tomoo Otaka, a friend of Schütz and former student of Husserl who, then living in Vienna, negotiated and helped finance the publication of Schütz's major systematic work, *Der sinhafte Aufbau der sozialen Welt* (published in English as *The Phenomenology of the Social World*).[14] Schütz initially took little interest in Husserl's *Logical Investigations* and *Ideas*. However, after encountering Husserl's discussions of time consciousness and intersubjectivity, Schütz recognized in phenomenology a philosophical framework adequate to rigorously ground a theory of both subjective and objective and public meaning.[15] He concluded, according to Wagner, that Husserl's account of time consciousness held "the key to a basic explanation of the transition from subjective experience to objective conceptions, and vice versa, leading from 'time objects' to objects in general." Further, wrote Wagner, Schütz came to understand the project of sociology in terms Husserl set out in *Logical Investigations*—as the "eidetic science" of the "regional ontology" of social phenomena.[16] Beginning in 1932, Schütz visited Husserl in Freiburg repeatedly, accompanying Husserl on the habitual "philosophical walks" where he held court with his closest associates, then Eugen Fink, Ludwig Landgrebe, and his American protégé Dorion Cairns. Husserl eventually asked Schütz to become one of his assistants, but Schütz was not able to accept.[17]

The Phenomenology of the Social World, written in 1932 and the only complete monograph published by Schütz during his lifetime, drew on Husserlian phenomenology to reconstruct Weber's methodology on a rigorous foundation. Schütz believed that Weber had failed to fully grasp the problem of how the sociologist understands the subjective meaning of another's action. Both purposively and inadvertently, Weber held, the body expresses information about an actor's mental state for direct observation, which the sociologist places within "a broader framework of meaning" using "motivational understanding" that allows an act to be interpreted as part of a "rationally purposive" series of behaviors. Schütz argued that an act's subjective meaning could not be "identical with the meaning which his perceived external behavior has for me as an observer." Observation of outward behavior, he maintained, requires a background of context for its meaning to be intelligible. For an actor and observer to share an identical "context of meaning" they would need to have lived perfectly identical lives. Thus, the possibility of studying subjective meaning as Weber understood it seemed to be foreclosed.[18]

Weber's concept of motivational understanding was also marked by ambiguity, failing to differentiate past motivations (the experiences and knowledge that informs one's comportment to a situation) and future motivations (the goal an action is performed to achieve). Notably, Schütz remarked, "in both cases the motive being sought after lies outside the time span of the actual behavior." The object of motivational understanding is, thus, always the "'accomplished act' . . . considered either as something really completed in the past or as something whose completed future form is now being envisaged." By contrast, in direct observation we "witness the action as it unfolds," not as complete, but "in the mode of actuality."[19] The analysis of observational and motivational understanding points to an important distinction between ongoing "action" and a finished "act." Ongoing action necessarily refers to the subject involved in its performance. However, although an act exists only through action, that action need not enter consideration of the completed act's meaning. Therefore, whereas "the action is a series of experiences being formed in the concrete and individual consciousness of some actor," Schütz wrote, "the act is, so to speak, performed anonymously."[20] This creates a dilemma: rather than a singular subjective meaning, the interpretive sociologist is now saddled with a pair of distinct meanings—that of the action and the act. To clarify the situation, Schütz turned to Husserl.

In *Logical Investigations*, Husserl identified meaning as the ideal unity of individuals expressing that meaning.[21] In his later work, however, he rejected this view, realizing that meanings are not "static" but constituted by the subject atop a background of meaningful experience. The meaning-endowing intentional act refers back to a substratum of previous intentions. This stratification occurs within inner time consciousness through the flow of the present into retention, synthesizing "polythetic" lived experience, with its various rays of attention, into a monothetic "meaning-context." While "immersed in the flow of duration," no action is complete, as the world is "only now being constituted" and "ever being constituted anew in the stream of my enduring ego."[22] Thus, the *completed* act can exist only in reflection on one's own experience, through which the object of attention becomes fixed and immutable because it is constituted through the retrospective gaze as something already elapsed. As a correlate, the subjective meaning of ongoing action can never become the object of the sociologist's study, since any effort to reflect upon action removes it from the flow of duration. Thus, Schütz concluded, "only the already experienced is meaningful, not that which is being experienced. For meaning . . . only becomes visible to the reflective glance."[23]

Of course, internal time consciousness reaches not only into the past as retention but forward through protention, which imagines a future in which the act has been completed. This protention contains the act's "in-order-to motive." Schütz distinguished this from the act's "because motive," which lies strictly in the past and is not fulfilled by an action's performance or unfulfilled in its failure. For instance, I might say that I open my umbrella because it is raining. Despite this sentence's syntax, however, it expresses an in-order-to motive: I open my umbrella *in order to* avoid the rain, projecting a future in which I remain dry. The genuine because motive of the action may be rendered as "If I expose myself unprotected to the rain I will get wet and soon it will become unpleasant." However, the rain attains relevance as an obstacle only when an actor begins the project of constructing strategies to cope with it. In other words, the because motive does not exist before the project. Rather, it is constituted from the strata of past experiences that are brought to attention when an action is considered in retrospect. Therefore, Schütz concluded, before the act of opening an umbrella is projected into the future as the fulfillment of an in-order-to motive, "there is given no meaning-context wherein the perception of rain and the opening of an umbrella are connected elements."[24]

Schütz was, thus, able to define the meaning of an action as "the meaning of . . . its corresponding projected act": its in-order-to motive. Having collapsed Weber's distinction between action and behavior, Schütz now restored the binary by differentiating their protensive contents. Action, he argued, was a subset of behavior distinguished by the unfulfilled protention of a completed act that is to be "constituted in the action." When spontaneous behavior is directed at another consciousness, it is "social behavior." When, moreover, this behavior has been projected, it is "social action." In this framework, rational action can also be defined as "an action with known intermediate goals," As Schütz explained, "The actor projects his action as if it were already over and done with and lying in the past . . . which the actor pictures and assigns to its place in the order of experiences given to him at the moment of projection."[25]

While clarifying the nature of subjective meaning was a significant advance, the project of interpretive sociology remained in danger so long as the possibility of intersubjective meaning had not yet been saved from the threat of solipsism. Turning to this problem, Schütz noted that the contemporary world's existence is taken for granted in the natural attitude, as is the existence of alter (other) egos with their own streams of consciousness. Of course, we have no access to the precise subjective meaning of the alter ego's acts.[26] However, he explained, the other's body is grasped as "a *field of expression* for the life-experience of that psychophysical unity we call the other self." Although indubitable knowledge of another's experience is a limit point that can never be reached, their bodily field of expression reveals "indications of the other person's inner life," albeit from within our own unique meaning-context.[27] Thus, our perception of the other person's inner life "does not involve inference or judgement." It is an "intentional Act which utilizes an already established code of interpretation directing us through the bodily movement to the other's underlying lived experience."[28] Through the expressive field of the body, therefore, it is possible to reach toward the meaning of their acts: we grasp their bodily field of expression and interpret their "expressive acts," attempt to "put ourselves in the place of the actor and identify our lived experiences with his," and finally "project the other person's goal as if it were our own."[29]

Schütz identified the general mode "in which I am aware of another human being as a person" as the "Thou-orientation." In thou-oriented intentional action, the experience of the other as alter ego is pre-predicative, already understood without being conceptualized, and does not require the other's reciprocity (e.g., in the case of observation). However, the possibility of thou-oriented experience, Schütz argued, is grounded in a foundational "We-orientation" that is "already given to me by the mere fact that I am born into the world of directly experienced social reality." The we-orientation is characteristic of the previously described face-to-face relations in which the other is grasped directly through one's bodily field of expression. "When you and I are immediately involved with each other," Schütz wrote, "every experience is colored by that involvement."[30] However, unlike reflective consideration of one's own experience, which takes up the already completed events one's own past, the other's inner life is perceived as it occurs in face-to-face encounters, synchronous with one's own. Subsequent reflection on this perception, therefore, implicates one's own consciousness as well as the other's "in a single intentional act which embraces them both." A sense of shared time—"the phenomenon of *growing old together*"—is, thus, intrinsic to the we-orientation.[31] "During all this time," Schütz wrote, "we are aware of each other's stream of consciousness as contemporaneous with our own . . . without a need to reflect on it. In a flash I see your whole plan and its execution in actions."[32]

Schütz further divided the intersubjective world into distinct domains. The closest domain is the realm of "directly experienced social reality." This is one's own "Here and Now" in which "fellow men" are always already given as alter-egos: I am aware of their consciousnesses and, further, am aware that these others are aware of my consciousness. Beyond the horizon of direct experience is the "world of contemporaries," which is, in principle, available to direct experience. However, unlike the fellows of directly experienced reality, "I do not directly and immediately grasp [contemporaries'] experiences but instead infer, on the basis of indirect evidence, the typical subjective experiences they must be having." Unreachable even in principle is the "world of predecessors," of which "I can only be an observer and not an actor." Likewise, a "world of successors" exists beyond the end of one's life that can be grasped only "vaguely," comprised of individuals "with whose subjective experiences I can have no personal acquaintance."[33]

Weber described interpretive sociology as the study of "social action," which he defined as action "oriented to the past, present, or expected future behavior of others."[34] In this framework, a "social relationship" exists when there is the possibility of reciprocal social action among a group of individuals.[35] However, in clarifying the meaning of social action by defining it in relation to another's consciousness rather than in relation to that other's behavior, Schütz had found that the phenomenological structure of an act oriented toward another's subjective experience was contingent on the proximity of those involved.[36] Whereas Weber made no distinction between actions directed at the behavior of others in the past, present, and future, Schütz argued that these were distinct modes of intentionality whose differences were significant to sociological analysis. Even we-relationships, he continued, do not form a monolithic class; in each, the relationship is experienced in "different degrees of directness," as is apparent in the contrast between a face-to-face interaction and a telephone conversation. Along this gradient, we move from the world of direct experience into the world of contemporaries. Indeed, relationships like friendship and marriage are discontinuous, Schütz wrote, "made up of many separate events occurring over a long period of time," in which those involved pass between the world of direct experience and the world of contemporaries. What endures these changes is "a storehouse of past experiences" that one assumes "can be reactivated in a revived We-relationship."[37]

The world of contemporaries is also composed of a diverse domain of entities. There are concrete individuals such as the absent friend and, more distantly, others known only by their reputation. Further still are persons known to me only as occupants of a social role, such as an airplane's unseen pilot. Still more distant are collective entities such as the airline pilots' union or the state, with which "I could never in principle have direct experience." At these further removes, Schütz wrote, entities "can only be known in the form of *general types* of subjective experience." Contemporaries are, therefore, *constituted* using the storehouse of our past experiences to construct "fixed" models from analogous situations. Unlike the thou-oriented acts of face-to-face encounters, the "They-orientation" that one adopts toward contemporaries is, therefore, a mode of intentionality that takes one's "own experience . . . of social reality in general" as its object. It accomplishes this through "interpretive judgements" in which "the subjective meaning-context has been abandoned as a tool of interpretation . . . [and] has been replaced by a series of highly complex and systematically interrelated objective meaning-contexts." In these fixed models, Schütz concluded, he had identified the basis of Weberian "ideal types."[38]

An ideal type must be constructed, Schütz held, to postulate the in-order-to or because motive of an anonymous individual's action. One begins from one's direct perceptions of similar actions and interprets them "within an objective context of meaning," taking their motives as generalizable for anyone performing the action, "regardless of . . . what his subjective experiences are at the time." With the action and motive established as a repeatable unity, one postulates an ideal typical agent who "typically intends this typical act." In other words, "a person is postulated whose actual living motive could be the objective context of meaning already chosen to define a typical action." However, the consciousness of this ideal type is necessarily "conceived in a simplified and tailored form."[39] As Schütz explained, this ideal typical agent lacks

> all the empty protentions and expectations that accompany real conscious experiences. It is not an open question as to whether the typical action will succeed in being a finished act. Such success has been built into it by definition. The ideal-typical actor never has the experience of choosing or of preferring one thing to another. . . . This completed act is at the same time the *major* goal of the actor's typical state of mind at the time. For if the act were merely a means to another goal, then it would be necessary for the interpreter to construct for his ideal actor another typical state of mind capable of planning out the wider goal.[40]

The idealized relationship between motive and action is merely a "frozen cross section of consciousness," chosen subjectively by the observer and "inserted into the consciousness of the personal ideal type" as its totality. Thus, Schütz wrote, "*it is a function of the very question it seeks to answer.*"

In other words, the ideal type is "so constructed that it must subjectively attach to its acts precisely the meaning that the interpreter is looking for." Any interpretation based on the supposition of an ideal type's behavior is "only a prophecy after the event."[41]

Schütz's observations were a precaution against a sociological reliance on ideal types without evidence of their accuracy. However, they also implied that ideal types were indispensable and, in fact, necessarily involved in a wide range of everyday behavior. When an ideal type is based on direct experience of an individual, it is, Schütz argued, "relatively concrete" and commensurably verifiable through comparison with its model's actions. However, types that are constructed through multiple iterations of idealization, such as "the state" or "habitual behavior," possess greater "anonymity" and resist conversion to the world of direct experience.[42] One of the principal tasks Schütz left to the sociologist was, therefore, the analysis of how habitual types and social collectivities are constructed in everyday life:

> It will be crucial to determine whether a social collectivity is essentially based on a direct or an indirect social relationship, or possibly on a relationship of both kinds, existing between the component individuals. It will also be necessary to study the exact sense, if any, in which a subjective meaning-context can be ascribed to a social collectivity . . . whether, by the subjective meaning-contexts of a collectivity, we do not really mean those of its functionaries.[43]

For instance, Schütz argued that analysis of the ideal constitution of cultural constructs revealed that the objective meaning of cultural objects cannot correspond with "the subjective meaning-context in the mind of a real individual." Rather, its meaning-context belongs to the "abstract and anonymous personal ideal type of its producer toward which we characteristically assume a They-orientation." Likewise, reaching Heideggerian conclusions via conventionally Husserlian avenues, Schütz argued that the in-order-to meaning of a tool referred to an ideal type of its user that was "absolutely anonymous," like Heidegger's das Man.[44] Thus, Schütz concluded, "it can hardly be [the social sciences'] function to understand the subjective meaning of human action in the sense that one person understands another's meaning when he is directly interacting with him." Rather, the sociologist must strive to understand the "process of construction" by which actors orient themselves to the indirect world of contemporaries, "for it is this process alone which gives a dimension of objectivity to his meaning."[45]

* * *

Schütz was in Paris, conducting business for Reitler and Company, when Hitler seized Austria in 1938. As a Jew and a banker, he faced certain persecution if he returned to Vienna. Although Schütz acceded to the reality of his situation, remaining in France, his escape was made bitter by forced separation from his wife and two children, and by the knowledge that his family remained in peril. Through his correspondents, Schütz learned of the fates of friends and colleagues, and of the frantic efforts being made to facilitate a scramble for survival mediated through state and institutional bureaucracies that required displaced and terrorized peoples to prepare credentials, authorizations, and the other diverse modality of official documentation that, in the modern imagination, constitute proof of one's existence and rights. Fritz Machlup, who then held a position at the University at Buffalo, notified Schütz that as of April 5, 1938, he had already received requests to write immigration affidavits in support of eleven individuals. With Paris becoming a hub of émigré activities, Schütz was well situated to receive and disseminate information and, because of his work for the bank, was connected with a wide network of government and private institutions. From this position, he took up the cause of friends and acquaintances, working to facilitate the movement of money and people across borders. These activities consumed him, leaving little opportunity for philosophy but at the same time fostering connections with other members of Husserl's circle, such as Aron Gurwitsch and Paul Landsberg. Still, the matter of greatest importance to Schütz was his family, whose passage from Vienna to Paris was allowed only after the Nazi government secured their commitment never to return. While Schütz's wife and children experienced difficulties leaving Austria, their struggles were overshadowed by the "bureaucratic torture" to which Schütz's parents and mother-in-law were subjected before finally being permitted to leave Austria. Nazi officials seized the home of Schütz's parents at gunpoint. Already beset by health issues, the couple was forced into an itinerant life of long lines, changing demands, delays, and cruel reversals of policy as they struggled to win approval to emigrate.[46]

Even before the seizure of Austria, Reitler and Associates had been exploring the possibility of establishing a greater presence in the United

States. Indeed, Schütz first met Marvin Farber in 1937 while traveling in America on business for Reitler. With conflict consuming Europe, Reitler's American activities took on a new urgency, and, in 1939, Schütz was chosen to act as liaison between its New York and Paris offices. This allowed Schütz and his wife, Ilse, to secure immigration visas, the last available under that year's quota.[47] Ilse's influence was the deciding factor in the family's choice to leave France. Alfred's 1937 visit to the United States had left him wary of life in America. He was warned by his colleagues that Jews in America faced discrimination that limited their social and professional opportunities. Schütz was also shocked by America's racial segregation, its gender inequality, and the repression of its laboring underclass, who worked in conditions he considered inhumane.[48] The color line remained central to Schütz's understanding of his adopted country, exemplified in an anecdote he reported to the political theorist Eric Voegelin:

> An American journalist is being conducted through the marble-decorated Moscow subway by his Russian guide. The American says: "But there are no trains! Where are the trains?" The Russian replies: "So there are no trains! And what is the matter about lynching in the South"?[49]

However, after relocating his family to the United States in 1939, Schütz adopted a more "upbeat morale" toward America, reaping the benefits of the New York Public Library and cultural institutions such as the Metropolitan Opera.[50] While Schütz did not reconcile himself with America's social inequalities, the United States became his home. Schütz was free to return to Europe after the war's conclusion but was disillusioned by what he saw of the postwar Continent. Now, Michael Barber wrote, Schütz "found painful the growing European anti-Semitism and the decadence and hopelessness of France." No longer entirely a stranger in America or entirely at home in Europe, he elected to remain in the United States.[51]

Schütz's experience adapting to American life was at once less fraught and more complicated than most of his intellectual peers'. Unlike émigré academics who found temporary, often marginal appointments and depended on a strained network of émigré organizations for support, Schütz's position with Reitler provided financial security and the ability to live in one of America's intellectual and cultural centers. On the other hand, this arrangement required Schütz to divide his time between intellectual and professional responsibilities. Schütz continued to work on behalf of friends and relatives in Europe, dispensing funds, negotiating American employment opportunities, and helping to secure visas, running through his own savings in the process.[52] He was also devoted to his family, on whom he bestowed love and attention generously. One letter to Ilse, written while their son was enduring a health crisis, declared that "you and the children are the only true meaning of my life"—a heavy phrase from one dedicated to the study of meaning.[53] Balancing these obligations became increasingly difficult, however, as Schütz attested to Aron Gurwitsch: "As you know, by night I am a phenomenologist, but by day an executive. At the moment my day life is taking over my night life."[54]

By 1940, Farber had drafted Schütz into the core group of philosophers responsible for overseeing *PPR*. Even within this circle, however, Schütz was one of Farber's closest confidants and collaborators. His "night life" was now largely consumed by his editorial responsibilities and the work of managing the journal's affairs. At the same time, however, Schütz remained doubtful of phenomenology's future, as he conveyed in a letter to Aron Gurwitsch: "Are you still enough of an optimist to believe that phenomenology will save itself out of the ruins of this world—as *philosophia aere perennius*? I simply don't believe that any more [*sic*]." His continuing efforts on the movement's behalf, Schütz explained, signified that his despair didn't "stop [him] from wanting to die as [he] lived. . . . Therefore we have to try to create in our world that order which we have to do without in our world." It was, of course, not only the world of philosophy that was out of order. "In these dreadful times," Schütz wrote, "all words have received a perverse meaning: Springtime is the code word for offensive, moonlight no longer interests lovers and poets but rather the night bomber."[55] For the refugees of Hitler's Europe, whose world had been lost, a lifetime's stratified experience could no longer provide a meaning-context for confident projection into the future. Nevertheless, Schütz remained committed to his family, his work, and his new country.

Despite the need to balance the demands of his employment as a banker and his philosophical pursuits, the period between 1939 and 1943 was fruitful for Schütz, who published new works, participated in the Unity of Science Conference at Harvard, and presented a paper titled "William James's Concept of the Stream of Thought Phenomenologically Interpreted" at the 1940 annual meeting of the American Philosophical Association.[56] He also delivered a paper on the meaning of "rational action" to the Harvard Faculty Club and wrote a lengthy review of the Talcott Parsons's *The Structure of Social Action*.[57] Schütz's editorial work for *PPR* further expanded his range of contacts within American academia, introducing him to contributors such as the New School's Albert Salomon, who brought Schütz to the university's interdisciplinary "General Seminar" in 1942. Through his work placing refugee intellectuals, Schütz was already acquainted with the New School's president, Alvin Johnson, who invited him back to deliver a lecture at the university in 1943.[58] Schütz held a part-time appointment at the New School as a visiting professor until 1952, when he was named as a full professor in both philosophy and sociology.

At the New School, Schütz was an avid defender of its Graduate Faculty's interdisciplinary organization. As he argued in a 1953 memorandum titled "The Scope and Function of a Department of Philosophy within the Graduate Faculty":

> The unique educational advantage we have to offer is that we are teaching the social sciences as a faculty, that is, on an interdepartmental basis. Our "departments" are merely administrative units. We are convinced that the study of human affairs is only possible within the unified field of the social sciences in their totality, not within a particular discipline alone. . . . Elsewhere it is possible to study social psychology without sociology, sociology without the history of ideas, government without political philosophy, economics without reference to the other disciples; but Graduate Faculty students become aware of the social sciences as an integrated whole.[59]

Schütz's teaching at the New School also highlighted the intersection of traditions not only between disciplines, but within philosophy itself. For instance, his 1957 course, "Other Minds," featured readings by Gordon Allport, A. J. Ayer, Rudolf Carnap, and Edmund Husserl.[60] Likewise, the reading list for his course "Sign and Symbol" included works by Max Black, Ernst Cassirer, Susanne Langer, Sigmund Freud, Bertrand Russell, and John Wild.[61]

Schütz did not complete another philosophical monograph after immigrating to the United States, although he prepared a preliminary manuscript for a work titled *Strukturen der Lebenswelt* (*The Structures of the Life-World*), which represented the culmination his decades-long efforts to provide a comprehensive phenomenological account of social reality.[62] In an obituary for Schütz, Hans Jonas wrote:

> The trials of emigration and exile, the demands of a new language, doubly exacting to his artistic sensitivity, the burden of two simultaneous professions, a delicate health—from these his untiring energy and devotion wrested the heroic harvest. As it is, we are left with an unfinished symphony; but what is there is enough to serve as a measure of what we have missed.[63]

Even without completing his magnum opus, however, Schütz was a productive scholar, publishing numerous articles that continued to advance his phenomenological analysis of social life. For instance, his 1946 essay titled "On Multiple Realities" provided a phenomenological reconstruction of William James's claim that reality exists as different realms, each of which is "real after its own fashion."[64] To avoid a lapse into psychologism, Schütz redefined these realms as "*finite provinces of meaning* upon each of which we may bestow the accent of reality." Because reality is constructed from meaningful intentional acts, each of these provinces of meaning "show a specific cognitive style." Everyday life, for instance, is characterized by the suspension of disbelief about the external world, a "wide-awakeness originating in full attention to life," intersubjective sociality, bodily involvement in one's projects, and temporal experience marked by the intersection of inner *durée* and objective time.[65] Schütz contrasted this to the cognitive styles adopted in other realms, such as the world of hallucination, the world of dreams, and the world of scientific theory, showing how each was constituted through different modes of intentionality. The scientist, for instance, must "leap" outside the natural attitude, bracketing their own existence and body, so as to inhabit a "preconstituted world of scientific contemplation handed down to [them] by the historical tradition of his science." One distinctive feature of this world's cognitive style, Schütz noted, is the lack of a "vivid present" on which the we-orientation is grounded in the natural attitude. Instead, the theoretician's sense of time reaches back to a problem's formulation and forward into "the open horizons" of an experiment's anticipated outcomes.[66] Identifying scientific theorization as a specific mode of intentionality that constitutes its own reality, Schütz's work opens space to consider the limits of science and the nature of knowledge into nonscientific domains.

Schütz's postwar writings explored a range of difficult philosophical topics, such as the problem of relevant knowledge in his "The Well-Informed Citizen" (1946) and the limits of conceptual meaning in his "Making Music Together" (1951), which concluded that music is fundamentally different from linguistic expressions insofar as it is an "*essentially* polythetic" mode of communication that cannot be abstracted from the experience of inner time.[67] However, Schütz's scholarly corpus, only partially and briefly described above, is often overshadowed by his achievements as a teacher and a mentor whose students carried his work further than he could travel on his own. Counted among Schütz's progeny are Thomas Luckmann and Peter Berger, considered two of the most influential sociologists of the twentieth century. He also oversaw the work of Richard Zaner, Helmut Wagner, and Maurice Natanson, important figures in the American phenomenological movement during the second half of the twentieth century who continued to explore the application of phenomenological methods to the problems of social life.[68]

In 1959, at the age of sixty, Alfred Schütz died from complications of a chronic heart condition.[69] Jonas, his colleague at the New School, wrote:

> If a thinker also teaches through his life, a servant of truth through the manner of his service, then Alfred Schutz leaves a legacy beyond the last achievements of his work: the example of a pure and noble soul whose loyalty to the spirit could not be deflected by suffering and the adversity of fate.[70]

Only during the last seven years of his life did Schütz have the opportunity to dedicate himself solely to scholarship and teaching without the competing obligations other professional responsibilities or political turmoil. Despite these limitations, he left an indelible mark on the worlds of his contemporaries and successors as a teacher, a scholar, and a "noble soul."

4

· Who Rules Philosophy?

Perhaps, however, it is not good for us to agree; perhaps difference,
opposition and heresy are the lifeblood of philosophy; perhaps, even,
philosophy is the one realm in which anarchy is a good thing, for it may be
that in philosophy the human mind recovers and savors the primeval chaos
out of which the cosmos was created.
—Raphael Demos

Almost no philosophers are good administrators.
—Edwin G. Boring

On December 30, 1979, turmoil within the American Philosophical Asso-
ciation spilled onto the pages of the *New York Times*. An article titled
"Philosophical Group's Dominant View is Criticized" on page 23 of the
Sunday paper recounted the fracas that had taken place at the Sheraton
Centre Hotel in New York City, where the APA Eastern Division's annual
meeting was held:

> Charging that the American Philosophical Association has become "a mono-
> lith" and "intolerant," that its programs "neglect basic philosophic issues"
> and that its leadership "has lost contact with other philosophers," the Com-
> mittee for Pluralism in Philosophy of the A.P.A. spent two hours Friday
> night severely criticizing the leaders of the philosophical group and said it
> planned to try to replace them.

What followed were accounts of a discipline beset by bitter acrimony.
Analytic philosophy, Hofstra's Evelyn Shirk told the *Times*, "presents
itself as *the* philosophical position." William Barrett of NYU complained
of interviewing a graduate candidate who boasted that he "had never read
a page of Whitehead." The dogmatism of American analytic philosophers,
the pluralists charged, maintained a "historyless present" in which the

field's mainstream leaders had lost contact not only with their nonanalytic peers, but with the debates and texts that had defined philosophy as a discipline.[1]

The so-called "pluralist revolt" that occasioned the *Times* coverage had erupted when a dissenting faction within the APA organized supporters to attend the group's 1979 nominating committee meeting en masse and elect their preferred candidates to its leadership. Using procedural maneuvers they had initiated the previous year, the pluralists forced a floor vote on APA executive positions and elected Yale's John Smith, a nonanalytic philosopher, as vice president of the APA, putting him in line for the presidency the following year. While some leading analytic philosophers challenged the vote, claiming that nonmembers and students had improperly cast ballots, the results were upheld by the division's president, Richard Rorty.[2]

When the APA reconvened the following year, the *New York Times* was on the scene to cover the controversy. This time the analysts came prepared, circulating a letter signed by nine of the association's former presidents that accused the Committee for Pluralism of seeking "to obtain through political means a position of influence which it members have not been able to obtain through their philosophical work." Responding to the pluralists' charge that the APA limited opportunities for support and distinction to those within the analytic mainstream, Ruth Barcan Marcus, a pioneering logician and the chair of the board of officers of the APA, replied: "Philosophers do philosophy, not associations."[3]

The style, methodologies, and priorities of American philosophy had changed significantly between 1940 and 1979, as Richard Rorty recounted in 1982:

> In the early 1950s, analytic philosophy began to take over American philosophy departments. . . . By 1960, a new set of philosophical paradigms was in place. A new sort of graduate education in philosophy was entrenched—one in which Dewey and Whitehead, heroes of the previous generation, were no longer read, in which the history of philosophy was decisively downgraded, and in which the study of logic assumed an importance previously given to the study of languages. . . . As a result, most of today's teachers of philosophy in American colleges and universities assimilated some version of Reichenbach's picture of the history of philosophy in graduate school. They were brought up to believe themselves the lucky participants in the beginnings of a new philosophical age—an Age of Analysis, in which things would finally be done properly.[4]

In the early twentieth century, Jamesian pluralism was an important if inconsistently upheld ideal for Harvard's Philosophy Department and many of the institutions that took it as a model. Somehow, by the end of the 1970s, pluralism had become the ideology of philosophy's misfits and rebels. To the established leaders in the field, it represented "the suppression of serious scholarly and intellectual standards under the false banner of openmindedness."[5] The insurgent pluralists, however, saw this appeal to merit as a false front and replied, with some evidence, that the philosophers who disparaged them had not actually read their work.[6] In the words of John McDermott, whose writings focused on William James, what the analysts really questioned was "whether some of us are actually in the profession."[7]

Setting aside the question of these particular philosophers' talent or merits, this chapter examines America's changing metaphilosophical commitments alongside the meteoric rise of analytic philosophy during the postwar era. In 1979, when the insurgent pluralists charged leading analytic philosophers with ignoring or dismissing those outside their own tradition, many did not dispute the factual basis of this claim. Rather, they held that those who did not share an analytic approach had little to contribute to the discipline. Thus, attitudes toward one of American philosophy's organizing principles not only changed but reversed in the second half of the twentieth century. However, the tendencies for which the pluralists reprehended mainstream American philosophy—including its increased specialization, disengagement with the humanities, and disregard for history—were not straightforward consequences of analytic philosophy's dominance. Although there may have been superficial truth to this allegation, it did little more than raise the question of why many postwar analytic philosophers embraced a narrow view of their discipline. Indeed, the analytic movement's own topical and methodological range broadened significantly during the same era, so much, Rorty wrote, that there was "no more consensus about the problems and methods of philosophy in America [at the time] than there was in Germany in 1920."[8] As a consequence, he provocatively claimed, analytic philosophy had evolved into a family of practices now unified only by "stylistic and sociological" features.[9] Why, at the same time, did hostility to philosophy outside of the analytic tradition deepen?

If we consider the authorship of texts to be the full extent of philosophical labor, Ruth Barcan Marcus was right that it is philosophers, on their own or collectively, who "do philosophy." However, such restrictions provide few resources for explaining the analytic movement's growth or the enduring success of analytic philosophy as a kind of "normal science" that provides epistemic stability for philosophers, assuring them that their work is legitimized by practices and methods that are generally successful in providing answers to philosophical problems, even as its precepts change. A focus on individual invention also risks overlooking the innumerable points of contact between philosophers and the institutions in which their profession is situated. Philosophers work within a discursive community that includes fellow philosophers, scholars in other disciplines, students, and nonspecialists. Their writings contribute to a dialogue both between contemporaries and across generations. However, the production of novel ideas and provocative texts is only one aspect of the work that is required to sustain philosophical discourse. Without *reproductive* labor—work that includes hiring faculty, constructing curricula, training students, reviewing articles, and running professional organizations—philosophy can be only a personal indulgence.

The reproductive capacities of philosophy are the infrastructure that allow it to endure as a collective endeavor. The faculties of philosophical reproduction are dispersed throughout the institutions through which philosophy is conducted, such as universities, journals, professional organizations, and grant programs. These institutions mediate the practice of philosophy by providing standards by which someone is accredited as a philosopher, determining which ideas are taught or published, or serving as a forum in which a particular kind of work receives attention. In these reproductive activities, the practice of philosophy is less autonomous than in the production of texts. One is ordained as a philosophy professor, for example, only by the consent of departments and administrators, responding to the needs of their academic institutions. Students of philosophy are trained not by the fiat of individuals, but in accordance with the curriculum and expectations set out by an academic department. Both explicitly in course requirements and reading lists, and implicitly through departmental rankings and rituals like the thesis defense, students of philosophy are taught not only a body of philosophical knowledge, but an interlinked set of practices, values, and taboos that inform them of how to be a philosopher. These points of contact between philosophers and institutions provide a medium of influence for a complex of administrative, political, and cultural forces. This chapter, therefore, focuses on the social dynamics of intellectual reproduction, exploring the ways in which institutional demands shaped local conditions of philosophical practice in twentieth-century America, and how those practices spread throughout a network of the discipline's elite institutions. As it demonstrates, both the intra-university mandates of new interdisciplinary formations and changing inter-university dynamics of hiring and promotion after World War II transformed the ecosystem of philosophical reproduction, catalyzing the rise of analysis and decline of humanistic pluralism in American philosophy.

*   *   *

World War II was a point of rupture in the history of American universities. Hiring of philosophers, which had lagged during the 1930s, stagnated with America's entry to the war. At Harvard as at many other universities, faculty who remained at their posts were asked to contribute to the Allies' cause. After the bombing of Pearl Harbor, chairmen of all Harvard departments were instructed to "report as soon as possible" on their ability to offer courses that could aid the war effort: both "technical training for specific war service" and classes "contributing to the orientation of the citizen towards the war."[10] W. E. Hocking responded that members of the Philosophy Department might contribute to instruction in foreign languages and mathematics. However, he opined that "the best contribution that we can make to the emergency" would be to offer courses on the ethical, political, and religious foundations of Western civilization that deepened and shaped students' understanding of the "world situation."[11] Between 1942 and 1945, Harvard's new philosophy offerings included "Fundamental Issues of the War," "Philosophical Problems of the Post War World," "Ethics and the Social Order," "Development of the Democratic Idea," "Economic and Social Philosophies of the Last Three Centuries," and "American Philosophy and Its European Sources."[12]

A generation later, such courses would have seemed incongruous. However, offering instruction that contextualized the conflict between fascism and democracy required little modification to the interwar curriculum of Harvard's Philosophy Department. During previous decades, the task of synthesizing knowledge produced by fields such as economics, politics, biology, and psychology within a discourse on American values had been the purview of philosophers. For instance, Harvard's philosophers had offered such courses as "Philosophy of the State," which was described as "the principles of political life—liberty, democracy, rights, property, etc.— and of international relations studied with reference to psychology, ethics, and metaphysics." Likewise, the listing for a course on the "Philosophy of Evolution" promised "a survey of the more important conceptions of evolution in nature and society, with some considerations of the consequences for natural sciences, ethics, and social theory." Harvard's interwar curriculum also included "The Ethics of Democracy" and "American Ideals and Standards, with special reference to Puritanism and Democracy," reflecting an understanding that philosophers owned a share in the task of interpreting and shaping national character.[13] The waning of these subjects in Harvard's Philosophy Department after World War II did not reflect a collapse of interest, at least among undergraduate students. Rather, efforts to foster this discourse in the university more broadly had the paradoxical effect of removing it from philosophy's purview and relieving a new generation of philosophers of responsibilities many were content to have lifted from their shoulders.

The need to adapt higher education to serve the state in wartime prompted reflection on the purposes of the university and gave academic administrators unprecedented leeway to enact significant reforms at their otherwise conservative institutions. "What kind of a College should we have after the new peace?" asked the dean of Northwestern in an annual report to its president. It should be "an institution which attempts to stimulate young men and women to intellectual attainment, to help them to a sense of values and a philosophy of life, to acquaint them with the experience and culture of the society in which they live toward the end that the world may ultimately become a better place to live."[14] Such thinking was not restricted to university administrators. Yale's Philosophy Department reported in 1945 that returning soldiers were "turning with special interest toward the humanities. The result of two or three years of immersion in an intensely practical life [was] to send many of them back to college with a feeling of starved need for the values of reflection and appreciation."[15] As the war concluded, a number of America's most prominent colleges and universities set to the task of devising new programs for instruction in critical thinking, the history of Western civilization, and social theory— the background for productive and responsible citizenship in a modern democracy. The chair of Yale's Philosophy Department, Charles Hendel, reported to the university's president in 1953:

> Since Yale College started its post-war program most of the liberal arts colleges have followed suit according to the individual genius of their systems and their particular vision of education in the humanities. The country now abounds with "humanities programs" in which philosophy plays an essential part.[16]

For American philosophers, however, the effects of these efforts were not monolithic, as the creation of new interdisciplinary spaces in the humanities influenced philosophy's departmental priorities and role within the university curriculum.

Harvard spearheaded America's most ambitious effort to create a holistic program for educating a democratic citizenry. Under the direction of its president, James Bryant Conant, a committee of Harvard faculty that included the philosopher Raphael Demos conducted interviews and collected data for a report on America education.[17] Conant challenged the General Education Committee to devise a plan for shaping American mass society—not, as had been achieved in totalitarian states, into an uncritical regiment of ideologues, but into a republic of citizens, able to make informed, reasoned decisions that comported with the nation's traditions and values. Such skills, Conant believed, could be developed by fostering the student's capacity for critical judgment and cultivating an appreciation of the good. For instance, students might "develop an appreciation of criteria that can be used in judging values" through the study of art and literature, illuminating "subsequent discussion of what criteria can be used in passing judgment on complex social and ethical problems." While democratic commitments barred authorities from being "dogmatic as to what is right or wrong, beautiful or ugly, or good or bad," it remained possible to promote "an approach to the questions involved which is in accord with the fundamental premises of a free society."[18]

The committee's final report, *General Education in a Free Society*, was both a set of practical pedagogical recommendations and a philosophical reflection on the paradoxes of democracy and modernity. Taking the synthesis of contrasting tendencies as its theme, it was also an archetypal example of postwar liberal consensus ideology. The work represented, its authors emphasized, "a unanimity of opinion not based on compromise between divergent views." "General Education" was a program of instruction intended for a nation marked by contrasts: a highly decentralized system of education with curricula ranging from vocational instruction to the liberal arts. To this, the authors claimed, the only solution was a synthesis of opposites: combining "Jeffersonian" traditions of individual excellence with a "Jacksonian" dedication to principles of equality; joining medievalism's holistic cosmologies with the atomism of science; tempering the pursuit of innovation and freedom with traditions that would provide stability and meaning.[19]

The report also contained suggestions for the establishment of a new program of "General Education" at Harvard College that would ensure undergraduates received instruction focused on "general relationships and values" in addition to specialized training in a particular field.[20] The most significant precedent for Harvard's collegiate General Education was Columbia's Core Curriculum, which had been created in 1919 under the designation "Contemporary Civilization." Like its later counterparts, this program emerged from the university's response to war. During World War I, Columbia had offered a course to members of the Student Army Training Corps called "War Aims," which consisted of "Allied apologetics, with no pretense at objectivity or balance."[21] After the war's conclusion, "War Aims" was reimagined as "Peace Aims." Under the direction of the philosopher John Coss, it became a course of instruction, required for all freshman, on the political, economic, and social foundations of "Contemporary Civilization." The focus was eventually expanded beyond politics and the social sciences to give greater attention to European history, the arts, literature, music, and philosophy. A second year of coursework was also added, focusing on the economic and political challenges facing contemporary America, as well as an application-only "Great Books" seminar for upperclassmen, called "General Honors," taught by members of the English and Philosophy Departments such as John Erskine, Lionel Trilling, and Jacques Barzun. Finally, during the 1930s, these courses were consolidated into a humanities sequence for freshmen and sophomores, covering Western literature, music, and fine arts.[22]

As described in a 1927 report, philosophers at Columbia believed that it was their discipline's responsibility to "appraise" developments in the "biological and human sciences" and "develop their implications for every field," address the "human problems of scientific and industrial civilization," and adjust the "values of the religious, ethical, and esthetic traditions to the world revealed by contemporary science."[23] Although this vision of philosophy did not originate with Columbia's program in Contemporary Civilization, the Philosophy Department's role within the interdisciplinary spaces of Columbia College as "the only department that regularly supplies instructors in Contemporary Civilization, Humanities, Advanced Humanities and Colloquium, and even Oriental Studies" appears to have bolstered its historical and humanistic focus by establishing instruction in these areas as one of its functions within the university. However, it also brought the Philosophy Department into conflict with the Columbia administration and established an institutional framework in which philosophers with humanistic interests were distinguished from their colleagues. By February 1960, reports of growing departmental dysfunction had prompted Columbia's President Grayson Kirk to appoint a Committee on the Future Planning of the Philosophy Department to review its operations, to the chagrin of some members of its faculty.[24] "I suppose that by this time I ought no longer be surprised by anything that the Columbia administration does," Ernest Nagel wrote, "but its resources for incompetent and discourteous action seem to be inexhaustible."[25] Nagel was on leave while the review took place, so he was not interviewed by the committee—a fact that should be considered in assessing its report on relations between the departmental factions. However, his correspondence with Robert Denoon Cumming, then chairman of the department and an expert on both ancient philosophy and phenomenology, provides a window into the affair and complicates the committee's picture of ideological conflict at Columbia. As Nagel ended another letter to Cumming: "But don't let Columbia get you down—all we need is a new administration and not more than a hundred million dollars to remedy our ills."[26]

Cumming and Nagel saw the review as an effort by Columbia's administration to assert control over a department concerned more with its philosophical imperatives than its obligations to the university. However, among the report's more damning observations was its judgment that the department had become "inbred and limited in the philosophical positions presented," suggesting a system of outside review for senior appointments.[27] The propensity of Columbia's Philosophy Department to hire its own graduates was, in fact, uniquely pronounced, which left it iconoclastic and isolated. However, the committee report also alleged growing divisions within the department itself, stating that "almost without exception, our colleagues in the Department of Philosophy agreed that the Department is divided into two factions." The minority faction believed that the department's traditional emphasis on the history of philosophy and "theoretical or 'creative' philosophy" was outdated. The majority faction, by contrast, believed too much attention was already being given to logic and the philosophy of science. This situation was not, the report stressed, unique to Columbia. However, it declared, "there is general agreement among our colleagues here and elsewhere that both Yale University and the University of Michigan are the acknowledged leaders in this field at present, with departments that seem strong, healthy, well-balanced, and harmonious to an extent not true at Columbia."[28]

Some members of the department saw matters differently. Horace Leland Friess, for instance, wrote to President Kirk that "our Departmental democracy has not been a matter of bloc outvoting bloc. Its spirit in the main has more nearly resembled an enduring effort to attain as much consensus as possible."[29] Friess, of course, belonged to the majority faction, so his testimony to his department's democratic governance has limited value as evidence. However, as a whole, the archives paint a picture of a department less at war with itself over philosophical ideology than in conflict with an administration over the competing objectives of philosophical excellence and service to the university. For instance, discussions within the department of a replacement for the recently retired logician John Cooley appear to have focused on leading analytic philosophers such as Hilary Putnam and Burton Dreben.[30] However, the committee report advised replacing him with a "logician in the more traditional sense," citing a "distinguished philosopher at another institution" who expressed doubt that symbolic logic "belongs in the field of philosophy at all."[31] Jacques Barzun, then serving as Columbia's provost and dean of faculties, instructed the department in 1960 that two new tenure lines "should be used in a way that would preserve the 'balance' . . . between 'analysts' and 'humanists,'" wedding "humanism" to a particular type of philosophy—one that eschewed the prevailing philosophical trends in America—by administrative fiat.[32] When informed by Cumming of this mandate, Nagel wrote:

> Just how does that great intellect qualify to tell us how we should make our appointments? And what on earth is the contrast between "analysts" and "humanists"? I have no doubt that on his books I count as an "analyst"—but I resent being so labelled by him, and I think that we are in for a bad time if, on the assumption that anyone who tries to deal with philosophic questions in a reasonable way is classified as <u>not</u> a humanist, we permit Barzun's predilections for empty chatter to determine any part of the future of the department.[33]

These efforts understandably provoked hostility from many philosophers, who were concerned with the reputation of their department and the standards of excellence they believed it should uphold. Cumming—who would presumably have been classified as a "humanist"—replied to Nagel, "With regard to your irritation over Jacques' babbling and labeling, I take a Manichean view of the academic world, and I don't see any reason why one should confidently expect administrators to be anything but beneath intellectual contempt." The letter then turns to Columbia's Core Curriculum. Complaining that his appointment to a committee on the program's future had forced him to endure a year of "Jacques' drivel (and Trilling's too)," Cumming explained that he would have resigned but for his hope to put CCB, the sophomore year component of the Core Curriculum, "out of its misery."[34] Returning to the matter of the philosophy appointments, Cumming wrote:

I'm ready to take his [Jacques's] money, if and when it becomes available, however he may label what _we_ decide to do with it. I have at present no reason to anticipate that his "predilection for empty chatter" will determine in any other way "any part of the future of the Department." His labels leave plenty of lee-way, and all that counts is the stature of the appointee or appointees we might hope to bring.[35]

Cumming's assessment proved correct: in the following years, those hired by Columbia were overwhelmingly analytic in orientation.

In contrast to Columbia, philosophy would play a minor role in the General Education program at Harvard. Two of the philosophers who might have contributed most to the program, W. E. Hocking and R. B. Perry, retired from the department in 1943 and 1945. Its leadership then fell to C. I. Lewis, and, later, Donald Cary Williams. With Lewis as chair, the department hired Henry Aiken, Morton White, and Henry Bugbee between 1946 and 1948. This trio seemed well equipped to fill the gaps left by the departure of Perry and Hocking. However, the new generation took a more modest view of philosophy's subject matter than did their predecessors, ceding the discipline's traditional scope to the empirical studies of specialists in other fields. In 1931, Perry had described philosophy as "that branch of knowledge which seeks to be both profound and comprehensive, even at the risk of abstractness and inexactness. . . . Philosophy, then, is that branch of knowledge which attempts to get to the bottom of things, and embrace the whole of things."[36] By contrast, in 1946, Lewis wrote to Harvard's Committee on General Education that "a professional student of philosophy is merely one who specially devotes himself to those residual problems which, by being common to all branches of study, do not fall within the special field of any."[37]

White and Aiken both split their attention between logical analysis and a broader tradition of philosophical engagement with society and humanistic scholarship. White initially offered courses on American intellectual history, social philosophy, and civilization. However, after the publication of _Social Thought in America_, he lost interest in courses he viewed as redundant on his published work, and, as he wrote, "stopped teaching any courses in what I jokingly called 'Americanology,' for I had become tired of serving as Ralph Barton Perry's successor in the interdepartmental program on American civilization." In graduate instruction, White explained, he also found it difficult to go against the departmental grain "because the topics I dealt with, such as historical explanation, were not the central concerns of philosophers and not likely to be asked about in the preliminary examinations of their first year."[38]

Aiken was a Harvard-trained analytic philosopher of aesthetics and ethics who also saw engagement with culture and the humanities as critical to philosophy's purpose. In his early years at Harvard, Aiken's courses included "The Conflict of Ideals in Modern Civilization," "Philosophy of Art," and "Philosophy of the State." While extolling the virtues of logical analysis, Aiken bristled at the restrictions many of his analytic colleagues placed on the discipline:

> The linguistic philosophers have placed at our disposal powerful intellectual tools which can be put to use clarifying the leading concepts of the educational vocabulary itself. . . . Yet, with few exceptions, the very philosophers who might contribute most to the removal of these confusions have avoided the philosophy of education and of human culture like the plague.[39]

At Harvard, he concluded, "the proper complaint could not be that we had too much linguistic analysis, but that we had too little else."[40] Making matters worse, he wrote, "we in the philosophy department were made to feel that our subject was peripheral to the main intellectual, social, and political enterprises to which the university's resources were committed." Philosophers "were generally viewed by people in other departments within the humanities as pariahs." While Harvard's philosophers did have a greater degree of interaction with the "social and psychological sciences," Aiken claimed that these occasions "were exceptions, and most of the passages were one-way."[41] Through General Education, Aiken found space to engage in a broader humanistic sort of philosophy. However, these circumscribed opportunities did not change his general view of the university as "a cloister whose classrooms and studies were so many beautifully appointed cells, each sequestered from the rest." In 1964 Aiken left Harvard in search of a more humanistic departmental home at Brandeis.[42]

Initially, if tentatively, philosophers at Harvard had been supportive of General Education's synthesizing mission. Lewis reported that the philosophy faculty was in "enthusiastic accord" with the report on General Education.[43] However, within the first year of its inclusion as a requirement in Harvard's curriculum, General Education had already become a source of conflict over departmental resources and begun to circumscribe the Philosophy Department's autonomy by creating obligations within an administrative space over which it had little control. Philosophers initially feared reduced enrollments because their department did not attract a large number of majors and General Education requirements left fewer elective slots for undergraduates.[44] Although the expansion of the student body after the war's conclusion quieted these fears, the Philosophy Department found that providing faculty to General Education created logistical difficulties. For instance, D. C. Williams had to request funds for a substitute instructor from Dean Paul Buck in 1949 because Aiken's obligations in General Education precluded him from teaching his regular course on aesthetics.[45] While the department secured funding to appoint Roderick Chisholm as a visitor, the arrangement had left the department reliant on Harvard's administration for support.[46]

Moreover, philosophy fit poorly within the framework of General Education, which was trifurcated into the Humanities, Social Sciences, and Natural Sciences Divisions. Philosophers, who were generally placed in the humanities, found that many of the subjects to which they might have contributed were allotted elsewhere. For instance, a 1946 list of faculty suggestions for General Education courses included offerings of "Cosmologies," "Philosophies in Literature and Life," and "Appraisal of Current Events" by D. C. Williams. The Philosophy Department had also offered to make Aiken's "American Ideals" a General Education course during the 1950/51 year. However, as David Owen, who was chairman of the Committee on General Education, wrote: "For better or worse, we are committed to reliance on the classics as the principal material in the humanities courses."[47] The Philosophy Department even considered taking a strong stance against the General Education program in 1949 when it was reorganized and made mandatory for freshmen. However, knowing this to be a losing battle, its members resigned themselves to tolerating General Education while privately bemoaning that "lacking concise factuality on the on hand and philosophical precision on the other, [General Education] is sure to be merely journalistic and literary loose talk."[48] With the Philosophy Department consigned to the "classics," courses like "Interpretations of American Institutions" and "Democratic Theory and Its Critics," which might have been offered by philosophers in the interwar period, were instead given in the Social Science Division of General Education by figures such as the political scientists Louis Hartz and John Gaus.[49]

During the 1950s, philosophy's primary contribution to General Education was "Ideas of Man and the World in Western Thought," which was offered most years between 1952 and 1960 by Henry Aiken and Morton White.[50] White wrote that he believed that the course, which enrolled as many as seven hundred students in a single year, "performed a very valuable service for many undergraduates, for many graduate students, and for the Department of Philosophy itself."[51]

> It provided a course in the humanities that could be followed with understanding by students who did not take very well to what was provided in more literary elementary courses in General Education. It also provided employment for philosophy graduate students who taught discussion sections in it, and it helped somewhat to restore the department to a position in the university from which it had been removed by self appointed custodians of Harvard culture.[52]

However, others within the department, such as D. C. Williams, took a dim view of these offerings. He wrote to D. W. Gotshalk, chairman of the Philosophy Department at the University of Illinois, that White and Aiken's course had at least "come nearer and nearer to being a history of philosophy rather than just a hash of Platonic ideas and miscellaneous poetry." However, Williams would have preferred to "insert at least a general history of philosophy and a course in general and applied logic, since we rather deplore the loose introduction to salon conversations which most general education becomes."[53]

Unlike Columbia's Core Curriculum, in which philosophy served a central synthesizing function, philosophy was one voice among many at Harvard. As Williams lamented: "Raphael Demos argued so persuasively that philosophy has become just another technical specialty that we were not given the directive role which philosophy has at Columbia and elsewhere in programs of General Education."[54] Harvard philosophers viewed the economists, historians, sociologists, and others who offered philosophical courses under the aegis of General Education as interlopers who had, in the words of D. C. Williams, "nearly supplanted our prerogatives."[55] Likewise, as Williams complained to Dave Owen, "With the word 'philosophy' on nearly every page (I speak without actual statistical canvass) of the [General Education report], and with philosophical works and ideas fairly teaming in your course descriptions, it seems a most extraordinary anomaly that <u>philosophical</u> philosophy should contribute so small a part in your program."[56] Thus, General Education at Harvard separated discourse about humanistic philosophy from its technical subfields and, locating this discourse among a diverse group of nonphilosophers, contributed to the view that these subjects were extraphilosophical.

Despite a disdain for the "loose salon conversations" of General Education, members of the Philosophy Department discovered a use for this new administrative unit.[57] Faculty from General Education would occasionally be asked to cover gaps in the Philosophy Department's course offerings, such as when Philip Rhinelander was loaned to teach "The History of Modern Philosophy" during the 1949/50 academic year.[58] Likewise, Frederick Olafson, a specialist in phenomenology and existentialism who was serving as an instructor in General Education in 1952, was called to teach a course on the philosophy of history when its regular instructor, Johannes Auer, fell ill.[59] The Philosophy Department also skirted Harvard's onerous restrictions on hiring by making joint appointments with General Education. For instance, the Philosophy Department hired Stephen Marshall Cohen and Robert Paul Wolff in 1958, with their appointments (and salaries) split between Philosophy (three-fifths) and General Education (two-fifths).[60] Peculiar to Harvard was a system of appointments and retirements governed by actuarial tables devised by the mathematician William Graustein. Under this system, permanent appointments occurred on a set schedule, with a system of debits and credits, allowing for flexibility but ultimately forcing departments to return to a preestablished size. Permanent appointments became available in the Philosophy Department once every five years.[61] By sharing appointments with General Education, therefore, Harvard's Philosophy Department could provide for course instruction in underrepresented areas without forcing the department to expend its own tenure lines.

Yale University provides a third example of collegiate efforts to grapple with the problem of educating a democratic citizenry in postwar America. Yet, while Yale's aims were similar to those of Harvard and Columbia, the program's influence on philosophy differed substantially. As universities became increasingly secular during the 1930s, Bruce Kuklick has explained, Yale philosophers "self-consciously determined to make New Haven stand for speculative philosophy and the sacred," committing the department to a "faux-Christian theism" that was difficult to reconcile with the growing importance of logical positivism and analytic philosophy.[62] In the words of Charles Hendel, Yale's Philosophy Department stood for "the spiritual tradition of our civilization."[63]

Although Christian ideology continued to inform the development of Yale's Philosophy Department into the 1950s, an exclusive focus on Yale's religious values draws an incomplete picture of its philosophical commitments. Yale's concern for Western civilization's spiritual tradition is best understood as one face of American universities' multifaceted efforts to make academe a bulwark against fascism and totalitarianism in the wake of World War II. As described in a 1956 article on philosophy in the *Yale*

Alumni Magazine, "The growth of philosophy at Yale has been part of a tidal movement of opinion in the nation at large regarding the aims of education." At Yale, the driving force behind these changes was the dean of the college, William DeVane, who initiated a series of curricular reforms that emphasized the importance of humanistic education and gave philosophy a central role within the humanities.[64] Yale's continuing commitment to humanistic philosophy is, therefore, misunderstood if it is seen merely as an iconoclastic effort to revivify a nineteenth-century vision of the university in which religion played a central role. Rather, in the context of World War II, Yale philosophers shared the concerns of many of their peers, and contemporary assessments show that Yale's Philosophy Department was perceived as a leader in the discipline: a 1948 assessment by the American Association of Universities ranked Yale's Philosophy Department the best in the country, and a 1957 survey by the University of Pennsylvania ranked Yale's Department second in the country.[65]

Postwar curricular reform at Yale had two major components. The first was the introduction of a new requirement in "Formal Thought," fulfilled during the freshman year by courses in mathematics, linguistics, or philosophy. For Yale this was a major change. Brand Blanshard explained:

> To allow [undergraduates] to plunge into philosophy at the very threshold of their college career was a daring step on the part of the Course of Study Committee and one whose success was not assured; philosophy has been traditionally regarded as a subject that is most appropriately taught by the president of the college to members of the graduating class.[66]

Those who chose to fulfill the "Formal Thought" requirement through philosophy took a first semester course on logical thought, which covered both traditional Aristotelian and modern symbolic logic, and a second-semester course on ethical thought.[67] At least in comparison to mathematics and linguistics, philosophy appealed to Yale's undergraduates. Philosophers were caught entirely off guard when enrollments for the first semester course exceeded five hundred students and neared seven hundred for the second semester.[68] With lecture halls overflowing, Blanshard joked that classes might be relocated to Yale's football stadium. "If called upon," he wrote in his annual report to the university's president, "the department will do its best to groom a team of philosophers for appearance in the Bowl, stipulating only that the cheerleaders be duly coached in pronouncing 'Epistemic Correlation.'"[69]

A second element of Yale's postwar curricular reform was the creation of a two-year program in the humanities called Directed Studies. This program was designed both as the university's response to the civilizational challenge of World War II and as foray against "the Balkanization of knowledge which rigid departmentalization [had] so tended to produce" since the development of the elective system at the start of the century.[70] Unlike Harvard and Columbia's programs, Directed Studies was selective, admitting approximately forty students per class. Participants in the program took an interconnected group of courses during freshman and sophomore years that focused on literature, philosophy, language, history, and the natural sciences.[71] Whereas Columbia's "Western Civilization Course" had placed significant administrative burdens on its Philosophy Department and philosophy became merely one discipline among many within Harvard's General Education, Yale's Philosophy Department enjoyed congenial relations with the Directed Studies program, and philosophy assumed a central position within the program itself. As Brand Blanshard described the program's first year under Monroe Beardsley:

> Conceiving philosophy as the central and correlating subject among the Directed Studies, he has sought, through his own regular participation in the courses in literature and mathematics, to keep in intimate touch with all sides of the students' work. His program in the philosophical seminars has been as follows: he begins with an analysis of common-sense knowledge, and moves on into a consideration of the purposes, methods and claims of the sciences which the students are pursuing simultaneously—of empirical science on the one hand and mathematical science on the other. He then goes on to consider the nature of poetry, taking examples from literature which the students are currently reading. Toward the end of the year he pushes on into the underlying issues that belong to the theory of knowledge and metaphysics.[72]

In Harvard's General Education courses, the task of finding meaning in the human and natural sciences, traditionally the role of philosophy, was forfeited to technical experts in those disciplines. By contrast, though Beardsley soon retired, philosophy retained its mandate for interdisciplinary synthesis at Yale. By 1952, Directed Studies engaged nine philosophy instructors; a full professor, Theodore Greene, was appointed to oversee their work. Like Harvard and Columbia, most positions in Directed Studies were not tenure track. However, as the program expanded, the Philosophy Department requested that it allow instructors to retain one-third of their time for "general work in the department"—particularly, aiding in its large new freshman courses. After a year or two of service, instructors would be released to offer courses in their own field so that they might pursue "opportunities for advancement on the strength of their own specialties in scholarship." Indeed, it was not uncommon for instructors in Directed Studies, such as Irwin Lieb and James Haden, to be promoted to tenure-track positions.[73] Thus, according to Richard Bernstein, who served in Directed Studies before joining Yale's Philosophy Department as an assistant professor, a posting in Directed Studies was seen as a "plum" appointment.[74]

More than any of America's other elite philosophy departments, Yale continued to emphasize humanistic methodologies during the second half of the twentieth century, serving as a nexus for analytic and Continental traditions until conflict brought about its collapse. This was, of course, not reductively attributable to the influence of its Directed Studies program. However, it would also be ill considered to conclude that ideology or philosophical commitments alone could explain Yale's iconoclasm. This is not to say that philosophers embraced or rejected ideas from a mercenary sense of opportunity. However, in a postwar era marked by the rapid expansion of institutional control, a growing portion of the philosopher's work was undertaken in the professional realm, where individuals were in constant negotiation with administrative forces. These negotiations had effects on the meaning, function, and value attributed to philosophy within institutions that outlasted the administrative projects that created them. Indeed, after Yale eliminated its freshman-year "Formal Thought" requirement in 1956, enrollments in introductory philosophy courses actually increased.[75]

* * *

The most significant changes to postwar American universities did not originate from within the academy. As the war concluded, the state regularized its efforts to use the university as a site for the development of economic, military, and technocratic resources. At the same time, Congress committed to provide the opportunity for a college education to American veterans, bringing a wave of new students into the university system. These changes had important ramifications for philosophers, as departments expanded and adapted to the new circumstances. The changes also acted as a catalyst for the emergence of analytic philosophy as the dominant philosophical tradition in America, overcoming barriers of both institutional culture and demographics that had inhibited any one school or viewpoint in philosophy from becoming orthodoxy during the first half the twentieth century.

The partnership that formed between universities and the government during the Second World War continued to thrive after its conclusion, facilitating the development of a new institutional formation that Clark Kerr, the former chancellor of the University of California, Berkeley, called "the federal grant university." While federal engagement with universities did not begin with World War II, the war affected a sea change in its scope and magnitude. Indeed, by 1960, annual federal spending on higher education had reached a rate one hundred times what it had been in 1940. Although the government did not exercise formal control over academic research, Kerr explained, its deep pockets afforded substantial influence: "A federal agency offers a project. A university need not accept—but, as a practical matter, it usually does."[76] As Rebecca Lowen has argued, the federal grant regime changed the balance of power between academic departments and university administration, as administrators worked to make their institutions competitive for research funds. This was most profoundly transformative in the sciences, where departmental balance and teaching were subordinated to research and "decisions about hiring and about which fields of research to emphasize . . . implicitly included estimations of their significance to federal patrons." These effects were less dramatic in the humanities, where there were fewer "steeples of excellence" on which a university might position itself for federal patronage. In some institutions, however, philosophers navigated these same currents. At Stanford, for instance, Joel Isaac has shown that government and private contracts were "crucial to the [Philosophy] department's viability," orienting it toward research in "logic, applied mathematics, and problems in econometrics and psychological scaling" in which analysts tended to predominate.[77] Moreover, if federal grants were offered to scholars as a carrot, some were ready to protect their prize with the metaphorical stick. According to Hubert Dreyfus, a phenomenologist whose writings criticized the foundations of artificial intelligence research, computer scientists at MIT petitioned their provost to oppose Dreyfus's tenure, claiming that his promotion jeopardized the substantial grants their program received from DARPA.[78]

The growing portion of students studying social and natural sciences also affected administrative expectations of philosophy departments. As the APA Committee on Employment observed during the Depression, the emergence of the elective system had made philosophy a "service" or "distribution" department: its students were not, for the most part, studying for a degree in philosophy, but enrolled in a philosophy course because of its relevance to their own field of study, university requirements, or individual interest. Moreover, as philosophers began to cede courses in social and humanistic philosophy to the social sciences and new interdisciplinary programs, their responsibility for instruction in formal logic grew in importance.[79] Finally, as Roderick Firth wrote to Harvard's dean of the Graduate School of Arts and Sciences, in 1958: "Although philosophy is classified as one of the humanities, it demands some of the same skills as mathematics and natural sciences, and many of our best students have come to us after undergraduate training in those fields." Thus, in postwar America, the profile of a graduate candidate in philosophy was also changing. They were less proficient in foreign languages, and some were less broadly read in the discipline's traditional canon, but many possessed tremendous powers in mathematics and abstract reasoning and a background that included some formal education in the sciences.[80]

Federal policies had their greatest impact on the reproductive capacities of American philosophy. Increased federal spending on education and surging enrollments fostered a hiring boom in American universities. To identify the effects of these changes on philosophers, I have compiled a database of philosophy faculties for eleven of the discipline's most prestigious midcentury departments: Berkeley, Chicago, Columbia, Cornell, Harvard, Michigan, Pennsylvania, Princeton, Stanford, UCLA, and Yale.[81] Throughout this work I will refer to this set of institutions as "elite" or "leading" departments. However, I want to reiterate that this verbiage refers only to their exclusive social position and reproductive power within the American philosophical profession and is not intended to confer a normative judgment. While subsequent analysis will not avoid evaluation of these departments' reputations entirely, this terminology does not address that issue. Rather, as this chapter will show, "elite" institutions led American philosophy's development because the profession's social organization made them primary sites for the reproduction of professional and disciplinary norms.

In 1945, a total of sixty-nine assistant professors, associate professors, and professors made up the faculties of the eleven elite departments, an average size of 6.3 regular positions.[82] The University of Chicago's Philosophy Department was largest, with ten members. Harvard had the second largest department, with eight. The smallest departments had five members. In 1969, 190 philosophers held positions of the same ranks in those departments, an average size of 17.3 regular positions. The largest department was Yale, which had swollen to twenty-nine (this would fall to twenty-two by 1972), and the smallest was the University of Pennsylvania, which had only eleven philosophers. Harvard's department was now the

FIGURE 4.1 Average Size of Leading Departments, 1930–1979. Average number of assistant professors, associate professors, and professors with appointments in philosophy at the leading eleven departments. See also the appendix.

second smallest, with only fourteen philosophers affiliated with its faculty. By comparison to the period 1930 through 1944, during which these departments hired new faculty, on average, only once every three and a half years, each hired an average of 1.2 philosophers per year during the period of 1945 to 1969.

In and of itself, the increasing size of philosophy departments may have affected the professional practice of philosophy. As departments expanded, the teaching demands placed on individual professors changed. In a department of five or six, professors must be conversant in a variety of subjects if they are to teach and advise students with a range of interests. In a department of fifteen or twenty, there is more room for specialization. Therefore, as departments expanded, their need for philosophers who were proficient across a broad range of subjects declined. Moreover, because of lagging hiring during the 1930s and early 1940s, the faculties of these departments were of an advanced age by the end of World War II. Only twelve of their rank from 1945 remained on their faculties in 1969 (of 190 total). 78.4% had received their PhD (or highest degree) in 1945 or later, and almost half (47.9%) had been awarded a doctorate in the past ten years. Thus, by the end of the 1960s a demographic revolution had taken place, filling the profession's ranks with philosophers who had been educated within a relatively narrow window of time.

Although the selection of departments I surveyed comports with contemporary graduate rankings, it was not based on them. Rather, it reflects an analysis of *reproductive* influence, measured by identifying the sites of graduate training for members of elite departments. Beginning with Princeton, whose status as a leading department I considered uncontroversial, I compiled a list of assistant professors, associate professors, and professors who served on its faculty from 1930 to 1979 and determined where each of these philosophers received their PhD or highest degree in philosophy.[83] Using this data, I performed the same analysis for each department whose graduates comprised a significant portion of Princeton's faculty. I iteratively repeated this procedure for each of those departments until all universities that placed a significant number of graduates at these schools had been surveyed. This produced a portrait of a group of eleven elite departments that hired almost exclusively from within their own ranks. Harvard was alone at the center of the network. Although entry to this caste was not altogether impossible, the group remained remarkably stable during the fifty-year period of 1930 to 1979, even as the discipline underwent its dramatic expansion.

Graduates of all other American philosophy programs had virtually no prospect for employment by the elite departments. Accordingly, elite

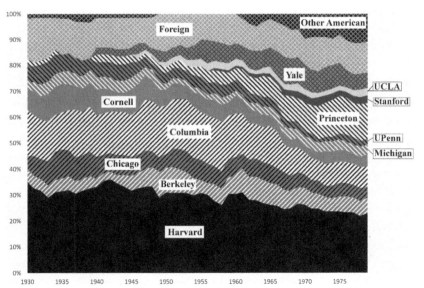

FIGURE 4.2 Composition of Leading Departments by Faculty Degree, 1930–1979. Degree-granting institutions of PhD or highest degree in philosophy for faculty of the leading eleven departments. See also the appendix.

faculties were united almost entirely by common educational experiences within a small number of institutions. This regime of exclusion facilitated their convergence on common pedagogical practices, styles, and norms— ones shaped first and foremost at Harvard University, which dominated the group. Because of this sociological reality, philosophers trained at these institutions in the early postwar years could see the common influences in their colleagues' work, recognize their style, and evaluate their arguments by shared standards.

To be clear, the "regime of exclusion" I identify was neither explicitly constituted nor intentionally upheld. There was no conspiratorial scheme to preserve the power and prestige of certain departments, no unethical arrangement to place pedigree before merit. Rather, under the prevailing norms of faculty appointments, this was the profession's homeostatic condition. As the Harvard-trained analytic philosopher Robert Paul Wolff explained:

> The old boy network was not merely alive and well [in 1957]; it was the only mechanism for placing new Ph.D.'s in entry-level teaching positions. When a department had an opening, the Chair would write to the handful of graduate departments known to be turning out philosophers, and would ask whether they had anyone suitable at the moment. A few phone calls or a note to a friend would lead to an interview, and the young aspirant would be placed.[84]

There was a rationality to this system. Elite departments distinguished themselves by monopolizing the discipline's most esteemed scholars, and promising students were channeled to them for the opportunity to study under these eminences. Most important, the longstanding professional and personal relations between members of these faculties meant that peer institutions could be relied on for assessments of faculty candidates by shared standards. This applied to graduate admissions as well. A 1948 letter from Harvard's C. I. Lewis put the matter bluntly: "There is no member of the faculty of Oklahoma or Tulsa whom we in the Department know well enough so that we could regard a letter from him as decisive ground of judgment on a candidate for admission to the Graduate School."[85]

However, there were flaws in the logic that identified philosophical talent with institutional affiliation and pedigree. Because the elite departments prioritized research, their members taught fewer classes with more support than most American philosophers. This was an obstacle for émigré phenomenologists such as Herbert Spiegelberg, who subsisted in marginal positions at the discipline's periphery. Before immigrating to the United States, Spiegelberg had published two book-length works on ethics and the philosophy of law, *Antirelivatismus* (Antirelitavism) and *Gesetz und Sittengesetz* (Law and moral law), and completed the manuscript of a third, *Sollen und Dürfen* (Ought and may). However, in his position as an instructor at Lawrence College, Spiegelberg's opportunities for research and scholarship were limited, and his work on social ethics was effectively abandoned. As he explained, "The adjustment to the American academic world required a complete reorientation since my first chance for teaching was on the introductory undergraduate level. For the first fifteen years the preparation of manuscripts, especially in a language in which I was not yet at home, was out of the question."[86] *Sollen und Dürfen* would not be published until after Spiegelberg's death. Thus, the scholarly achievements of American philosophers reflected a combination of ability and opportunity, complicating comparisons of talent with individuals whose institutional obligations were an impediment to focused research. Finally, some number of brilliant students were invariably denied admission by elite departments, while others chose to pursue graduate education outside their ranks because of proximity, curriculum, or funding. Therefore, prevailing hiring practices predetermined that appointments were constrained not just by talent or ideology, but by the limits of a philosopher's professional world—a network of pupils, mentors, and former colleagues that defined the range of who might be considered for a position. As Wolff concluded, this system was "easy, efficient, comfortable, and thoroughly unfair."[87]

On average for the years 1945 to 1969, graduates of the eleven elite departments accounted for 87% of assistant, associate, and full professors on their own faculties; 11.4% of their faculties were educated at foreign universities. Only 1.6% of their faculties received doctorates from American departments outside their own ranks. If we exclude assistant professors, this number drops to 0.6%. The caste of elite departments can also be divided into core and peripheral groups. The first consists of Harvard and the six other most influential departments: Berkeley, Chicago, Columbia, Cornell, Princeton, and Yale. Their students alone account for 77.4% of the faculty at the leading eleven schools in this period. The second tier of schools, Michigan, Pennsylvania, Stanford, and UCLA, thus accounts for 9.6% of their faculty. Even excluding all philosophers hired by the university at which they received their doctorate, eliminating the effect of bias toward an institution's own students, 79.1% of philosophy faculty of the leading departments came from within their own ranks between

1945 and 1969, with only 2.4% coming from all other American universities combined.

Harvard held a metropolitan position within this network of departments. Its singular influence over the discipline's norms and agenda was ensured by the overwhelming prevalence of Harvard graduates in its leading departments. In total, Harvard-trained philosophers accounted for 29.6% of all faculty and 32.2% of associate professors and professors at these eleven programs between 1945 and 1969. Indeed, in the decade following the conclusion of World War II, there is no year in which Harvard graduates constituted less than 29.5% of the overall composition of these departments. Further, if we exclude those hired by their own universities to assess these institutions' external influences, we find that Harvard graduates account for 36.9% of philosophers on their faculties during 1945 to 1969.

Not all Harvard graduates found employment in the leading departments, and few began their careers there. Thus, Harvard's influence extended throughout the professions. Indeed, some Harvard philosophers saw the promotion of their department's standards and culture as part of its philosophical mission. When Harvard's Dean Clifford Moore suggested limiting the number of graduate students in philosophy in 1927, allowing resources to be dedicated to the best rather than the "pretty good," C. I. Lewis replied:

> The next generation will receive the bulk of the college instruction from "pretty good" men. There are the state universities, for instance. I should like to think that a goodly portion of such men will form their scholarly ideals and their conception of what a university ought to be under Harvard auspices. That is one great thing Harvard may do for this country.[88]

The placement of its graduates was not the only means through which Harvard influenced disciplinary norms. New philosophy departments and those attempting to revise their curricula also appealed to Harvard for guidance directly. For instance, when philosophers at Brown debated whether to institute comprehensive examinations for their students, C. J. Ducasse, himself a Harvard graduate, wrote to his alma mater requesting past copies of their exams, explaining that Harvard's example would "be of a good deal of help to us."[89]

Columbia was America's next most prolific philosophy department, accounting for 16.4% of faculty within the leading departments between

1945 and 1969. However, more than half of those philosophers were employed by Columbia itself. Thus, unlike Harvard, this number significantly diminishes when we exclude those hired by their own university. In comparison to Harvard's 36.9%, Columbia graduates accounted for only 11.4% of outside hires. However, no other school accounted for more than 8% of overall faculty (or 7% of outside hires), so Columbia represented the most significant counterweight to Harvard's influence in the early decades of postwar America. It was only in the 1970s that Princeton surpassed Harvard as the most common site of graduate training for new appointments. Still, since Harvard graduates comprised 43.5% of Princeton's faculty from 1960 to 1979, Princeton's ascendance was more akin to a colonial uprising than a coup against Harvard's leadership in the field.

*   *   *

Harvard graduates also composed the core of the analytic movement in the United States at the beginning of the postwar era. To track the development of philosophical traditions, I have coded the faculties of America's leading departments as "analytic," "nonanalytic," or "historical," allowing individual philosophers to carry multiple classifications. I must stress that I am not identifying these men and women *as* analytic or nonanalytic philosophers. Rather, classifications reflect my determination of whether a philosopher's work addresses problems and projects within these discourses. In other words, these philosophers were conversant in and intellectually engaged with—but not necessarily members of—the traditions with which they are identified.[90] Of the sixty-nine philosophers on the faculties of the leading departments in 1945, I have identified 16 (23.2%) as engaged, either in part or entirely, with analytic subjects (five of the sixteen participated in both analytic and nonanalytic discourses). Among these, 7 (43.8%) had received their PhD at Harvard.[91] Three had received PhD at foreign universities.[92] The remaining six came from Berkeley, Chicago, Columbia, Cornell, Michigan, and Yale.[93] With just under a quarter of their faculty working in analytic fields, analysis was a minority position within the discipline, albeit a significant one. By comparison, the work of 68.1% included nonanalytic methods and traditions, and 23.2% worked on the history of philosophy. However, the sixteen analytic philosophers were clustered in several of the group's most influential departments, constituting significant blocs of the faculties. With the retirements of Hocking and Perry, Harvard's department had shrunk to eight philosophers, three of whom worked in analytic fields. At Chicago, four in a faculty of ten were analytic philosophers; at Michigan and Yale, two in a faculty of five; at Cornell, two in a faculty of six.[94]

Between 1946 and 1955, the eleven leading departments made ninety appointments. I have identified forty-eight as engaged with analytic subjects either in part or entirely. Overall, 53.3% of those hired worked in analytic fields, 27.8% worked in the history of philosophy, and 41.1% worked in nonanalytic fields. Of the forty-eight analytically inclined philosophers, fifteen had received their PhD from Harvard. Within a decade, this influx of new philosophers had changed the intellectual demographics of philosophy departments significantly. By 1955, 43.7% of their faculties worked either in part or entirely in analytic fields, almost matching the 46.6% who engaged with nonanalytic subjects. Critically, however, several of the elite departments had become major centers of analytic thought. At Harvard, eight of thirteen faculty members worked in fields that included analytic philosophy. At Cornell, seven of nine faculty members worked in fields that included analytic philosophy. At Michigan, all seven members of the Philosophy Department were analytic philosophers. However, all the eleven leading departments had at least two analytic philosophers on their faculties.

Thus, analytic philosophers did not yet constitute a majority in most of the discipline's leading institutions in 1955, but they held a commanding position in three of its most prestigious departments, including Harvard. Even at this point it was not inevitable that analytic philosophy would emerge as an orthodox position throughout the discipline. However, preventing this outcome would have required departments to deviate from prevailing norms, both in terms of their curricular emphases and their hiring practices. With so many new positions opening, simply hiring the best-recommended graduates of the leading departments ensured an eventual analytic majority. Because of this, preserving departmental diversity required active intervention and consistent commitment to iconoclasm. Few of the leading departments took such measures.

By 1969, 128 of the 190 philosophers (67.4%) at the eleven leading departments worked, either in part or entirely, on analytic subjects. 25.3% worked in the history of philosophy, and 26.8% worked on subjects that included nonanalytic topics and methods.

Some departments, such as Chicago, Columbia, Pennsylvania, and Yale, did attempt to preserve methodological balance or other nonanalytic emphases during the 1950s and 1960s. Indeed, R. B. Perry's description of Harvard's commitment to methodological diversity at the beginning of the twentieth century echoes in the *Yale Alumni Magazine*'s 1956 report on its department:

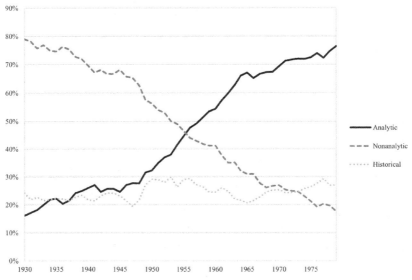

FIGURE 4.3 Composition of Leading Departments by Method, 1930–1979. Percentage of philosophers at the leading eleven departments whose work included analytic philosophy, nonanalytic philosophy, and the history of philosophy. Philosophers who worked in multiples fields are counted in each. See also the appendix.

> The policy in general is to seek distinction in every major appointment and the promise of it in all other ranks, to aim at balance in provision for the various branches of philosophical study and teaching, and to oppose Yale's being committed to any one philosophy, system, or orthodoxy.[95]

However, upholding these values meant losing ties with the other leading departments, whose students increasingly focused on analytic subjects. By the 1980s, Yale alone supported a faculty in which analytic philosophers did not predominate. Columbia preserved its distinctive departmental culture for some time by fielding a faculty composed primarily of its own students. Between 1950 and 1964, when Harvard graduates held 29.9% of regular positions in the leading departments overall, they composed 0.4% of Columbia's. By comparison, 79.2% of Columbia's faculty had received their PhD at Columbia. The university's standing in American philosophy dramatically declined in the two decades following the end of World War II. Whereas its graduates accounted for 18.8% of the leading departments' faculties in 1950, this number had dropped to 8.4% in 1970. In the mid-to-late 1960s, Columbia appointed analytic philosophers almost exclusively, including four from Harvard. By 1970, Columbia was solidly analytic.

During the first half of the twentieth century, American philosophy had been a field already marked by rigid hierarchies, in which a commitment to departmental balance had, often failingly, fostered intellectual diversity within the narrow confines of its membership. However, the postwar hiring boom produced a demographic revolution that made the domination of philosophy by a new generation of philosophers a fait accompli. The metaphilosophical commitment to pluralism that had promoted diversity at Harvard during the early twentieth century had already begun to erode by the 1930s. As the gulf separating Harvard's present from the era of James grew, its culture changed to embody a concept of philosophical talent measurable in absolute terms. This can be seen, for instance, in a report on possible candidates for a 1944 appointment in Harvard's Philosophy Department. One candidate is "first place among living scholars in the field of mediaeval philosophy." Another would be "accounted one of the first three or four men in this country" in aesthetics. The third, however, was "probably the best man in Aesthetics in this country." The last they declared "the most widely influential living representative of Aristotelian and Thomistic realism . . . in the front rank of the many philosophers in every civilized country who are participating in that revival of philosophia perennis."[96] In the years that followed, Harvard distinguished itself as a department that prized philosophical talent and scholarly excellence above all else.

At last, the ideal of departmental balance simply could not hold against the pace of hiring after World War II, which left the profession in the hands of a new generation of American philosophers by the end of the 1960s. Under their leadership, according to Robert Paul Wolff:

> There [was] a steady attrition, a progressive atrophy of the vigor and breadth of philosophical studies in this country, with more and more graduate programs concentrating narrowly on only those texts readily available in English, by and large written by Americans and English men during the past century and a half.[97]

These philosophers—most of them educated within a narrow window of time and at a small number of densely connected schools—shared, if not a unified vision, a common set of texts, problems, and experiences from their education that informed their opinions on the proper boundaries and norms of professional philosophy. With the traditions and practices of these departments as a pattern against which philosophers and programs could be evaluated, mainstream American philosophers, most of whom now identified as analytic philosophers, were able to experience their work as participation in a stable project, even as many abandoned earlier programs and methodologies. Analytic philosophy became a dominating ideology, first and foremost, because it *was* dominant. Its prevalence within philosophy's elite institutions became the fact of its virtue and the grounds on which the discipline's leading members could dismiss their pluralist critics. To be clear, I do not deny analytic philosophy's real philosophical virtues. However, as we will see, it was not a lack of intellectual merit, but the fact that phenomenology was rooted in institutions that were, effectively, lower caste that insured most of its practitioners would not join the ranks of philosophy's elite. Without reproductive ties to philosophy's leading institutions, phenomenology became a sort of boutique philosophy, which might or might not catch the interest of some within the discipline's core but in any case could not demand their attention.

C

Hubert Dreyfus

People have begun to think of themselves as objects able to fit into the inflexible calculations of disembodied machines. . . . Our risk is not the advent of superintelligent computers, but of subintelligent human beings.
—Hubert Dreyfus

Hubert Dreyfus was the elder son of a poultry wholesaler from Terre Haute, Indiana, whose success as a high school debater secured his admittance to Harvard's undergraduate class of 1951. His time at Harvard straddled two eras, entering the college amid its first experiments with General Education and the wave of new appointments that would transform its Philosophy Department's emphases and culture. Dreyfus intended to study physics, but he was drawn to philosophy by the lectures of C. I. Lewis, eventually combining his interest in an honors thesis, "Causality and Quantum Theory," written under W. V. O. Quine.[1] Despite his technical talents, however, Dreyfus was not a narrow technician. His life was marked by serious and sustained scholarly engagement with the humanities that manifested in his teaching, his writing, and his commitment to providing a nonreductive, humanistic account of lived experience.[2] As such, Dreyfus had a rare ability to engage both analytic and Continental audiences, exemplifying the potential for synthesis and cooperation that this liminal moment at Harvard briefly engendered.

Dreyfus benefited from the sort of unprogrammatic education that still remained available to a privileged few in the 1950s. After completing his undergraduate studies, he began an extended and disjointed graduate education at Harvard, during which he served as a teaching fellow in General Education, an instructor in philosophy at Brandeis, and an assistant professor of philosophy at MIT.[3] In 1953, Dreyfus received Harvard's Sheldon Fellowship, funding a year's study of French existentialism and the philosophy of religion in Europe. His recommendation, written by

W. V. O. Quine, noted the breadth of Dreyfus's interests, which reached from the philosophy of science to "the opposite edge of the philosophical continuum," stating, "I am sure he could find no adequate substitute in America for study with Karl Jaspers and Karl Barth."[4] Unlike during the interwar years, however, postwar Sheldon fellows were required to remain in a particular location for no more than one month. Thus, Dreyfus spent the year "drifting around Europe arranging to meet various influential Continental philosophers such as Martin Heidegger, Jean-Paul Sartre, and Maurice Merleau-Ponty, thereby getting, if not their arguments, at least a sense of their engaged approach to philosophy."[5]

When Dreyfus returned to Harvard in 1954, he landed amid a new phenomenological current that carried him still deeper into the field. John Wild, preparing to offer courses on phenomenology and existentialism, began to translate division I of *Being and Time* and drafted Dreyfus as a collaborator. At nearby Brandeis, the émigré philosopher Aron Gurwitsch was completing his systematic work *Théorie du champ de la conscience*, later published in English as *Field of Consciousness*.[6] During this period, Gurwitsch held regular dinners and discussion sessions at his home with local students and practitioners of phenomenology. In addition to Dreyfus, attendees of these meetings included Samuel Todes, John Wild, Harold Garfinkel, and Susan Sontag.[7] Finally, supported by a Fulbright award, Dreyfus traveled to Belgium in 1956 to conduct research at the Husserl Archives in Louvain. He returned to Boston in 1957 to assume a position as an instructor in philosophy at Brandeis and was appointed as an assistant professor of philosophy at MIT in 1960.[8] Dreyfus's term at MIT was turbulent, epitomizing the widening and increasingly acrimonious schism in the discipline. He was a gadfly whose views put him at odds with his colleagues, both in his own department and in one of the university's major research programs. When he left for a position at Berkeley 1969, MIT's James Thompson bluntly told an excited colleague in Dreyfus's new department: "Your gain is our gain."[9]

Despite the disdain he earned at MIT, Dreyfus was dedicated to showing the importance of phenomenology and continental European philosophy to his American peers. His interpretations of Husserl, Merleau-Ponty, and, most notably, Heidegger rendered their works into language that was accessible to analytic philosophers. Admittedly, Dreyfus was less successful in advancing Heidegger's cause than some of his Harvard colleagues would be with Husserl's. However, selling analysts on Heidegger presented challenges that Husserl did not, obvious issues of style and Heidegger's personal history aside. The structure of Husserlian intentionality rested on a distinction between thought and its objects that accorded with the account of human activity offered by analytic philosophers of mind such as John Searle. By contrast, Heidegger's radical rejection of the subject-object distinction precluded any appeal to mental activity as a foundational structure of existence.[10] Given this, Dreyfus's limited success at making a credible case to mainstream American philosophers that Heidegger's work was not only not-nonsense but comprehensible, relevant, and even insightful was no minor victory.

Today Dreyfus is best known through *Being-in-the-World: A Commentary on Heidegger's "Being and Time"*, published in 1991. This was neither the first major English work on Heidegger's thought—a distinction belonging to Marjorie Grene's 1948 *Dreadful Freedom*—nor even the first companion to *Being and Time*. In fact, it was at least the fifth.[11] It was, however, according to a 1993 writeup in the *Philosophical Review*, "the best commentary we have on Heidegger's *Being and Time*, Division I."[12] In *Being-in-the-World*, Dreyfus took Heidegger's narrative circles and, as best one could, ironed them flat. The work followed the thematic organization of *Being and Time* but drew from across the text and into the wider phenomenological tradition to provide fixed meanings where Heidegger gave only mutable gestures for a practice of hermeneutic inquiry. Thus, Dreyfus introduced the key analytic virtue of clarity to existential phenomenology. However, in so doing, *Being-in-the-World* alters Heidegger's text. Martin Woessner, for instance, calls it a "philosophical Frankenstein," assembled from "pieces borrowed from the philosophy of mind, existentialism, pragmatism, and both the analytic traditions." Thus, Dreyfus's approach to Heidegger's philosophy, called "Dreydegger" honorifically by his followers and derisively by his detractors, has garnered criticism from some phenomenologists who maintain that too many of Heidegger's fundamental insights are lost in Dreyfus's conceptual translation.[13] Whatever his virtues or shortcomings as an interpreter, however, Dreyfus was also an original philosopher whose unique contributions to American thought bridged traditions and disciplines, establishing his peculiar status as the oracular humanistic critic of the electronic age.

* * *

Dreyfus's academic career began in a moment of unchecked confidence that a revolution in the field of artificial intelligence (AI) was close at hand. In recent decades, the term *AI* has become associated with a range of tools that take advantage of the technological capacity to perform enormous numbers of algorithmic computations at high speeds for data analysis and content creation. However, in the late 1950s and early 1960s, *AI* identified a more robust project. Artificial intelligence was a mirror to the human mind. By studying and replicating the processes of the brain, computer scientists sought to create machines that could think—quite possibly more quickly and deeply than their human creators. The thinking machine appeared widely and variously in popular culture, from the villainous HAL 9000 of Stanley Kubrick's *2001: A Space Odyssey* (1968), which became all-too-human in its descent into madness, to the benevolent Siegfried von Shrink of Frederik Pohl's *Gateway* (1977), programmed with GOTO statements to probe the human psyche. These were not merely the expectations of a naïve public. Rather, computer scientists were among the most exuberant promoters of artificial intelligence. In 1957, Herbert Simon, a future winner of the Turing Award and the Nobel Prize in Economics, predicted that within ten years, computers would be crowned the world's chess champion and prove "an important new mathematical theorem." Perhaps even more strikingly, he held that by 1967 "most theories in psychology [would] take the form of computer programs, or of qualitative statements about the characteristics of computer programs."[14] That none of these goals had been realized in 1970 did not seem to diminish the confidence of those scientists who predicted in *Life* magazine that a machine with the "general intelligence of an average human being" would be created within three to fifteen years.[15]

Almost invariably, these predictions were accompanied by promising initial results. For instance, Simon debuted a chess-playing program in 1958, albeit "not yet fully debugged." By 1960, the program had advanced to the point where it could play a losing game of legal chess with a "ten-year-old novice." If a computer could be taught to play chess, it was thought, teaching it to play chess *well* should not be any more difficult than teaching a child. Indeed, in subsequent decades, computer scientists succeeded in designing programs that could beat amateur players, renewing proclamations in both scientific and popular literature that the creation of master-level chess computers was all but accomplished.[16] Logically, building a chess-playing computer was a perquisite to creating a program that played chess at a master level. In a sense, therefore, this initial accomplishment moved AI science "closer" to its objective. But to define this movement as "progress," Dreyfus argued, would imply that "the first man to climb a tree could claim tangible progress toward reaching the moon."[17] This "fallacy of the successful first step," he held, explained the trajectory of AI research: "success with simple mechanical forms of information processing, great expectations, and then failure when confronted with more complicated forms of behavior."[18]

AI researchers failed to recognize the fallacy behind their predictions of progress, Dreyfus argued, because of an entrenched and fundamental misunderstanding of the human mind. The entity that scientists sought to simulate was a simulacrum that, as conceived, could no more reach the goal of intelligence than the man who searched for a tree tall enough to climb to the moon. Of course, this error did not belong to computer or cognitive science solely or originally. Rather, Dreyfus called artificial intelligence theorists the "last metaphysicians" in a tradition that reached back to Socrates, whose demand that Euthyphro define criteria for right action assumed that the requirements for piety must be systematizable. Plato went further, distinguishing knowledge from intuition and belief by the criterion that only knowledge could be defined explicitly. As Enlightenment astronomers derived mechanical laws that succeeded in predicting the movement of heavenly bodies, it became plausible to consider whether deterministic principles of the mind's movements might also be revealed.[19] In a mechanistic universe, the mind is an engine of reason, operating on the inputs of sensible phenomena and memory to produce thoughts and actions. Its facility for separating the true from the false reveals an innate or learned capacity for analysis that mirrors the objective principles of logic. Finally, with the discovery of a logical algebra, complex statements could be analyzed mechanically using simple rules. Even if Socrates's formula for piety remained elusive, formal validity was now merely a matter of simple computations that a rational mind appeared to reproduce.[20]

To Kant and Hume, the mind already resembled an "information processing device," constructing experience by applying rules to phenomenal inputs or reflexively responding to physical stimuli. This, Dreyfus argued, "prepared the ground" for a model of thinking as "a third person process in which the involvement of the 'processor' plays no essential role." With the advent of digital computers, the metaphor of the mind as an analytic engine became far less abstract, replacing the mysterious "homunculus" of Kant's transcendental ego with a physical entity.[21] In the 1950s and 1960s. cognitive scientists and philosophers proposed and increasingly embraced a "computational theory of mind" that characterized the brain as a computing machine. Different versions of the theory defined mental states either in relation to their antecedents and consequents in the overall functional organization of a biological system, or as manipulations on symbolic representations of primitive concepts.[22] However, each held that the mind "functions like a digital computer" at either the level of biology or psychology, performing tasks similar to "computer processes such as comparing, classifying, searching lists, and so forth."[23]

In the abstract, this was a plausible account of the mind's activities. Yet, as Merleau-Ponty noted, in our everyday habitus we do not catch ourselves searching a matrix of memories and associations to weigh hypotheses about the entities we encounter. Seeing the gesture of an actress, meant to evoke the form of a classical statue, does not prompt us to consider that she might be marble. We simply see the actress and her evocative gesture, immediately and certainly. Indeed, experience is filled with both congruous illusions and incongruous realities that an algorithmic process would hold in abeyance. However, we do not mistake the daydream of a familiar friend for her actual presence, even at a place and time it might be expected. Neither do we dismiss the unfamiliar sights and sounds of modern life as fantasy. Unlike the computer, our minds are tasked with navigating the chaos of a world that refuses reduction to rational principles.[24]

Although the brain is a physical entity that processes information, the analogy to a digital computer rests on the premise that "experience can be analyzed into isolable, alterative choices," building up thoughts and actions from countless discrete operations on bits of experience.[25] This involves several important assumptions that Dreyfus held to be, at minimum, lacking empirical justification. First, he charged philosophers like his MIT colleague Jerry Fodor with evading the problem of the phenomenal field's constitution by appealing to the nebulous concept of "stimulus input." Perceptions can be legitimately described on purely biological or phenomenological levels. At the biological level one appeals to entities such as patterns of light and vibration that cause chemical changes within a physical organism. At the phenomenological level, one may speak of agents and objects, encountered by a perceiver.[26]

However, the concept of "stimulus input" sits ambiguously between these levels of explanation. Dreyfus called attention to this tension in Fodor's analysis of a listener's ability to identify variations of a melody. Fodor argued that the mind performs operations on sensory inputs (e.g., the frequency, intensity, and duration of sound waves) that identify patterns so that the mind "expects" subsequent inputs based on past experience. However, as Dreyfus wrote, "we do not 'expect' any 'absolute values' at all. We expect notes *in a melody*." Indeed, the melodic similarity between two cadences that may differ significantly in pitch, rhythm, tempo, and instrumentation follows a logic that can be meaningfully explained only at the phenomenological level, in terms of the embodied and cultured experience of listening to music. In other words, the process Fodor described relies on a prior step in which the physical energy of sound waves is transformed into a computational representation of melody, accompaniment, background noise, and any other elements of the phenomenal field. This, Fodor asserted, is achieved unconsciously by a computational program. The difficulty of what he suggested is obscured by the language of "stimulus input," which does the work of equating biological sense organs and a computer's data inputs. However, this analogy is fundamentally flawed. Unlike biological sense organs, a computer is given formatted data, written so that it can be parsed by known computational processes. Indeed, image recognition had proved an insoluble problem for AI in the 1960s, and it remains difficult today despite the advent of computational methods fundamentally different than those Dreyfus criticized. Thus, Dreyfus considered the proposition that perception involves a preliminary stage of data processing through "complicated mental operations" implausible. At the very least, he argued, this position was unsupported by evidence, requiring empirical justification that had not been obtained. Instead, researchers in AI presupposed that this *must* be the structure of cognition and made this unproven theory the basis for the claim that their heuristic algorithms simulate the operation of a human mind *in fact*.[27]

Still, other scientists and philosophers argued that a machine could be programmed to mirror the results of mental processes even if a digital computer was not able to replicate the processes themselves. For example, it would be exceptionally difficult to construct a digital computer that perfectly simulates the movement of each particle of sand in an hourglass; however, a computer can mark the passage of an hour quite easily. By analogy, a computer might be constructed that produces the same outputs as a human mind even if it does not think in the same manner as a human mind. Here, however, Dreyfus identified another problematic assumption. A computer's behavior is dictated by a formal set of instructions, either built into its architecture or given as an input. If human behavior is to be reproduced by a digital computer, it must, then, be describable in terms of formal laws.[28] However, humans are able to cope with unlawlike situations, such as when semantic rules are broken as a means of poetic expression. As Dreyfus wrote, "Logically it is hard to see how one could formulate the rules for how one could intelligibly break the rules," since the human capacity for understanding violations of these "metarules" leads to an infinite regress.[29] Instead, Dreyfus argued, communication that violates syntactic norms is possible because speakers "take for granted common situational assumptions and goals." The practice of language *use*, therefore, implicates "the speaker's understanding of his situation" as well as formal rules. This suggests that even a "general theory of syntax and semantic competence" would not be sufficient ground for a theory of linguistic "performance" that could be used by a computer to simulate human behavior. "Neither physics nor linguistics offers any precedent for such a theory," Dreyfus wrote, "nor any comforting assurance that such a theory can be found."[30]

Finally, Dreyfus challenged the assumption that the world itself can be represented by a digital computer. All data input for a computer is encoded in binary digits. There is no intermediate state between "on" and "off" in a logical circuit. While sophisticated algorithms allow complex data structures to be encoded using only these two states, the binary nature of digital data implies that every property of a represented entity is explicitly defined through a finite number of yes-or-no choices. Properties unable to be so defined cannot be encoded. Thus, digital representations are necessarily "discrete, explicit, and determinate."[31] This compounds the difficulties implied by the first two assumptions. First, while the physical properties of sensory inputs can be represented by binary values, the logic of intelligent behavior involves phenomenological entities, such as objects and melodies, rather than physical properties. Second, this logic is based in a theory of "performance" that implicates its local context or, in Heideggerian terms, a "situation" as well as general norms. However, it is far from obvious that a situation can be rendered "as an explicit description."[32]

AI researchers had come to realize that tasks like language recognition require a computer to draw on data about the "context" of utterances. Given the nature of digital data, such background information would be organized in a structure that relates discrete "facts" to particular "objects." However, this creates a problem. To make use of contextual data, a computer requires the means to decide which facts are relevant. This had eluded AI researchers, but, relying on the assumption that the human mind must employ similar data structures, they maintained that better heuristics would eventually provide a solution.[33] Dreyfus disagreed, arguing that context was an implicit structure of one's "understanding of the human situation," and could not be reduced to a set of explicable rules.

> Even a chair is not understandable in terms of any set of facts of "elements of knowledge." To recognize an object as a chair, for example, means to understand its relation to other objects and to human beings. This involves a whole context of human activity of which the shape of our body, the institution of furniture, the inevitability of fatigue, constitute only a small part. And these

factors in turn are no more isolable than is the chair. They all get *their* meaning from the context of human activity of which they form a part.[34]

Two different situations—such as signing a contract in front of a witness and writing one's name before an onlooker—might involve the same physical data. Yet, Dreyfus noted, "Writing one's name is not always signing, and watching is not always witnessing."[35] This sort of situation is an irreducibly human affair. It is only through "the broader context of social intercourse that we see we must normally take into account what people are wearing and what they are doing, but not how many insects there are in the room."[36]

The social context of human life is a holistic unity. As Heidegger explained, the entities of the world, encountered primordially as equipment, cannot be isolated from one another because they are originally disclosed within an already-discovered totality of relations. As there could be no tool for hammering without objects to be hammered, equipment is inextricable from this referential manifold.[37] So, too, the world is not an entity that can be defined over and against Dasein's Being-in-the-world:

> The fact that this referential totality of the manifold relations of the "in-order-to" has been bound up with that which is an issue for Dasein, does not signify that a "world" of Objects . . . has been welded together with a subject. It is rather the phenomenal expression of the fact that the constitution of Dasein . . . is primordially a whole.[38]

As such, Dreyfus wrote, the human world is "prestructured in terms of human purposes and concerns in such a way that what counts as an object or is significant about an object already is a function of, or embodies, that concern." The field of experience "is not neutral to us but is structured in terms of our own interests and our capacity for getting at what is in it."[39] The complexity and ambiguities inherent in the human situation resist reduction to a set of facts and rules such as a computer might employ. Thus, while AI researchers continued to search for theories and heuristics that would explain how the mind's functions were achieved computationally, Dreyfus urged a different approach: human intelligence could best be understood through phenomenological description.[40]

*   *   *

A preprinted quotation from Aldous Huxley adorns the first page of a 1964 datebook used by the existentialist philosopher William Earle:

Every man who knows how to read has it in his power to magnify himself, to multiply the ways in which he exists, and to make his life full, significant, and interesting.[41]

The words "full," "significant," and "interesting" have been underlined by Earle, who added the commentary: "He doesn't have enough Dasein."[42] This, in a nutshell, was Dreyfus's critique of AI and the computational theory of mind: "Intelligence requires understanding, and understanding requires giving a computer the background of common sense that adult human beings have by virtue of having bodies, interacting skillfully with the material world, and being trained into a culture"[43] Human experience is not a mental computation; it is Being-in-the-world. The original fact of our existence is its there-ness, *Dasein*, which is precisely what a computer lacks. No more could a computer simulate human thought without living in a human situation than could a person lead a significant life merely by reading about events that have no bearing on his or her own existence.

The challenges AI researchers encountered in the 1960s demonstrated the difficulty of providing discrete instructions for tasks that are simple to most humans, such as recognizing a face or understanding the meaning of a sentence. To play an adequate game of chess, for instance, a computer would consider tens of thousands of possible positions before making each move. However, the best human players appeared to consider no more than two hundred.[44] The conclusion that the human mind subconsciously performs similar calculations, asserted by AI researchers, was not empirically evidenced. It was, rather, a consequence of the metaphysical premise that the mind was a Turing machine. Dreyfus turned this argument on its head, maintaining that the failure to simulate human intelligence using heuristic approaches to digital computation was evidence that the computational theory of mind was in error. As an alternative, a phenomenological description of consciousness could provide an explanation for the ability of humans to identify strong chess moves without explicitly analyzing all possibilities.

An expert human player can anticipate threats and opportunities by "zeroing in" on particular areas of the chessboard while ignoring others. This rests on a kind of "global" awareness of a situation that provides a context for making such decisions. Drawing from Husserl, Dreyfus argued that intelligent behavior involves both inner and outer horizons of experience. Unlike a digital image, in which each pixel is independent, ontologically equal, and defined by an explicit value, the outer horizon of perception is an implicit background laden with meaning that guides the intentional act. For instance,

Dreyfus wrote, "the hazy layer which I would see as dust if I thought I was confronting a wax apple might appear as moisture if I thought I was seeing one that was fresh. The significance of the details and indeed their very look is determined by my perception of the whole."[45] Husserl also argued that the transcendental object presents itself in perspectives, with aspects and elements always hidden. However, once an element is revealed, it remains in our perception of the object even when it is not visible. This indeterminate "something-more-than-the-figure-is" is the inner horizon of perception. Thus, in lived experience, new information is incorporated into an already-structured perception of the object as a whole. To the experienced chess player, this inner horizon is constituted as the game is played, incorporating information into a "sense of the whole" that allows her to identify lines of play without explicitly counting out moves.[46]

It is crucial to understand that the horizons of experience are not mechanisms for data processing. They are not structures that allow the mind to make meaning from a neutral stream of sensory inputs. Rather, the perceptual object can appear only within the horizon of a whole situation in which certain "details" are expected to occur. Dreyfus illustrated this by examining a case of breakdown in which our expectations are subverted:

> If you reach for a glass of water and get milk by mistake, on taking a sip your first reaction is total disorientation. You don't taste water, but you don't taste milk either. You have a mouthful of what Husserl would call pure sensuous matter or hyletic data, and naturally you want to spit it out. Or, if you find the right global meaning fast enough, you may recover in time to recognize the milk for what it is. . . . One might well wonder how one knows enough to try "milk" rather than, say, "gasoline." Doesn't one need some neutral features to begin this process of recognitions? . . . But the process seems less mysterious when we bear in mind that each new meaning is given in an outer horizon which is already organized, in this case a meal, on the basis of which we already have certain expectations.[47]

A digital computer might be programmed with heuristics to aid in object recognition. However, Dreyfus argued, it is doubtful that a comprehensive list of rules for anticipating the identity of beverages could even be enumerated, and it is simply implausible that we go about our lives carrying this list in our heads, along with innumerably many others that cover the full range of human experience. Indeed, Merleau-Ponty's analysis of the Schneider case (see chapter 1) had shown the strict limitations faced by one who could not act without recourse to rules. Thus, Dreyfus turned to his *Phenomenology of Perception* to provide an alternative account of intelligent behavior.

The field of human experience, Merleau-Ponty held, is a gestalt in which figure and ground are mutually constitutive. While some AI researchers had attempted to program processes for "global recognition" that replicated this holistic phenomenon, Dreyfus argued that they had failed to understand this gestalt relationship between parts and wholes. A digital structure of background information is constructed from discrete data with independently defined meanings. A gestalt, by contrast, "defines what counts as the elements it organizes." Thus, for instance, although individual beats constitute a rhythmic phrase, there is "no such thing as a syncopated beat" except as part of such a phrase. Unlike the rigid rules a machine must use for data analysis, Dreyfus held that the gestalt relationship between parts and the whole allowed for flexibility.[48] This sort of global processing was possible, according to Merleau-Ponty, because the intentional arc is directed through the body, which acts as a whole to engage with the world without explicitly thematizing it. As Dreyfus summarized, "After all, it is our body which captures a rhythm. We have a body-set to respond to the sound patter. The body-set is not a rule in the mind which can be formulated or entertained apart from the actual activity of anticipating the beats." Even needs and intuitions announce themselves bodily, as a compulsion to "search to discover what allays our restlessness or discomfort." Unlike a computer, which executes operations through an explicit program, human behavior is "skillful." A skill might initially be acquired by following a set of rules, as when one learns to throw a ball or identify a species of bird. However, explicit consciousness of these rules disappears as the skill is mastered, becoming a way of Being-in-the-world that allows a person to "cope" in different situations without performing additional analysis. Indeed, the techniques employed by one who has mastered a skill may significantly differ from his or her training. Someone who has learned to throw a ball to first base, for instance, need not formulate a new set of rules to throw to second or from their knees. By contrast, explicit programming only allows computers to respond in predetermined ways. Thus, Dreyfus argued, "the question of whether artificial intelligence is possible boils down to the question of whether there can be an artificial embodied agent."[49]

* * *

In 2013, Dreyfus delivered the John Dewey Lecture at the annual meeting of the American Philosophical Association's Western Division. The Dewey

Lecture adds a personal element to the association's yearly gathering, inviting a distinguished senior member of the profession to reflect on his or her career and life as a philosopher. Dreyfus's talk, which focused on his experience as MIT's resident heretic, ended on an upbeat note:

> So, it turned out to everyone's surprise, including my own, that existential philosophy could influence the world outside of academic philosophy, making critical contributions in cultural and scientific domains.[50]

As Dreyfus certainly knew, this was only partially true. Almost five decades later, many of his predictions had been vindicated. Advances in machine intelligence have proceeded slowly; prophesized breakthroughs like general intelligence remain out of reach. Moreover, much of the progress that has occurred is attributable to new techniques such as neural networks, in which a computer "simulates a holistic system," unlike the "information processing" models Dreyfus criticized.[51] Yet, while movements in the field of AI research paralleled Dreyfus's conclusions, it is not evident that his influence was instrumental in these developments.

Dreyfus's work was almost universally ignored or met with derision by the AI researchers to whom it was addressed.[52] Of course, this was a predictable response of well-credentialed experts to an outsider who brashly declared that their enterprise was fundamentally flawed. Compounding Dreyfus's outsider status, however, was an attitude of contempt toward Continental philosophy, which discredited him by association. One computer scientist, Stanford's Edward Feigenbaum, dismissed Dreyfus's criticism, saying that he "bludgeons us over the head with stuff he's misunderstood and is obsolete anyway. . . . And what does he offer us instead? Phenomenology! That ball of fluff! That cotton candy!"[53] AI researchers who attempted to rebut Dreyfus objected that he refused to provide a scientifically rigorous alternative to their own theories of mind. Without enunciating a "formal set of rules" and precise definitions of entities, no explanation of mental activity offered by Dreyfus could amount, in their view, to a proper theory. A "scientific" explanation of human behavior, in other words, is one that "treats man as a device, an object responding to the influence of other objects, according to universal laws or rules." However, Dreyfus believed phenomenological analysis demonstrated that *no such theory* could account for human behavior. As such, he replied, the form of explanation AI researchers demanded was "determined by the very tradition to which we are seeking an alternative."[54] In this context, the implications of Dreyfus's critique are radical. He asserted the existence of physical entities that science, as so conceived, could not describe. Portions of the universe are closed to scientific discovery not only in practice but in principle. Yet, in this perplexing realm that cannot be measured, codified, or formalized, humanistic analysis remains a reliable guide. Perhaps Dreyfus did not succeed at bringing existential phenomenology's influence to scientific domains. However, he instead secured a place for the human mind against the circuitry of the digital age and identified an irreducibly humanistic field of knowledge beyond science's grasp.

5

Becoming Continental

What happened to me, as to many other young American philosophers, was
that in graduate school one learned what not to like and what not to consider
philosophy.
—Hilary Putnam

There is the kind of difference from another that is arrived at reluctantly
because one's own evidence seems to require it; such difference there must
always be. There is also the sort of difference that is cultivated for its own
sake, or for the witness it gives to the sturdy independence, the acumen, the
devastating dialectical powers, or the noble refusal to be anybody's echo,
of the man who begs to differ. It is harder in philosophy than in most other
disciplines to recognize the subtle undercover work of egoism. But where
it is indulged without check or limit, philosophy resolves itself into endless
dissidence of dissent.
—Brand Blanshard

"What is this oxymoron . . . American continental philosophy," asks the
back cover of *American Continental Philosophy: A Reader*, published in
2000 by Indiana University Press. It continues:

> Continental philosophy was first introduced to America by expatriate Euro-
> peans after World War II. During the 1950s and 1960s American-born philos-
> ophers assimilated the thought of Husserl, Heidegger, Merleau-Ponty, Sartre
> and others; through their teaching and writing, continental philosophy took
> root and developed its own particularly American character.[1]

This story is perplexing. We know that phenomenology came to America
well before the 1950s. Here, however, the movement's leading lights are
grouped with unnamed "others" as representatives of a postwar import
called "Continental philosophy." As these contradictions suggest, this new
term, which identified philosophers with a region rather than a method,
was no mere synonym. Its emergence as an organizing concept during the

second half of the twentieth century restructured the taxonomy of modern philosophy and facilitated the erasure of America's early engagement with phenomenology. This was not the only framework available for conceptualizing philosophical discourse in the postwar years. However, it was the idea of a "divide" between analytic and Continental traditions that took hold, becoming a gulf of neglect across the discipline.

During the second half of the twentieth century, most analytic and Continental philosophers simply ignored one another, and insofar as they did engage their counterparts, they did so through invective rather than argument. For many Continental philosophers, analysts were "narrow and sterile," interested more in mathematics and word games than in understanding fundamental philosophical questions. To many analysts, Continental thought was "fuzzy-minded" and "illogical," obscure, likely obscurantist, and irrelevant to contemporary discourse.[2] In 1964, Stanley Cavell observed:

> At the moment, analytic philosophy is the dominant mode of academic philosophizing in America and England, while existentialism (together with phenomenology) dominates the philosophizing of Western Europe; and there seems to be no trade across the English Channel. Mutual incomprehension and distrust between them is one of the facts of contemporary philosophical life.[3]

Little change is apparent in a 2003 assessment by Neil Levy:

> Western philosophy has been split into two apparently irreconcilable camps: the "analytic" and the "Continental." Philosophers who belong to each camp respond to their fellows almost exclusively; thus, each stream develops separately, and the differences become more entrenched. Relations between the camps are characterized largely by mutual incomprehension and not a little hostility.[4]

In contrast to the hopes that had motivated interwar efforts to integrate phenomenology into American philosophical discourse, the framework of "Continental philosophy" rendered it as an alien "other." Phenomenology's trajectory in postwar America cannot be understood without explaining how it became "Continental."

* * *

In the years following the founding of the International Phenomenological Society, the phenomenological movement enjoyed growing exposure

in America. In 1940, the Program Committee of the American Philosophical Association's Eastern Division organized a symposium on
phenomenology—one of the seven sessions held at that year's annual
meeting—intended introduce its members to "those aspects of the movement which promise to be most fruitful for the further development of
philosophy in this country."[5] The symposium featured Marvin Farber,
Alfred Schütz, Dorion Cairns, and Herbert Spiegelberg. In a letter to Fritz
Kaufmann, Farber reported that the session had been "well attended and
seemed to achieve the desired results. The general tone," he wrote, "was
cordial and cooperative." In particular, Farber mentioned in a letter to
Schütz, Curt Ducasse had reported that he perceived an affinity between
phenomenology and his own thought.[6] In 1943, phenomenology figured
prominently in another major philosophical meeting, the Inter-American
Conference of Philosophy. During the preceding years, phenomenology
had begun to blossom in Latin America. Phenomenology first appeared
in Spanish through the writing and editorial work of José Ortega y Gas-
set and spread to Latin America with refugees of the Spanish Civil War,
including Ortega, José Gaos, and Joaquín Xirau.[7] Among the conference's
Latin American speakers was also Eduardo Nicol, a Mexican Spanish philosopher influenced by Heidegger, and whose address on philosophical
anthropology included comments about phenomenology.[8] On the American side, Marvin Farber spoke to the conference about "The Significance
of Phenomenology for the Americas."[9] Each paper presented at the conference was subsequently published in *PPR*.

Throughout the 1940s, *PPR* continued to gain recognition on the
America scene. By 1941, the journal already had 190 individual subscrib-
ers and eighty library subscriptions.[10] Indeed, between 1945 and 1949,
only the *Philosophical Review* published more articles by members of the
leading eleven departments than *PPR*: to the *Philosophical Review*'s fifty-
two articles, *PPR* published forty-six—the same number published by the
Journal of Philosophy and more than double the next runner-up, *Ethics*,
which published twenty-two. In the tradition of Husserl's *Jahrbuch*, *PPR*
distinguished itself by publishing articles longer than those that ordinarily
appeared in Anglo-American journals.[11] While its first volumes consisted
primarily of phenomenological texts by European authors, *PPR* increasingly served as a forum for a diverse range of viewpoints. Cutting against
the current of specialized journals that proliferated during the second half
of the twentieth century, *PPR* sought to bring phenomenology into dialogue with American philosophers. In particular, it featured philosophical
symposia with extended exchanges between participants. Many symposia

featured discussion of trending topics in American philosophy from a variety of perspectives, including those outside the mainstream. For example, "A Symposium on Meaning and Truth," which began in 1943, included the phenomenologist Felix Kaufmann, analytic philosophers C. I. Lewis, Ernest Nagel, and Alfred Tarski, and others such as Curt Ducasse, Roy Wood Sellars, Gustavus Watts Cunningham, and Wilbur Marshall Urban.[12] As the symposium stretched into 1944 and 1945 it became a full-blown debate, featuring replies and replies to replies. *PPR* also held symposia on "Probability" and "The Unity of Science" in 1945 and 1946. The former brought together the phenomenologist Felix Kaufmann, the American philosophers D. C. Williams and Ernest Nagel, members of the Vienna Circle Rudolf Carnap, Hans Reichenbach, and Gustav Bergman, as well as the physicist Henry Margenau and the mathematician Richard von Mises. Otto Neurath, Charles Morris, Marvin Farber, Horace Kallen, and Raphael Demos each contributed to the discussion of the unity of science.[13]

With various and esteemed contributors and a willingness to publish iterative replies, *PPR* distinguished itself as a unique forum for a distinctive mode of philosophical engagement. The journal also invited discussions on topics neglected by other journals, such as its symposium on Harvard's report *General Education in a Free Society*.[14] In 1944, *PPR* published a symposium on Russian philosophy, featuring a range of articles on dialectical logic and Marxist philosophy.[15] Later, the journal featured a series of translated articles by Soviet authors, the outgrowth of an A.C.L.S. project that aimed to "raise somewhat the curtain between the Russian people and ourselves by publishing translations of books which were not intended for outside scrutiny."[16]

However, Farber's efforts to broaden *PPR*'s appeal fomented conflict within the organization he had created. Helmut Kuhn, one of the journal's original editors, began to petition Farber for changes in late 1946, objecting to the inclusion of logical positivists in the journal's symposia and the publication of works by Soviet philosophers, which he saw as mere propaganda "furnished wholesale indirectly by the Soviet Embassy." Kuhn also criticized the journal's discursive format and the "replies to replies" it generated.[17] In 1947, Farber received a letter from Kuhn, demanding that these policies be reconsidered by the organization and threatening resignation if they were not.[18] Farber wrote to the editorial staff of *PPR*, detailing Kuhn's objections and inquiring: "Do you approve in principle the policy of this journal?" "We still give, and shall always do so, due attention to phenomenology," the letter said, "but we never really intended to restrict ourselves to it. We were determined to not form a 'sect.'"[19] Subsequent correspondence indicates that Farber received a "positive response." However, in a gesture toward democracy, he indicated his intent to hold regular staff meetings so that "plans for the future may be discussed."[20] For his part, Schütz expressed his strong support for Farber, writing that "Herr Toscanini could not conduct his orchestra successfully if the second bass-fiddle had the right to vote upon the selection of works to be performed." "After all," Schütz continued, "that magazine is your personal work, you are the only one who made it with the greatest possible personal sacrifice a success, and, consequently, you are entitled to define what should and should not be included in our program."[21]

PPR's editors also struggled to navigate the growing divisions within the phenomenological movement. In 1940, Fritz Kaufmann contacted Farber to protest an article submitted by Walter Cerf that claimed Husserl's followers viewed Heideggerian philosophy as heresy. "Where is the 'old guard,'" Kaufmann asked, "who 'decries him as traitor and apostate'?" As Kaufmann explained, when Heidegger was denounced, it was not "for his ontology but his ontic behavior." He continued:

All phenomenologists I know of, and who could be in question, recognize their indebtedness to Heidegger—Landgrebe and even Fink no less than Becker, Lowith, Koyre, Hering, Lipps, myself. Gerhart Husserl may be the only exception for very personal reasons.

Husserl, Kaufmann pointed out, "never minded deviation from his philosophy." Rather, Heidegger's betrayal was political and personal: his abandonment of Husserl after joining the Nazi Party and his efforts to undermine Husserl's position with his students "by all means of craft and malice since the early twenties."[22] Yet, even despite these actions, the core of the journal's leadership in 1940 remained convinced that Heidegger could be relied on to help those connected to the movement. Another letter from Kaufmann dutifully relayed his wife Alice's rebuke of a remark Farber had made to Dorion Cairns. Farber had asserted that Heidegger would come to the aid of Malvine Husserl, Edmund Husserl's widow, because he "owed too much to [Husserl] to forget the fact." Alice responded through Fritz that Heidegger and his allies "have forgotten everything. Not one of them had a line for Mrs. Husserl at the death of her husband. . . . They are together responsible for this and every disaster, these Aryan students."[23]

Having faithfully conveyed his wife's message, Fritz Kaufmann proceeded to brush it aside, writing that "women have the right to be less objective and comprehending than we other scholars are."[24] Of course,

Alice Kaufmann was correct. Heidegger took no action on behalf of the wife of his former advocate and mentor. At the end of World War II, Heidegger would be banished from Freiburg for half a decade as punishment for his political crimes, which included leading the university's Nazification and persecuting dissenters and "undesirables."[25] Writing to the committee that would decide Heidegger's fate, the philosopher Karl Jaspers testified to Heidegger's factual complicity and warned that his "manner of thinking" was "in its essence unfree, dictatorial, and incapable of communications." While Jaspers advised that Heidegger "remain in the position to work and to write," he maintained that if Heidegger were allowed to resume teaching immediately, the "pedagogical effects would be disastrous."[26]

In Europe, dispute over the relation between Heidegger's politics and philosophy began in 1946 with the publication of Karl Löwith's "Les implications politiques de la philosophie de l'existence chez Heidegger" (The political implications of Heidegger's existentialism).[27] In America, Farber had anticipated this critique, emerging as one of Heidegger's earliest and most severe critics. In a 1945 article titled "Remarks about the Phenomenological Program," Farber decried Heidegger as an "international danger," stating that "the ease with which 'Existentialism' could accommodate itself to Nazi Germany is noteworthy."[28] Farber's argument paralleled Jaspers's, asserting that Heidegger's opaque verbiage and esoteric argumentation was tailored from the same cloth as the fanatically uncritical antilogic of Nazi ideology. For this eschewal of reason, Farber denied Heidegger's "good standing" as a phenomenologist, writing:

> It cannot be denied that he has promoted obscurantism in his systematic thought. The "Philosophy of Existence" is a type of philosophy which can only alienate one for whom the canons and ideals of logic are meaningful, and especially one for whom the ideal of philosophy as a rigorous science is definitive.[29]

That Heidegger's philosophy had gained a following in Japan, Latin America, and France, Farber concluded, "can only give us cause for concern."[30] Later, Farber would write to Schütz that Heidegger's effort to exculpate himself "reminds me in part of a story told by William James . . . of the foolish virgin who admitted that she had a child, 'but it was such a little one.' To be sure Heidegger became a Nazi—but he was such an innocent one."[31]

PPR had never shied from publishing harsh criticism, including criticism aimed at members of the phenomenological movement. However, Farber was the journal's editor, not merely another contributor, leaving some uncertain whether his remarks reflected personal opinion or editorial policy. Indeed, Farber reported to Hugo Bergmann that he had been reproached from Louvain, with Van Breda and even Malvine Husserl protesting his attack on Heidegger. They instead urged Farber to remain "nonpolitical." However, "I was adamant in my refusal to admit error," Farber wrote. "I can only suppose that a deadly fear grips such people."[32]

This was not the only source of conflict between America and Louvain. Before the invasion of Belgium, Van Breda had promised that *PPR* would be provided selections from Husserl's unpublished manuscripts for publication. Although the Nazi occupation had halted their collaboration, the journal's editors were hopeful it would resume with the war's conclusion. Indeed, *PPR* published a selection from Husserl's archives in March 1946, and Farber was confident enough that his journal would resume regular publication of Husserl's manuscripts to reject other projects that fall for the sake of preserving space.[33] However, disagreements about the extent of Louvain's authority over Husserl's work lingered. Attempting to force a resolution, Van Breda predicated the future publication of Husserl's manuscripts by *PPR* and the distribution of copied materials from Husserl's *Nachlaß* to researchers in Buffalo on the IPS's formal recognition of Louvain's claim to sole legal and editorial authority over Husserl's work.[34] While Schütz appeared ready to accept this proposal and Buffalo ultimately received the promised photocopies, no further Husserl manuscripts appeared in *PPR* until 1956.[35] Instead, beginning in 1950, Louvain oversaw the publication of selections from Husserl's papers by the Dutch academic press Martinus Nijhoff in a series called *Husserliana*. In 1958, this collaboration expanded with the creation of the series Phenomenologica, which has since published more than two hundred works by members of the phenomenological movement.[36] New European institutions dedicated to phenomenology that had no connections to the International Phenomenological Society also began to emerge during the 1950s, ending Farber's hopes that it would become an umbrella organization for the movement. Van Breda, controlling Europe's most important phenomenological institution, was protective of his prerogatives. Although Buffalo remained a nexus of activities for American phenomenologists, it receded into the background on the international stage.[37]

Division between branches of the phenomenological movement also fomented conflict within *PPR*. John Wild's position at Harvard was a valuable resource for the cash-strapped journal. However, Wild's priorities put him at odds with the Husserlian core of *PPR*'s editors. As Wild explained in a 1940 letter to Farber:

As you have so clearly discerned, I am doing all I can to dissociate phenomenology from the transcendental vagaries and technicalities of Husserl's idealism. Frankly,—if this cannot be done somehow by someone the whole movement in this country is doomed to collapse into a small group of German refugees. . . . I am not in the least interested in this. Neither are the philosophers here—except for a few exceptions who have studied at Freiburg. You know this! The great objections coming up again and again, in trying to "sell" phen. here, are the over-technicality, the transcendentalism, and the other vagaries of Husserlianism. Hence I feel that in attempting to free phen. from these dubious elements in emphasizing its Aristotelian roots, and more universal scope (as certainly Heidegger has done) I am performing, or rather, trying to perform a much needed service.[38]

It was true that idealistic philosophy had long been an endangered species on American shores. That the existential phenomenology of Heidegger and Sartre was better suited to the American scene was a more questionable assertion. Farber feared that emphasizing the often-enigmatic works of existential phenomenology would hinder the reception of their movement by Americans who had little prior exposure to it. As Farber tested the philosophical winds, he concluded that phenomenology's fate in America depended on finding common ground with the Anglo-American mainstream in the systematic rigor of Husserl's program. "If we do not succeed in injecting the strict phen. procedure into the general stream of philosophy," he wrote, "the larger aura of phen. influence . . . will be swept away by the growing trend of logical analysis."[39]

Wild, by contrast, believed that existential phenomenology, which he considered a close relative of William James's psychology, could serve as a link to American traditions that predated the rise of analytic philosophy and found a revival of realism rooted in lived experience. In his influential monograph, *The Radical Empiricism of William James* (1969), Wild presented the titular figure as a thoroughgoing critic of scientific reductivism who recognized the primacy of a lifeworld, grounded not in conceptual understanding but in the structures of pre-theoretical, lived feeling. Yet, while James took the whole of reality as his subject, Wild argued, the discipline of philosophy had since become a fragmented subfield, concerned with technical questions to which a rich and intrinsically vague human world could never be reduced.[40] Philosophy's diminished role in General Education illustrated this trajectory:

The need for general education in the humanities and in those subjects dealing with what are now commonly referred to as "values," is widely recognized. But academic philosophy has so far contributed very little to the meeting of this need. Hence on many campuses which have felt the recent general-education ferment, philosophy has been left behind to be replaced in the exercise of its integrative function by other discipline like history, literature, and social science.[41]

It is notable that Wild's first target of criticism was the administrative displacement of philosophy by disciplines that could not perform its synthetic and integrative function. Of course, Wild did not refrain from criticizing analytic philosophy, which, he wrote, "surrenders objective insight to focus on the logical and linguistic tools of knowledge . . . like a man who becomes so interested in the cracks and spots of dust upon his glasses that he loses all interest in what he may actually see through them."[42] However, he presented existentialism as a "challenge" not merely to logical analysis, but to the broad fragmentation of knowledge into technical disciplines that subordinate the data of experience to indirect observations and theoretical constructions. If phenomenology were to succeed in America, Wild calculated, it would be as a philosophy of existence that restored the discipline's traditional "cultural function" by bringing it back in touch with the "practical moods and feelings" of active human life.[43]

In his correspondence with Farber, Wild repeatedly cautioned against depending on Harvard's continuing financial support, casting himself as the journal's sole champion. Either Wild was uncommonly effective at securing subventions from a recalcitrant department or his correspondence with Farber overstated the opposition. Harvard's resources were clearly strained by war demands, and any extra expenditures would have faced serious scrutiny. Indeed, the Philosophy Department's minutes record in 1942: "[C. I.] Lewis suggests that [PPR] be warned that it will probably be harder to wangle any money for them hereafter." Yet, despite his repeated assertions that renewed funding was unlikely, PPR received subventions from Harvard totaling $1,200 between 1940 and 1947, allotted in every year except 1945.[44]

There are other reasons to treat Wild's representations with suspicion. After all, the department still included both Husserl's lifelong friend, W. E. Hocking, and R. B. Perry, who served on the journal's advisory committee. However, Wild repeatedly warned throughout the early 1940s that continued support from Harvard would be contingent on PPR adopting a broad focus and adding Americans to its editorial staff.[45] It is perhaps a coincidence that the reforms Harvard purportedly demanded were precisely those Wild himself wished the journal to adopt. However, a 1941 letter from Wild urged Farber to attract "young American philosophers to our pages who are fed up with pragmatism and positivism": an unlikely formula for Harvard's approval.[46] With little connection to the group of émigré Husserlians that Farber had assembled, Wild was an outsider on the *PPR* editorial board. Therefore, his demands that more Americans be added to its staff amounted to an effort to counterbalance the journal's dominant Husserlian faction with a bloc of Wild's allies. After all, the journal did not want for American editors, with Farber, Cairns, and McGill in addition to Wild. However, Cairns and Farber were strongly connected to both Husserl and the phenomenologists of the émigré community by shared history and outlook. Wild suggested adding Paul Weiss or Otis Lee, Harvard-trained philosophers who had studied phenomenology without falling into Husserl's orbit.[47] The following year, Farber authorized Wild to make an offer to Lee. As Farber explained in a letter to Schütz, "We are really compelled to make haste in this matter. In view of the uncertain future, Harvard's good will is of all the more importance to us."[48]

Wild was also willing to leverage his role as the journal's conduit to Harvard to amplify his editorial power. This was most apparent in a 1940 dispute over an article by Wild's former student Henry Veatch, reviewed by Cairns, Spiegelberg, and Felix Kaufmann, and rejected by all three.[49] Wild demanded that Farber overrule his editors, writing that, as president, it was Farber's responsibility to ensure that the journal's interests were served. If Farber could not "succeed in getting Veatch's paper through in some form," he wrote, "I shall have to conclude that you yourself are uninterested in appealing to more than a small sectarian group."[50] Likewise, Wild's commitment to methodological diversity in *PPR* extended only to his own preferred methods. For example, in response to Kuhn's criticism of *PPR*'s editorial practices, Wild informed Farber that "I do not agree with every aspect of the journal's recent policy, but I am willing to give a general vote of confidence . . . I do agree with Kuhn, however, that there has been too much lately along positivistic lines."[51] Farber replied that he was "not very much satisfied" with Wild's stance. "For one thing," he wrote, "you seem to forget that you were one of the persons who urged a broadening of our policy. That being the case, your opposition to positivism is hardly defensible."[52]

While Farber allayed concerns that his journal would be "forever rattling the bones of [the] beloved saint" Husserl, his own writings caused allies to question whether he was sufficiently committed to Husserl's vision of phenomenology.[53] Farber's "Experience and Subjectivism," published in a 1949 volume he coedited with Roy Wood Sellars and V. J. McGill, was the first public sign of a break with Husserl. However, despite calling Husserl's idealistic framework "a fatal limitation to his philosophy," the essay was not wholly critical. It offered a nonidealistic reinterpretation of Husserl's *Ideas*, treating the phenomenological reduction as an intermediate "auxiliary" method that clarifies the structure of experience by holding certain beliefs in abeyance, but does concern the existence of reality itself.[54]

Farber now endorsed a methodological pluralism in which phenomenology and naturalism were adopted as complementary methods with separate domains and "all who contribute parts of truth should realize that they can coexist."[55] Given Farber's reconstruction of Husserl's phenomenology as a scientific first philosophy in his 1928 *Phenomenology as a Method and as a Philosophical Discipline*, the heterodox analysis of "Experience and Subjectivism"—which abandons the quest for apodicticity to advocate for phenomenology's place in a pluralistic discourse—undoubtedly surprised some of his colleagues. However, it was consistent with the trajectory of Farber's career and ideological commitments. Farber had been interested in reconciling phenomenology with dialectical materialism since at least the 1930s, when he had asked Husserl whether he "had taken a stand, qua phenomenologist, toward the historical materialism of Marx and Engels."[56] Now, Farber concluded that "the 'given' in experience is . . . historically conditioned" and that the significance of philosophy "should never be detached from its social-historical context." There could be no final, transhistorical account of experience, making phenomenology an ongoing project that "must be undertaken again and again, in each cultural generation at least." This project, Farber argued, is naturalistic, guided by scientific results, and expounds the conditions of experience "*within the framework of physical nature.*"[57] Some of these conclusions resonate with Merleau-Ponty's *Phenomenology of Perception* and share the concerns of Husserl's late work on intersubjectivity. However, throughout the essay, Farber inveighed against idealistic philosophy as "a trap for metaphysical purposes."[58] He dismissed Husserl's account of the lifeworld's transcendental constitution, without seriously engaging it, as "sheer dogma, which is characteristic of the writings of Husserl's last period." That Husserl could even have considered it plausible, he wrote, could mean only that "Husserl had lived alone too much . . . and combed over his self-consciousness to such an extent, that to him the term 'everything' came to mean only the set of correlates of his own consciousness."[59]

Despite his equivocations, Farber's essay could not have been considered anything but a strong rebuke of Husserl by his Freiburg-era followers. As a philosopher, Farber was, of course, free to criticize Husserl. However, when Farber reprised his critique two years later in a *PPR* article titled "Experience and Transcendence," the ambiguity of his status as a philosopher and as the editor in chief of *PPR* prompted unease from some. Both Spiegelberg and Gurwitsch wrote to Schütz, asking him to clarify whether Farber's attack on Husserl was a statement of the journal's official position.[60] Schütz relayed their concerns to Farber, who replied in a brief, scribbled note:

1) Naturally (obviously!) I wrote as an individual
2) You misquoted me when saying I accused E. H. of irrationalism. The Existentialists are referred to!
3) My fidelity to E. H. remains—<u>after my fashion</u>, which is now no different than when I was his admiring personal student.[61]

Encouraging his colleagues to separate Farber's personal writings from his editorial stance, Schütz averted further conflict. *PPR* would continue to publish a diverse range of perspectives, both within the phenomenological movement and outside of it. However, Farber's leadership and even his standing as a phenomenologist remained suspect.[62]

Thus, by the end of the 1940s, *PPR* had emerged as a significant philosophical journal, publishing work from the era's leading luminaries and facilitating dialogue between a range of thinkers. Farber had engineered *PPR*'s rise by abandoning sectarian commitments and appealing to a broad audience. When, in 1950, Farber invited the analytic philosopher Paul Henle to assume an editorial post at *PPR* left vacant by Felix Kaufmann's death, Henle replied, "Since I consider your journal by far the best published in this country, I regard it as an honor even to be considered for the editorial staff."[63] This was the sort of forum phenomenologists required to introduce their work to mainstream American philosophers. Yet, at least some of its founders had conceived of *PPR* not merely as a vehicle for publishing phenomenological works, but as the successor to Husserl's *Jahrbuch*. While Husserl had always tolerated heterodoxy among his followers, the *Jahrbuch* realized the ideal of a collaborative program under the title phenomenology. It upheld phenomenology's distinction, unity, and identity against other contemporary movements, while providing a survey of its scope. *PPR*, which instead took Husserl's ideal of a scientific philosophy only as a starting point, could not replace the *Jahrbuch*, particularly as fault lines within the phenomenological community widened.[64] Thus, despite *PPR*'s success, American phenomenologists lacked an institution suited to representing the unique identity of their movement to other American philosophers. Of course, this did not immediately change the terms in which phenomenologists understood their own work. However, their lack of organization *as phenomenologists* left few means to resist discursive formations adopted by mainstream American philosophers who sought to understand and define phenomenology on their own terms, in reference to the places and situations in which *they* encountered it.

*   *   *

World War II fundamentally altered the landscape of intellectual relations between America and Europe. In the interwar years, young Americans had crossed the Atlantic as provincial elites from a former colonial fringe on a pilgrimage to learn from the sages of the old world's esteemed academies. Students like Farber and Cairns believed their *Wanderjahr* with Husserl provided an opportunity for participation in an epochal event in the history of Western ideas. By contrast, Americans after World War II surveyed a devastated Europe with the eyes of victors. Forrest Williams, a student of the philosopher William Earle, reported from the Sorbonne in 1950: "Paris is as lovely as ever to me, but everything in Europe seems even more doomed than it did twelve or thirteen years ago. Then it was a question of what elements in Europe would prevail; now it seems that nothing European can possibly prevail."[65] In the postwar world, America set the high-water mark of western civilization, not only as a military and economic power but, having absorbed the flood of intellectuals who fled Nazism during the 1930s and 1940s, as the world's center of research and scholarship. Most postwar American philosophers encountered twentieth-century European philosophy on their own shores, where it was a foreign import, considered either as a subject of cultural interest or for its suitability to an American environment. There were, of course, exceptions. Some, such as Hubert Dreyfus, Stanley Cavell, and John Glenn Gray, who traced the itinerant paths of their interwar predecessors, succeeded in building bridges between American and European traditions. However, for most Americans who encountered it during the postwar era, the reception of contemporary European philosophy was mediated by translators and popularizers who took on the task of its adaptation and by academic authorities who decided how, where, and by whom it would be taught. Indeed, most American philosophers would now encounter contemporary European philosophy, first and foremost, as a professional problem, as their institutions struggled to provide instruction in a constellation of subjects that included Hegel, Nietzsche, Marx, phenomenology, and existentialism.

During the first half of the twentieth century, it made little sense to identify the contemporary philosophy of continental Europe as a distinct or unified tradition. The phrase had a long been employed to describe the eighteenth- and nineteenth-century opposition of British empiricism and German idealism. However, when used to describe contemporary philosophy, the phrase had only geographic meaning. Even in 1948, an article in the journal *Nineteenth Century and After* referred to the logical positivists Hans Reichenbach and Rudolf Carnap as "continental philosophers."[66] This changed, however, as the logical positivists' flight from Berlin and Vienna to America made it possible to conceive an imagined geography that separated the thought and culture of the Anglo-American world from continental Europe.

During the early 1950s, a new idiomatic use of the phrase *Continental philosophy* began to appear in philosophical publications, principally invoked in discussions of existentialism. For instance, Frederick Copleston wrote in "The Human Person in Contemporary Philosophy":

> I can well imagine some British philosophers rejecting many of the theories which I have narrated as meaningless nonsense. But I think that it would be a mistake to allow one's natural impatience with vague or unfamiliar language to lead one into rejecting the modern continental philosophers unheard, that is, without one's making any real attempt to understand what they are getting at.[67]

The first occasion I have identified in which the idea of a modern "Continental" tradition was invoked to separate Hegelian, phenomenological, and existentialist tendencies from other contemporary philosophical currents was a 1949 course at Harvard titled "Hegel and His Influences on European Thought." Taught by John Ladd, it was described as a "study of present-day continental philosophies, particularly dialectical materialism and existentialism, in the light of their essentially Hegelian setting" that promised to stress "the fundamental assumptions underlying the whole development of recent continental thought."[68] Similar language appears in the description of a new course, titled "Recent European Philosophy," that Ladd was scheduled to offer in the fall of 1950. It would have covered Wilhelm Dilthey, Husserl, Heidegger, Jaspers, and Sartre, and emphasized "those traits that differentiate continental from Anglo-Saxon thought—especially historicism, the phenomenological movement, anti-naturalistic human-ism, and existentialism."[69] In the decades that followed, this framework would continue to resurface as Harvard and other universities struggled to determine where and how contemporary European philosophy would be incorporated into their curricula.

Peter Gordon and Michael Friedman have called attention to the 1929 encounter between Heidegger and Ernst Cassirer at Davos as a seminal event in the history of twentieth-century philosophy. Friedman writes that "before [the Davos] encounter there was no such split" as exists today between analytic and Continental philosophers. Davos, here, marks the first visible cracks in a fissure between traditions that would undergo "thoroughgoing intellectual estrangement" with the rise of Nazism and emigration of analysts from Europe, ultimately resulting in those tradi-tions' "almost total lack of mutual comprehension."[70] It is true that Carnap's withering critique of Heidegger in "Überwindung der Metaphysik durch logische Analyse der Sprache" ("The Elimination of Metaphysics through Logical Analysis of Language"), written shortly after he attended the Davos conference, was widely cited in subsequent decades.[71] Legitimized by the eminence of its author, the article's logical reconstruction of selective quo-tations from "Was ist Metaphysik?" ("What Is Metaphysics?") promoted an image of Heidegger as a purveyor of meaningless mysticism and turned the phrase *das Nichts selbst nichtet*, along with its glib English translation "the Nothing noths," into shorthand for the fatuity of phenomenology and exis-tentialism.[72] Yet, despite the notoriety that Davos has since gained, records of the conference's proceedings did not become publicly available until the 1960s. Thus, it seems unlikely that the event held great significance for most American philosophers during the critical period of the 1950s when the concept of Continental philosophy was being defined.[73] However, a dif-ferent conference, the 1953 International Congress of Philosophy in Brus-sels, offered Americans abundant material for constructing a new vision of a divided discipline.

The *Journal of Philosophy* and the *Philosophical Review* both published accounts of the 1953 International Congress, written by the philosophers Max Rieser and Walter Cerf, respectively.[74] As World War II refugees who had established themselves in the United States as philosophers, Rieser and Cerf held a privileged status as interpreters of European philosophical tra-ditions. Writing for an American audience that perceived itself at the cen-ter of the postwar world, both fused the language and idea of "Continental philosophy" with anti-Catholicism and classic Orientalist tropes, ironi-cally inverted to testify against their German and French progenitors.[75]

Rieser's review of the Congress observed a "deep cleavage between Anglo-American philosophy on the one side and continental philosophy on the other," describing philosophers "intellectually not on speaking terms but rather uttering soliloquies in a vacuum."[76] He continued:

> The Continentals do their philosophizing by themselves without any reference to or interest in the Anglo-American group, and vice versa; the two groups move in parallels that never meet. The history of philosophy can show few examples of such a cleavage since philosophy became an international enterprise in the West. There is no real discussion between these two groups, and at the Congress there was none.[77]

Rieser placed the blame for this on "Continental philosophers, steeped in the idiom of phenomenology and its existentialist stepchild, [who] use as a matter of course an array of notions which arouse bewilderment and incredulity among the English-speaking philosophers."[78] While Anglo-American philosophy was a "cognitive enterprise," Continental philosophy, he argued, was "at bottom largely an emotional Stimmungsphilosophy, the exhibition of a mood totally alien to the more sober thinkers in the Atlantic sphere."[79] Indeed, Rieser concluded, Continental philosophy "has a strong flavor of Orientalism, despite its Western origin; it seems closer to Hindu contemplation than to rational analysis."[80]

Like Rieser, Cerf portrayed the congress as a failure. In the first paragraph of his essay, he declared: "If the Lord could make rhyme and reason out of the Brussels congress, he would indeed be of infinite intelligence."[81] With the Lord presumably otherwise occupied, Cerf offered himself the lesser task of summarizing the works presented and providing suggestions for future endeavors. Cerf's article also indulged in Orientalist tropes, depicting the Brussels conference as a space outside the norms of rational civilization: "Cranks, exhibitionists, odd females, and black-frocked dogmatists are, I suppose, a curse on any congress; but I have never seen more and worse examples of these groups than at Brussels."[82] The proclamations of existentialists were thus dismissed as "prophetic and orphic monologues," whose eschewal of clarity "makes us rightly suspicious of their ideas."[83] However, unlike Rieser, Cerf called for renewed dialogue, albeit one that placed the onus of reconciliation on the Continental side of the divide. As Cerf concluded his essay: "Let our next International Congress of Philosophy be a meeting ground of empiricists and existentialists. As long as there is a chance of being enriched by existentialist thinking, let us give the existentialist a chance to make his experiences clear to us—and to himself."[84]

Throughout this report and several other articles, Cerf used the new framework of an analytic-Continental divide to illustrate an Orientalized vision of European thought, positioning himself as an essential conduit to its esoteric insights. German philosophy might seem "unfathomable and ridiculous," but, he intimated, it held "positive characteristics of new beginnings, of a powerful new tackle of old questions."[85] Such insight that might elude the rational empiricist minds of his readers became accessible through the intermediary efforts of this graduate of both Bonn and Princeton. For instance, a 1940 article in which Cerf set out "to build a bridge from Anglo-Saxon empiricism to Heidegger's existential analysis" characterized Heidegger as "one of 'those deep and obscure German metaphysicians,'" testifying: "I believe Heidegger's voice would be able to carry new life and greater depth into the shallow and insipid philosophy of today." However, Cerf warned that Heidegger's "books belong indeed to the hardest reading in philosophy":

> This voice will sound so exceedingly strange to anybody educated in the Anglo-Saxon philosophical tradition that my task today can only be to lead the reader from his own philosophical training and background to a point from which Heidegger's thought may sound more comprehensible, or at least less incomprehensible.[86]

A 1951 article, "Logical Positivism and Existentialism," called the titular movements "the two most antagonistic schools in contemporary Western philosophy . . . having nothing in common but the name of philosophy, and even that they deny each other." This piece also appealed to Orientalist logic: "Although, ironically enough, both Logical Positivism and modern Existentialism originated in German speaking countries, the split between the two goes vaguely in parallel with, and may have found some ready echo in, the different cultural inheritance of the Anglo-Saxon and Latin races."[87]

Concurrent with Cerf's report on the International Congress of Philosophy, the *Journal of Philosophy* published his bleak portrait of intellectual life in postwar Germany, "Existentialist Mannerism and Education," drawn from his experiences attending lectures in West Germany for two months during 1953. Cerf described a nation in which Heideggerian existentialism was taught in schools as dogma and in which the "degenerate romanticism of the recent past apparently has made the students prefer deep-sounding nonsense in philosophy to rational communication," undermining their "intellectual and moral resistance" to the rise of a new Hitler.[88] The essay prompted a scathing reply from Husserl's former assistant Ludwig Landgrebe.

"I can say unconditionally," he wrote, "that no proof of such predominance of existentialism can be found."[89]

Despite their dubious details, these insider reports provided American philosophers material to forge opinions about philosophy in Europe. In a 1954 letter, W. E. Hocking wrote to Henry Bugbee:

> You may have noticed the latest number of the Journal of Philosophy, a report on the XIth International Congress, which declared an opening gulf between Continental and Anglo-American thought on just this ground. (If you haven't noticed that article, do get it: it is revealing).

In the next sentence, Hocking stated that Bugbee's thought "has something in common with this 'Continental' trend." Notably, Hocking placed "Continental" in quotes, suggesting that he attributed the term to Rieser.[90] In his reply, Bugbee also used Rieser's language to discuss "the gulf between Anglo-American and Continental thought." However, he stressed the need to ensure that "the will to communicate and meet on common ground" between these lines of thought "does not temper."[91] Indeed, some philosophers had taken up this task, even at the Brussels congress. Richard McKeon, an influential philosopher at the University of Chicago presented a paper (mentioned by Rieser, as promoting "tolerance" but dismissed for "a lack of clarity, precision, and determination in thought") in which he defended an "all-inclusive" view of experience as action that he associated with both Dewey and Sartre. Rather than taking European philosophers to task for their obscurity, McKeon argued that analytic and Continental philosophers found themselves at odds because the distinctions denied by an inclusive philosophy of experience ("subject and object, theory and practice, art and science, emotion and knowledge") were the same concepts used by philosophers of language "to differentiate cognitive, emotive, persuasive, and evocative uses of discourse." Without ignoring this important difference, McKeon cast the divide between analysts and their peers on the Continent as a normal philosophical dispute, not a contest between incommensurable views of the discipline itself.[92]

Ultimately, McKeon's approach did not predominate. Despite the many differences between existentialists, Marxists, phenomenologists, Hegelians, and the many other cousins, nephews and stepsiblings of the Continental family, most mainstream American philosophers would learn to recognize these movements, through the unifying framework of "Continental philosophy," as a foreign tradition disconnected from the mainstream of American thought. Given this, the idea of Continental philosophy is fundamentally misunderstood if it is treated merely as an empty framework through which Anglo-American philosophers organized and evaluated contemporary European thought. Maintaining the imagined geography of this divide required American philosophers to forget their earlier engagement with phenomenology.

* * *

The success of Continental philosophy as an otherizing concept also reflected the peculiar interest European philosophy garnered outside the academy in postwar America. In the mid-1940s, America was struck by the "vogue" of existentialism. America's first direct contact with Sartre's work was a journalistic essay with an existential inflection titled "Paris Alive," published in 1944 by *Atlantic Monthly*. Soon, middlebrow publications such as *Vogue, Life,* the *New York Times Magazine,* and *Harper's Bazaar* teemed with profiles and essays on thought they characterized as a new Parisian fashion. These periodicals romanticized Jean-Paul Sartre, Simone de Beauvoir, and Albert Camus as members of the French Resistance both literally and in literature: pioneers of a new kind of writing that addressed the condition of man without illusions and with confidence borne of their discovered freedom. Interest in existentialism grew, along with the belief that it had something to say that was urgently relevant to the mass society of Cold War America. As George Cotkin observed: "A cult of personality developed whereby the general renown of existentialism became intimately connected to the personal life of the philosopher and even to the circumstances of the nation he or she represented."[93]

At the same time, Christian existentialism brought Heidegger and Sartre to the attention of religious intellectuals in America. Most influential among this group was the liberal theologian Paul Tillich, who had served as Heidegger's colleague at Marburg before immigrating to the United States. Tillich's 1952 work, *The Courage to Be,* which reinterprets the ontological analysis of *Being and Time* into "explicitly theological language," became an essential text in religious debates over the postwar crisis of "meaninglessness" that followed two world wars and the emergence of mass society. Thus, interest in existential phenomenology mushroomed among diverse American audiences during the 1950s. When the Macquarrie and Robinson translation of Heidegger's *Being and Time* was published in 1962, it sold out repeatedly, "establishing all kinds of new records" for sales and shocking its publisher Harper & Row.[94]

This upsurge of interest in existential philosophy distressed some phenomenologists, who saw it as a pollutant in their presuppositionless waters.

"There were those," Calvin Schrag recalled, "who sought to continue more or less the program of phenomenology as defined . . . [by Husserl] and who were openly suspicious of the 'foreign elements' supplied by existentialism."[95] However, Sartre's popular appeal provided opportunities—even to his detractors in the phenomenological movement, who were nonetheless well prepared to teach his works. Thus, as postwar American undergraduates, hungry for novel European philosophy, turned to their philosophy departments in search of French and German fare, curricula and institutions increasingly subsumed phenomenology under a broader category of contemporary "Continental" philosophy.

America's most prestigious philosophy departments were not immune from the outbreak of existentialist excitement in their student bodies. A 1950 report from Harvard's Philosophy Department noted the "current great demand" for instruction in both linguistic analysis and Continental subjects.[96] Roderick Firth went further in 1958, describing the visiting appointment of the Sartre specialist William Earle as "very successful," since it "helped meet the demand of our undergraduates for more <u>real</u> philosophy—i.e., existentialism." To be clear, Firth was no great admirer of existentialist thought. His invocation of "<u>real</u> philosophy" was facetious, mocking the presumption of college students who deigned to lecture Harvard's faculty on the nature of philosophy.[97] Yet, the students' attitude paralleled a reality of growing exhaustion, even within the American philosophical mainstream, with the programs of positivist and linguistic analysis as they had developed in the interwar years. Brand Blanshard, for example, wrote to D. C. Williams in 1960 that there was "a plainly perceptible wave of boredom with linguisticism and all its ways."[98] As a result, analytic philosophy expanded into fields it had previously neglected, such as metaphysics and political philosophy, albeit *within* the framework of philosophical analysis. However, in the late 1950s, the popular appeal of existentialism and positivism's decline raised the specter that the hard-won rigor of logical analysis would be overshadowed by a philosophical movement seen as hostile to reason. At least some American philosophers took this threat seriously. In his reply to Blanshard, Williams wrote: "I think that [a wave of boredom with linguisticism] does exist. . . . The danger is that the reaction will take people only into the arms of superstition, e.g., existentialism."[99] Williams put the matter less delicately in a letter to the philosopher Paul Wienpahl: "I just do not see in what respect the analytic and inductive intellect has failed mankind that it deserves to be scuttled at the hest of spiritual pirates."[100]

While illustrating the steep gradient of enthusiasm for existentialism between America's philosophers and their undergraduate students, these interactions hint at another issue: the practical difficulty American philosophy departments faced incorporating contemporary European philosophy into their curricula. This reflected an absence both of qualified philosophers and of philosophical texts. While interest in existentialism prompted literary engagement with Sartre's work, much of the product was of dubious philosophical worth, written or directed by specialists in other disciplines. It was not, for instance, philosophers but members of Yale's French Department who invited Sartre to lecture at the university in 1945 and offered the university's first course on existentialism.[101] Popularizations that eschewed careful attention to philosophical argument in order to appropriate existentialism as therapeutic psychology were particularly problematic for those who hoped existentialism would be taken seriously by American philosophers. One such philosopher, Asher Moore, wrote:

> Frankly, I'm getting sick and tired of existentiallSM. Everytime [*sic*] I go to the library there are six new books about it. . . . Don't you think it's absolutely the most infantile thing you ever heard of—all these grown men getting worked up because someone told them they get born and die and aspire and fall in love and have to scrape together the courage somewhere?[102]

During the 1940s, the scarcity of philosophically rigorous texts on existentialism was particularly acute. Among the first such works to appear in English was William Barrett's 1947 essay *What Is Existentialism?* In an invitation to deliver a lecture at Harvard shortly after his essay was published, D. C. Williams commended Barrett: "Now, our people have a chronic but uninformed interest in 'Existentialism,' and your pamphlet is one of the few treatments of the subject which a competent student of technical philosophy has produced."[103]

In the decade following the end of World War II, a handful of significant secondary works on existentialism were published for an English-speaking audience. These included Marjorie Grene's *Dreadful Freedom: A Critique of Existentialism* (1948), Ralph Harper's *Existentialism, a Theory of Man* (1948), Helmut Kuhn's *Encounter with Nothingness: An Essay on Existentialism* (1949), Jean Wahl's *A Short History of Existentialism* (1949), John Wild's *The Challenge of Existentialism* (1955), and Walter Kaufmann's *Existentialism from Dostoevsky to Sartre* (1956).[104] Additionally, due to the work of Farber and others who had studied in Germany during the inter-war era, a modest secondary literature on Husserl's phenomenology was available to Americans.[105] However, vanishingly few philosophical works from the canonical figures of the phenomenological and existentialist tra-ditions existed in English translation before the mid-1950s. The British philosopher William Boyce Gibson had translated Husserl's *Ideas* in 1931, but none of Husserl's other published work had been translated in the sub-sequent two decades.[106] Sartre was best represented, with his short essay "L'existentialisme est un humanism" published in English twice under the titles *Existentialism* (1947) and *Existentialism and Humanism* (1948). Of Sartre's other philosophical writings, his early epistemological work *L'Imaginaire: Psychologie phénoménologique de l'imagination* (*The Psychol-ogy of Imagination*, 1948) was available, as were *Esquisse d'une Théorie des Emotions* (*The Emotions: Outline of a Theory*, 1948), *Réflexions sur la ques-tion juive* (*Antisemite and Jew*, 1948), and *Qu'est-ce que la littérature* (*What Is Literature*, 1950).[107] By contrast, only a few essays by Heidegger had been translated into English, published with commentary by Werner Brock in *Existence and Being* (1949), although the collection did include Heidegger's influential essay "What Is Metaphysics?"[108] From Karl Jaspers even less was available in English: only several essays, published as *Existentialism and Humanism: Three Essays* (1952).[109] Even Jaspers, however, was better represented than Merleau-Ponty, whose work did not begin to appear in English until 1962.[110] It was only when academic publishers initiated series dedicated to phenomenological and existentialist philosophy in the 1960s that a significant body of these figures' work would became available in English translation.

While many American philosophy departments were vexed by the vogue of existentialism, those that had developed connections with émi-gré phenomenologists during the 1940s had stumbled upon a valuable resource. Several built on this groundwork, seizing the opportunity for distinction in an emerging field of popular interest. For instance, Marvin Farber recruited Fritz Kaufmann to Buffalo's faculty in 1947. While the department remained small, the presence of *PPR*'s editor in chief and one of Husserl's former assistants gave it outsize importance.[111] Still, it was the New School that became America's first and most significant center for phenomenological study. With Felix Kaufmann, Alfred Schütz, Dorion Cairns, and Aron Gurwitsch on its faculty, it was the institution par excel-lence for Husserlian studies in the United States in the three decades following the conclusion of World War II. After opening an American branch of the Husserl Archives in 1968 with a complete set of Husserl's

Phenomenologists of the New School for Social Research							
	1940	1945	1950	1955	1960	1965	1970
Felix Kaufmann	███						
Alfred Schütz		███	███	███			
Werner Marx			███	███	███	███	███
Dorion Cairns				███	███	███	███
Hans Jonas				███	███	███	███
Aron Gurwitsch					███	███	███
Hannah Arendt						███	███

FIGURE 5.1 Phenomenologists of the New School for Social Research.

manuscripts photocopied from Louvain, realizing a plan begun by Alfred Schütz and Herman Van Breda in 1958, no university in the world except Louvain itself had greater resources for research on Husserl's thought than the New School.[112]

Gurwitsch and Cairns played the role of Husserl's "disciples," dedicated to their mentor and his vision of rigorous science. However, because species of their dedication demanded that they carry Husserl's project further than he himself had conceived and correct his work when it fell into error, phenomenology remained an ongoing project at the New School.[113] Following the model of their mentor, Husserl's former disciples challenged their own students to join in their undertaking. In so doing, they made it an "intellectual home" for American students of phenomenology and an important reproductive institution for the American phenomenological movement.[114] Graduates of the New School, including Maurice Natanson, Richard Zaner, Lester Embree, Helmut Wagner, and Thomas Luckmann, were counted among the leading figures in the postwar generation of American phenomenologists.[115] New School graduates also organized the Center for Advanced Research in Phenomenology (CARP) in 1971. Founded as a repository for the unpublished writings of American phenomenologists, the center's activities included sponsoring conferences and workshops on phenomenology and overseeing the Series in Continental Thought, established by the Ohio University Press in 1978.[116]

The émigrés who found refuge on the New School's faculty also led the effort to Americanize phenomenology or, in Schütz's words, "show that phenomenology is not quite a stranger in this country." This contributed to a growing discourse on the relation between phenomenology and American pragmatism as movements that viewed lived experience as the foundation of philosophical analysis. In his paper for the phenomenology panel at the 1940 APA conference, Schütz made the connection between phenomenology and James's epistemology explicit, identifying an affinity in their insistence on the personal nature of experience. Both rejected the possibility that reductive epistemologies, epitomized by Locke and Hume, could construct the "unity of continuously streaming cogitations" from material first rendered as depersonalized units of sensation.[117] Thus, Schütz's lecture not only invited Americans to embark upon the phenomenological project, but informed them that they had already taken significant steps on that journey.

Gurwitsch's influential work *The Field of Consciousness* (1964) also explored these affinities. Building on James's division of the perceptual field into focus and margin, Gurwitsch argued that perception comprises three "domains": the focus of attention, or "theme"; the "thematic field" of relevant surroundings; and a "margin" of experience that is irrelevant to the theme. James held that the margin of consciousness is unorganized. If so, however, it is unclear how the mind determines whether contextual phenomena outside of its direct focus are relevant to an experience.[118] Contra James, Gurwitsch argued that the theme, field, and margin of experience were all organized, and, contra both James and Husserl, he denied that "sense-data depend entirely upon, and are determined exclusively by, the corresponding physical stimuli." Maintaining that the perception of order is not purely the result of cognition, Gurwitsch drew on Gestalt theory to explain that "organization must be an autochthonous feature of the stream of experience and of the experiential field in its original form."[119] From this premise and in ongoing reference to James, Gurwitsch expounded his own field-theory of consciousness, which detailed the importance of contextual relevance for conscious activity through a phenomenological account of experience that described the intentional theme's "emergence" within an already-organized Gestalt that "the theme carries . . . along with it."[120]

Northwestern University, another institution with early connections to the phenomenological movement, also established itself as a significant American center for the study of phenomenology, particularly in connection with existentialism. With help from the Emergency Committee in Aid of Displaced Foreign Scholars, Fritz Kaufmann had obtained a position in Northwestern's Philosophy Department in 1938. Two years after Kaufmann's 1947 departure, Northwestern appointed William Earle as an instructor. Earle had been mentored in phenomenology by Gaston Berger while studying at France's Aix-Marseille University under the aegis of a Rockefeller Foundation scholarship. Earle was particularly drawn to Sartre's *Being and Nothingness*, although he claimed to be "about the only person in France who [was] reading it" on account of its enormous length and small print.[121] Beginning in 1951 with "Existentialism and its Sources," Earle offered courses in contemporary European philosophy at Northwestern.[122] He also contributed to the growing literature on phenomenology and existentialism through his connection with Cecil Hemley and Arthur Cohen. Hemley and Cohen, friends of Earle from the University of Chicago, founded the Noonday Press in 1951 as an American venue for works of avant-garde poetry, literature, and philosophy. Earle served as its philosophy editor, selecting manuscripts and keeping its editors "abreast of current philosophy."[123] Between 1955 and 1958, Noonday published translations of works by Jaspers, Sartre's *Transcendence of the Ego*, and a work by Earle titled *Objectivity: An Essay in Phenomenological Ontology*.[124] Meridian Books, an offshoot of Noonday under Cohen's control, also published Walter Kaufmann's highly influential *Existentialism from Dostoevsky to Sartre* in 1956.

In 1961, John Wild left Harvard to join Earle at Northwestern. Although he quickly departed for a position at Yale, his impact at Northwestern was significant, marked by the founding of the Society for Phenomenology and Existential Philosophy (which will be discussed in chapter 6). These events initiated an influx of philosophical talent to Evanston, as phenomenologists such as James Edie and Sam Todes joined the department in 1961 and 1965. However, despite an emphasis on European philosophical traditions, Northwestern's faculty aimed to ensure that analytic philosophy was not neglected. In a letter to Karl Popper, whom Northwestern attempted to hire in 1964, William Earle explained that the department was "pluralistic, and welcomes any authentic and disciplined mode of philosophizing."[125] Another departmental self-assessment asserted: "We must not be merely 'a mirror reflection' of those American departments which emphasize analytic philosophy to the exclusion of practically everything else" by failing to represent analytic thought.[126] Whatever their intentions, however, Northwestern's faculty acknowledged their "relative weakness" in areas related to analytic philosophy when compared to leading American departments.[127]

The trajectory of Northwestern's Philosophy Department also paralleled the grant-seeking creation of "steeples of excellence" in scientific disciplines, described by Rebecca Lowen.[128] Indeed, a 1960 departmental report argued, Northwestern's unique stock of specialists in contemporary European philosophy created an opportunity to seek funding from the NDEA for an "'institute' for the study of 'Phenomenology and Existentialism.'"[129] A center of expertise, as Northwestern had become for existential phenomenology, is a social formation that facilitates collaboration and the creation of new institutional organization. This reproductive process is autocatalytic: its own products are the material for creating programs, institutes, publications, and societies that spur further activities centered on those sites. In fact, once a critical mass of engagement is achieved, the creation of additional institutional organization becomes the lowest energy path for many activities to proceed. For example, Northwestern's Philosophy Department began a collaboration with Northwestern University Press in 1962 to publish the text of lectures on existentialism given by members of the department.[130] The project evolved into a series, with James Edie and John Wild as its editors, titled Northwestern University Studies in Phenomenology and Existential Philosophy. A brochure for the series' first volume, a translation of essays by Merleau-Ponty titled *In Praise of Philosophy*, proclaimed "a radical renewal of philosophy" for the "many American philosophers" who were "interested in this new style, this return to experience in all its existential richness and density."[131] Over the next decade, the Northwestern series would publish more than forty titles, including ones with canonical status in the phenomenological tradition such as *The Crisis of European Sciences and Transcendental Phenomenology* and *Experience and Judgment* by Husserl, *Sense and Non-sense* by Merleau-Ponty, a collection of essays by Paul Ricoeur titled *History and Truth*, and *The Structures of The Life-World* by Alfred Schütz.[132]

Along with Yale, which will be discussed later, the New School and Northwestern were the most important institutions for the organization and promotion of phenomenology in the United States during the 1950s and 1960s. However, they were among a growing group of departments and societies that promoted research and instruction in contemporary European philosophy and facilitated the organization of professional activities focused on these methods and traditions. Often these were institutions that had taken in émigré philosophers during the 1940s, such as the University of North Carolina at Chapel Hill, which gave refuge to the German philosopher Helmut Kuhn and subsequently hired the New School–trained phenomenologist Maurice Natanson.[133] Likewise, the German émigré Hans Freund helped establish Pennsylvania State University's Philosophy Department as an incipient hub for existential phenomenology. Freund was hired in 1946 along with John Anderson, a 1939 graduate of Berkeley, trained in both philosophy and mathematics. At Penn State, Anderson's focus turned to phenomenology, to which he would make significant contributions as an author, a translator, and a founding member of the "Heidegger Circle," which held annual conferences on Heidegger's philosophy.[134] In 1965, Penn State's faculty added Joseph Kockelmans, a prolific Heidegger scholar and philosopher of science who had trained at Catholic universities in Rome and Louvain. The university also hosted the Catholic phenomenologist Anna-Teresa Tymieniecka between 1957 and 1961; she founded the World Phenomenological Institute and served as editor of the influential series *Analecta Husserliana.*

Catholic universities—where philosophy's disciplinary privileges remained robust despite the receding tides of twentieth-century curricular reforms—also ranked among the premier phenomenological institutions in postwar America. In fact, Catholic neoscholastics who encountered phenomenological analysis through Husserl's *Logical Investigations* had been among the first groups of Europeans drawn to phenomenology, perceiving Husserl as fellow defender of realist metaphysics. Early twentieth-century Catholic philosophers such as August Messer, Léon Nöel, and Joseph Geyser hoped to use phenomenology as a bridge between scholastic and modern thought, allowing them to participate in contemporary discourses in which scholasticism had become an anachronistic non sequitur, and to recover the foundational Thomistic principle that human knowledge of the world is objective. By transcending subjectivity, they believed, phenomenology "could help secular thinkers recognize God's order in the world." Thus, as Ed Baring explains, progressive neoscholastics turned to phenomenology, hoping it could "convert modern philosophy to their ends, and overturn a process of intellectual secularization they traced to the reformation."[135]

Because of phenomenology's early circulation through European neoscholastic institutions, Catholic philosophy departments in America were able to draw on an international network of contacts that was largely distinct from the currents that brought phenomenology to their secular counterparts.[136] The graduates of Louvain, where Father Van Breda had established the Husserl Archives, were particularly important vectors for phenomenological expertise and influence into American Catholic institutions. However, Catholic universities were also characterized by an "isolation" that was, according to Bruce Kuklick, both self-imposed and a result of "the closed anti-Catholic professionalism of non-Catholic philosophers."[137] Thus, while Catholic institutions played an important role in bringing phenomenology to the attention of secular European philosophers outside Germany, their direct influence on mainstream philosophical discourse in America was limited.

As with secular universities, phenomenology first took root in Catholic philosophy departments that had been touched by the wave of phenomenological émigrés. In 1940, Fordham University hired the phenomenologist Dietrich von Hildebrand, an influential contributor to Catholic discourse on marital love and sex, who fled Europe facing a death sentence for his anti-Nazi activities in Austria.[138] Hildebrand remained at Fordham until 1960, during which time the university hired three more phenomenologists. All three—Balduin Schwarz, Quentin Lauer, and W. Norris Clarke—were Europeans, trained at Munich, the Sorbonne, and Louvain, respectively. After Schwartz's retirement in 1964, Fordham appointed the phenomenologists William Richardson and Patrick Heelan, both also graduates of Louvain.[139]

Duquesne University, under the leadership of Father Henry Koren, also proved to be fecund soil for phenomenological studies. Although Koren's background was Thomistic, he believed that phenomenology would allow Catholic philosophers to address important modern issues "untouched" by traditional Thomistic thought. As chair of the university's Philosophy Department, Koren arranged visiting appointments for a series of European phenomenologists as well as permanent appointments for Alphonso Lingis and André Schuwer, graduates of Louvain, Manfred Frings from Cologne, and John Sallis, who had earned a PhD at Tulane.[140] Duquesne's Psychology Department was also led by a phenomenologist, Father Adrian Van Kaam, and included Amedeo Georgi, an expert on Husserl and Merleau-Ponty. From Duquesne, they advanced the field of phenomenological and existential psychology, an effort to redirect the discipline toward methods and practices grounded in a nonreductive humanistic self-understanding of existence. As with Northwestern and the New School, this concentration of expertise in existential-phenomenological psychology had autocatalytic reproductive benefits for the movement. In 1970, Giorgi founded the *Journal of Phenomenological Psychology* at Duquesne, and, the following year, he oversaw the publication of the first of four volumes in the series Duquesne Studies in Phenomenological Psychology. In 1980, he and John Sallis established the Simon Silverman Phenomenology Center at Duquesne as a repository of phenomenological texts and materials and a site for lectures, symposia, and programs on phenomenology. By 1981, both the University of Dallas and Seattle University had created clinical programs in phenomenological and existential psychology, founded by graduates of Duquesne.[141]

By the late 1950s, phenomenology was represented at most of America's leading Catholic universities: Notre Dame employed Frederick Crosson, adding Guido Kung in 1962; at Georgetown were the Sartre scholar Wilfrid Desan and the Marxist philosopher Louis Dupré; at Boston College was the Heideggerian philosopher Thomas Owens; and, though lagging behind their peers, the Catholic University of America hired Kenneth Schmitz and

Robert Sokolowski in the 1960s, while DePaul hired Bernard Boelen and Manfred Frings from Duquesne.[142] Some secular universities began to accumulate phenomenological and existentialist expertise as well. The faculty of NYU included both Harmon Chapman and William Barrett. Calvin Schrag and Richard Grabau held positions at Purdue, which added William McBride in 1973. At Rice were James Street Fulton and Louis Mackey. Claremont Graduate University boasted Frederick Sontag and Stephen Erickson.

*   *   *

As a new network of institutions formed, connected by their focus on Continental philosophy, phenomenology's status in its first American home, Harvard University, was in flux. John Wild had begun offering classes on contemporary European philosophy at Harvard in 1952. Intent on teaching Heideggerian philosophy, Wild collaborated with Hubert Dreyfus, Robert Trayhern, and Cornelius de Deugd on a partial translation of Heidegger's notoriously abstruse *Being and Time* for use in a new course titled "Phenomenology and Existentialism."[143] As one student wrote: "[Wild] shares our feelings about the crap that has been translated while the good things go begging. His motive for translating *Sein und Zeit* (the first half) was that he didn't want his students to read crude popularizations."[144] According to Richard Rorty, who assigned the manuscript to his students at Wellesley, mimeographs of Wild's translation became "the basis for most teaching of Heidegger in the United States prior to the publication, in 1962, of the Macquarrie and Robinson translation."[145]

In a bid to further bolster its course offerings in Continental philosophy, Harvard's Philosophy Department offered a visiting appointment to Jean-Paul Sartre in 1958.[146] Failing to entice Sartre, Harvard turned to Northwestern's William Earle. During Earle's four-month stay in Cambridge, he developed a close association with Harvard's phenomenologists. His datebook lists ten meetings with Hubert Dreyfus, then a graduate student, and at least eighteen meetings with John Wild.[147] In 1960, one year after Earle's visit, Wild informed his colleagues that he intended to leave Harvard for a position at Northwestern. Learning of his decision, the department's senior members hastily wrote to Wild in the hope "that it is not yet too late to influence you in behalf of Harvard and us." The letter was heartfelt, expressing their respect for their colleague and desire that he remain. He would be missed, the letter explained, "more than the somewhat raucous style of some of us would lead you to guess."

The gist of what we would say, of course, is that we shall be very glad if you decide to stay and very sorry if you do not. We should miss you, John, more than the somewhat raucous style of some of us would lead you to guess. We value the unique and powerful contribution you make to the department's curriculum and to its councils, to our relations with other groups in the university, to the university as a whole, to philosophy at large, and to that great part of the wider public who are serious about the things you are so admirably serious about. We are grateful for your humanity, your scholarship, your widely searching thought, and your kind and whimsical humor. When it comes to a showdown, where could Harvard find your equal in the important and prophetic parts you have so effectively taken? (And who knows, conversely, how many roots you have in the alkaline Harvard soil which would be none the better for transplanting?) We value you, in fine, for you inimitable John-Wildness and your long friendship.[148]

With its reference to the department's "raucous style," the letter hints at the conflict Wild's philosophical differences no doubt occasioned with his analytic colleagues. Despite this, it made clear the deep personal and philosophical esteem in which Wild was held. Harvard seemed to breed such ambiguous intellectual and personal coexistences. A similar dissonance was apparent in the relationship between W. V. O. Quine and the heterodox American existentialist philosopher Henry Bugbee, who was denied tenure at Harvard in 1953. In a letter to W. E. Hocking, Bugbee expressed his confusion at the "paradox . . . that of all the members of the Harvard Department, Quine has given me the closest and most sympathetic philosophical companionship." Quine had read Bugby's work, offered him "the strongest encouragement," and helped him obtain the Santayana Fellowship. Yet, Bugby wondered, "how can he think officially as he does and fail to take philosophical offense at the kind of thing I've been fumbling along with?"[149] This paradox is an important reminder that, even for philosophers, the intimate and personal is always present alongside and even against the rational or ideological. It is an irreducible element of this history that will at times resist the more durable logics of intellectual and social structures. Here, however, it did not win out. Wild departed. The "essence of the matter," Harvard's Dean McGeorge Bundy wrote, was that Wild had been invited to lead a department "along what he calls 'non-analytic, non-positivistic lines.'" This was, Bundy concluded, "an opportunity which he has wanted for years, and we must wish him well in it."[150]

During the 1950s and 1960s, representation of Continental philosophy at the leading eleven departments remained essentially constant, except

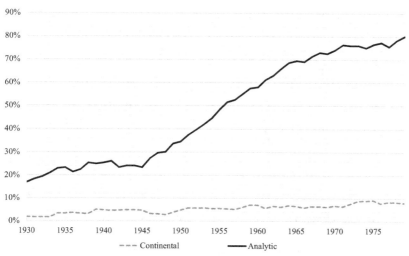

90%
80%
70%
60%
50%
40%
30%
20%
10%
0%

1930   1935   1940   1945   1950   1955   1960   1965   1970   1975

--- Continental   ——Analytic

FIGURE 5.2 Total Representation at Leading Departments (Yale Removed), 1930–1979. Percentage of analytic and Continental philosophers at leading departments, not including Yale. See also the appendix.

at Yale, which was increasingly iconoclastic, dedicating significant attention to phenomenology and existentialism. At midcentury, Yale was distinguished primarily by its commitment to speculative philosophy and a Christian-inflected humanism.[151] While Continental subjects were somewhat better represented at Yale than other leading institutions in the 1950s, it was only in the mid-1960s that Yale significantly broke from its peers in its emphasis on phenomenology and existentialism. In 1960, Yale employed only two philosophers whose work intersected with Continental discourses: George Alfred Schrader and Richard Bernstein. However, Yale hired nine philosophers between 1963 and 1968 who specialized in or were significantly engaged with Continental thought: John Wild, Karsten Harries, David Carr, Kenley Royce Dove, William McBride, John Findlay, Merold Westphal Jr., Edward Casey, and James Ogilvy. Although most appointments were at the rank of assistant professor, Yale had assembled the largest contingent of Continental philosophers of any department in the United States by the late 1960s. At least on paper, Yale's faculty represented analytic and Continental tendencies in roughly equal proportion. As the department's chair, Robert Fogelin, explained in 1970, this was the result of the Yale's pedagogical tradition, which held that "a balanced program" was a critical resource for training future scholars. However, Fogelin added that "the idea of a balanced program presents a difficult challenge" and warned that, if Yale could not make more tenured appointments "of the very highest quality" in the analytic field, "the Department will remain largely isolated from the other major departments in this country and our students will continue to receive what is generally thought to be a one-sided education."[152]

In 1945, only three of sixty-nine philosophers with permanent appointments in the leading departments had a record of engagement with phenomenology and existentialism: Columbia's Horace Leland Friess, Harvard's John Wild, and Stanford's Henry Lanz. In 1950, the situation was virtually unchanged, with four of ninety-six philosophers engaged in the field: Friess at Columbia, Wild at Harvard, Walter Kaufmann at Princeton, and George Schrader at Yale.[153] By 1959, despite undergraduate demand for courses in Continental philosophy, this number had increased only slightly in absolute terms, to 8 of 114 philosophers. This suggests that leading American philosophy departments faced a second obstacle to integrating phenomenology into their curricula: a deficit of trained faculty. Ironically, this problem was particularly acute for the discipline's leading departments. While phenomenology proliferated within a subset of American institutions during the postwar era, it was not until the 1960s, when Yale's Philosophy Department began to emphasize Continental subjects, that phenomenologists had more than a token presence on the faculties of any graduate program that ranked among the discipline's best. Accordingly, few recent graduates qualified to teach and supervise research in these subjects could be found within the elite caste's traditional hiring network.

Of course, institutions like the New School and Catholic universities were not without talented students or the resources for excellent instruction. However, they drew fewer of the highest-caliber students than did the top-ranked mainstream departments. These dynamics were summarized in a 1959 report from Northwestern's Philosophy Department: "We attract, year after year, some good graduate students, but very few really excellent ones; for the most part, the very best young men still go to Harvard and Yale."[154] As the department distinguished itself as a center of phenomenology and existentialism, the situation was only partly ameliorated. The 1966 annual report noted that the Philosophy Department received approximately 150 applications for graduate admissions. Among these was "a goodly little number of candidates of the highest quality." However, from this "highest quality" group, approximately half were "lured by Yale, Princeton, Harvard, Chicago, Stanford, etc."[155] Of course, admissions is a fallible system, and the leading departments did not monopolize all the field's most promising students. But even acknowledging the irreducible subjectivity in appraisals of philosophical quality, it is impossible to dispute that far more of America's best philosophers were trained at its traditionally most prestigious departments than those on the periphery, where they were more likely to engage with phenomenology and existentialism.

Because the leading departments offered appointments only to those students considered most promising (even among the rarefied ranks of their own graduates), the number of plausible candidates for a position in any particular specialty would be a fraction of recent graduates who specialized in that field. Moreover, choices were, as a practical matter, confined to graduates of the leading eleven departments, reflecting both the limitations of their "old boys'" hiring network and a perception that graduates of smaller and heterodox departments were simply less talented. There was, further, a disconnect between the overall perception of peripheral departments and their strength in fields that were neglected by the majority. Although Northwestern was "among the leaders in continental philosophy," a 1980 report stated, it did not have a strong national reputation:

> So long as the division [between American and European philosophy] persists, a department like Northwestern's, which has been one of very few departments in a major U.S. University to provide a home for distinguished philosophers working in the phenomenological tradition, but which has not been able to attract and retain equally distinguished philosophers working in the analytic tradition, is bound to suffer in its rating within the profession in this country.

For most American philosophers, it was implicitly understood that excellence in phenomenology and existentialism was not, on its own, sufficient to distinguish a department as a premier philosophical institution. This hinged on the unstated premise that Continental philosophy was a boutique specialization—a subfield, like Kant studies or aesthetics. Yet, one might ask, if Continental philosophy is a subfield, is not analytic philosophy as well? If we deny this valuative distinction, the leading departments appear in an entirely different light. "Harvard, for example, offers little in the history of philosophy and hardly anything in contemporary Continental philosophy," the Northwestern report noted. "Its eminence rests on the reputations of a few brilliant contributors to contemporary philosophy and, of course, on the eternal truth that Harvard is Harvard."[156]

Harvard's search for faculty candidates who were qualified to instruct students in contemporary European philosophy indicates how these perceptions both shaped and were shaped by the everyday professional experiences of American philosophers. In its search for a successor to John Wild,

Harvard made inquiries of Princeton, Michigan, Berkeley, and Yale.[157] Harvard also solicited the advice of two philosophers who were not members of the leading departments' faculties: Maurice Mandelbaum, a professor at Johns Hopkins, and Richard Brandt, a professor at Swarthmore. However, both were graduates of Yale, and Mandelbaum was the incoming president of the APA. Both also recommended only graduates of the leading departments.[158] Their search was, thus, circumscribed by boundaries that confined their view to only one other department in which contemporary European philosophy was beginning to receive serious attention. What they discovered seemed to confirm accounts of a fundamental split between analytic and Continental philosophers and a distinction in ability between members of those groups. For instance, Ledger Wood responded to D. C. Williams's request for information on Princeton's recent Continental graduates:

> These men on the whole are much inferior to our men in the fields of logic, philosophy of science and theory of knowledge. There is among these men only one . . . whose graduate record would justify his consideration by Harvard. Although I cannot recommend him unqualifiedly, I have no doubt that he would rate among the best men in his age group whose interests are historical, religious, and existentialist.[159]

Williams wrote back to Wood: "I am considerably impressed by your judgment that the existentialist type of philosopher is, at least on average, much inferior in sheer ability to his analytic brother (if 'brother' is the correct word)."[160] In fact, Wood had only been speaking of Princeton's current crop of graduate students, but the reasoning was easily extended to the whole field. Indeed, Wood's assessment made such an impression on Williams that he would discuss it in subsequent correspondences with two different philosophers, writing that he had been informed by a colleague at Princeton that "such men average much less intelligent than analytic philosophers," and "the spiritual types are so likely to be so much stupider than the others!"[161]

To fill the void left by Wild's departure, Harvard turned to Dagfinn Føllesdal, a Norwegian logician and doctoral student of Quine who had developed an interest in phenomenology prior to his graduate studies at Harvard. In a productive and wide-ranging philosophical career, Føllesdal injected Husserlian ideas into analytic discourse. His first major work on phenomenology, "Husserl's Notion of Noema," was published in 1969 by the *Journal of Philosophy*. In it he argued that Husserl's noema is a close analogue of "sense" in Gottlob Frege's philosophy of language.[162] Because

Husserl's noematic structure characterizes all intentional acts, not merely linguistic utterances, Føllesdal hoped that Husserl could provide a framework through which the techniques of linguistic analysis could be applied to an expanded range of mental states.[163] In this new philosophical synthesis, phenomenology could be used as a tool of linguistic analysis. This project was fundamentally rooted in the ethos of Harvard. It was while writing his dissertation on the interpretation of quantified modal logic that Føllesdal developed his understanding of Husserl's relation to Frege.[164] Indeed, his 1977 application for a Guggenheim Foundation grant to complete a book that would "make Husserl's phenomenology intelligible to philosophers belonging to other philosophical traditions" explained that the work's core was "a 280 page lecture manuscript which I wrote for a course on Husserl that I taught at Harvard in 1962."[165]

Føllesdal left Harvard in 1965 to return to Norway, ultimately negotiating a contract with Stanford that allowed him to split semesters between Oslo and Palo Alto. In need once more of a philosopher qualified to give courses on existentialism and phenomenology, Harvard's Philosophy Department agreed to fund a portion of Frederick Olafson's appointment, which Harvard's Graduate School of Education had initiated. Olafson, an expert on Heidegger, was also a Harvard graduate, a student of John Wild.[166] Harvard's response to the challenge of representing phenomenology and existentialism fit an emerging pattern of institutional norms that informed American philosophers' perceptions of their discipline's boundaries and internal gradients of value. Its department would host one or two experts (but no more) in contemporary European philosophy, ideally by courtesy appointment. Of course, little else could be done at Harvard. The Graustein formula, which established a set schedule for appointments, limited its ability to hire new faculty, and an extreme institutional exceptionalism restricted who could be considered for employment. As we have noted, however, Harvard provided a model of professional organization for many American philosophy departments. This seems to have been no less true with respect to the representation of Continental philosophy. Despite a rapid postwar expansion, most departments would not hire more than one or two philosophers with expertise in modern European philosophy— enough to provide course coverage, but too few to influence departmental priorities. In 1965, as the average size of the elite departments exceeded fourteen, none except Yale employed more than two specialists in contemporary European philosophy.

While this disparity in methodological representation was largely the product of structural dynamics, philosophers did, at times, act purposively to prevent their Continental colleagues from gaining power. In 1970, Stuart Hampshire stepped down as chair of Princeton's Philosophy Department to accept a position at Oxford. Among those considered to replace Hampshire as department chair was the Nietzsche scholar Walter Kaufmann, who was one of the department's longest-serving members. Kaufmann had also achieved rare celebrity for a philosopher of the postwar era through his popular collection *Existentialism: From Dostoevsky to Sartre*.[167] However, a group of Kaufmann's departmental colleagues argued that his philosophical interests should disqualify him from leadership at Princeton. Gilbert Harman wrote to the university's president, Robert Goheen: "Kaufmann would want to carry us off in a direction that most of us do not want to travel" and "lacks the element of taste" that "built up this department from the one that was clearly moribund in the early fifties."[168] Ledger Wood warned that Kaufmann "might be inclined to press for new appointments in the department in the areas of his own interest," asserting that "these happen at the present time to be areas in which there are few really distinguished philosophers."[169] As Richard Rorty described the situation to President Goheen:

> There is very little agreement within the department on how we are to keep up our reputation. . . . [On] the one hand there are the tough-minded technicians (e.g., Harman, Benacerraf, Grandy, Lewis, Field) who often brush aside work which doesn't seem to them in the "main stream" of current concern in the philosophy of language and related areas. On the other hand are more broad- and tender-minded types (e.g., Kaufmann, Smith, Vlastos, me) who talk about the need for "greater balance" in the department (a phrase which these days has become a euphemism for "fewer logicians and philosophers of language"). . . . The nightmare of the former group is that the department will become a "zoo"—with one specimen of each philosophical school. The nightmare of the latter group is that history of philosophy, contemporary European philosophy, etc., will be pushed to one side in order to devote more and more faculty slots to people working in a few currently fashionable areas.[170]

The letter is an itinerary of the philosophical divide's metaphorical landscape, invoking an opposition between "balance" and analysis and the vaguely gendered language of "tough-minded" analysts and "tender" Continentalists. While he lamented the situation, Rorty was forced to acknowledge that "Walter Kaufmann, alas, simply [doesn't] have the respect of enough of the department to succeed in the job."[171]

Efforts to marginalize heterodox philosophers could be even less subtle. Hubert Dreyfus claimed that he was "never informed of any faculty meeting" during his seven years on the faculty at MIT. Because these meetings were held off campus in the homes of department members, this procedure was quite effective at ensuring his exclusion. With no dissenters in attendance, the majority was free to set pretense aside. Indeed, Dreyfus wrote, a "friendly assistant professor told me that at one such meeting it was decided that no library funds were to be spent on continental philosophy books devoted to 'Stone Age Philosophy.'"[172]

* * *

Even before World War II, Continental and analytic discourses were becoming increasingly technical and self-referential. The styles and lexicons of both movements were opaque to many American philosophers trained in the early twentieth century, as W. E. Hocking noted to Henry Bugbee in 1954:

> The symbolic logicians are doing their best to develop a technology which only they can read. . . . the followers of Husserl have gone far in the direction of scholastic jargon; and the Existentialists together with the neo-ontologists have begun explorations of great importance which tend to terms and manners of expression peculiar to themselves.[173]

The generation of American philosophers educated in the postwar era, by contrast, benefited from significant exposure to symbolic logic and analytic texts. At the same time, the narrow boundaries of the professional network from which elite departments hired facilitated the development of common stylistic and curricular norms, and the overlapping gradient of prestige around this group marked those norms as correct. Thus, social conditions favored disciplinary narrowness and exceptionalism. Few within this network would be trained to engage with Continental philosophy and, for those who had learned philosophy reading Russell, Wittgenstein, Carnap, and Quine, the unfamiliar verbiage and style of Continental works immediately marked them as "other." In existentialism, Hocking had perceived a "kinship with poetry and music and drama and all art," which assured him "that it has an import like that of Plato in his day." Indeed, he believed it had "the most substantial stuff to say to our time," even if much of it was "chaff." However, these sensibilities reflected the education of an era that had already ended. As disciplinary boundaries solidified in the modern university, philosophy was reconstructed as a professional enterprise in the image of the sciences. The same qualities that recommended existentialism to Hocking now meant that "to much of British and American thought it is moonshine."[174]

Still, differences in language and style go only so far in explaining American attitudes toward European thought, raising the question of why these differences existed and persisted. Further, they do not account for the emergence of "Continental philosophy" as a framework that included phenomenologists such as Husserl and Merleau-Ponty whose works comported with many norms of analytic discourse. Indeed, in the fight against irrationalism and obscurity, analytic philosophers could have found committed allies among the ranks of Husserlian phenomenologists, whose philosophical project aimed to make the discipline a "rigorous science." Yet, as Continental philosophers, Husserlians in America fared no better than followers of Heidegger or Sartre. The term *Continental philosophy* remained salient beyond the initial incidents from which it was coined, not because of its intellectual coherence but because it identified a professional problem that manifested in the everyday experience of American philosophers. The unifying feature of the thinkers it circumscribed— including Hegel, Marx, Nietzsche, Kierkegaard, Husserl, Heidegger, Sartre, and Merleau-Ponty—was that few philosophers trained in America's mainstream departments were qualified to teach courses or evaluate work that emphasized their philosophy. These traditions became conspicuous when demand for instruction made their absence a problem.

The term *Continental philosophy* began to appear in discussions of appointments and departmental planning by the late 1950s. In 1959, Harvard received a request for information about job candidates from the University of Illinois that specified "contemporary continental European philosophy" as one of the desired areas of competence. That same year, a report from Northwestern's Philosophy Department announced that it was "on [its] way to becoming a small-scale sampler of the European continental philosophy of twenty or thirty years ago," alluding to a "continental phenomenological-ontological-existential wing of philosophy." Likewise, a 1961 letter that discussed a potential appointment at Harvard stated: "We are still trying to decide whether our most desperate need is for someone in ancient philosophy, someone in recent continental philosophy, or someone in philosophy of science."[175] Viewed as a specialization, it was logical that departmental representation of Continental philosophy would be limited. This qualitative distinction between the categories of analytic and

Continental philosophy was materially inscribed in the discipline through professional activities such as job postings and conferences. In the 1970s, 2,513 jobs were posted in Jobs for Philosophy, citing 6,679 desired areas of research. Counterintuitively, more positions were posted for specialists in "Continental Philosophy" (6%) than "Analytic Philosophy" (3.2%). Of course, this did not reflect diminished demand for analysts. Rather, analytic philosophy had been normalized so that analytic philosophers could be classified by a topical subfield alone (e.g., epistemology, logic, political philosophy).[176] Thus, the question of analytic philosophy's overrepresentation would not even be posed in most leading departments because of a discursive formation that rendered its factual normativity as rational.

The virtual absence of phenomenologists from mainstream departments limited possibilities for professional relationships like that between Quine and Bugbee and foreclosed possibilities for autocatalytic reproduction within the nation's most influential institutions. It also meant that work in analytic subjects generally provided students greater opportunity to build relationships with faculty. In the leading departments, it was principally analytic philosophers who wrote recommendations and evaluated students for fellowships, awards, and positions. All of these were strong incentives to pursue work in analytic subjects. Most important, however, the absence of phenomenologists and existentialists meant that Continental philosophy was constructed as an imaginary. Rather than engaging the thing itself in texts, talks, and personal interactions, most American philosophers encountered Continental philosophy through the testimony of like-minded colleagues and within the domain of common knowledge, where Heidegger's association with Nazism was among its most salient features. Indeed, one needed look no further than the front cover of Dagobert Runes's translation of *German Existentialism* (1965), featuring a swastika that dwarfs its title font, to form a strong opinion of Continental philosophy.[177] Philosophers in America's most prestigious universities could also see that the departments where contemporary European philosophy received significant attention were at the periphery of the profession. This offered an object lesson, as Hilary Putnam put it, in "*what not to consider philosophy*," as the valuative distinction between peripheral or idiosyncratic institutions and their own departments was easily mapped onto the philosophical traditions prioritized within them.[178]

Reports from philosophers such as Rieser and Cerf helped make sense of these professional experiences. Their account of a Continental mindset steeped in unreason and producing thought that was "totally alien to the more sober thinkers in the Atlantic sphere," provided intellectual justification for the institutional neglect of contemporary European thought.[179] As the profession expanded, these categories became increasingly important as a tool for classifying, distinguishing, and ultimately evaluating philosophers. However, it would be unjustified to conclude that analytic philosophers cynically deployed otherizing accounts of European philosophy to maintain control over the discipline. Rather, to appropriate a line from Paul E. Johnson, if we are to render the analytic-Continental divide intelligibly, we must understand that American philosophers in elite philosophy departments experienced their struggle to hire suitably esteemed philosophers *as a philosophical problem*—a problem that had to do not with only the practices of their institutions, but the "rightness" of their beliefs.[180] Just as the faculties of philosophy's leading departments found their suspicions regarding Continental thought confirmed by their experiences conducting faculty searches, their students would see the idea of an incommensurable divide between philosophical traditions reified in its absence from their curricula. Thus, the institutional organization of American philosophy reproduced both the ranks of a professional class that, particularly in its elite strata, consisted primarily of analytic philosophers and an ideology that took the profession's division as natural.

The potential impact of this framework on American philosophical attitudes did not go unnoticed by contemporary European philosophers. Indeed, when Kurt Fischer was invited to teach "Contemporary Continental and Analytic Philosophy" at Harvard in 1964, he explained that he was happy to give a course on the subject but was "particularly dissatisfied with contrasting 'analytical' with 'continental' in spite of the obviousness of these labels."[181] However, like any discursive formation, the idea of "Continental philosophy" was available for other uses by those it had been created to define. Regardless of whether the designation had a valid historical basis, Continental philosophy had become a social reality by the 1970s, reflected in the organization of philosophical institutions, curricula, and resources in the United States. Organizations like the Society for Phenomenology and Existential Philosophy, which will be discussed in chapter 6, drew on the membership of this larger community to counterbalance the power of the analytic majority, accepting the Continental paradigm. Indeed, in 1978, the Center for Advanced Research in Phenomenology began a new book series with the Ohio University Press, called the Series in Continental Thought. The name was chosen by Lester Embree, a New School–trained phenomenologist. As he explained, "Previously at a SPEP meeting at Catholic University I had heard somebody classify Theodor Adorno as a phenomenologist [and] decided we needed a new and broader rubric than 'Phenomenology and Existentialism.'"[182] If it was unavoidable that phenomenologists would be lumped together professionally with Hegelians, existentialists, Frankfurt School Marxists, and others, then Embree hoped that at least the idea of a "Continental" tradition would provide space for each of these discourses to exist on its own terms.

D

Iris Marion Young

Iris Marion Young was born in 1949, the daughter of an insurance under-writer and a "homemaker" with a master's degree in English who spurned the tedium housework to indulge her appetite for literature, language, art, and music. Young was a "city girl," whose early years in a Flushing apartment nourished her belief in the pluralistic possibility of urban sociality. Her parents, however, idealized suburban family life and relocated their family to central New Jersey when they had sufficient savings, purchasing a midpriced house in a new development. Their split-level home was one of four models in the development, promising potential owners a prefabricated American dream: a generic form of life that could be worn like a suit off the rack. As Young discovered, for those who deviated from the development's norms, it was, instead, a straitjacket.[1]

At the age of eleven, Young lost her father, who died suddenly from a brain tumor. Her grieving mother drank, and her refusal of housework deepened, which did not escape the attention of her suburban neighbors:

> A woman alone with her children in this development of perfectly new squeaky clean suburban houses. She is traumatized by grief, and the neighbors look from behind their shutters, people talk about the disheveled way she arrives at church, her eyes red from crying. . . . A woman alone with her children is no longer a whole family, deserving like others of respectful distance.

One day, an officer appeared without explanation, taking Iris and her siblings to a teen reform school. Her mother had been charged with neglect. "The primary evidence," Young wrote, "was drinking and a messy house. We ate well enough, had clean enough clothes, and a mother's steady love, given the way she gave it. . . . We were a family in need of support, but we children were not neglected." After two months, Iris was returned to her mother.

However, an accidental fire the following summer brought authorities back to her home. The firemen found beer cans and mess, and her mother was arrested for neglect. Iris and her siblings were sent to live with family friends. After a year, her mother was released from jail, and, not much later, Iris's foster father died. The state concluded that the foster home, "headed now only by a woman," was no longer a suitable environment. Iris and her siblings were returned to their mother, who "wasted no time packing up" and moved the family "back to the safe indifference of New York City."[2]

⋆　⋆　⋆

Young attended public high school in New York and enrolled in Queens College in 1966. Following her mother's path of study, she entered college as an English major, but was drawn to philosophy by writers like Nietzsche, Kierkegaard, Sartre, and Camus, whose works permeated the collegiate intellectual atmosphere.[3] Young graduated from Queens College in 1970 and in 1974 entered the doctoral program in philosophy at Penn State University, one of the programs that had developed an emphasis on and strong reputation in Continental philosophy during the early postwar era. Young completed her dissertation on the later work of Ludwig Wittgenstein under the direction of the polymath philosopher John Anderson, whose interests spanned the fields of existential phenomenology, mathematics, computer science, religion, and logic. Young's dissertation is, likewise, notable for its breadth, drawing from Heidegger to read Wittgenstein as a hermeneutical philosopher, engaged in a critique of positivism and Cartesianism that provided important insights into the logic of modern technological society.[4]

After completing her doctorate, Young held appointments in the Philosophy Departments of Rensselaer Polytechnic Institute (1975–1976) and Miami University (1976–1979) before joining the Philosophy Department of Worcester Polytechnic Institute. As much as the academy, however, Young's engagement in feminist and socialist politics was essential to her professional and philosophical identity. Patchen Markell described Young as "one of those scholars who practiced—who lived, in the texture of her everyday life—what she preached; in her case, a systematic egalitarianism and opposition to hierarchy."[5] Ann Ferguson wrote, "I always admired Iris for the way that she was able to work in social justice coalitions as a local activist yet also continue her very important theoretical work on the feminist theory."[6] Politics thoroughly suffused Young's life, so much that the birth announcement for her daughter declared: "Another socialist feminist has come into the world!"[7] Young credited the Society for Women in Philosophy (SWIP) as "an important training ground" for her as a philosopher and a feminist. Founded in 1972, SWIP was both a vital professional nexus for women philosophers and a font of novel feminist theory. "We had intense meetings twice a year," Young wrote, "where we were inventing feminist philosophy, and then we had evening parties!"[8] Young was also active in SOFPHIA (the Socialist-Feminist Philosophers Association) and its precursor, MAP (Marxist Activist Philosophers). Ferguson recalls Young as "one of the intellectual leaders of this group from the beginning, not only in creating and critiquing social theory, but also in making practical connections to that theory, which included encouraging the group to go to antiwar, pro-union, and other social justice demonstrations when they were in the venue of the conference."[9]

During the 1970s, Young recalled, socialist feminists "took on an ambitious theoretical project. We wanted to remain continuous with and retain many of the insights of . . . Marxism, but at the same time transform it into a theory in which male domination is at least as important conceptually as class domination." In her 1981 essay "Beyond the Unhappy Marriage: A Critique of Dual Systems Theory," Young argued that patriarchy and class exploitation should not be theorized as distinct systems of oppression that feminist and Marxist critique addressed respectively and separately. Such attempts at union made for an "unhappy marriage" in which gender oppression was either dehistoricized and abstracted from material relations or relegated to a separate, limited sphere within the capitalist mode of production. Young rejected this approach, maintaining that "the situation of women is not conditioned by two distinct system of social relations which have distinct structures, movement, and histories." Rather, their analyses required "a single theory . . . which can comprehend capitalist patriarchy as one system in which the oppression of women is a *core* attribute."[10] In such a theory, she explained, the division of labor would have equal standing with class as a primary analytical category. Whereas class analysis provides "a vision of the system as a whole," analyzing the division of labor "proceeds at the more concrete level of particular relations of interaction and interdependence in a society according to their position in laboring activity." Because gender is the axis along which unpaid domestic work is distinguished from other forms of necessary labor, Young argued, "analysis of the economic relations of production in a social formation requires specific attention to the gender division of labor."[11]

Although "Beyond the Unhappy Marriage" examines the implications of overlapping identities for social theory, it leaves the nature of identity unexplored, addressing "the social division of labor in gender specific terms" without stipulating that women in general face "a common and unified situation."[12] However, Young entered the feminist movement at a moment when it faced an internal challenge from women who rejected its traditionally white, bourgeois leadership's claim to represent universal interests of their gender. Indeed, recognition of the heterogeneity of women's experiences initiated a debate over the political utility and even ontological grounding of the category "woman." At the same time, as the consciousness-raising efforts of left-wing groups affirmed ethnic and cultural diversity, some feminists began to question the assumption that all gender differences are intrinsically invidious. "My own reflections on the politics of difference," Young recalled, "were ignited by discussions in the women's movement on the importance and difficulty of acknowledging differences of class, race, sexuality, age, ability, and culture among women."[13]

As feminists split over issues like the exclusion of lesbians and the marginalization of minorities, the consequences of neglecting identity's philosophical foundation became apparent to Young. If women shared a common identity qua women, the diversity of their experiences made its contents elusive. The emerging distinction of female gender identity and biological sex in feminist discourse provided a temporary escape from essentialism, but it left an individual's relationship to her identity unclear. "The absurdity of trying to isolate gender identity from race or class identity becomes apparent," Young wrote, "if you ask of any individual woman whether she can distinguish the 'woman part' of herself from the 'white part' or the 'Jewish part.'" Some, such as Judith Butler, argued that even sex could not be taken as a fixed category without classifying behaviors as normal or deviant along an axis of heterosexual relations. "The insistence on a subject for feminism," whether "woman" or "gender," Butler concluded, ossified norms that feminists should instead approach critically.[14]

Searching for a path forward, Young attempted to clarify the concept of identity without reifying it as an essence or property. Like Husserl, she cautioned against "theory": self-enclosed discourse that attempts to provide a totalizing, systematic account of phenomena. At the same time, however, she maintained that gender was not a concept that could be discarded without harming feminist politics.[15] Refusing to theorize identity, Young adopted a pragmatic orientation that addressed its implications for the "political dilemma generated by feminist critiques of the concept 'woman.'" The decision whether to conceptualize women as a group was consequential, since "without conceptualizing women as a group in some sense, it is not possible to conceptualize oppression as a systematic, structured, institutional process." However, because the practical difficulties that arose from subsuming women under a single shared identity appeared "insurmountable," Young appealed to Sartre's distinction between a "group" and a "series" for clarification.[16]

While members of a group (e.g., a sports team) mutually identify one another "as in a unified relation," members of a series (e.g., subway commuters) are "unified passively by the objects around which their actions are oriented or by the objectified results of the material effects of the actions of the others."[17] In other words, the basis of a series lies not in shared attributes or an experience of belonging, but in factical conditions that delimit possibilities of action. As Young explained:

> Membership in serial collectives define an individual's being, in a sense—one "is" a farmer, or a commuter, or a radio listener, and so on, together in series with others similarly positioned. But the definition is anonymous, and the unity of the series is amorphous, without determinate limits, attributes, or intentions.[18]

Like the never fully explicit "milieu of action" that organizes seriality, the boundaries of a series remain blurry and in flux. Yet, while a series does not have definite criteria for inclusion or exclusion, thrownness into the "practico-inert reality" of an always-already constituted world establishes serial relations, such as gender, race, and class, as social facts. The series "women," so understood, is a "loose unity" constituted through "a vast, multifaceted, layered, complex, and overlapping set of structures and objects" that orient its members toward "the same or similarly structured objects." This series is defined by the social rules that govern the female body (which is itself a "practico-inert object") as well as "a vast complex of other objects and materialized historical products [that] condition women's lives as gendered." In particular, Young argued, women are organized through norms governing biological processes, like menstruation and pregnancy, the institutionalization of heterosexual relations, which places women "in a relation of potential appropriation by men," and by a gendered division of labor that proliferates practico-inert artifacts such as "offices, workstations, locker rooms, uniforms, and instruments of a particular activity [that] presuppose a certain sex."[19]

By treating gender as a more or less shared position within a historically constituted milieu of action, the concept remained available for analyzing social structures that constrain women's opportunities and freedom without denying that the "subjective experiential relation that each person has, and sometimes groups have, to the gender structure, are infinitely variable."[20] Yet, while refusing gender the status of an essence, Young maintained that women's lived experience is distinctive in its very structure. Although patriarchal society makes femininity into a tool of "confinement" by "enforcing behavior in women that benefits men," Young argued that gender difference is not necessarily invidious. To understand femininity only as a maimed or deformed mode of being is to accept uncritically the aims and pursuits of the dominant culture as those that are most fundamentally human. Instead, Young advocated a "gynocentric feminism" that critiqued "the devaluation and repression of women's experience by a masculinist culture that exalts violence and individualism" over nurturing, cooperation, and continuity with nature. Women's oppression was not, in this view, reducible to the denial of opportunities to participate in society on the same terms as men. Participation still required submission to institutional rules and norms that were modeled on values drawn from male experience, even when it was allowed. Privileging male aims and masculine ways of acting and knowing, Young argued, is itself oppressive of women, whose desires, achievements, and abilities are evaluated by their comportment to a male model.[21]

Young's writings explore both how patriarchal femininity narrows women's ontological freedom and how a positive femininity, taken up creatively by women from within the horizon of gendered existence, might become "the source of a conception of society and the subject that can not only liberate women, but also all persons."[22] Her early investigations of women's experience focus on the subject of embodiment. As Young explained, "oppression typically involves the marking or control of the bodies of the oppressed." Workers must adapt their "movements to the relentless rhythm of the assembly line." Others, such as the elderly, disabled, and LGBTQ persons, "are reduced to bodies understood as being deviant or unhealthy." For women, she wrote, "our being is largely reduced to our bodies, the media of male pleasure and procreation, and we find our ability to live and move freely restricted by that definition."[23] However, the subject of women's embodiment remained seriously neglected by philosophers. "Neither philosophical nor feminist-theoretical nor sociological literature," Young wrote, "contained many works engaged in such a project." Even those phenomenologists who were concerned with embodiment, such as Sartre and Merleau-Ponty, had uncritically taken the male body as normative. Sandra Bartky, Young recalled, "was the only philosopher I was aware of whose work aimed to bring ideas of existential phenomenology to analysis of women's gender-specific experience."[24]

Having held that the category "woman" could be neither reduced to biological sex nor identified with some gendered inner homunculus, Young required a new concept on which to ground an investigation of women's experiences. She addressed this problem in her 2002 essay, "Lived Body vs Gender: Reflections on Social Structure and Subjectivity," which outlines a phenomenology of gendered experience grounded in the concept of the "lived body." As Young explained, "The lived body is a unified idea of a physical body acting and experiencing in a specific socio-cultural context; it is body-in-situation." This framework avoids biological reductivism, recognizing the "plural possibilities of comportment" toward the situation of gendered embodiment as well as situational differences along spectra such as sexual orientation, race, and class, but it also rejects "a nature/culture distinction that considers gender as 'merely cultural.'" A person's relation to her body is immanent and, in a sense, originary. Yet, experience of the body is not unmediated: "The body as lived is always enculturated: by the phonemes a body learns to pronounce at a very early age, by the clothes the person wears that mark her nation, her age, her occupational status, and in what is culturally expected or required of women."[25] This is, for example, how gender creates biological sex as a seemingly pre-theoretical reality. While the physical form of male and female bodies is, in fact, infinitely variable, one's bodily experience is given as always already within the horizon of the normative binary between "masculine" and "feminine." There is no original relationship to an ungendered body that can be recovered. The facticity of gender demarcates the situation in which the body is constituted. Likewise, other historical and cultural sources of identity contribute to the body's constitution, not as definite characteristics or cellular elements, but in a holistic unity: "The individual person lives out her unique body in a socio-historical context of the behaviour and expectations of others, but she does not have to worry about constituting her identity from a set of generalized 'pop-beads' strung together."[26]

Young's best-known essay, "Throwing Like a Girl: A Phenomenology of Feminine Body Comportment Motility and Spatiality," is a landmark text in the philosophy of embodiment and gender. The article appeared in a 1980 issue of the journal *Human Studies*, founded by George Psathas as a forum for work that explored connections between existential phenomenology and the social sciences. In "Throwing Like a Girl," Young reflected on the discovery by kinesthetic and psychological researchers that male and female children employed different bodily movements to throw a ball, even before the development of physiological differences that might affect the act of throwing. Girls, these studies found, "do not bring their whole bodies into the motion as much as the boys. They do not reach back, twist, move backward, step, and lean forward. Rather, the girls tend to remain relatively immobile except for their arms, and even the arm is not extended as far as it could be." Going further, Young noted that women's restricted bodily habitus contrasted men's physical capaciousness in various arenas:

> Though we now wear pants more than we used to, and consequently do not have to restrict our sitting postures because of dress, women still tend to sit with their legs relatively close together and their arms across their bodies. When simply standing or leaning, men tend to keep their feet further apart than do woman, and we also tend more to keep our hands and arms touching or shielding our bodies. A final indicative difference is the way each carries books or parcels; girls and women most often carry books embraced to their chests, while boys and men swing them along their sides.

Because gendered variations manifested even in the absence of physiological differences, as the ball-throwing study demonstrated, Young argued that attribution of these discrepancies to biology merely begged the question, invoking a "mysterious feminine essence." Such reification was proscribed by Young's phenomenological and feminist commitments both.[27]

Having identified femininity with "a set of structures and conditions which delimit the typical situation of being a woman in a particular society," Young argued that these structures are reflected in women's purposive bodily comportment. It is, therefore, to be expected that feminine motricity would "exhibit [the] same tension between . . . subjectivity and being a mere object" described in de Beauvoir's account of women's experience as in "a basic tension between immanence and transcendence."[28] Here, however, Young seriously complicated Merleau-Ponty's account of motive behavior as an intentional arc through the body, referring "not onto itself, but onto the world's possibilities." For Merleau-Ponty, our embodied habitus is "a transcendence which moves out from the body in its immanence in an open and unbroken directedness upon the world in action. . . . The lived body as transcendence is pure fluid action, the continuous calling forth of capacities, which are applied to the world."[29] Young countered that women, objectified by the male gaze and acculturated to doubt their physical abilities, are hindered from attaining the easy fluidity or unbroken transcendence of male embodiment:

> [Women] experience our bodies as a fragile encumbrance, rather than the media for the enactment of our aims. We feel as though we must have our

attention directed upon our body to make sure it is doing what we wish it to do, rather than paying attention to what we want to do through our bodies.[30]

Thus, women's dual existence in patriarchal society produces the situation that "the body frequently is both subject and object for itself at the same time and in reference to the same act."[31] In women's relationships to their bodies and bodily relationships to the world, this tension is manifest as "an ambiguous transcendence, an inhibited intentionality, and a discontinuous unity with its surroundings" that makes the body "a burden, which must be dragged and prodded along, and at the same time protected."[32]

In subsequent essays on breasted embodiment, pregnancy, and menstruation, Young challenged the terms in which women's bodies are constituted under the male gaze, working to recover a positive phenomenology of women's originary bodily experience that could be "used to refigure social values."[33] This project aimed toward both women's liberation and the liberation of Western philosophy from inherited orthodoxies. For instance, in her 1990 essay "Breasted Experience: The Look and the Feeling," Young noted that Cartesian metaphysics is committed to an epistemology modeled on sight that assumes a hard boundary between the perceiving subject and perceived object that women's experience subverts.

> If we move from the male gaze in which woman is the Other, the object, solid and definite, to imagine the woman's point of view, the breasted body becomes blurry, mushy, indefinite, multiple, and without clear identity. . . . Fluids, unlike objects, have no definite borders; they are unstable, which does not mean they are without pattern. Fluids surge and move, and a metaphysic that thinks being as fluid would tend to privilege the living, moving, pulsing over the inert dead matter of the Cartesian worldview. This is, simply, a process metaphysics, in which movement and energy is ontologically prior to thingness and the nature of things takes its being from the organic context in which they are embedded.

A philosophy "spoken from a feminine subjectivity," Young suggested, "might privilege touch rather than sight"—a reciprocal relationship in which the grasping hand cannot take hold of its object without simultaneously making itself an object to be touched. "Inasmuch as women's oppression derives to a significant degree from literal and figurative objectification," she continued, "subverting the metaphysics of objects can also be liberating for women."[34]

Like breasted embodiment, Young argued, pregnancy complicates standard assumptions about identity, revealing "a paradigm of bodily experience in which the transparent unity of self dissolves and the body attends positively to itself at the same time that it enacts its projects." Even while describing intentional arcs as decentered subjectivity, Merleau-Ponty maintained that experience must be unified through the body. However, pregnancy erases the boundary "between what is within, myself, and what is outside, separate. I experience my insides as the space of another, yet my own body."[35] Indeed, it puts "the boundaries of the body . . . themselves in flux." As the expectant mother's body changes, her "automatic body habits become dislodged; the continuity between [her] customary body and [her] body at this moment is broken." Insofar as the pregnant woman's bodily habitus is interrupted by her growing size and changing center of gravity, her body ceases to function as a "transparent medium," revealing itself in its physicality as present-at-hand. Yet, the lived experience of pregnant embodiment also complicates Heidegger's account presence-at-hand as a situation of breakdown. This, Young explained, would assume that "such awareness of my body must cut me off from the enactment of my projects; I cannot be attending to the physicality of my body and using it as the means to the accomplishment of my aims."[36] However, she wrote,

> contrary to the mutually exclusive categorization between transcendence and immanence that underlies some theories, the awareness of my body in its bulk and weight does not impede the accomplishing of my aims. This belly touching my knee, this extra part of me that gives me a joyful surprise when I move through a tight place, calls me back to the matter of my body even as I move about accomplishing my aims. Pregnant consciousness is animated by a double intentionality: my subjectivity splits between awareness of myself as body and awareness of my aims and projects.[37]

Focusing on these experiences, Young held, could ground liberating alternatives to the medicalization of women's bodies, which inscribes them with the "implicit male bias in medicine's conception of health." Western medicine, taking the young-adult male as its model, "assumes that the normal healthy body is unchanging," which defines experiences like menstruation, pregnancy, and menopause as "conditions" subject to medical intervention. By identifying healthy women's bodies as medical problems, women are alienated from themselves and instructed to distrust their immediate bodily knowledge. For instance, while "discomforts . . . such as nausea, flatulence, and shortness of breath can happen in the healthiest of women . . . discussions of the fragility of pregnancy may lead her to define such experience as signs of weakness."[38] Phenomenology provided a competing framework that, Young hoped, could help women recover an authentic relationship to their bodies.

Young's efforts to recover a positive understanding of women's experience were not restricted to her work on embodiment. In "House and Home: Feminist Variations on a Theme," Young explored the experience and meaning of domesticity for women. If homemaking is merely "the confinement of women for the sake of nourishing male projects," she wrote, "then feminists have good reason to reject home as a value." However, while affirming that enforced domesticity "deprives women of support for their own identity and projects," Young maintained that "the idea of home also carries critical liberating potential because it expresses uniquely human values."[39] Drawing critically from Heidegger's account of "dwelling" as "man's mode of being," Young rejected Heidegger's choice to emphasize aspects of "construction" over those of "cultivation" or "preservation." For Heidegger, she wrote, construction is "the heroic moment of place" in which, projecting into the future, "man establishes a world and his place in the world."[40] Construction is also, Young noted, the aspect of dwelling from which women are most often excluded. Thus, the privilege Heidegger seemed to grant construction reflects a male viewpoint and fails to apprehend that "human meanings enacted in the historicality of human existence depend as much on the projection of a past as of a future." The work of homemaking has a distinct temporality, grounded in the past. It involves organizing the "objects, artifacts, rituals, and practices that configure who we are in our particularity," teaching children "stories, practices, and celebrations that keep the particular meanings alive," and continually rearranging and reinterpreting the fluid world of the home. In contrast to construction, "the activities of preservation"—where women traditionally exercise authority—provide "some enclosing fabric to this ever-changing subject by knitting together today and yesterday, integrating the new events and relationships into the narrative of a life, the biography of a person, a family, a people."[41] The work of preservation could, of course, be mundane and conservative. Moreover, the gendered division of labor that disproportionately assigns the uncompensated work of caring and nurturing to women is purely exploitative. Nevertheless, Young argued, women could recover the positive value of their experiences in the home, looking to phenomenology to affirm that "much of typically women's work . . . is at least as fundamentally world-making and meaning-giving as typically men's work."[42]

In 1990, Young left Worcester Polytechnic Institute for the University of Pittsburgh, where she was elevated to the rank of full professor in 1993. However, her appointment was in Pittsburgh's School of Public and International Affairs rather than its Philosophy Department, and her subsequent position at the University of Chicago would be in its Department of Political Science. Thus, as would be the case for an increasing number of Americans in the Continental tradition, Young obtained professional rewards for philosophical achievement by stepping outside the realm of professional philosophy. However, just as Young's political commitments informed her phenomenological writings, her political philosophy drew from her phenomenological studies of embodied experience and identity, displaying a phenomenological suspicion of theoretical artifice that subordinated actual human experience. In particular, against an American political tradition defined by an ideal of civic impartiality, the embrace of meritocratic hierarchies within a melting-pot culture, and a vision of liberty modeled on the image of formally unfettered markets, Young insisted that justice could not be obtained under a regime of formal individual equality that did not recognize the legitimacy of political rights grounded in group history and culture.

Young's most significant political work, *Justice and the Politics of Difference* (1990), is a critique of "positivism and reductionism in political theory," which assails the positivistic tendency to "[assume] as given institutional structures that ought to be brought under normative evaluation" and the reductionist tendency "to reduce political subjects to a unity and to value commonness or sameness over specificity and difference." Young's foil was John Rawls, whose *Theory of Justice* was uniquely influential among works of postwar American philosophy. Rawls argued that legitimate uses of political authority are those that would win unanimous consent from individuals in a hypothetical "original position": deprived of any knowledge about the role they would take in society. In this situation, Rawls asserted, a reasonable person would hedge by supporting policies that maximize the minimum allotment of "primary social goods" (e.g., liberties, rights, opportunities, and wealth) that any individual might receive. Subtly modifying the criterion of Pareto efficiency used by many economists, Rawls enunciated this strategy as the "difference principle," which permits unequal distributions of primary goods only if doing so provides a net benefit to the least-advantaged members of society.[43]

It is difficult to overstate the influence of Rawls's work on late twentieth-century political philosophy and liberal politics. Like its conservative counterpart, public choice theory, *A Theory of Justice* claimed to secure nonideological objectivity by obtaining a set of normative criteria for fairness solely from the premise that agents will pursue rational self-interest. In providing purportedly objective grounds for redistributive policies within a capitalist framework, Rawls broke the monopoly of laissez-faire intellectuals over claims of value neutrality, deducing an approximation of Great Society liberalism from first principles.[44] However, Young noted, from the phenomenologist's stance, the kind of objectivity that Rawls achieved is "illusory," since "there is nothing but what is, the given, the situated interest in justice, from which to start."[45] Moreover, the price of this illusory objectivity—restricting the domain of political theory to "laws, policies, the large-scale distribution social goods, [and] countable qualities like votes and taxes"—was the exclusion of lived experiences such as "bodily reactions, comportments and feelings." Social phenomena like racism, sexism, ageism, and homophobia are thus reduced to their formal elements. If informal norms, implicit structures, and unconscious biases of the dominant culture produce the cultural devaluation, social marginalization, and abjection of oppressed groups, this falls outside the scope of political judgment. When "normative philosophy ignores these aspects of oppression enacted in practical consciousness and the unconscious," Young reproached, "it contributes not only little to ending oppression, but also something to the silencing of the oppressed."[46]

Beyond her phenomenological commitments, it is apparent that Young's political philosophy was rooted in her personal experiences with bureaucratic state power. Welfare capitalist practices, she wrote, "define policy as the province of experts, and confine conflict to bargaining among interest groups about the distribution of social benefits." State efforts to rationalize the distribution of opportunities and assets under capitalism during the twentieth century had empowered elite policy makers while "depoliticizing the process of public policy formation."[47] *Justice and the Politics of Difference* was, thus, a rebuke of the limits that technocratic rationalization and redistributionist political theory place on the liberal imagination. Justice, Young argued, cannot be reduced to the distribution of goods:

> Such a model implicitly assumes that individuals or other agents lie as nodes, points in the social field, among whom larger or smaller bundles of social goods are assigned. The individuals are externally related to the goods they

possess, and their only relation to one another that matters from the point of view of the paradigm is a comparison of the amount of goods they possess. The distributive paradigm thus implicitly assumes social atomism, inasmuch as there is no internal relation among persons in society relevant to considerations of justice.[48]

Submission to a distributionist paradigm, Young argued, "reifies aspects of social life that are better understood as a function of rules and relations than as things."[49] A thicker concept of justice would not be exhausted by the equitable distribution of goods *within* an institutional context. Rather than assume the validity of prevailing social and cultural structures, it would consider "what people are doing, according to what institutionalized rules, how their doings and havings are structured by institutionalized relations that constitute their positions, and how the combined effect of their doings has recursive effects on their lives."[50]

Many important social questions, Young argued, cannot be adequately addressed under a strictly distributionist paradigm because they involve both distributive and nondistributive elements. For instance, the division of labor produced professional hierarchies of prestige, power, autonomy, and respect that evaded scrutiny when analysis is restricted to the permissibility or impermissibility of material inequalities:

> As a distributive issue, division of labor refers to how pregiven occupations, jobs, or tasks are allocated among individuals or groups. As a nondistributive issue, on the other hand, division of labor concerns the definition of the occupations themselves. Division of labor as an institutional structure involves the range of tasks performed in a given position, the definition of the nature, meaning, and value of those tasks, and the relations of cooperation, conflict, and authority among positions.[51]

To reorient political philosophy toward the lived phenomenon of social experience, Young proposed a theory of justice rooted in analysis of "domination" and "oppression." Structures of domination ("phenomena which exclude people from participating in determining their actions or the conditions of their actions") and oppression (processes that prevent people from developing and exercising capacities to learn, create, communicate, play, feel, and be heard) are nonreducibly implicated in both the collective form of life under a sociocultural regime and relations between different social groups within it. Unlike the distributive paradigm, therefore,

Young's theory of justice also requires a social ontology with a domain that is not restricted to individual actors.[52]

Class relations, for example, cannot be subsumed under an atomistic distribution paradigm because class is a social formation that is nonindividualizable. It exists in action, through structures and institutions that hierarchically organize social relations and perpetuate class difference. Similarly, gendered oppression is not merely an expression of uneven distribution of assets and opportunities between men and women. It involves a cultural formation of expectations about childrearing, intimacy, and household labor that do not enter into a theory of justice if the family is taken as the basic unit to which goods are distributed.[53] Indeed, Young held, the attempt to analyze nonmaterial goods such as "opportunity," "rights," and "respect" under a distribution paradigm mistakes social relationships for things. These concepts refer to constraints and "condition[s] of enablement" that are given through "the rules and practices that govern one's action, the way other people treat one in the context of specific social relations, and the broader structural possibilities produced by the confluence of a multitude of actions and practices."[54] They are, in sum, part of the human "world," which we grasp holistically, exactly as it is given, and which cannot be reduced to a set of rules or entities.

Young enumerated five aspects of oppression: exploitation, marginalization, powerlessness, cultural imperialism, and violence. "Distributive injustices may contribute to or result from these forms of oppression," she explained, "but none is reducible to distribution and all involve social structures and relations beyond distribution." Neither could these categories be reduced to relations between individuals; they implicate structures that organize a society not on the basis of its members' individuality, but according to those members' situation within a network of historically constituted identities and roles. "The oppression of violence," for instance, "consists not only in direct victimization, but in the daily knowledge shared by all members of oppressed groups that they are liable to violation, solely on account of their group identity."[55] Insofar as relatively stable categories are the basis of social belonging, Young argued, "group meanings partially constitute people's identities in terms of the cultural forms, social situation, and history that group members know as theirs." Although a person's characteristics or a group's contours might change over time, it is not possible to precipitate an autonomous subject out of this solution. "Group affinity," Young wrote, "has the character of what Martin Heidegger calls 'thrownness': one *finds oneself* as a member of a group, which one experiences as always already having been." Insofar as groups are subject to oppression, their members must struggle against a received identity, inscribed in dominant culture, that predetermines them as abject. Nevertheless, Young rejected the conclusion that group identity was necessarily invidious, holding instead that "group differentiation is both an inevitable and a desirable aspect of modern social processes."[56]

To theorize justice while remaining faithful to the phenomenology of social life, philosophy cannot evade the problem of group conflict by limiting the domain of political theory to the rights and liberties of abstract, identity-less individuals, among whom difference can only be unjust. Rather, Young insisted, "oppressed groups have distinct cultures, experiences, and perspectives on social life with humanly positive meaning." The right to "full participation in social life" cannot be conditioned on a group's submission to dominant cultural norms.[57] Rejecting cultural imperialism requires the creation of a public in which difference is affirmed and protected. For a model, Young looked to her childhood refuge of the city:

> In the city persons and groups interact within spaces and institutions they all experience themselves as belonging to, but without those interactions dissolving into unity or commonness. City life is composed of clusters of people with affinities—families, social group networks, voluntary associations, neighborhood networks, a vast array of small "communities." City dwellers frequently venture beyond such familiar enclaves, however to the more open public of politics, commerce, and festival, where strangers meet and interact. City dwelling situates one's own identity and activity in relation to a horizon of a vast variety of other activity, and the awareness that this is unknown, unfamiliar activity affects the condition of one's own.

Thus, while rejecting the atomistic individualism of liberal capitalism, Young also denied the communitarian vision of a unified social whole, advocating an "unrealized ideal" of city life as the "openness to unassimilated otherness" and "being together of strangers."[58]

Taking group identity as a fundamental element of political theory was a novel intervention. Liberal political theorists conventionally understood social groups either as aggregates (sets of persons sharing some characteristic or characteristics) or associations (formal institutions with defined membership). In both cases, the individual subject was given ontological priority over their group identity, underpinning an assimilationist logic that regards social identity skeptically as an obstacle to a universal public and ideal of equality. However, as has been discussed, Young held that neither model of group membership could support the "fluid and often shifting, but nevertheless real" experience of social identities.[59] Since neither relations between different groups nor the relationship between a group and its members could be reduced to an expression of individual preferences, a political theory concerned with oppression must accept that social identities provide legitimate ground for group-specific protections and privileges. Still, Young maintained, political efforts to secure space for group difference would regress into bargaining over distributive benefits without genuinely pluralistic participatory democracy. The ethos of pluralistic democracy, therefore, had to be pervasive, providing "mechanisms for the effective recognition and representation of the distinct voices and perspectives of its constituent groups that are oppressed or disadvantaged," both in government and the institutions through which groups organize.[60]

* * *

Iris Marion Young's life and career were cut tragically short by cancer in 2006. Fifteen years later, her work appears remarkably prescient, reaching the heart of debates about identity, equality, and difference that consume American culture and politics. Disputes around the intersection of bodies, identities, and rights remain contentious. The increasing visibility of transgender persons in American life has evoked backlash from communities and legislatures. Men's capacious appropriation of space on public transportation has become a cultural motif with political ramifications. Rawlsian liberalism, while still dominant in mainstream American politics, is besieged by competing claims for social justice. While Young was not alone in addressing these problems, the clarity with which she perceived them and her efforts to ground their analysis in a rigorous methodology makes her work an invaluable resource and illustrates the foresight of phenomenological critique.

6

Flanking Maneuvers

There are two Establishments in American philosophy nowadays, a Major, or
so-to-speak Establishment Establishment, which is firmly oriented to the
Anglo-American, basically empiricist, tradition, and a minor, so-to-speak Anti-
Establishment Establishment, engaged in reporting, developing, interpreting
and assimilating twentieth century continental, that is, European, thought.
—Marjorie Glicksman Grene

During the period of 1940 to 1960, phenomenologists in the United States
struggled to reestablish Husserl's enterprise on American shores. While the
tactics they employed included the creation of new institutions in which
their movement could play a principal role, their strategic objective was
the integration of phenomenology into the American mainstream. Beginning in the 1960s, however, many American philosophers working under
the rubric of Continental philosophy adopted a new strategy, creating a
parallel establishment that provided professional alternatives to the discipline's mainstream institutions. Over the next two decades, the practice
of Continental philosophy in the United States both expanded and transformed as this new antiestablishment facilitated the tradition's growth,
Continental outposts at Yale and the New School collapsed, and Continental ideas gained a foothold as "theory" in a wide variety of extraphilosophical disciplinary contexts.

Founded in 1962, the Society for Phenomenology and Existential Philosophy, or SPEP, was the first philosophical association to organize along
lines coincident with the boundaries of Continental philosophy.[1] The
principal architects of SPEP were John Wild and William Earle, the latter
having lured the former to Northwestern to organize a department that
emphasized phenomenology and existentialism as its core strength.[2] Wild's
departure from Harvard was a turning point in twentieth-century American philosophy for two reasons: First, since the beginning of the twentieth century, no other philosopher had left a tenured position at Harvard

for another American university. Wild's exit presaged the closing of an era that had lasted almost a century, during which Harvard's preeminence in American philosophy went uncontested. Second, it signaled a strategic shift for American phenomenologists, many of whom largely abandoned their campaign to gain a foothold in American philosophy's mainstream.

The most important exceptions to this trend were those Wild left behind at Harvard. This second generation of Harvard phenomenologists included Dagfinn Føllesdal, Hubert Dreyfus, Samuel Todes, Charles Parsons, and Stanley Cavell. The first group of Harvard students to become devotees of Husserl and Heidegger—those who encountered them personally before the outbreak of World War II—had returned to the United States, hoping to plant the seed of phenomenological thought in American soil. While they worked to adapt phenomenology to America's intellectual climate, they remained committed to programs like Husserl's "rigorous science" or Heidegger's *Destruktion* in which phenomenology was a *foundational* methodology. Although this did not inhibit them from engaging productively with members of other philosophical traditions, their objective was the development of phenomenological discourse. The second generation, by contrast, attempted to graft phenomenology onto a branch of America's native flora. Their work drew on the phenomenological tradition to contribute to Anglo-American philosophical discourse, arguing that thinkers like Husserl, Heidegger, and Merleau-Ponty had important insights on problems within the analytic tradition. With Føllesdal at Stanford, Dreyfus at Berkeley, and Føllesdal's protégés David Woodruff Smith at UC Irvine and Ronald McIntyre at California State University, Northridge, a new base of phenomenological activities emerged in California. The phenomenological paradigm introduced by the second generation of Harvard phenomenologists, characterized by its engagement with analytic philosophy and identification of Husserl's *noema* with linguistic meaning, became known as "West Coast Phenomenology."[3]

The West Coast phenomenologists enjoyed some success in engaging analytic philosophers and drawing their attention to phenomenological ideas through events such as the 1980 NEH Summer Institute on "Phenomenology and Existentialism: Continental and Analytic Perspectives on Intentionality," organized by Dreyfus and John Haugeland at UC Berkeley.[4] Notably, John Searle, one of the most influential analytic philosophers of the postwar era, published his own work on intentionality in 1983, which used the framework to explore the relation between speech acts and mental states as well as topics such as the mind-body problem.[5] More recently, Michael Dummett's *Origins of Analytic Philosophy* (1996) argued that

Husserl and Frege would have appeared "remarkably close in orientation, despite some divergence of interests" to a German student in 1903. However, in contrast to Føllesdal, Dummett argued that a linguistic noema cannot be generalized to encompass the full noemata of acts like perception. This, he held, made the "linguistic turn" impossible for Husserl, laying the groundwork for a schism between phenomenologists and analysts.[6]

While second-generation Harvard phenomenologists like Dreyfus and Føllesdal continued a program of engagement with analytic thought into the late twentieth century, most within the phenomenological movement would be content to avoid it, flanking the dominant analytic camp by creating and occupying alternative spaces for the practice of Continental philosophy.[7] This was, of course, not the first attempt to build new institutions focused on contemporary European philosophy. However, it was fundamentally different than previous efforts. Philosophers at the New School had been united by the necessity of self-reliance, and *PPR* had served as a conduit for engagement between different philosophical schools. Wild, by contrast, believed that mainstream American philosophy had become disconnected from its ground in lived existence; he sought space for a program defined by its opposition to the Anglo-American mainstream. Unsurprisingly, the emerging framework of its "other," Continental philosophy, was easily mapped onto this new institutional formation.

Wild, who had begun discussing plans for a society dedicated to contemporary European philosophy while still at Harvard, became its central figure at Northwestern.[8] The first organizational meeting for the group that became SPEP took place in 1961. Five philosophers were involved: John Wild, William Earle, and James Edie from Northwestern, George Schrader from Yale, and Calvin Schrag, who was then an assistant professor at Purdue.[9] Its creators conceived of SPEP as an alternative to the APA, which offered few slots on the program of its annual meetings to Continental philosophers. As Robert Scharff recalled, their hopes for phenomenology in America hinged on the prospect of establishing "good, continentally oriented graduate programs at good schools, with the intention of making and sustaining at these centers a decidedly pluralistic faculty." SPEP was not, however, intended as a replacement for the APA. It would not host job interviews, and activities related to recruitment were discouraged. Annual meetings of SPEP would be devoted to cultivating philosophical dialogue and fostering connections within the far-flung community of American phenomenologists.[10]

The fledgling society's early activities were marked by their informality. Philosophers invited to SPEP's first conference were simply those known by its founders to have interest in the field. Mimeographed newsletters announcing SPEP's subsequent meetings were mailed out to a growing list of contacts and sent to any American universities that supported graduate programs in philosophy.[11] According to Edward Casey, who attended the first annual meeting of SPEP as a graduate student, the defining feature of SPEP was the social "proximity" its informal atmosphere produced, fostering "an intense form of intersubjectivity" that engendered "reciprocity" between philosophers.[12] For American Continentalists, accustomed to intellectual isolation, SPEP provided the rare opportunity for intellectual community:

> For the less and the more seasoned alike, SPEP became an event to look forward to year after year, for it provided a unique venue, at once timely and necessary, for the exchange of ideas that were percolating up in Continental philosophy. Other than SPEP, there was no other public space in which to be recognized and heard.[13]

At the same time, Scharff recalls, while SPEP had been "founded in dissent—as a living objection to the oppressive philosophical atmosphere and attitude of the Anglo-American mainstream," its members did not consider themselves as "a group of rebels or critics." Rather, SPEP was conceived as a "society in which anyone whose approach to philosophical issues was in some sense existential and phenomenological would be welcome." Indeed, early meetings included papers from analytically inclined philosophers such as Wilfrid Sellars, John Searle, Bas van Fraassen, and Jaakko Hintikka.[14]

Meetings of SPEP also allowed young philosophers to encounter Continental thought in a environment where it was treated as serious philosophy rather than an eccentric Parisian fad. David Carr described his first experience of SPEP in 1964 as a dive into the unknown:

> We thought of phenomenology, and especially existentialism, as rather anti-establishment currents, and the idea of an academic conference devoted to them seemed incongruous. I remember Chip Dallery wondering if there would be an "existentialist smoker." Some of you may find this hard to believe, but "smoker" was the name given to the evening receptions at conferences like the American Philosophical Association (APA) in those days. The word perfectly encapsulated the hugely male-dominated, tweed-jacketed, pipe-smoking atmosphere of the era. We wondered: Would there

be black sweaters and black berets instead of tweeds and Gauloises instead of pipes?

Indeed, he reflected, "SPEP did seem to be made up of oddballs and outsiders."[15] However, graduate students "slowly got a sense of the great learning and intellectual integrity of our elders and also eventually picked up the excitement of being an embattled minority struggling for survival and recognition." At SPEP, these elder Continentalists became "secondary mentors" for the group's younger participants: "figures who are not in one's own department or university but who have a powerful mark on one's thinking and way of proceeding in the profession."[16]

While SPEP was an important haven to some of American philosophy's outcasts, it was not immune from other prejudices. Despite the prominence of women such as Edith Stein and Simone de Beauvoir in the Continental tradition, SPEP remained for years assiduously uninterested in gender as either a philosophical subject or a professional concern. As Nancy Fraser recalled, "SPEP's brand of phenomenology and existential philosophy was, in a word, depoliticized and patriarchal."[17] The organization's first session on de Beauvoir was not held until 1978, and its Committee on the Status of Women was not formed until 1984.[18] At least in part, these absences reflected SPEP's undemocratic structure, which gave control of its program to unelected directors and eschewed practices such as blind review of proposals. Thus, not unlike the discipline as a whole, the primary American organization for Continental philosophers developed its own hierarchies, which were hostile to groups that challenged its orthodoxies. As Fraser remarked, it was "at best an old boys' network, at worst a private fiefdom."[19]

As Continental philosophers such as Julia Kristeva, Luce Irigaray, and Judith Butler gained prominence in the 1980s, a combination of philosophical interest and activism made feminist philosophy impossible to ignore.[20] Tensions reached a peak in 1986 when a group of dissidents led by Nancy Fraser, Iris Marion Young, and William McBride campaigned for the society's democratization, introducing a resolution at its annual business meeting calling for an elected leadership with a requirement that at least one of SPEP's two codirectors be a woman.[21] Nancy Holland recalled the isolated but vital community of women she found during her early days at SPEP, stating, "For me, SPEP has always been about the women." Many of them committed to feminist praxis as well as theory, these women led the campaign to reform SPEP, opening its program not only to feminist philosophy, but also fields such as African American and LGBTQ philosophy. Later generations would experience SPEP differently as reformers' labors bore fruit in the diversification of SPEP's membership and the society's growing emphasis on a wide range of critical, literary, poststructuralist, and postmodern theory.[22] These methods were rooted in phenomenological and existentialist traditions, but had developed their own canons of foundational texts, which sometimes posed an obstacle to mutual comprehension with conventional phenomenologists. However, as Continental philosophy became both increasingly diverse and increasingly fragmented, SPEP continued to function, at times uneasily, as an overarching organization for work in the field.

As phenomenology inspired a growing range of work in diverse academic disciplines, new groups formed or broke away from SPEP to organize activities around particular disciplinary, methodological, or topical niches within the phenomenological family. For instance, the sociologist George Psathas led the creation of the Society for Phenomenology and the Human Sciences (SPHS) in 1981 as a splinter group of SPEP. SPHS would provide space for philosophers to engage with anthropologists, sociologists, psychologists, and political scientists to discuss work in areas such as ethnomethodology, critical theory, and poststructuralism.[23] SPEP also inspired Herbert Spiegelberg's experimental series of phenomenological workshops, which were held in 1965, 1966, 1967, 1969, and 1972. As Psathas recalled, the idea for the workshops originated in Spiegelberg's discussions of phenomenological pedagogy with John Wild and William Earle during SPEP's first meeting. For Spiegelberg, they were an attempt to realize Husserl's vision of a genuinely intersubjective συμφιλοσοφειν, philosophizing together. Over the course of two weeks, Spiegelberg guided participants in cooperative phenomenologizing, asking them to reflect on experiences such as looking at Claude Monet's paintings, viewing the closed-eye visual field, and moving through air. Spiegelberg organized a total of five workshops with funding from such unlikely sources as the National Science Foundation and the Monsanto Corporation.[24] "I want to thank you for arousing me to the kind of questioning in which I am currently engaged," wrote an attendee of Spiegelberg's third workshop. "No, I do not agree with you, but I want you to know that I am convinced that my disagreement has been most important for my intellectual development."[25]

Other phenomenological institutions developed organically in parallel with SPEP, such as the Lexington Conferences organized by the psychiatrist Erwin Straus to promote phenomenological discussions of humanistic approaches to psychology and psychiatry.[26] The emergence of these groups reflected both the growing momentum of the American phenomenological movement and its internal divisions. For instance, the antecedents of the Heidegger Circle first convened at Drew University in 1964. The circle was formally established at Penn State University in 1967, eventually becoming an affiliate of SPEP. In 1969, approximately thirty philosophers assembled for the first meeting of the Husserl Circle, created because its founder perceived "a need to offer an alternative to the flood of Heideggerian efforts to appropriate the name of phenomenology and philosophy." Reflective of their fear that Husserl's phenomenology had been co-opted and distorted, joining the circle required the sponsorship of one of its members. Not to be left out, members of the Merleau-Ponty Circle organized their first meeting at the University of Akron in 1976.[27]

While the foundation of societies, conferences, and circles provided a vital organizational link for the growing number of American Continental philosophers, two of America's most important institutions of phenomenological education, the Philosophy Department of Yale and the Graduate Faculty of the New School, entered periods of crisis in the 1970s. Beyond the practical effects of their collapse, these affairs held considerable symbolic significance. To philosophers in the analytic mainstream, they illustrated the infeasibility of pluralistic organization and the mediocrity of Continental institutions. To those outside the mainstream, they confirmed the conviction that analytic philosophers were willing to use institutional power to crush dissent and destroy the careers of their ideological foes. On both sides, however, these events have been misunderstood, at least in part.

During the 1960s and 1970s, Yale attempted to sustain a balance between analytic and Continental traditions within its philosophy department, seeking preeminence in both fields. These efforts failed. In subsequent decades, Yale became a metonym for the tension between these movements and, as its standing in the profession plummeted, shorthand for the folly of striving for departmental balance. However, this interpretation is misleading, neglecting the complex mixture of difficult personalities and unsustainable institutional practices that undermined Yale's Philosophy Department. Although differences in philosophical approach could provide occasion for tensions to erupt, Yale's primary fault line was metaphilosophical, falling between philosophers who prioritized a broad representation of topics and methods and those who believed appointments should be based, first and foremost, on an "objective" determination of merit and ability, signified by a candidate's reputation and success within the elite institutions of American philosophy.

Between 1957 and 1979, Yale's Philosophy Department hired forty-three individuals at the rank of assistant professor. Among them, only two—Karsten Harries and Richmond Thomason—were granted tenure by Yale.[28] This was, in and of itself, an unstable situation that signified a major failure of departmental governance. However, dysfunction was deeply rooted in the department's culture. "I have gained some appreciation of what it must be like being the Premier of Italy or the Mayor of New York," wrote Robert Fogelin to Yale's president, Kingman Brewster, after resigning as department chairman in 1972. "Beyond this, I do not think that I have accomplished much of permanent value. The antagonisms in the Department run deep, originating in events prior to my coming to Yale."[29] After surveying junior faculty for opinions on Fogelin's replacement, the historian Howard Lamar reported they "felt no great confidence in any senior man."[30]

Tensions in Yale's Philosophy Department had been high since 1965, when the decision to deny tenure to Richard Bernstein threw the university into turmoil. Bernstein was a popular teacher and broad-minded philosopher who drew on diverse intellectual sources, including American pragmatism, Continental philosophy, and the analytic works of Wittgenstein. Although he was prolific as an editor of both collected volumes and the journal *Review of Metaphysics*, however, Bernstein came up for tenure without having published a major work of his own scholarship. The Philosophy Department unanimously recommended Bernstein's promotion, but it was rebuffed by the Yale Appointments Committee. This decision prompted a flurry of agitation, including a meeting of more than four hundred students around Yale's Beinecke Library, a three-day vigil outside the university administration building, and the creation of the group STOPPP (Students to Oppose Publish Perish Pressure).[31] These protests were treated as major news, even earning coverage in the *New York Times*, and won a new hearing of Bernstein's case.[32] However, under reconsideration, the committee insisted that the Philosophy Department testify to their confidence that "promotion to professorship within a period of five years will be justified by his continuing scholarly achievement." Under this standard, the department reversed its decision, voting against Bernstein. This vote, however, was not unanimous and sparked bitter recriminations. The philosopher of science Norwood Russell Hanson told the *New York Times* and *Yale Daily News* that his initial support of Bernstein had been based on conversations and student appraisals, but a closer inspection of Bernstein's work led him to conclude he was "distinctly undistinguished." Paul Weiss, who supported Bernstein, responded that Hanson was unqualified to judge work in the pragmatist tradition and implied that divisions between humanistic and analytic philosophers affected Hanson's judgment.[33]

Compounding these difficulties, Yale struggled to retain talented analytic philosophers. This contributed to a perception, among its peers and some members of its own faculty both, that Yale was out of touch with the main thread of postwar American philosophy. Yale lost the eminent positivist Carl Hempel to Princeton in 1955 and the promising young analyst Arthur Pap to kidney disease in 1959. Then the logicians Nuel Belnap and Alan Anderson left Yale in 1963 and 1965 amid cluster of analytic hires by the University of Pittsburgh, which had committed to making its Philosophy Department a leader in the field.[34] Norwood Russell Hanson died in a 1967 plane crash, and the logician Richmond Thomason, who had received tenure at Yale in 1971, accompanied his wife, Sarah Thomason, to Pittsburgh, where she had an appointment in linguistics.[35] Additionally, the talented assistant professors Bas van Fraassen and Robert Stalnaker left Yale for positions at the University of Toronto and the University of Illinois. Despite these impediments and growing turmoil among senior faculty, Yale's annual report in 1970 reiterated its commitment to balance. In his view, Fogelin explained, this meant a department "composed in about equal measure of tenured members working in contemporary Continental philosophy, members dealing with issues in contemporary Anglo-American philosophy, and, finally, those carrying out research in the historical fields of philosophy."[36]

In 1973, Yale hired Ruth Barcan Marcus, expanding the ranks of its tenured faculty to nine full professors. With the retirement of John Findlay, the department's senior ranks now included two specialists in analytic philosophy, Marcus and Fogelin, as well as the broad-minded logician Frederic Fitch and two specialists in Continental philosophy, Karsten Harries and George Schrader. As a woman who achieved distinction in one of the most male-dominated subfields of a male-dominated discipline, Marcus had been tempered by experience: self-confident, uncowed, and merciless to those she believed were undeserving. She was, in the recollection of her friend Bruce Kuklick, "one of the most formidable people and intellects I have met . . . totally committed to intellectual excellence as she defined it; and also to moral principles as she defined them." As a result, "She did not suffer people whom she perceived to be fools gladly."[37]

The first major issue of departmental governance Marcus confronted at Yale was the tenure case of David Carr, a Yale-educated specialist in the philosophy of history who had recently completed the manuscript of his first major work, *Phenomenology and the Problem of History* (1974).[38] Carr's promotion was recommended by Yale's Philosophy Department by a vote of 6–2 with one abstention and was subsequently approved by the Senior Appointments Committee by a vote of 7–0 with one abstention. However, tenure decisions at Yale were subject to final approval by a majority vote of the Joint Board of Permanent Officers of the Faculty of Arts and Sciences. This board convened at regular intervals to consider a slate of recommendations for appointments or promotions to tenured positions. All full professors in the Faculty of Arts and Sciences were eligible, but not required, to attend and vote in meetings of the joint board. Normally, the *Yale Daily News* explained, the joint board accepted "all recommendations" from a candidate's department and the Appointments Committee. However, when it met to consider Carr, Marcus delivered a lengthy speech to the Permanent Officers, opposing her department's recommendation. Breaking with tradition, eighteen voted against Carr and ten abstained. Although a plurality of twenty-five voters supported Carr, with fifty-three members in attendance, he fell two votes shy of a majority and promotion was denied.[39]

Although Marcus offered a variety of arguments against Carr's promotion, her speech to the Joint Board focused on two claims. First, Marcus argued that senior appointments in Yale's Philosophy Department should be reserved for thinkers who had developed "an original philosophical voice." Carr's scholarship, she asserted, merely recapitulated Husserl, and "beyond the illumination it might bring to some of the discontinuities and impasses in phases of Husserl's thought," it provided no evidence of an "independent and vigorous philosopher at work."[40] John Smith, who was among those in the Philosophy Department supporting Carr's appointment, found this claim galling. Responding to Marcus in a letter to Yale's Dean Horace Taft, Smith claimed that Carr's outside evaluators contradicted this testimony, writing that it was the "height of irony that a person who has no competence in the field should be able to overturn the judgement of those who do."[41] Indeed, although Marcus claimed some familiarity with Continental philosophy, gained during her tenure at Northwestern, her assessment of Carr did not appreciate that the fragmentary and protean character of Husserl's later writings made reconstructing his work on history, the lifeworld, and intersubjectivity as systematic philosophy a task that required significant independent insight.

Marcus's other argument was that Karsten Harries and George Schrader already provided sufficient representation of Continental philosophy at Yale. Senior appointments, she argued, should be used to fill curricular gaps in areas such as political philosophy or the philosophy of science. This position was superficially at odds with her opening remarks to the joint board, which asserted that the fight over Carr was not "a struggle between competing philosophical traditions, i.e.[,] Anglo-American Analytic versus Continental Non-analytic." However, Marcus supported her assessment of departmental needs with an empirical evaluation of dissertation subjects. Carr's supporters objected to the range of Marcus's dataset, which included years prior to Yale's efforts to emphasize Continental philosophy. Data from recent years, they argued, demonstrated the need for a third appointment in the field.[42]

All sides viewed the matter of Carr's promotion as a decision with implications beyond its immediate effects. For Marcus, at issue was whether Yale would continue to uphold the professional standards of a leading institution. Marcus wrote to Yale's President Brewster that "an appointment as mediocre and unimaginative as Carr is part of a larger dreary picture" and to the Executive Committee that "if the Carr appointment is finally approved then future agreement in the department will at best be a compromise with mediocrity."[43] Smith feared that Marcus's actions had established a dangerous precedent. He noted that Carr was the only tenure candidate from the Division of Humanities under consideration during that meeting of the joint board. Thus, most who attended the meeting were scientists, "not accustomed, as those in the Humanities are, to dealing with the brute fact of ideological differences." In the future, he feared, factions would use the joint board as a veto on departmental decisions to which they objected. Carr's supporters were convinced that Marcus was committed overturning the department's traditional commitment to balance. As Smith wrote to Dean Taft, "Although Mrs. Marcus cleverly slid over the point, the fact is that her underlying objection is ideological. . . . She simply does not believe in this area of philosophy."[44] Previous events had, indeed, bred mistrust of Carr's opponents. At the beginning of Carr's tenure review, Marcus and Robert Fogelin had sent letters to the director of the Humanities Division, Howard Lamar, in which one or both had petitioned that they be allowed to choose Carr's outside readers. This was revealed when Lamar wrote to Karsten Harries, who was serving as the department's chairman, that he would not object to this arrangement but thought the phenomenologist Louis Dupré was better qualified to identify experts in his field.[45] Harries replied incredulously: "I don't know whether anyone has seriously suggested to let Fogelin and Marcus pick outside readers. We all know how easy it is to call on readers who can be counted on to make their decision in one way or another."[46]

The wound that the Carr affair left on Yale's Philosophy Department was severe but not immediately fatal. President Brewster reaffirmed his commitment to supporting a "diversity of traditions and perspectives in the study of Philosophy" at Yale. The Philosophy Department would be allowed to make two senior hires in the coming year, and Brewster stipulated that one be in the field of modern Continental philosophy, writing: "This seems to us essential if the diversity first mentioned is to be sustained."[47] The appointments of Harry Frankurt, an analytic philosopher, and Maurice Natanson, a phenomenologist, would be approved by the department, both by unanimous votes. However, in the Carr affair's aftermath, Harries resigned as chairman, and the department's 1976 annual report declared that "junior faculty morale [was] at a low ebb."[48] Marcus had also been wounded in the conflict. She wrote to Harries in 1975, "I should say at the outset that my first two years here were among the most painful and unproductive of my entire career." In particular, Marcus wrote, she was shocked that members of the department had used the *Yale Daily News* to publicly advocate for Carr and "berate those of us who disagreed." As a result, she claimed, her students had become "disaffected" and even hostile, hindering effective instruction. Marcus, for her part, assiduously refused the student paper's requests for comments on the affair. Although she admitted to no mistakes, Marcus's letter did end on a conciliatory note. "But it does seem to me," she wrote, "that our differences can be settled in rational and professional ways. At least it is worth a try."[49]

Whether or not such attempts were made, the department was headed for disaster. The ensuing conflict was not a simple result of or reaction to the Carr affair. However, the fight exacerbated problems of departmental administration that predated it and left the senior faculty with few resources and little will to mitigate future conflict. As a 1976 report to President Brewster conveyed, the consequences of Yale's failure to advance junior faculty was becoming apparent: "Already 'up-tight' with the assumption that they will not receive tenure here . . . junior faculty additionally bears a heavy teaching load. Their commitment to teaching here is lessened by their need to establish credentials for the eventual move beyond Yale."[50] The perception that junior positions in philosophy at Yale were dead-end jobs also hampered its ability to attract top tier junior candidates. Marcus reported in 1977: "Since I have been at Yale, no junior candidate who has had competing offers from remotely comparable institutions has accepted ours."[51] In the fifteen years following the Carr affair, Yale's Philosophy Department failed to award tenure to a single member of its junior faculty. At the same time, tensions among Yale's senior faculty did not abate, manifesting as personal rancor that eschewed ideological lines. When asked by the *Chronicle of Higher Education* to explain his department's dysfunction, Harry Frankfurt is reported to have replied: "demonic possession." Hemorrhaging talent amid the infighting, Yale's standing within the profession and national rankings plummeted. Citing the "level of discord and disagreement and incivility among the senior members," the university's administration put its Philosophy Department into receivership in 1990, conferring control over hiring and promotion on an outside committee.[52]

On the heels of the Carr affair, phenomenologists at the New School faced a crisis of their own, with a moratorium placed on graduate admissions while administrators considered their department's elimination. In 1977, a review of the New School's Graduate Faculty conducted by the New York State Board of Regents found that several of its departments, including its Philosophy Department, failed to meet minimum standards for graduate education. The Rating Committee tasked with evaluating the New School was led by the analytic philosopher Maurice Mandelbaum and included Vere Chappell, Ernan McMullin, Manley Thompson, and Richard Rorty.[53] Albert Hofstadter, who had joined the New School's Philosophy Department the previous year, reproved the group as "a 'mainstream' committee appointed in Albany and never in touch with the New School."[54] To Hofstadter and many nonanalysts, it appeared that philosophers representing the discipline's dominant wing were committed to destroying a heterodox institution. Two decades later Richard Rorty would reflect on his participation in the New School affair, concluding that the "project was a bad idea.... [Nonanalytic philosophers] thought that this was an assault by the analytic establishment against everybody who was non-establishment, and in retrospect I think they were right."[55]

As a member of the committee responsible for evaluating the New School, Rorty was indisputably well placed to assess it. Nevertheless, I believe that Rorty's revisionist recollections are off the mark, mistaking the effects of bureaucratic management and economic rationalization for a conflict between philosophies. A confluence of events led to the suspension of the New School's graduate program in philosophy. First, as academic departments expanded during the 1960s graduate admissions ballooned, soon outpacing the number of positions available for graduates. When the job market collapsed with the onset of economic recessions in the late 1960s and the 1970s, the disparity between job seekers and positions was further amplified.[56] Most efforts to address this crisis focused on managing and rationalizing advanced graduate education: limiting the number of doctorate earners to bring their numbers in line with the demands of the market. In 1969, the New York Department of Education created the Fleming Commission, tasked with making recommendations for the improvement of graduate education. Critically, however, it stipulated that these improvements be achieved without new expenditures. To this end, the commission instituted a regime of evaluations for both public and private universities. Outside reviewers were tasked with assessing a doctoral program's quality of graduate education. Ultimately, it was hoped, educational standards could be raised and job placements could be improved simply by eliminating low-quality doctoral programs and creating regional consortia, allowing several universities to combine their doctoral programs, using resources more efficiently by eliminating overlapping functions.[57]

In 1976, the New York Department of Education initiated a review of the Graduate Faculty of the New School. This could not have come at a worse time for its Philosophy Department. After the deaths of Aron Gurwitsch and Hannah Arendt and the retirement of Hans Jonas, only one full professor, J. N. Mohanty, and three assistant professors, James Nichols, Reiner Schürmann, and Stewart Umphrey, remained on the department's faculty. To restore the department, the New School hired two full professors, Albert Hofstadter and Anthony Quinton, who began in the fall semester of 1976.[58] Thus, when the Fleming evaluation began, the New School's Philosophy Department consisted of six members, three of whom were full professors. By comparison, the smallest of the leading philosophy departments in 1976, Harvard and Pennsylvania, each had twelve members. The largest, Princeton and Pennsylvania, had twenty-one. Evaluators appear to have set seven or eight full-time members as the minimum standard for a department to support graduate study.[59] The administration of the New School argued that the graduate faculty's freedom from undergraduate teaching and interdisciplinary organization changed the calculus of faculty requirements. However, before the committee's findings had officially been announced, Quinton and Mohanty resigned from the New School, accepting positions elsewhere.[60] Thus, by the time of the committee's final report, the department had been reduced to a faculty of four, with only one full professor, making the point moot. Facing the threat of disaccreditation, the New School's President John Everett placed a moratorium on graduate admissions for philosophy, withdrawing the department from evaluation. The Sociology and Political Science Departments, which also faced failing evaluations, shared the Philosophy Department's fate.[61]

The charge that the New School's Philosophy Department had been targeted because of its curricular emphases resonated with the experiences of many heterodox philosophers. Under the name "Saturday Group," some began to holding meetings to consider tactics for resistance. These activities gave birth to the Committee for Pluralism in Philosophy (discussed at the beginning of chapter 4), which briefly seized control over the Eastern Division of the American Philosophical Association in 1979. Bruce Wilshire, one of the Saturday Group's organizers, repeated this charge in 2012:

> Evaluators from the nutshell world had judged that one of the very few schools that allowed graduate students another option, some breadth of choice for study, was too narrow. *It* was too narrow! They assumed that the analytic and neo-positivistic methods constituted the whole range of philosophy, and then had broken this down into many subspecialties which added up, they believed, to a broad and balanced program.[62]

It is, of course, possible that the Mandelbaum Committee would have exercised leniency with a mainstream department that shared the New School's deficiencies. However, the draft evaluation of the New School's graduate program in philosophy does not evidence ideological bias. This contrasted with the committee's report on the New School's graduate program in sociology, whose reviewers asserted that other institutions already provided sufficient representation of European thought and claimed that "the students who are attracted to the present program recognize that it is not a mainstream one and they do not compete nationally for faculty positions in graduate programs of sociology."[63] The Mandelbaum Committee instead praised the Philosophy Department's focus on Continental thought as "distinctive and valuable," stating that its curricular emphasis was "not a subject for criticism." The report did state: "It would be fortunate if at least some of the new appointments which we hope will be made were people familiar with contemporary work in analytic philosophy, even though their own interests lay elsewhere," suggesting that students' professional opportunities might be diminished if they had no exposure to the field. However, it acknowledged that a consortium arrangement with other universities in the city might make representation of analysts at the New School unnecessary.[64] When the review was complete, Rorty wrote to Dean Greenbaum, now in a private capacity, that he was "very distressed" that the review might result in the discontinuation of graduate instruction in philosophy at the New School. "Certainly I and all my colleagues on the Rating Committee for Philosophy," he explained, "are horrified at the thought that we might have made more likely the end of a tradition which has been so valuable."[65]

What threatened the Graduate Faculty of the New School was not analytic philosophy but enthusiasm for technocratic management and the rationalization of public life. A philosophical curriculum that eschewed mainstream philosophical trends mattered far less to its evaluators than the New School's institutional eccentricities, such as an admissions policy that ballooned its nominal enrollment by admitting applicants with "inadequate" undergraduate records as nonmatriculating students and allowing them to qualify for enrollment toward a terminal degree if they excelled in graduate coursework.[66] More fundamentally, because the Graduate Faculty had been organized by scholars who were "fighting against [the] departmentalization . . . going on in other universities," an expectation that students would work across disciplines reduced the importance of any given department's size.[67] This organization reflected the material necessities the New School faced in assembling a faculty of refugees with limited and uncertain resources, which forced educational innovations, such as its joint seminars, to overcome the limitations of its faculty's size. However, much as Husserl had seen phenomenology as a first science on which the unity of all disciplines could be grounded, the New School's curriculum was designed to embody "the organic unity of the social sciences and [strove] to realize cooperation between the social sciences."[68]

For all these reasons, the New School was a different kind of institution than its peers. Whether or not its graduate faculty was sufficient to maintain a PhD program in 1977, it did not fit the state's model of a healthy department. That being said, the Rating Committee's report had not necessarily been fatal, allowing the Philosophy Department to continue graduate admissions on the condition that the New School hired two additional professors. However, the New School's graduate faculty was further imperiled by the attitudes of its own administration. In December 1978, President Everett appointed Allen Austill, the dean of the university's School of Adult Education, to serve as interim dean of the graduate faculty.[69] In March 1979, Austill issued a report on the graduate faculty, maintaining that the departments under moratoria had been unable to resolve the committee's concerns. It stressed that the Graduate Faculty was "a deficit operation and has been for many years," estimating that restoring the departments would cost the university in excess of $1 million.[70] Faculty and students vigorously rebutted these conclusions. Writing on behalf of the departments of sociology, philosophy, and political science, Arthur Vidich charged that, throughout Austill's report, "the intellectual needs of students—and by extension the intellectual needs of society—have been discussed solely in terms of instrumental utility. The intellectual stewardship which is the obligation of any responsible graduate faculty is altogether neglected." Vidich also charged Austill with fundamentally misrepresenting the administration's actions:

> During the years of moratorium, the administration has been negligent in its duty and has failed to take any steps or permit the departments to take any steps which might constitute proper legal responses to the conditions of moratorium. The crisis to which Dean Austill repeatedly refers is in fact a product of administrative paralysis—a paralysis remarkable in the face of the legal obligation undertaken by the administration to the State Education Department.

The Philosophy Department had not, for instance, been unable to locate "satisfactory replacements" for Mohanty and Quinton, as Austill claimed. Rather, presented with possible replacements, the administration had refused to authorize hiring.[71] The New School's administration, in this account, had prolonged and deepened the crisis of its graduate faculty in order to present drastic cuts or its outright elimination as a fait accompli.

As news spread that the Graduate Faculty was in danger, scholars from outside the university wrote to President Everett. Those writing on behalf of its Philosophy Department included Alan Donagan, Alasdair MacIntyre, Paul Ricoeur, and Jürgen Habermas.[72] Even Harvard's W. V. O. Quine advocated for the Philosophy Department, writing:

> Word has reached me that it may be found necessary to terminate the philosophy department at the New School. This saddens me, for I have long thought of that department as a rare and important point of contact between American philosophers and the philosophical trends on the continent of Europe.[73]

Everett nonetheless remained noncommittal about the Graduate Faculty's future. Suspicions of his intentions continued to build, culminating in a letter from the New School's Executive Faculty to its trustees in May 1979, charging that Everett had "failed to maintain the bonds necessary between a President and his faculty and students" and calling for his ouster.[74] In September, the trustees released a statement that specified their support for the Graduate Faculty's continued existence and announced the formation of a study committee to recommend a program for the Graduate Faculty's reconstruction.[75] The Study Committee, which was led by F. Champion Ward, strongly supported the continuation of all departments of the

Graduate Faculty at "the highest level of excellence," regardless of whether they required subsidization.[76] In the wake of the Ward Committee's report, President Everett committed to supporting the continuation of all departments of the Graduate Faculty. However, Everett's remarks to the trustees show that the suspicions of students and faculty had been justified:

> I must confess that I had hoped that the Ward Committee would recommend that we abolish or telescope some departments so that the costs might be decreased. During the course of their discussions, they concluded that the present six departments should be maintained and all of them restored to the doctoral level of excellence. At first I was reluctant to go along with them. However, I found their arguments to be overwhelming.[77]

Thus, "saved" by the university trustees, the Graduate Faculty entered a period of rebuilding in 1982. Nevertheless, significant damage had been dealt to phenomenological education in the United States. The New School's Philosophy Department would not accept new students until 1989.[78]

*   *   *

In 1960, Herbert Spiegelberg published the first edition of *The Phenomenological Movement: A Historical Introduction,* the first work in any language to describe the lives and works of the phenomenological movement's canonical figures within a single narrative that traced the intellectual and historical logics of the movement's development. The idea for the volume was suggested to Spiegelberg by William Frankena, an analytic philosopher who had briefly studied with Heidegger while traveling Europe on a Sheldon Fellowship from Harvard. Spiegelberg had become acquainted with Frankena during a semester he spent as a visiting professor at the University of Michigan. According to Spiegelberg, Frankena advised him that his "best chance of making a contribution to American philosophy would be to provide a concise Anglo-American focused introduction to the phenomenological movement . . . 'not more than 100 pages after the model of Marjorie Grene's *Dreadful Freedom.'*" With the support of Paul Henle, Frankena's colleague at Michigan, Spiegelberg applied for project funding from the Rockefeller Foundation. However, assuming that Spiegelberg intended to conduct research on the movement in Europe, the Rockefeller Foundation offered additional funding for travel. This unexpected boon changed the character and scope of Spiegelberg's project dramatically, with far-reaching consequences for the phenomenological movement.[79]

Spiegelberg's subsequent research produced a seven-hundred-page volume, remarkable for the historical details in its reconstruction of phenomenology's development, its breadth in the presentation of a diverse group of philosophers as members of a movement, and the clarity of its analysis and explanation of the movement's major works and thinkers. While American publishers had asked Spiegelberg to cut the volume's length by half, Herman Van Breda recognized the work's importance and arranged for it to be published in its entirety in the Phaenomenologica series.[80] According to retrospective assessments by William McBride and Karl Schuhmann, *The Phenomenological Movement* effectively settled debates over the movement's boundaries, defining its membership and essential characteristics.[81] In a review of the work for *Philosophical Review*, Samuel Hart called it "an invaluable source of information for readers not acquainted with the phenomenological philosophy." Spiegelberg, he continued, "deserves credit for enriching the Anglo-American reader with a badly needed book on a philosophy which dominates the European scene today."[82] Peter Simons dubbed Spiegelberg the "official biographer of phenomenology."[83] In the preface to his history's first edition, Spiegelberg quoted a 1950 article by Herbert Schneider:

> The influence of Husserl has revolutionized continental philosophies, not because his philosophy has become dominant, but because any philosophy now seeks to accommodate itself to, and express itself in, phenomenological method. . . . In America, on the contrary, phenomenology is in its infancy. The average American student of philosophy, when he picks up a recent volume of philosophy on the continent of Europe, must first learn the "tricks" of the phenomenological trade and then translate as best he can the real import of what is said into the kind of analysis with which he is familiar.[84]

From 1960 onward, Americans interested in phenomenology enjoyed the benefits of having a history of the phenomenological movement and guide to understanding its texts that was written in their own language and an accessible style. The American phenomenological movement, in turn, benefited from their interest.

Two years after Spiegelberg's *Historical Introduction* first appeared in print, Noonday Press published *Phenomenology and Science in Contemporary European Thought*, written by the Polish émigré Anna-Teresa Tymieniecka. The work was inspired by Tymieniecka's discussions with the émigré logician Alfred Tarski, whom she had engaged in a reading of Husserl's *Logical Investigations* in 1958. Tarski, to her consternation, dismissed Husserl's phenomenology as mere theory that could provide no solutions, plans, or innovations of practical consequence.[85] Thus, where Spiegelberg examined the phenomenological movement's philosophical core, Tymieniecka surveyed the application of phenomenological techniques by European scholars across a range of disciplines. The phenomenological lineage of these works was evident in their rejection of reductive causal mechanisms as the only valid foundation for rigorous explanation. In the past century, Tymieniecka wrote:

> a strong reductionist attitude stemming from scientific premises gradually infiltrated all fields of intellectual activity. . . . Complex cultural configurations, for example, were supposed to be explained when they were reduced to particular social conditions. The social phenomena could be further reduced to economic and psychological factors—thus the dream of ultimate explanation in strictly scientific, physical terms.[86]

The rigorous search for precise and verifiable knowledge, Tymieniecka held, need not be so restricted. However, taking the natural sciences as the model of all properly "scientific" research implied a metaphysical commitment to the uniformity of reality as a domain governed by causal relations, which are the only mode of explanation they admit. As we have repeatedly seen, phenomenology allows for an account of reality as a "many layered structure," whose overlapping domains "cannot be understood as effects of preceding ones, but which are 'motivated' in the way meanings which cannot act on each other can yet have bearing on each other."[87] On this basis, Tymieniecka argued, phenomenology had inspired methodological innovations in aesthetics by Roman Ingarden; in psychology and psychiatry by Max Scheler, Ludwig Binswanger, and Eugène Minkowski; and in sociology by Alfred Schütz and Georges Gurvitch. "By concentrating solely on the direct analysis of the structure of phenomena," Tymieniecka held, these thinkers had "superseded the construction of explanatory hypotheses and revealed far more complexities in many fields than the older methods had admitted."[88] Specifically, she concluded, "science has again become meaningful for man's personal and human pursuits, promising him understanding on the human level." *Phenomenology and Science in Contemporary European Thought* was an immediate success, selling more than ten thousand copies during its first year in print.[89]

In the decades that followed, as phenomenology took root in departments such as SUNY Stony Brook, UC Irvine, and Vanderbilt University, a new generation of Americans pioneered original avenues of phenomenological studies. Notable among these philosophers and research programs are: Sandra Bartky and Iris Marion Young (philosophy of gender), Elizabeth Behnke and Alphonso Lingis (philosophy of embodiment), John Caputo and Dallas Willard (philosophy of religion), David Carr (philosophy of history), Kah Kyung Cho (comparative philosophy), Edward Casey (aesthetics and philosophy of psychology), Lester Embree and Calvin Schrag (philosophy of the human sciences), Nancy Fraser and William McBride (political philosophy), Karsten Harries (philosophy of architecture), Don Ihde and Robert Scharff (philosophy of technology), Maurice Natanson (philosophy of the social sciences and literature), Robert Sokolowski (philosophy of language and religion), and Richard Zaner (philosophy of medicine). However, facilitated by its new accessibility in Spiegelberg and Tymieniecka's works, the influence of phenomenology also spread beyond philosophy into disciplines such as anthropology, architecture, comparative literature, gender studies, geography, psychology, and sociology. "At many universities in the United States," Arthur Vidich remarked during the debates over the future of the New School's Graduate Faculty, "there are students who are dissatisfied with the programs in analytical philosophy and who have transferred into Literature, Religion or Psychology."[90] As a result, growing numbers of phenomenologists and Continental theorists occupied new disciplinary sites, which became the principal context for work within those traditions at most American universities. In turn, these scholars participated in, contributed to, and helped sustain the organizations and publications created by American Continental philosophers, outflanking analytic philosophy's disciplinary dominance.

Since phenomenology was first conceived in a moment before philosophy and psychology had been decisively severed into distinct disciplines, the idea that phenomenological philosophy was introduced to psychologists as an extradisciplinary import is somewhat confused.[91] However, in the context of psychology and psychiatry as American disciplines, an account of phenomenology's influence need not be concerned with such ambiguities. At Dusquene, where Adrian van Kaam's vision and organizational impetus fostered a program in phenomenological and existential psychology, Amedeo Giorgi led the development of the new field's methodology.[92] Appointed by Duquesne in 1962, Giorgi, a graduate of Fordham's program in experimental psychology, believed that psychology should become a "human science," bypassing the theoretical idealizations of the natural sciences by grounding its methodology "directly" in descriptive analysis of the prereflexive *Lebenswelt*. Phenomenological psychology pursued an understanding of the human being "as a person and not an object" through nonreductive qualitative analysis, treating psychological phenomena as "more than biological and less than logical."[93]

Phenomenology also left a distinctive imprint on postwar American sociology through the work of Alfred Schütz. Schütz's influence is most clearly seen in the theory of social constructionism, first enunciated in 1966 by his students Peter Berger and Thomas Luckmann in *The Social Construction of Reality*. This text, as ranked by a 1997 survey of the International Sociological Association, was the fifth most influential work of sociology published in the twentieth century.[94] Berger and Luckmann argued that the sociologist is given two tasks: (1) describing the body of knowledge a particular society uses to identify reality, and (2) understanding "the process by which *any* body of 'knowledge' comes to be socially established *as* 'reality.'" Foreclosed by this project is any attempt to determine the "ultimate validity or invalidity" of the "social construct" of another's reality.[95] Rather, sociology would provide an accurate theoretical understanding of the processes by which that intersubjective reality was constituted and maintained through the thoughts and actions of "ordinary members or society." To clear a presociological starting point, Berger and Luckmann turned to phenomenological analysis: "The method we consider best suited to clarify the foundations of knowledge in everyday life," they explained, "is that of phenomenological analysis, a purely descriptive method and, as such, 'empirical' but not 'scientific.'"[96] The only footnote to the work's first chapter states that this "entire section of our treatise is based on . . . *Die Strukturen der Lebenswelt*," Schütz's uncompleted manuscript, which was compiled from his notes by Luckmann following Schütz's death.[97] Thus, social constructionism rejected both purely structural-functional explanation, which ignores individual meaning, and psychologistic analysis, which is based on a posited ahistorical human nature. Rather, drawing on Husserl's analysis of the *Lebenswelt*, Berger and Luckmann argued that the objective reality of human society is constituted historically through the habituation and institutionalization of individually meaningful practices that are, however, performed within an intersubjective world in which the meaning of everyday behavior is always already given as "objective" knowledge within the integrated whole of its historically constituted social "logic." Thus, phenomenology provided sociology with a method that is both humanistic and holistic, which understands society as "a human world, made by men, inhabited by men, and, in turn, making men, in an ongoing historical process."[98]

Phenomenology also influenced the development of ethnomethodology, an important heterodox position in postwar American sociology, pioneered by Harold Garfinkel. While completing a PhD under Talcott Parsons at Harvard, Garfinkel was introduced to Alfred Schütz and Aron Gurwitsch, whose phenomenological study of Gestalt psychology, *The Field of Consciousness*, argued that the organization of perception "must be an autochthonous feature of the stream of experience and of the experiential field in its original form."[99] Garfinkel applied these Gestalt principles to the analysis of social reality, reconceiving social facts as "the local, endogenous workings" of holistic phenomena like traffic jams and conversational turn taking. Among the properties of organization that these phenomena express, he held, is "the coherence of its identifying orderliness as the population that staffs it."[100] As Garfinkel explained:

> It is the workings of the traffic that make its staff available as "typical" drivers, "bad" drivers, "close in" drivers, and anything else demographers need to have in order to administer a causal account of driving. Endogenous populations are a subject of recurring methodological interest. In order to specify an endogenous population you start with concerted *things*—traffic flow—not bodies.

Thus, ethnomethodology drew from phenomenology to reconceive the sociologist's task as the study of social organization through careful endogenous descriptions of social phenomena as "instructed action." This was not a replacement to traditional, formal sociological analysis, as Garfinkel emphasized, but an incommensurable and complementary alternative that reached toward the unspecified "what more" of social practice lost in formalization.[101]

Phenomenology's influence was felt across a range of other disciplines. Anthropologists used Husserl's methods for understanding the natural attitude to inform their approach to theorizing the "cultural configuration of reality."[102] Merleau-Ponty's phenomenology of embodiment was also a significant source of anthropological theory, providing a framework for scholarship that grounded "theorizing, description, and analysis in close examinations of concrete bodily experiences, forms of knowledge, and practice."[103] While feminist theory had traditionally been grounded in varieties of liberal, Marxist, and post-Marxist analysis, the appearance of pioneering phenomenological works on feminism and gender, such as those by Iris Marion Young, Sandra Bartky, and Judith Butler, demonstrated the contributions that a phenomenological analysis of experience could make to the emerging discipline. Phenomenology also entered the discipline of geography during the 1970s, as geographers in the United States such as Yi-Fu Tuan and Anne Buttimer identified it as a framework for analyzing the human experience of space.[104] Adopted as a corrective to the positivistic stance of traditional geographic practices, humanistic geography drew on phenomenology as a theoretical foundation that did not commit the geographer to a third person, empiricist account of the world. Because the analysis of phenomenologists such as Heidegger and Merleau-Ponty rejects the dichotomy between self and world, it provides a framework for understanding the environment as a sphere of human possibilities that is navigated according to a pattern of life manifested as embodied behavior.[105] Phenomenological influence can be seen in the study and practice of architecture as well, particularly in the postmodern style. By locating architectural meaning in immediate experience, phenomenology facilitated a break from the formalistic limitations of the architectural vocabulary of modernism, allowing postmodern architects to reintroduce a pastiche of elements from historical influences.[106]

Finally, a second wave of European thought, grounded in or in opposition to phenomenology, took root in American universities during the 1970s and 1980s. Mapping the influence of phenomenology on intellectuals such as Jacques Derrida and Michel Foucault falls beyond the scope of this work. The methods of poststructuralism and deconstruction, to which these men were important contributors, can be understood as a tradition of postphenomenology, which borrowed phenomenological techniques and insights but abandoned the goal of a presuppositionless philosophy rooted only in experience by turning to social, psychological, and literary analysis of ontic entities. While deconstruction enjoyed a period of significant influence among American literary critics during the 1970s and 1980s, it also provoked strong antagonism, earning charges of jargonistic esotericism. The accusation that it was "elite, obscure, [and] pretentious" was not entirely unfair.[107] Heidegger's suspicion of language—which he believed occludes Being behind the inauthentic categories and dichotomies of everydayness—bred a mode of expression that traffics in glimpses of meaning, purchased through the play of signifiers. Resisting conventional modes of writing, which attempt to achieve clarity by eliminating contextual elements of expression beyond the formalizable grammar and established dictionary of a language, the sense of deconstructionist works cannot be reduced from the act of reading in which a text's range of significances is given play. They are, thus, often unclear, but in and against that lack of clarity they are meaningful.

Poststructuralism and deconstruction became important cultural signifiers during the late twentieth century, affecting attitudes toward Continental philosophy and the prospects of the phenomenological movement in the United States. The reception of such works as "French theory" (often metonymically defined by the trio of Jacques Derrida, Jacques Lacan, and Michel Foucault) played out, according to Marc Redfield, as an "allegorical drama."[108] The appellation *theory* marked a distinction from philosophy in the Anglo-American world, and the boundary between "philosophy" and "theory" was policed by mainstream philosophers. For example, a group of nineteen philosophers published a letter in the *Times* of London, protesting the decision by Cambridge to offer an honorary doctorate to Jacques Derrida in 1992. The letter, which compared Derrida's work to "tricks and gimmicks . . . of the Dadaists or of the concrete poets," declared: "In the eyes of philosophers, and certainly among those working in leading departments of philosophy throughout the world, M. Derrida's work does not meet accepted standards of clarity and rigour."[109] Yet, because of shared influences and interests with phenomenologists and existentialists, literary and critical theorists in America regularly inhabited the alternative spaces created by Continental philosophers, such as SPEP. Thus, despite the sustained efforts of American philosophers to proscribe the canons of deconstruction and "theory" within their discipline, they continued to influence American philosophical discourse, admitted by its Continental antiestablishment.

* * *

From its early reception, concentrated within a single university's philosophy department, the phenomenological movement had diffused throughout the disciplines of America's humanities and social sciences by the century's closing decade. Although phenomenology had been introduced to America by the nation's most influential philosophical institution, its postwar spread relied on a network of departments and organizations that were defined by their resistance to the practices and influence of mainstream American philosophy. Outside the discipline of philosophy, phenomenology proved to be a vital current of American intellectual life, gaining currency as the groundwork for methodologies and modes of humanistic research neglected by the dominant ideology of scientism. In a half-century defined by the political empowerment of technocratic managers, the eclipse of organicism by mechanistic theory, and the computer's dominance as a metaphor for the mind, phenomenology provided tools to contest the hegemonic presupposition that scientific reductivism and Enlightenment rationalism provided an unassailable foundation of knowledge that could be challenged only on its own terms. However, as the influence of phenomenology and post-phenomenological theory spread outside the discipline of philosophy, its successes did not go unopposed. Thus, while phenomenologists outflanked their philosophical opponents to capture important ground in the American intellectual landscape, they encountered new foes who indicted Continental philosophy as a threat to the values of Western civilization and free society.

Elided with other theoretical traditions under the rubric of "postmodernism"—an inchoate group of contemporary theories and methods marked by skepticism toward the value of universal standards and the possibility of objective knowledge—phenomenology and Continental philosophy became embroiled in academic and popular controversies during the closing decades of the twentieth century. Heidegger was cast as a leading villain in *The Closing of the American Mind*, Allan Bloom's 1987 reactionary broadside against the latter half of the twentieth century, which bemoaned the democratization of the cultural sphere and denounced academe for permitting various forms of multiculturalism and relativism to pollute the waters of elite Western culture. Bloom wrote in admonition:

> Our stars are singing a song they do not understand, translated from a German original and having a huge popular success with unknown but wide-ranging consequences, as something of the original message touches something in American souls. But behind it all, the master lyricists are Nietzsche and Heidegger. . . . Our intellectual skyline has been altered by German thinkers even more radically than our physical skyline by German architects.[110]

While phenomenological innovations remained a critical alternative to mainstream methodologies in most fields, met with varying degrees of acceptance or skepticism, Bloom declared that "Heidegger's teachings" were "the most powerful intellectual force in our times," threatening to transform of the American university along the lines of Germany in the 1930s. *The Closing of the American Mind* was an opening salvo in the "canon wars" over efforts to broaden the curriculum of liberal arts instruction, and part of a wider "culture war" between reformers and defenders of tradition. It was also the first in a series of works—including Roger Kimball's *Tenured Radicals: How Politics Has Corrupted Our Higher Education* (1990) and Keith Windschuttle's somehow even less subtle *The Killing of History: How Literary Critics and Social Theorists Are Murdering Our Past* (1994)—that condemned left-wing radicals, deconstructive literary theorists, and Continental philosophers for disseminating moral relativism and perverting the aims of education.[111]

Already burdened by a reputation for "abstruseness" and insincerity, deconstruction was also rocked by scandal in 1987 when a Belgian graduate student discovered that Paul de Man had written more than a hundred pieces from 1941 to 1942 for *Le Soir,* a Belgian collaborationist newspaper. Among them was found praise for "Hitlerism" and an article titled "The Jews and Contemporary Literature" that decried "Jewish influence" over Western culture.[112] Appearing prominently in the *New York Times,* the story was quickly picked up by publications across America.[113] That same year, the publication of Victor Farías's *Heidegger et le nazisme* brought renewed attention to Heidegger's association with the Nazi party and renewed debate about the relationship of Nazi and antisemitic ideology to his hermeneutic philosophy.[114] As we have seen, the phenomenologist Marvin Farber was among the first philosophers to allege fascist affinities in Heidegger's work. Heidegger was also denounced by his former student Hans Jonas in the keynote address of a 1964 conference of theologians at Drew University. Jonas's indictment, that Heidegger's philosophy could not be divorced from the Nazi ideology its author had embraced, made a significant impact on the growing community of American theologians interested in Heidegger's work and received national coverage in the *New York Times.*[115]

The Heidegger controversy of the late 1980s echoed these events. However, it also reiterated a motif of suspicion, perennial in twentieth-century Anglo-American thought, about the relation between German philosophy and the politics of the German state. During the First World War, John Dewey argued that German militarism was rooted in Kantian idealism, which left the German people obedient state subjects by elevating a "substantively empty" concept of duty and forbidding consequentialist ethical considerations.[116] During the World War II era, German totalitarianism was explained as the fruition of a Hegelian lineage by Karl Popper, A. J. Ayer, Bertrand Russell, and H. H. Price.[117] Now, the two points of Heidegger and de Man seemed to define a line across the Continental tradition that connected the entire enterprise to Nazi crimes. In *Telling the Truth about History,* Joyce Appleby, Lynn Hunt, Margaret Jacob wrote: "Although most theorists of postmodernity have clearly rejected the protofascist and anti-Semitic implications of the works of Nietzsche and Heidegger, doubts remain about the ease with which one can separate the strands in their thought."[118] Free from doubt was David Hirsch, who argued that "Heidegger's thought lends itself not only to a 'nondemocratic view of the world,' but to a view of the world that led to Auschwitz."[119] Even well-meaning philosophers and theorists had, in Hirsch's view, "become ensnared in the trap set by de Man and his hordes of privileged and self-blinding followers."[120]

More recently, responding to the assertion that "contemporary philosophers are largely embarrassed by the positivists," the analytic philosopher Clark Glymour wrote:

> There is a larger reason I do not find the positivists embarrassing: the contrast case on the continent. The positivists, not just those two I have emphasized, wrote with scientific and liberal ambitions, and at least with a passing connection with mathematics and science; in a time in which philosophy on the continent was embracing obscurantism and vicious, totalitarian politics they stood for liberal politics. When National Socialism came, they left home and country, but not in some cases, as with Hempel, before helping to ferry Jews out of Germany. Compare Heidegger, whose defenses of National Socialism echo some of his philosophical views.[121]

Glymour's remarks exemplify a common attitude of easy disdain toward the Continental tradition, which insists that Heidegger's personal history reveals the inner meaning of Continental philosophy. However, they erase the suffering that most phenomenologists endured under Nazi tyranny, as well as the courageous acts of those in the movement who resisted. Absent is Husserl, the phenomenological movement's founder, who spent his last years in exile from the academy. Absent, too, is Husserl's student Edith Stein, killed in Auschwitz. Fritz Kaufmann, who taught *Volkshochschulkursen* to expelled Jewish youths until that also became untenable. Maximilian Beck, who fled Europe rather than accept the Nazification of his journal. Dietrich von Hildebrand, tried and sentenced to death *in absentia* for his anti-Nazi activities. So too the labors of those like Alfred Schütz, who, having escaped to the United States, worked on their own and with the Emergency Committee in Aid of Displaced Foreign Scholars to secure positions in America for endangered colleagues still in Europe. The nobler legacies of these philosophers, erased in this narrative about the Continental tradition, must also be counted among the victims of Heidegger's misdeeds.

Conclusion

In 1982, three years after the pluralist revolt against the APA, Richard Rorty criticized the internecine struggles between America's philosophical factions in an essay titled "Philosophy in America Today." This article followed closely in the wake of *Philosophy and the Mirror of Nature* (1979), in which Rorty rejected the foundational theories of mind and truth espoused by many analytic philosophers as barren, commending the antifoundationalist insights of figures such as Heidegger and Dewey. Rather than calling for reconciliation between philosophy's divergent traditions, Rorty argued that philosophy need not be a unitary *Wissenschaft* to contribute to the modern university. What mattered was that, whether it was "Gadamer or Kripke, Searle or Derrida," when a student studied a work of philosophy, they could "find somebody to talk with about it."[1] Thus, Rorty recommended to philosophers an attitude of pluralistic tolerance and a disciplinary commitment to "let a hundred flowers bloom [and] admire them while they last."[2] While embracing Continental philosophy as an important source of ideas, Rorty maintained that it was simply not relevant to philosophy as analytic philosophers conceived of it. "If we put aside wistful talk of bridge-building and joining forces," he wrote, "we can see the analytic-Continental split as both permanent and harmless. We should not see it as tearing philosophy apart. There is no single entity called philosophy that once was whole and now is sundered."[3] For his own part, Rorty left professional philosophy, joining the faculty of UVA in 1982 as its Kenan Professor of the Humanities and addressing most subsequent work to specialists in political theory and comparative literature.[4]

Much in America's philosophical history recommends Rorty's attitude of pragmatic pluralism and suspicion of disciplinary closure. Analysis flourished in America during the twentieth century, and the United States, hitherto a minor province in the world of philosophical discourse, emerged as its metropole. At the same time, phenomenology's status as an unassimilated other in the American academy provided the movement space to develop a critical orientation on the totalizing vision of scientistic reductivism that eclipsed different forms of knowledge and reason. Economists eschewed the contingency of history for equilibrium equations and game-theory calculations. Political theorists embraced public choice theory as an ostensibly rational tool for decision-making. In legal thought, formalist approaches like textualism and "law and economics" gained influence. Indeed, new disciplines such as cognitive and computer science reduplicated the image of the mind as a great Turing machine. Although these traditions developed within their own institutional and disciplinary matrices, analytic philosophy provided them a rigorous formal foundation and, at times, occupied shared spaces within the academy.

Many of these collaborations were fruitful, helping philosophy to establish itself as a modern discipline that could contribute to the regime of applied research that dominated the postwar university. However, they accompanied the transformation of the philosopher into a disciplinary expert, focused on theory and technical problems. By contrast, the nineteenth-century American philosopher had been a central figure in the university. He was, as Bruce Kuklick wrote, "the custodian of certain truths necessary to the successful functioning of civilized society," whose teachings edified a generation of students and "provided the rationale for an entire way of life."[5] As America's academic institutions liberalized, democratized, and professionalized, this kind of cultural authority became untenable. Its recovery is now neither possible nor desirable. Nevertheless, the history of the American phenomenological movement complicates our understanding of American philosophy's professionalization by showing that it did not foreclose alternatives to this technical turn. Phenomenology approached the world with human wonder rather than detached calculation. As my portraits of American phenomenologists illustrate, philosophy could admit the reality of a human world, defined by its intrinsic ambiguity and shaped by its inexplicit fringes, without abandoning the methodological rigor that vouchsafed philosophy's modern legitimacy. Allowed to bloom on its own, phenomenology endured as a stronghold of nonreductive humanistic methodology against the hegemony of scientistic reductivism in American academia. In preserving this tradition and serving as a wellspring of humanistic critique, it made an essential contribution to American intellectual life not only in philosophy, but in disciplines such as sociology, psychology, geography, architecture, and anthropology.

Rorty's essay is also an insightful reflection on the sociology of philosophical knowledge. Rorty aptly perceived many of the ways in which the division of postwar American philosophy reflected conflicts over institutional power rooted in mundane professional activities:

> My story has been one of struggles between kinds of professors, professors with different aptitudes and consequently with different paradigms and interests. It is a story of academic politics—not much more, in the long run, than a matter of what sorts of professors come under which departmental budgets.[6]

Rorty likewise deserves credit for recognizing how the postwar expansion of American universities fueled the explosive growth of philosophical analysis. Among his essay's most explosive charges, however, is its claim that only "style," not method, unified analytic philosophers of the 1980s. While I believe that Rorty's diagnosis of disunity goes too far, I have identified many of the social and institutional formations through which the common style of postwar analytic philosophy was created, even as analytic discourse broadened: ones rooted in the narrow hiring network within which the discipline's most influential members shared educational and professional experiences, and catalyzed by the surge of academic appointments and disciplinary reorganization of the humanities following the end of World War II. Nevertheless, Rorty's analysis misses the mark on several points, including his prediction for philosophy's future in the United States:

> One may expect, by the end of the century, that philosophy in America will have gotten over the ambiguities that have marked the last thirty years and will, once again, begin to develop a clear self-image. One possibility is that this image will be of a new discipline, one not much more than fifty years old, which . . . does not try to link up with, or even to argue with, what is practiced under the heading of philosophy in other parts of the world.[7]

In fact, no such transformation has occurred. The division between analytic and Continental traditions has persisted as an institutional and curricular phenomenon in America, and disputes over the nature and demarcation of philosophical inquiry endure.

The antipodal impulses to secure foundations and slip their tethers directed the development of American philosophy during the twentieth century. However, like whitewater rushing over boulders, the currents that these tendencies produced were not entirely predictable. Both the phenomenological and analytic movements arrived in America at a moment when philosophy was being freed from sectarian institutional commitments that narrowly delimited the range of correct belief. Under the auspices of President Charles Eliot and William James, Harvard's Philosophy Department modeled a pragmatic pluralism that, although limited in its scope, advanced the novel and influential principle that institutions of philosophy were better served by disagreement than consensus. At the same time, however, American philosophers were redefining their role in the emerging disciplinary academy, compartmentalized into units of experts on a particular methodology or subject. With new disciplines annexing institutional and epistemological terrain, philosophers like Bertrand Russell, Rudolf Carnap, and Edmund Husserl appealed to Americans who faced both intellectual and practical demands to establish philosophy's foundations and define its subject.

By midcentury, many analytic philosophers and phenomenologists had abandoned foundationalist programs. Although phenomenologists followed this trajectory farther than Quinean holism or late Wittgenstein took analysis, it is an oversimplification to characterize the postwar era of American philosophy as narrow. While some analytic philosophers, in varying degrees, neglected historical and nonanalytic discourses, they also pioneered novel areas of research. With academic departments expanding at an unprecedented rate, philosophy's place in the academy was secure, lowering the practical stakes of the discipline's search for a method and subject. Even if it grew increasingly difficult to define philosophy's scope and purpose qua philosophy, its importance to the university was reestablished through programs like Columbia's Core Curriculum and course offerings that supplemented education in departments such as mathematics and cognitive science. Thus, Rorty's essay does not propose a new disciplinary paradigm as much as it calls on philosophers to understand one that was already becoming a practical reality. Nevertheless, the implications of Rorty's analysis were radical. While his plea for pluralistic toleration and vision of philosophy as a tool for personal edification recalled the ethos of the early twentieth century superficially, that resemblance is misleading. The diversity James promoted was both narrowly limited and essentially instrumental. Harvard employed R.B. Perry, W.E. Hocking, and James Haughton Woods, not to "admire them while they last," but so that they could argue with one another and learn from their arguments.

"Philosophy in America Today" is also peppered with references to Thomas Kuhn's *The Structure of Scientific Revolutions*.[8] Given Rorty's rejection of Kuhn's incommensurability thesis and his professed hermeneutical "hope" that "agreement is never lost so long as the conversation lasts," his conviction that reconciliation between analytic and Continental philosophy was impossible is somewhat puzzling.[9] However, Rorty accepted Kuhn's analysis that there could be no neutral language between certain paradigms of any "help whatever in bringing decision between theories under an algorithm."[10] Although Rorty rejected the possibility of a foundational criterion for comparing conceptual schemes and, therefore, considered the concept of commensurability incoherent, his engagement with Kuhn instructed his understanding of the conflict between analytic and Continental philosophers. Insofar as the history of the analytic and Continental movements does fit this model, my own story provides an opportunity to consider the conflict between disciplinary paradigms concretely and historically.

The work of reconciliation between analytic and Continental philosophy was futile, Rorty argued, because they were not "two sides . . . attacking common problems with different methods."[11] Without the possibility of shared concept–independent content, philosophy was relieved from the task of coordinating between and adjudicating among various modes of knowledge; analytic and Continental philosophy were free to go their separate ways.[12] Consistent with Kuhn's later writing, Rorty considered paradigms, or conceptual schemes, to be semantic structures. However, Kuhn's shifting characterizations of paradigm shifts in *The Structure of Scientific Revolutions* goes further, claiming that "after a revolution scientists work in a different world" and "see different things when they look from the same point in the same direction." Rorty considered these earlier remarks by Kuhn to be unfortunate distractions, leading down an idealistic rabbit hole from which modern empiricism had escaped, to its own benefit.[13] However, a theory implicates not merely concepts and entities, but the devices, techniques, traditions, and social situation in which science is practiced, complicating its reduction to a semantic structure. As the historian of science Peter Galison has argued:

> The meaning of instruments should include not only what we say about them but the often unspoken patterns of their functional location with respect to other machines, patterns of exchange, use, and coordination. Like theoretical concepts, these knowledge-producing machines acquire meaning through their use within the physical laboratory and, in complex ways, through their material links to machines far from physics.[14]

Indeed, the philosophers surveyed in this work have provided powerful counterarguments to the claim that thought is reducible to language.

Heidegger held that the meaning of entities is disclosed though a network of historically constituted uses and relations. Merleau-Ponty and Iris Marion Young stressed that the body is a necessary element of epistemological analysis, maintaining that concepts like space are founded on experience that cannot be abstracted from motricity. Dreyfus argued, further, that human thought cannot be described by formal semantic rules, paralleling Kuhn's description of paradigms as "prior to, more binding, and more complete than any set of rules for research that could be unequivocally abstracted from them."[15]

In places—particularly in his discussion of Wittgenstein and game playing—Kuhn appeared to recognize that scientific paradigms cannot be distilled from the social and technological dimensions of scientific practice. Indeed, he noted:

> the process of learning a theory depends upon the study of applications, including practice problem-solving both with a pencil and paper and with instruments in the laboratory. If, for example, the student of Newtonian dynamics ever discovers the meaning of terms like "force," "mass," "space," and "time," he does so less from the incomplete though sometimes helpful definitions in his text than by observing and participating in the application of these concepts to problem-solution.[16]

Phenomenology suggests that these insights must be taken further. Without Being-in-the-world of institutional and social practices through which knowledge is generated, and without the readiness-to-hand of experimental equipment, we cannot share the researcher's perspective on the world because it is through and in relation to these that the meanings of scientific concepts are disclosed. In other words, theoretical holism requires that we are holistic not only with respect to a theory's idealized concepts, but also the nonsemantic situation through which they are encountered.

From this perspective, the development of twentieth-century philosophy provides a useful corollary to Galison's account of microphysics research during the same period. In the field of high-energy physics, the high cost and staffing requirements of experimental instruments moved research from isolated laboratories to spaces shared by hundreds or even thousands of researchers. This forced scientists with adversarial experimental philosophies and fundamentally different theoretical commitments to coordinate and even collaborate, creating what Galison called "trading zones." As he explained, "Cultures in interaction frequently establish contact languages, systems of discourse that can vary from the most function-specific jargons, through semispecific pidgins, to full-fledged creoles rich enough to support activities as complex as poetry and metalinguistic reflection."[17] In a trading zone, Galison wrote, a language's meaning holism partially breaks down:

> People have and exploit an ability to restrict and alter meanings in such a way as to create local senses of terms that speakers of both "parent" languages recognize as intermediate between the two. The resulting pidgin or creole is neither absolutely dependent on nor absolutely independent of global meanings.[18]

As a consequence, while different groups of theorists or engineers might have been committed to incommensurable worldviews, they were able to develop local languages and nonlinguistic "wordless creoles" to coordinate practices and exchanges of information for mutually beneficial purposes. Thus, for example, two scientists might "hammer out an agreement that a particular track configuration found on a nuclear emulsion should be identified with an electron and yet hold irreconcilable views about the properties of the electron."[19]

Unlike in the world of microphysics, there were few philosophical trading zones where analytic and Continental philosophers could "come to a consensus about the procedure of exchange [or] about the mechanisms to determine when goods are 'equal' to one another." Their situation did not require "the continuation of exchange [as] a prerequisite to the survival of the larger culture of which they are a part."[20] While analytic philosophy and phenomenology originally shared a disciplinary domain without unusual rancor, growing impediments of language, style, and culture hindered dialogue between these groups. More fundamentally, however, opportunities for practitioners of these traditions to encounter one another as colleagues were limited by transatlantic migration and the institutional networks of American philosophy. With few Continental philosophers in America possessing the pedigree or mainstream recognition sought by hiring committees of elite departments, efforts to increase their representation would too often be seen, in Ruth Barcan Marcus's words, as "a compromise with mediocrity."[21] Indeed, connections outside one's own group had few practical benefits for most philosophers. Given the mutual hostility between their members, acknowledgment of another tradition's merits could invite the scorn of one's peers, as Rorty and Dreyfus faced from analysts and Continental philosophers, respectively. As I have argued, these social determinants were not incidental to the concept of Continental philosophy but its foundation as such. Its genealogy as a signifier of professional marginality, curricular deficits, and Orientalized otherness determined the boundaries and status of the community it circumscribed. Thus, as historically contingent modes of knowing that implicated ideas, institutions, and practices, analytic and Continental philosophy were largely incommensurable within the situation in which they were constituted. However, this pragmatic incommensurability did not necessarily foreclose the possibility that shared meanings, projects, and evaluative criteria might emerge between their practitioners from a situation in which these discourses were no longer constituted through the social reality of their mutual alienation.

*   *   *

In this work, I have attempted to tell a story about both knowledge and institutional organization by refusing to consider ideas, practices, and the material formations in and through which both are generated as distinct kinds of determinate entities. Instead, my research and analysis reflect an effort to understand all these phenomena as processes, rejecting their ontological distinction. The cycles and rhythms intrinsic to the processes of human life structure recurrent patterns of existence. It is only through the repetition and replication of intellectual, cultural, and institutional forms that patterns of history emerge as meaningful grounds for explanation. Thus, reflecting on history as a process motivates a shift of focus from production and causation to reproduction. Whereas causal relations link ontologically distinct, temporally determinate events, reproductive processes are fluid yet enduring structures, overlapping and undifferentiated, that order social life through the dynamics of their interactions. Take, for instance, an observation by Morton White about the effects of Harvard and Columbia's different programmatic requirements on their students:

> While writing my thesis I kept admiring Harvard for abandoning the requirement that Ph.D. theses be published. Without question the Harvard system allowed a young philosopher to try being creative in a way that was rare at Columbia in my graduate days. On the other hand, I am convinced that the great thing about the Columbia system, by contrast to the Harvard system, was the fact that graduate students at Columbia did not have to take final examinations and to write term papers in their courses. . . . Columbia's relaxed standards permitted young philosophers to range widely in their interests.[22]

It would be facile to attribute the interests of any particular student of Columbia or Harvard merely to their university's publication requirements for doctoral theses. In the lives of individual philosophers, we will find more salient and causally efficacious events to explain their intellectual trajectory. However, because graduate education is an enduring structure with regular features, these requirements defined the characteristics of a reproductive process that fostered particular activities, values, and norms.

Time, as Marjorie Grene argued, "is not one dimension but a host of them." In choosing different themes and *durées* from the overlapping divisions of human life, we identify a multitude of temporal processes that combine constructively and destructively according to a logic of elective affinities and aversions.[23] Alfred North Whitehead also described these dynamics, adopting *society* as his term for a set of actualities defined by an ordering characteristic that is salient for its members because of their organization.[24]

> A society arises from disorder, where "disorder" is defined by reference to the ideal for that society; the favourable background of a larger environment either itself decays, or ceases to favour the persistence of the society after some stage of growth: the society then ceases to reproduce its members, and finally after a stage of decay passes out of existence.[25]

As an example of a society, Whitehead identified the set of actualities constituted by the union of each punctiform moment in the existence of an electron and a proton. "These occasions," he wrote, "are the reasons for the electromagnetic laws; but their capacity for reproduction, whereby each electron and each proton has a long life, and whereby new electrons and new protons come into being, is itself due to these same laws."[26] In treating the production of philosophical knowledge as a process, it is precisely these affinities and dynamics I have worked to identify, as they arose contingently within phenomenology's peculiar history in America. In history, we do not search for laws of nature like Maxwell's equations. We do not look for social certainties, like the "laws" economists ascribe to market economies. We do not describe how things must happen in any world, but how certain things *did* happen in *this* world: we define a subject and background by choosing one or another ordered phenomenon or principle of order, chart the dynamics that drove its growth or decay, and, perhaps, reflect on the contribution of these events to the broader "extensive continuum" of relations and possibilities between the entities of the world.

In this story we have seen that the development of interdepartmental programs in the age of departmentalization could either broaden or narrow a discipline's scope by imposing new obligations on departments. We have noted the autocatalytic effects of institutional concentration, which tend toward the creation of new, specialized organizations. Perhaps most important, however, the history of the American phenomenological movement suggests an affinity between hierarchical institutional structures and disciplinary division. The closed hiring network of philosophy's leading departments fostered the development of shared practices and norms among a generation of American philosophers. In turn, this intellectual framework established evaluative criteria that could be invoked as a meritocratic defense of these departments' generous representation in positions of leadership in philosophical organizations like the APA. While certainly not its cause, it was the elective affinity of restrictive metaphilosophical commitments to a certain kind of excellence with the narrow reproductive environment of the nation's leading departments that made philosophy's bifurcated organization so durable in the United States. Therefore, even if we do no more than admire the different blossoms of philosophical insight while they last, as Rorty suggested, it is essential that we cultivate their institutional terroir carefully, with attention to its history, and recognize that insights bloom most beautifully when they grow together.

Acknowledgments

This book is a testament to the love, influence, and encouragement of my mother and father, Anne and Robert Strassfeld, who have supported my intellectual development for more than three decades and whose high expectations have provided a standard toward which I continue to strive. They have made me who I am—at least, the best parts of me—and I hope this work reflects that. I am also grateful for the strength and support of my wider family. Among them, Daniel Strassfeld, Elisabetta Ronchi, Natasha Strassfeld, Shula Strassfeld, Mary Alice Hennigan, David Hennigan, Susi Hennigan, Patricia Hennigan, and Peter Hennigan have helped me in nearly every way one can throughout my studies, research, and writing.

I owe the deepest appreciation to Robert Westbrook, who directed the dissertation from which this work was adapted. Robb was everything I could have wanted in a mentor. Without his experience, insight, and candor, I would not be a historian and this book would not exist. Likewise, I am profoundly indebted to Bruce Kuklick, who gave me his time, help, and advice whenever I needed them, without limit. His influence suffuses this work, to its significant benefit.

Many other friends, colleagues, and mentors read my papers, drafts, and scribblings and, generous to think these were something, provided insightful comments, criticisms, and suggestions. Foremost among these are Warren Goldfarb, Robert Scharff, Brian Leiter, Daniel Borus, Jean Pederson, Anthony Grafton, Calvin Schrag, Ed Baring, Robert Paul Wolff, Bastiaan van Fraassen, David Carr, Ted Brown, Joan Rubin, Charles Parsons, Catherine Ludlow, and Ronald Jager. I am also grateful to Kyle Wagner, whose advice and editorial efforts steered my project from proposal to publication.

I am further indebted to Brian Leiter, who used his blog to help me compile the quantitative data that supports this work's central argument, and to Ned Hall, who allowed me to access Harvard Philosophy

Department records that were critical for my research. I am also grateful to those witnesses to the events that this work details who provided answers to my questions, informally or in formal interviews. These include Hubert Dreyfus, David Carr, Richard Bernstein, Richmond Thomason, and Bas van Fraassen. Additionally, I want to recognize the late Lester Embree, who helped me recognize the importance of institutional networks in the development of philosophical styles during the early stages of my research.

Throughout this project I have benefited from the help of friends who supported me intellectually and emotionally, with advice on translations, and, in many cases, by giving me a couch on which to sleep after a day in the archives: Lyle Rubin, Heather Le Bleu, Andrew Kinaci, Wendy Eisenberg, Sarah Outhwaite, Lucia Perasso, David Anderson, Anastasia Nikolis, Beau Madison Mount, William Sullivan, Shelly Kagan, Kyle Robinson, Charles Perry Wilson, Jon Feyer, Simon Kheifets, Zeb Blackwell, Daniel Kanter, Adam Francis, Daniel Gorman, Daniel Rinn, and Marsha Cohen.

Finally, I am indebted to the archivists of the following institutions, without whose help this project would not have been possible: Harvard University, Yale University, the New School, the University at Buffalo, Columbia University, Cornell University, the New York Public Library, Princeton University, the University of Chicago, Northwestern University, the University of Michigan, the University of Southern California, and the University of Pennsylvania.

Appendix: Quantitative Sources and Methods

Unless otherwise noted, quantitative analysis was performed using a database of employment and biographical information for faculty of the following eleven philosophy departments between 1930–1979:

University of California, Berkeley
University of Chicago
Columbia University
Cornell University
Harvard University
University of California, Los Angeles
University of Michigan
University of Pennsylvania
Princeton University
Stanford University
Yale University

The dataset includes only assistant professors, associate professors, and professors, excluding visiting faculty. The list is generally restricted to individuals whose primary appointment was in philosophy. However, I have included faculty with secondary appointments in philosophy on a case-by-case basis if they had significant duties within the philosophy department, including graduate instruction.

This information was compiled using faculty listings in course catalogs for Berkeley, the University of Chicago, Columbia, Cornell, Harvard, the University of Michigan, Princeton, the University of Pennsylvania, Stanford, and UCLA, available in their university archives. Also used was Michigan's online Faculty History Project and Princeton's online listing of faculty since 1949. Information on Yale faculty was drawn from the online Historical Register of Yale University.[1]

Information on the doctoral education of most American faculty was retrievable through the ProQuest Dissertation & Theses database. Other sources included the *Directory of American Scholars*, obituaries and memorials, faculty web pages, and direct inquiries.

Identifications of philosophers as "analytic," "nonanalytic," or "historical" were made by examining a philosopher's writings and, when available, discussions of their work. Multiple classifications for an individual philosopher were permitted. I must stress that I am not identifying these men and women as analytic or nonanalytic philosophers. Rather, I am identifying philosophers who participated in these types of discourse. Such classifications are disputable by their nature. Therefore, I posted my initial classifications on the philosophy blog *Leiter Reports*, soliciting comments and suggestions that I used to improve my dataset.[2]

Abbreviations

Alfred Schütz Papers	Alfred Schütz Papers, Beinecke Rare Book and Manuscript Library, New Haven, CT.
Columbia University Central Files, 1890–1984	Central Files, 1890–1984, Columbia University Archives, New York, NY.
Cornell Dept. of Philosophy Records	Dept. of Philosophy Records, 1892–1952, Division of Rare and Manuscript Collections, Cornell University Library, Ithaca, NY.
Emergency Committee Records	Emergency Committee in Aid of Displaced Foreign Scholars Records, Manuscripts and Archives Division, New York Public Library, New York, NY.
Ernest Nagel Papers	Ernest Nagel Papers, Columbia University Archives, New York, NY.
New School Graduate Faculty Collection	Graduate Faculty of the New School for Social Research collection, New School Archives, New York, NY.
Harvard Graduate Student Folders, Pre-1917	Graduate Student Folders, Pre-1917, Harvard University Archives, Cambridge, MA.
HPD1	Harvard University Department of Philosophy Records (1906–1979): Dept. of Philosophy and Psychology & Dept. of Philosophy: Minutes of Departmental Meetings and Correspondence Files, 1924–1960 (UAV 687.1), Harvard University Archives, Cambridge, MA.
HPD2	Harvard University Department of Philosophy Records (1906–1979): Dept. of Philosophy & Dept. of Philosophy and Psychology: Outgoing Correspondence, 1910–1915 (UAV 687.2), Harvard University Archives, Cambridge, MA.

HPD10	Harvard University Department of Philosophy Records (1906–1979): Dept. of Philosophy and Psychology; the Dept. of Psychology; and the Division of Philosophy and Psychology: Correspondence and Other Records, ca. 1927–1938 (UAV 687.10), Harvard University Archives, Cambridge, MA.
HPD11	Harvard University Department of Philosophy Records (1906–1979): Division of Philosophy and Psychology & Dept. of Psychology: General Correspondence, 1938–1965 (UAV 687.11), Harvard University Archives, Cambridge, MA.
HPD15	Harvard University Department of Philosophy Records (1906–1979): Dept. of Philosophy; Dept. of Philosophy and Psychology; Division of Philosophy and Psychology; and Dept. of Psychology: Administrative Records, including Correspondence, Memos, Reports and Other Material Relating to Departmental Issues (UAV 687.15), Harvard University Archives, Cambridge, MA.
President Kingman Brewster Records	Kingman Brewster Jr., president of Yale University, records, Yale University Archives, New Haven, CT.
Marvin Farber Papers	Marvin Farber Papers, University Archives: State University of New York at Buffalo, Buffalo, NY.
PPR Papers	Marvin Farber PPR Papers, University Archives: State University of New York at Buffalo, Buffalo, NY.
President Robert Goheen Papers	Office of the President: Robert F. Goheen, Princeton University Archives, Princeton, NJ.
Northwestern Philosophy Department Administrative Records	Philosophy Department General Administrative Records, Northwestern University Archives, Evanston, IL.
R. B. Perry Correspondence	Ralph Barton Perry Correspondence, Harvard University Archives, Cambridge, MA.
Sheldon Fund Records	Records from the Committee on General Scholarships and the Sheldon Fund, Harvard University Archives, Cambridge, MA.
Dean of FAS Records	Records of the Dean of Faculty of Arts and Sciences, Harvard University Archives, Cambridge, MA.
Records of Dean Simeon Leland	Records of the Dean, Simeon E. Leland, Northwestern University Archives, Evanston, IL.

Yale Secretary's Office Records, 1899–1953	Secretary's Office Records, 1899–1953, Yale University Archives, New Haven, CT.
USC School of Philosophy Records	University of Southern California School of Philosophy Records, USC Libraries Special Collections, Los Angeles, CA.
William Earle Papers	William A. Earle Papers, Northwestern University Archives, Evanston, IL.
W. E. Hocking Correspondence	William Ernest Hocking Correspondence, 1860–1979, Houghton Library, Cambridge, MA.
W. V. O. Quine Papers	W. V. O. Quine Papers, Houghton Library, Cambridge, MA.

Notes

INTRODUCTION

1. See Bruce Kuklick, *The Rise of American Philosophy, Cambridge, Massachusetts, 1860–1930* (New Haven, CT: Yale University Press, 1977).

2. See Edward Baring, *Converts to the Real: Catholicism and the Making of Continental Philosophy* (Cambridge, MA: Harvard University Press, 2019).

3. See George Cotkin, *Existential America* (Baltimore: Johns Hopkins University Press, 2003); Ann Fulton, *Apostles of Sartre: Existentialism in America, 1945–1963* (Evanston, IL: Northwestern University Press, 1999); Martin Woessner, *Heidegger in America* (Cambridge: Cambridge University Press, 2011).

4. See Peter Eli Gordon, *Continental Divide: Heidegger, Cassirer, Davos* (Cambridge, MA: Harvard University Press, 2010); and Michael Friedman, *A Parting of the Ways: Carnap, Cassirer, and Heidegger* (Chicago: Open Court, 2000).

5. Gordon Wood, "Intellectual History and the Social Sciences," in *New Directions in American Intellectual History*, ed. John Higham and Paul Keith Conkin (Baltimore: Johns Hopkins University Press, 1979).

6. See Karl Marx, *Capital: A Critique of Political Economy*, ed. Friedrich Engels and Ernest Untermann, trans. Samuel Moore and Edward B. Aveling, Modern Library of the World's Best Books (New York: Modern Library, 1936), 163–73.

7. Louis Althusser, *On Ideology*, trans. Ben Brewster (New York: Verso, 2008), 1–10.

8. See S. M. Amadae, *Rationalizing Capitalist Democracy: The Cold War Origins of Rational Choice Liberalism* (Chicago: University of Chicago Press, 2003).

CHAPTER ONE

Epigraph: Herbert Spiegelberg, *The Phenomenological Movement: A Historical Introduction*, 2nd ed., vol. 1, Phaenomenologica (The Hague: M. Nijhoff, 1965), 87.

1. Edmund Husserl, *Logical Investigations*, trans. Dermot Moran, vol. 1 (New York: Routledge, 2001), 168; Raymond Aron quoted in Simone de Beauvoir,

The Prime of Life, trans. Peter Green (London: Andre Deutsch and Weidenfeld & Nicolson, 1962), 112; Martin Heidegger, *Being and Time*, trans. John Macquarrie and Edward Robinson (New York: Harper, 1962), 58.

2. Barry Smith and David Woodruff Smith, *The Cambridge Companion to Husserl* (Cambridge: Cambridge University Press, 1995), 47–48, 139–41.

3. Husserl, *Logical Investigations*, 1:149–54.

4. Ibid., 155–61.

5. Ibid., 168, 77–79.

6. Edmund Husserl, *Ideas: General Introduction to Pure Phenomenology*, trans. William Ralph Boyce Gibson (New York Routledge, 2013), 177–82.

7. Spiegelberg, *The Phenomenological Movement*, 1:169–72.

8. Herbert Spiegelberg, *The Phenomenological Movement: A Historical Introduction*, 3rd rev. and enl. ed., ed. Karl Schuhmann (Boston: Martinus Nijhoff, 1982), 247–52.

9. Husserl, *Ideas*, 54–55, 101–3.

10. Ibid., 80, 91–92.

11. Ibid., 81, 108.

12. Eugen Fink, quoted in Maurice Merleau-Ponty, *Phenomenology of Perception*, trans. Donald A. Landes (New York: Routledge, 2012), lxxvii.

13. Husserl, *Ideas*, 112–16.

14. Ibid., 130–34, 38.

15. Edmund Husserl, *Cartesian Meditations*, trans. Dorion Cairns (The Hague: M. Nijhoff, 1965), 66.

16. Husserl, *Ideas*, 264.

17. Ibid., 233–34.

18. Ibid., 117–19.

19. Husserl, *Logical Investigations*, 1:260–61.

20. Husserl, *Ideas*, 246–51.

21. Ibid., 249, 61–62, 77.

22. Ibid., 272–79.

23. Ibid., 365–69.

24. Edmund Husserl, *The Crisis of European Sciences and Transcendental Phenomenology: An Introduction to Phenomenological Philosophy*, trans. David Carr, Northwestern University Studies in Phenomenology & Existential Philosophy (Evanston, IL: Northwestern University Press, 1970), 121–26.

25. Ibid., 129–35.

26.	Edmund Husserl and Ludwig Landgrebe, *Experience and Judgment: Investigations in a Genealogy of Logic*, trans. James S. Churchill and Karl Ameriks (Evanston, IL: Northwestern University Press, 1973), 32–39.

27.	Spiegelberg, *The Phenomenological Movement*, 1:275.

28.	Ibid., 275–83, 347–49.

29.	See, for example, Richard Wolin, ed., *The Heidegger Controversy: A Critical Reader*, European Perspectives (New York: Columbia University Press, 1991).

30.	Heidegger, *Being and Time*, 31.

31.	In fact, a dictionary of Heideggerian terms has been published: Daniel O. Dahlstrom, *The Heidegger Dictionary* (New York: Bloomsbury, 2013).

32.	Martin Heidegger, "Letter on Humanism," trans. Frank A. Capuzzi and J. Glenn Gray, in *Basic Writings*, ed. David Farrell Krell (San Francisco: Harper, 1993), 217–19.

33.	Heidegger, *Being and Time*, 43.

34.	Martin Heidegger, *History of the Concept of Time*, Studies in Phenomenology and Existential Philosophy (Bloomington: Indiana University Press, 1985), 106–7; Husserl, *Ideas*, 167.

35.	Heidegger, *Being and Time*, 78–80, 91–95; Hubert L. Dreyfus, *Being-in-the-World: A Commentary on Heidegger's "Being and Time", Division I* (Cambridge, MA: MIT Press, 1991), 90–91.

36.	Heidegger, *Being and Time*, 32.

37.	Martin Heidegger, *Ontology: The Hermeneutics of Facticity*, trans. John van Buren, Studies in Continental Thought (Bloomington: Indiana University Press, 1999), 14.

38.	Ibid., 6–8, 11.

39.	Ibid., 11–12.

40.	Heidegger, *Being and Time*, 63–64.

41.	Heidegger, *Ontology*, 14.

42.	Heidegger, *Being and Time*, 67–69.

43.	Ibid., 163–68.

44.	Ibid., 165.

45.	Ibid., 67–69, 219–24.

46.	Jean-Paul Sartre, *Existentialism Is a Humanism*, trans. Carol Macomber (New Haven, CT: Yale University Press, 2007), 20–22, 38–39.

47.	Ibid., 37.

48.	Ibid., 47–49.

49.	Heidegger, *Being and Time*, 63–64, 488; Jean-Paul Sartre, *Being and Nothingness: An Essay on Phenomenological Ontology*, trans. Hazel E. Barnes (New York:

Washington Square Press, 1992), 3–30; Herbert Spiegelberg, *The Phenomenological Movement: A Historical Introduction*, 2nd ed., vol. 2, Phaenomenologica
(The Hague: M. Nijhoff, 1965), 472–73. The introduction to *Being and Nothingness*, titled "À la Recherche de l'Être," also seems to invoke Marcel Proust's *À la
Recherche du Temps Perdu*, "In Search of Lost Time," gesturing with a wink at
the unwritten third division of *Being and Time*, prospectively titled "Time and
Being," in which Heidegger had promised "the explication of time as the transcendental horizon for the question of being." Heidegger, *Being and Time*, 63–64.

50. Heidegger, *Being and Time*, 67; Heidegger, "Letter on Humanism," 229; Sartre,
Existentialism Is a Humanism, 20–22. *Wesen*, which translates as "essence,"
is bracketed in quotations, signaling that the term is used only provisionally,
not meant to invoke the concept of *an* essence as traditionally understood.
Likewise, "its existence" is written as *"seinem Zu-sein"* (literally "its to-be," with
Zu-sein used as a noun in a manner akin to the substantival infinitive constructions of ancient Greek) and *Existenz*.

51. See Heidegger, "Letter on Humanism," 232, 37–38.

52. Jean-Paul Sartre, *The Transcendence of the Ego: An Existentialist Theory of Consciousness*, trans. Forrest Williams and Robert Kirkpatrick (New York: Hill and
Wang, 1991), 40–41, 50–52, 115.

53. Ibid., 40–41.

54. Ibid., 41; Sartre, *Being and Nothingness*, 11.

55. Sartre, *Transcendence of the Ego*, 40.

56. Ibid., 38–40.

57. Ibid., 48–49.

58. Ibid., 46–47.

59. Sartre, *Being and Nothingness*, 53–56.

60. Ibid., 41–42.

61. Ibid., 43.

62. Merleau-Ponty, *Phenomenology of Perception*, xxvii.

63. Ibid., 13–16, 60–62.

64. Ibid., 44.

65. Ibid., 286–88.

66. Ibid., 204–5.

67. Ibid., 209.

68. Ibid., 334.

69. Ibid., 332.

70. Ibid., 106.

71. Ibid., 137.

72. Ibid., 114.

73. Ibid., 131–32.

74. Ibid., 139.

75. Ibid., 140.

76. Ibid., 143–48.

77. Ibid., 137.

78. Ibid., 240–42.

79. Ibid., 248.

80. Ibid., 307, 10–11.

81. Ibid., 358–60.

CHAPTER TWO

Epigraph: Marvin Farber to James Woods, April 28, 1923, box 25, folder "Woods, James," Marvin Farber Papers.

1. See E. Murray, "Summaries of Articles: 'Psychologische Prinzipienfragen,' by H. Cornelius," *Philosophical Review* 16, no. 1 (1907): 101–12; Oscar Ewald, "Contemporary Philosophy in Germany (1906)," *Philosophical Review* 16, no. 3 (1907): 237–65; Oscar Ewald, "German Philosophy in 1907," *Philosophical Review* 17, no. 4 (1908) : 400–26; Oscar Ewald, "German Philosophy in 1908," *Philosophical Review* 18, no. 5 (1909): 514–35; Oscar Ewald, "German Philosophy in 1913," *Philosophical Review* 23, no. 6 (1914): 615–33; and J. R. Tuttle, "Summaries of Articles: 'Philosophie Als Strenge Wissenschaft,' by Edmund Husserl," *Philosophical Review* 20, no. 5 (1911).

2. See Josiah Royce, "Recent Logical Inquiries and Their Psychological Bearings," *Psychological Review* 9, no. 2 (1902): 111–12.

3. Hugo Münsterberg, quoted in W. E. Hocking, "From the Early Days of the 'Logische Untersuchungen,'" in *Edmund Husserl, 1859–1959*, ed. the editorial committee of Phaenomenologica (The Hague: M. Nijhoff, 1959), 5.

4. W. E. Hocking to Hugo Münsterberg, December 3, 1902, box 18, folder "Hugo Münsterberg (1 of 2)," W. E. Hocking Correspondence.

5. Hocking, "From the Early Days of the 'Logische Untersuchungen,'" 5; W. E. Hocking to Hugo Münsterberg, December 19, 1902, box 18, folder "Hugo Münsterberg (1 of 2)," W. E. Hocking Correspondence.

6. Walter Pitkin, *On My Own* (New York: C. Scribner's Sons, 1944), 250, 319.

7. While some remnants of the correspondence between Pitkin and Houghton Mifflin exist, they cannot verify Pitkin's account and provide no evidence of

James's involvement. Herbert Spiegelberg, *The Context of the Phenomenological Movement* (The Hague: Martinus Nijhoff, 1981), 105–18.

8. Roy Wood Sellars, "Reflections on the Career of Marvin Farber," in *Phenomenology and Natural Existence: Essays in Honor of Marvin Farber*, ed. Dale Maurice Riepe (Albany: State University of New York Press, 1973), 21–22.

9. H. H. Fisher, "Henry Lanz," *American Slavic and East European Review* 5, no. 1/2 (1946): 222; Gustav Shpet, *Appearance and Sense: Phenomenology as the Fundamental Science and Its Problems*, Phaenomenologica (Boston: Kluwer Academic, 1991), xvii.

10. Osborn attributed his interest in Husserl to the influence of Columbia's Horace L. Friess. Andrew D. Osborn, *Edmund Husserl and His "Logical Investigations"* (New York: Garland, 1980), 5.

11. Kuklick, *The Rise of American Philosophy*, 85, 235; Philip F. Gura, *American Transcendentalism: A History* (New York: Hill and Wang, 2007), 26–31; George Herbert Palmer and Ralph Barton Perry, "Philosophy, 1870–1929," in *The Development of Harvard University since the Inauguration of President Eliot, 1869–1929* (Cambridge, MA: Harvard University Press, 1930), 3–19.

12. Moritz Geiger to Henry Noble MacCracken, November 5, 1933, box 11, folder "Geiger, Moritz (1 of 2)," Emergency Committee Records.

13. Harvard University, *Reports of the President and Treasurer of Harvard College, 1908–09* (Cambridge, MA: Harvard University Press, 1910), 22.

14. Kuklick, *The Rise of American Philosophy*, 244.

15. Laurence R. Veysey, *The Emergence of the American University* (Chicago: University of Chicago Press, 1965), 227, 31.

16. Palmer and Perry, "Philosophy, 1870–1929," 3–4.

17. Veysey, *Emergence of the American University*, 232–33.

18. On the shared philosophical commitments of "Harvard pragmatism" and the limitations of Harvard's pluralism, see Kuklick, *The Rise of American Philosophy*, xx–xxvii, 451–80.

19. W. E. Hocking, "What Does Philosophy Say?," *Philosophical Review* 37, no. 2 (1928): 136.

20. Palmer and Perry, "Philosophy, 1870–1929," 25.

21. "Responses to Committee of 9 Memorandum," November 3, 1937, box 5, folder "Murdock, Dean R. B. (Committee of 9)" Murdock, HPD10; Kenneth Murdock to C. I. Lewis, October 21, 1937, box 5, folder "Murdock, Dean K. B. (Committee of 9)," HPD10.

22. "Departmental Questionnaire: Philosophy," 1927, box 1, folder "Mining and Metallurgy to Romance Languages," Reports of the Academic Departments to President N. M. Butler, Columbia University Archives, New York.

23. William Adams Brown to R. B. Perry, May 4, 1921, box 4, folder A–B, R. B. Perry Correspondence.

24. By contrast, James wrote, Yale had "a school but no thought." William James, *The Correspondence of William James*, vol. 10 (Charlottesville: University Press of Virginia, 1992), 324.

25. Bruce Kuklick, *A History of Philosophy in America, 1720–2000* (New York: Clarendon Press, 2001), 2.

26. R. B. Perry, *A Defense of Philosophy* (Cambridge, MA: Harvard University Press, 1931), 11–12.

27. Arthur Lovejoy, "On Some Conditions of Progress in Philosophical Inquiry," *Philosophical Review* 26, no. 2 (1917): 133.

28. Edwin Holt et al., "The Program and First Platform of Six Realists," *Journal of Philosophy, Psychology and Scientific Methods* 7, no. 15 (1910): 393.

29. Walter Pitkin, "Is Agreement Desirable?," *Journal of Philosophy, Psychology and Scientific Methods* 9, no. 26 (1912): 715.

30. Richard Grathoff, ed., *Philosophers in Exile: The Correspondence of Alfred Schutz and Aron Gurwitsch, 1939–1959*, trans. J. Claude Evans (Bloomington: Indiana University Press, 1989), 31 (December 19, 1940).

31. Marvin Farber, *Phenomenology as a Method and as a Philosophical Discipline* (Buffalo, NY: University of Buffalo, 1928), 9.

32. See Harry Todd Costello and Grover Smith, *Josiah Royce's Seminar, 1913–1914: As Recorded in the Notebooks of Harry T. Costello* (New Brunswick, NJ: Rutgers University Press, 1963), 44, 81, 160.

33. Albert Chandler, "Plato's Theory of Ideas Studied in the Light of Husserl's Theory of Universals" (PhD diss., Harvard University, 1913); Harvard University, *Reports of the President and Treasurer of Harvard College, 1911–12* (Cambridge, MA: Harvard University Press, 1913), 106; Karl Schuhmann, *Husserl-Chronik: Denk-Und Lebensweg Edmund Husserls* (Den Haag: Martinus Nijhoff, 1977), 169.

34. Robert Lindley Murray Underhill to R. B. Perry, March 3, 1915, box 3, folder 3, R. B. Perry Correspondence.

35. "Biography of Dr. Winthrop Pickard Bell," http://www.mta.ca/wpbell/bio.htm; "Further Education," http://www.mta.ca/wpbell/fureduc.htm.

36. R. B. Perry to Winthrop Pickard Bell, April 11, 1914, HPD2.

37. R. B. Perry to Dean C. H. Haskins, April 11, 1914, HPD2.

38. Winthrop Pickard Bell to R. B. Perry, March 31, 1914, box 2, folder 116, Harvard Graduate Student Folders, Pre-1917; R. B. Perry to Winthrop Pickard Bell, June 1, 1914, HPD2.

39. Winthrop Pickard Bell to R. B. Perry, May 2, 1914, box 2, folder 116, Harvard Graduate Student Folders, Pre-1917; Perry to Bell, June 1, 1914, HPD2.

40. Winthrop Pickard Bell to Herbert Spiegelberg, September 25, 1955, box 8550/1/101, Winthrop Pickard Bell Fonds, Mount Allison University Archives, Sackville, New Brunswick.

41. R. B. Perry to Abbott Lawrence Lowell, September 25, 1914, HPD2; William Phillips to Frank W. Hunnewell, October 1, 1914, box 2, folder 116, Harvard Graduate Student Folders, Pre-1917.

42. Hocking, "From the Early Days of the 'Logische Untersuchungen,'" 8–11.

43. Kuklick, *The Rise of American Philosophy*, 445–47.

44. "Biography of Dr. Winthrop Pickard Bell"; R. B. Perry to Kenneth Murdock, November 3, 1937, box 5, folder "Murdock, Dean K. B. (Committee of 9), October–November 1937," HPD10.

45. Marvin Farber to W. E. Hocking, July 2, 1923, box 8, folder 19, Marvin Farber Papers; Marvin Farber to W. E. Hocking, January 8, 1923, box 8, folder 19, Marvin Farber Papers.

46. Jude P. Dougherty, "Paul Weiss, 1901–2002," *Proceedings and Addresses of the American Philosophical Association* 77, no. 5 (2004): 174–75.

47. Farber to Hocking, July 2, 1923, box 8, folder 19, Marvin Farber Papers.

48. Susanne Langer to Marvin Farber, February 19, 1929, box 12, folder "Langer, Susanne," Marvin Farber Papers.

49. John Wild, *The Radical Empiricism of William James* (Westport, CT: Greenwood, 1980), 28.

50. Farber, *Phenomenology as a Method*, 21.

51. Ibid., v.

52. Ibid., 7.

53. Ibid., 37.

54. Ibid., 39–40.

55. Ibid., 1, 40.

56. Lovejoy, "On Some Conditions of Progress," 133; Holt et al., "The Program and First Platform of Six Realists," 394.

57. Farber, *Phenomenology as a Method*, 8.

58. Ibid., 1.

59. Ibid., 1–2.

60. Section 2, "The Object of Intentional Experience," section 4, "The Thing of Nature," and section 5, "The Phenomenological Description of Perception," are original to the dissertation, as well as the majority of section 6, "The Object of Reflection and the Polarity of Objects." Additionally, an entire paragraph is added to the end of section 1. Ibid., 101–20.

61. Marvin Farber, "The Perceptual Object," 1924, page 2, box 32, folder 6, Marvin Farber Papers.

62. Farber, *Phenomenology as a Method*, 102.

63. Farber, "Perceptual Object," 1924, box 32, folder 6, Marvin Farber Papers.

64. Marvin Farber to James Woods, April 7, 1923, box 25, folder "Woods, James," Marvin Farber Papers.

65. W. R. Boyce Gibson and Herbert Spiegelberg, "From Husserl to Heidegger: Excerpts from a 1928 Freiburg Diary by W. R. Boyce Gibson," *Journal of the British Society for Phenomenology* 2 (1971): 65.

66. Ibid., 63.

67. Ibid., 63–67.

68. Ibid., 72.

69. Woods and Hocking, quoted in "Charles Hartshorne—2G," box 12, folder "Sheldon Fellowship, 1923–1924 (1)" Sheldon Fund Records.

70. Charles Hartshorne to L. B. R. Briggs, March 3, 1924, box 12, folder "Sheldon Fellows, 1923–1924," Sheldon Fund Records.

71. Charles Hartshorne, review of *Jahrbuch für Philosophie und Phänomenologische Forschung*, by Edmund Husserl, *Philosophical Review* 38, no. 3 (1929): 285, 89.

72. Ibid., 290–91.

73. Ibid., 288–89.

74. C. I. Lewis to Dean L. B. R. Briggs, January 30, 1924, box 13, folder "Sheldon Fellowships," Sheldon Fund Records.

75. W. E. Hocking to Dean L. B. R. Briggs, February 3, 1924, box 13, folder "Sheldon Fellowships," Sheldon Fund Records.

76. Dorion Cairns, "My Own Life," http://thenewschoolhistory.org/wp-content/uploads/2014/07/cairns_myownlife-web.pdf; W. E. Hocking to Edmund Husserl, June 20, 1924, box 12, folder "Edmund Husserl (4 of 4)," W. E. Hocking Correspondence.

77. Cairns, "My Own Life."

78. Dorion Cairns to James Woods, February 3, 1925, box 13, folder "Sheldon Fellows," Sheldon Fund Records.

79. Ibid.

80. Ibid.

81. Lester Embree, "Editorial Foreword," in *The Philosophy of Edmund Husserl, by Dorion Cairns*, ed. Lester Embree (Dordrecht: Springer, 2013), vi.

82. "Vivian Jerould McGill—3G," box 14, folder "Sheldon Fellows," Sheldon Fund Records. Cairns, "My Own Life."

83. Vivian Jerould McGill to Sheldon Fellowship Committee, October 23, 1925, box 14, folder "Sheldon Fellows," Sheldon Fund Records.

84. James Woods to C. H. Moore, October 6, 1926, box 15, folder "Sheldon Fellowships, 1926–1927," Sheldon Fund Records.

85. Cairns, "My Own Life."

86. Lester Embree, "The Legacy of Dorion Cairns and Aron Gurwitsch," in *American Phenomenology: Origins and Developments*, vol. XXVI, ed. Eugene Francis Kaelin and Calvin O. Schrag, Analecta Husserliana (Boston: Kluwer Academic, 1989), 125; Lester Embree and Michael Barber, "The Golden Age of Phenomenology: At the New School for Social Research, 1954–1973," in *The Reception of Husserlian Phenomenology in North America*, ed. Michela Beatrice Ferri (New York: Springer, 2019), 103.

87. Embree, "Editorial Foreword," vi–vii.

88. Dorion Cairns to R. B. Perry, April 9, 1932, box 4, folder C–F, R. B. Perry Correspondence.

89. See Dorion Cairns, "The Philosophy of Edmund Husserl" (PhD diss., Harvard University, 1933).

90. "Ralph Monroe Eaton," http://www.gf.org/fellows/all-fellows/ralph-monroe -eaton/; Ralph Monroe Eaton, *General Logic* (New York: C. Scribner's Sons, 1931); "17: Ralph M. Eaton," box 1, folder "Milton Fund—Clark Behest Applications, 1926–27," Records from the Committee on the William H. Milton Fund and the Joseph R. Clark Bequest, Harvard University Archives, Cambridge, MA.

91. Jason Bell, "Phenomenology's Inauguration in English and in the North American Curriculum: Winthrop Bell's 1927 Harvard Course," in *The Reception of Husserlian Phenomenology in North America*, ed. Michela Beatrice Ferri (New York: Springer, 2019), 26–27, 30–32, 44.

92. Harvard University, *Official Register of Harvard University: Announcement of the Courses of Instruction Offered by the Faculty of Arts and Sciences, 1926–27*, vol. XIII, no. 36 (Cambridge, MA: Harvard University, 1926), 126; James Woods to Dean C. H. Moore, February 8, 1927, box 3, folder "Woods, J. H. (2)," Dean of FAS Records.

93. Alward Brown to James Woods, March 8, 1934, box 2, folder "Brown, AE," HPD10.

94. "Preliminary Examination for the Ph.D.: Logic," Spring, 1930, box 15, folder "310—Preliminary Exams, 1930–1939," HPD15; Dorion Cairns to R. B. Perry, November 4, 1932, box 4, folder C–F, R. B. Perry Correspondence; R. B. Perry to M. M. Bober, November 19, 1930, box 7, folder B, R. B. Perry Correspondence; W. E. Hocking to Edmund Husserl, October 24, 1932, box 12, folder "Edmund Husserl (4 of 4)," W. E. Hocking Correspondence.

95. Paul Weiss to James Woods, November 21, 1929, box 9, folder "Weiss, Prof. Paul, 1935–6," HPD10.

96. Paul Weiss to R. B. Perry, October 7, 1931, box 4, folder T–Z, R. B. Perry Correspondence.

97. Everett John Nelson to the chairman of the Committee on the Sheldon Fund, July 9, 1930, box 17, folder "Sheldon Fellows, 1929–1930," Sheldon Fund Records.

98. "John Daniel Wild," http://www.gf.org/fellows/all-fellows/john-daniel-wild/; C. I. Lewis to C. H. Moore, August 26, 1927, box 3, folder "Woods, J. H. (1)," Dean of FAS Records; C. I. Lewis to C. H. Moore, April 6, 1928, box 4, folder "Philosophy (and Psychology) (1)," Dean of FAS Records.

99. Woessner, *Heidegger in America*, 29.

100. John Wild to R. B. Perry, May 24, 1931, box 5, folder W–Z, R. B. Perry Correspondence.

101. See Dorion Cairns, Lester Embree, and John Wild, "A Letter to John Wild about Husserl," *Research in Phenomenology* 5 (1975): 155–81.

102. John Wild to R. B. Perry, December 31, 1934, box 9, folder "Wild, Dr. John," HPD10; Harvard University, *Official Register of Harvard University: Announcement of the Courses of Instruction Offered by the Faculty of Arts and Sciences, 1935–36* (Cambridge, MA: Harvard University, 1935), 208.

103. W. E. Hocking to W. S. Ferguson, February 12, 1940, box 11, folder "Harvard University, Dean's Office," W. E. Hocking Correspondence; Harvard University, *Official Register of Harvard University: Announcement of the Courses of Instruction Offered by the Faculty of Arts and Sciences, 1936–37* (Cambridge, MA: Harvard University, 1936), 199.

104. See Cairns, "Philosophy of Edmund Husserl"; Charles Malik, "The Metaphysics of Time in the Philosophies of A. N. Whitehead and M. Heidegger" (PhD diss., Harvard University, 1937); and Erminie Greene Huntress, "The Phenomenology of Conscience" (PhD diss., Radcliffe College, 1937).

105. R. B. Perry to Fritz Marti, February 6, 1937, box 5, folder Ma–Mu, HPD10; C. I. Lewis to Dewitt Parker, March 4, 1937, box 5, folder Ma–Mu, HPD10; William Frankena to R. B. Perry, May 10, 1936, box 8, folder 4, R. B. Perry Correspondence; Ruth Allen to W. E. Hocking, March 19, 1938, box 11, folder "Harvard University Department of Philosophy (3 of 10)," W. E. Hocking Correspondence.

106. Frankena to R. B. Perry, May 10, 1936, box 8, folder 4, R. B. Perry Correspondence.

107. William Frankena to Roderick Firth, May 23, 1961, Burton Dreben Papers (unorganized), private collection of Warren Goldfarb, Cambridge, MA.

108. Charles Malik to W. E. Hocking, February 1, 1936, box 16, folder "Charles Malik (1 of 5)," W. E. Hocking Correspondence.

109. Ibid.; see also Heidegger, *Being and Time*, 231.

110. Malik to W. E. Hocking, February 1, 1936, box 16, folder "Charles Malik (1 of 5)," W. E. Hocking Correspondence.

CHAPTER A

1. Marjorie Grene, "Intellectual Autobiography," in *The Philosophy of Marjorie Grene*, ed. Randall E. Auxier and Lewis Edwin Hahn (Chicago: Open Court 2002), 10.

2. Benjamin Cohen, "An Interview with Marjorie Grene," *Believer*, no. 22 (March 1, 2005), https://believermag.com/an-interview-with-marjore-grene/.

3. Marjory Grene, "Reply to Charles M. Sherover," in *The Philosophy of Marjorie Grene*, ed. Randall E. Auxier and Lewis Edwin Hahn (Chicago: Open Court 2002), 547–50.

4. Marjorie Grene, "The Reception of Continental Philosophy in America," in *Philosophy in and out of Europe*, ed. Marjorie Grene (Berkeley: University of California Press, 1976), 29.

5. Grene, "Intellectual Autobiography," 5.

6. Marjorie Grene, "A Note on the Philosophy of Heidegger: Confessions of a Young Positivist," in *Philosophy In and Out of Europe*, ed. Marjorie Grene (Berkeley: University of California Press, 1976), 44.

7. Ibid., 39.

8. Grene, "Intellectual Autobiography," 5.

9. Marjorie Grene, "The Concept of 'Existenz' in Contemporary German Philosophy" (PhD diss., Radcliffe, 1935), 21–22.

10. Ibid., 35.

11. See Rudolf Carnap, "Überwindung der Metaphysik durch logische Analyse der Sprache," *Erkenntnis* 2 (1931): 513–32.

12. Grene, "Intellectual Autobiography," 7–8.

13. Ibid., 9, 18; Marjorie Grene, preface to *The Knower and the Known* (Berkeley: University of California Press, 1974).

14. Heidegger, *Ontology*, 14.

15. Marjorie Grene, "On Some Distinctions between Men and Brutes," *Ethics* 57, no. 2 (1947): 122.

16. Charles Virtue to Roderick Firth, November 29, 1961, box 17, folder M, HPD11.

17. William R. Greer, "Susanne K. Langer, Philosopher, Is Dead at 89," *New York Times*, July 19, 1985.

18. "Marjorie Glicksman Grene: Curriculum Vitae," https://www.phil.vt.edu/people/MGreneCV.pdf.

19. For an explanation of this data, see appendix B.

20. National Education Association, "Teacher Supply & Demand in Colleges and Universities: 1955–56 and 1956–57," 1957, box 25, folder "Ford Foundation—Fund for the Advancement of Education," Alfred Schütz Papers, 34–35, 45.

21. Grene, "Intellectual Autobiography," 8–12; Marjorie Grene, "In and On Friendship," in *Human Nature and Natural Knowledge: Essays Presented to Marjorie Grene on the Occasion of Her Seventy-Fifth Birthday*, ed. Alan Donagan, Anthony N. Perovich, and Michael V. Wedin (Boston: D. Reidel, 1986), 860.

22. Marjorie Grene, "Philosophy of Medicine: Prolegomena to a Philosophy of Science," *PSA: Proceedings of the Biennial Meeting of the Philosophy of Science Association, 1976* (1976): 77–92.

23. Grene, "Intellectual Autobiography," 8–12; "Marjorie Glicksman Grene: Curriculum Vitae."

24. Grene, "Intellectual Autobiography," 10; Elaine Woo, "Marjorie Grene Dies at 98; Historian of Philosophy Known as Independent Thinker," *Los Angeles Times*, March 22, 2009.

25. Grene, "Intellectual Autobiography," 12.

26. See Marjorie Grene, *Dreadful Freedom: A Critique of Existentialism* (Chicago: University of Chicago Press, 1948); and Marjorie Grene, *Martin Heidegger* (New York: Hillary House, 1957).

27. Grene, "Intellectual Autobiography," 4.

28. Grene, *Dreadful Freedom*, 47–48.

29. Ibid., 47.

30. James T. Kloppenberg, *Uncertain Victory: Social Democracy and Progressivism in European and American Thought, 1870–1920* (New York: Oxford University Press, 1986), 37–63.

31. Grene, "Intellectual Autobiography," 11.

32. Marjorie Grene, "Kierkegaard: The Philosophy," *Kenyon Review* 9, no. 1 (1947): 58.

33. Grene, *Dreadful Freedom*, 51.

34. Grene, *Martin Heidegger*, 35, 51–52.

35. Grene, *Dreadful Freedom*, 69–72.

36. Grene, *Martin Heidegger*, 55.

37. Grene, *Dreadful Freedom*, 75.

38. Ibid., 145.

39. Grene, *Martin Heidegger*, 13–14.

40. Ibid., 17.

41. Ibid., 27.

42. Heidegger, *Being and Time*, 95–107.

43. Grene, *Martin Heidegger*, 22.

44. Ibid., 14–15.

45. Ibid., 82.

46. Ibid., 83.

47. Ibid., 29.

48. Grene, "In and on Friendship," 361–62.

49. "Marjorie Glicksman Grene: Curriculum Vitae."

50. Grene, "In and On Friendship," 361–62.

51. Marjorie Grene, *A Philosophical Testament* (Chicago: Open Court, 1995), 69.

52. Ibid., 80.

53. Marjory Grene, "Reply to Phillip R. Sloan," in *The Philosophy of Marjorie Grene*, ed. Randall E. Auxier and Lewis Edwin Hahn (Chicago: Open Court 2002), 257; Grene, "Intellectual Autobiography," 20–21.

54. Grene, "Intellectual Autobiography," 14.

55. Grene, *The Knower and the Known*, 185.

56. Ibid., 228.

57. Ibid., 185.

58. Ibid., 233.

59. Ibid., 238, 41.

60. Ibid., 217–19.

61. Ibid., 241.

62. Ibid., 242.

63. Marjorie Grene, *The Understanding of Nature: Essays in the Philosophy of Biology* (Boston: D. Reidel, 1974), 352–57.

64. Grene, *The Knower and the Known*, 173, 176.

65. Ibid.

66. Grene, *The Understanding of Nature*, 354.

67. Ibid., 357.

68. Merleau-Ponty, *Phenomenology of Perception*, 379–80.

69. Grene, *A Philosophical Testament*, 18.

CHAPTER THREE

Epigraph: Aron Gurwitsch, "April 20, 1941," in *Philosophers in Exile: The Correspondence of Alfred Schutz and Aron Gurwitsch, 1939–1959*, ed. Richard Grathoff, trans. J. Claude Evans (Bloomington: Indiana University Press, 1989), 36.

1. Scott Soames, *Philosophical Analysis in the Twentieth Century*, vol. 1 (Princeton, NJ: Princeton University Press, 2003), xii.

2.   In this, I am informed by E. P. Thompson's analysis of the emergence of working-class identity: "And class happens when some men, as a result of common experiences (inherited or shared), feel and articulate the identity of their interests as between themselves, and as against other men whose interests are different from (and usually opposed to) theirs. . . . Class-consciousness is the way in which these experiences are handled in cultural terms: embodied in traditions, value-systems, ideas, and institutional forms." E. P Thompson, *The Making of the English Working Class* (New York: Vintage, 1966), 9–10.

3.   Giuseppe Peano, quoted in Paolo Mancosu, *The Adventure of Reason: Interplay between Philosophy of Mathematics and Mathematical Logic, 1900–1940* (Oxford: Oxford University Press, 2010), 7.

4.   See ibid.

5.   Felix Kaufmann, *The Infinite in Mathematics: Logico-mathematical Writings*, Vienna Circle Collection (Boston: D. Reidel, 1978), 199.

6.   As Edward Huntington wrote, logical propositions are "blank forms in which the letters a, b, c, etc. may denote any objects we please and the symbols + and × any rules of combination." Quoted in Mancosu, *The Adventure of Reason*, 15.

7.   Gottlob Frege, "Sense and Reference," *Philosophical Review* 57, no. 3 (1948): 209–30.

8.   Bertrand Russell, "On Denoting," *Mind* 114, no. 456 (2005): 876–78.

9.   Herbert Feigl, "The Wiener Kreis in America," in *The Intellectual Migration: Europe and America, 1930–1960*, ed. Donald Fleming and Bernard Bailyn (Cambridge, MA: Belknap Press of Harvard University Press, 1969), 630–38.

10. Ibid., 651–58.

11. "A Statement of Policy," *Analysis* 1, no. 1 (1933): 1.

12. Greg Frost-Arnold, "When Did 'Analytic Philosophy' Become an Actor's Category?," *Obscure and Confused Ideas*, May 2011, http://obscureandconfused .blogspot.com/2011/05/when-did-analytic-philosophy-become.html; Eric Schliesser, "Nagel's Philosophic Prophecy . . . Or How Analytic Philosophy as We Know It Was Invented . . ." *New APPS: Art, Politics, Philosophy, Science*; Eric Schliesser, "On the Invention of Analytic Philosophy by Ernest Nagel (II)," *New APPS: Art, Politics, Philosophy, Science*, http://www.newappsblog .com/2011/10/on-the-invention-of-analytic-philosophy-by-ernest-nagel-ii.html.

13. Ernest Nagel, "Impressions and Appraisals of Analytic Philosophy in Europe. I," *Journal of Philosophy* 33, no. 1 (1936): 6.

14. Ibid., 5, 7–8.

15. Henry Sheffer to Lebaron Russell Briggs, October 23, 1910, box 2, folder "1909–11, R–Z," Sheldon Fund Records.

16. See Harvard University, *Official Register of Harvard University: Announcement of the Courses of Instruction Offered by the Faculty of Arts and Sciences 1924–25*, vol. XXI, no. 37 (1924), 114–18.

17. Harvard University, *Harvard University Catalogue: 1915–16* (Cambridge, MA: Harvard University Press, 1916), 472.

18. Harvard University, *Harvard University Catalogue: 1917–18* (Cambridge, MA: Harvard University Press, 1917), 122.

19. "Preliminary Examination for the Ph.D.—Spring 1929. LOGIC," Spring 1929, box 14, folder "309: Preliminary Exams 1929 and Earlier," HPD15.

20. In 1930, Harvard's Philosophy Department consisted of seven full professors (W. E. Hocking and R. B. Perry, C. I. Lewis, David Wight Prall, Alfred North Whitehead, Harry Astryn Wolfson, and James Haughton Woods), one associate professor (Henry Sheffer), and one assistant professor (Ralph Monroe Eaton).

21. Perry, *A Defense of Philosophy*, 17.

22. Jerome Greene to R. B. Perry, October 11, 1934, box 3, folder "Greene, J. D. + W. G. Land—Tercentenary 1934–5, 1935–6," HPD10; "Ballots," box 3, folder "Greene, J. D. + W. G. Land—Tercentenary 1934–5, 1935–6," 1935–6, HPD10; R. B. Perry to Jerome Greene, October 30, 1934, box 3, folder "Greene, J. D. + W. G. Land—Tercentenary 1934–5, 1935–6," HPD10.

23. Perry to Greene, October 30, 1934, box 3, folder "Greene, J. D. + W. G. Land—Tercentenary 1934–5, 1935–6," HPD10.

24. R. B. Perry to Jerome Greene, December 4, 1934, box 3, folder "Greene, J. D. + W. G. Land—Tercentenary 1934–5, 1935–6," HPD10.

25. Jerome Greene to R. B. Perry, December 5, 1934, box 3, folder "Greene, J. D. + W. G. Land—Tercentenary 1934–5, 1935–6," HPD10.

26. R. B. Perry to W. B. Land, December 12, 1934, box 3, folder "Greene, J. D. + W. G. Land—Tercentenary 1934–5, 1935–6," HPD10.

27. "Proceedings of the American Philosophical Association, 1938: Twelfth Annual Report of the Board of Officers," *Philosophical Review* 48, no. 2 (1939): 187–88.

28. Ibid., 188–89; C. I. Lewis to Albert Balz, January 31, 1938, box 1, folder "American Philosophical Association," HPD10.

29. R. B. Perry to Arthur Mitchell, June 6, 1932, box 4, folder M–Q, R. B. Perry Correspondence.

30. "Proceedings of the American Philosophical Association, 1931," *Philosophical Review* 41, no. 2 (1932): 189.

31. Henry Boynton Smith to R. B. Perry, March 2, 1932, box 4, folder R–S, R. B. Perry Correspondence.

32. R. B. Perry to Henry Boynton Smith, April 7, 1932, box 4, folder R–S, R. B. Perry Correspondence.

33. Department rankings were compiled through a survey of prominent philosophers. The top ten departments listed were (1) Harvard, (2) Columbia, (3) Chicago, (4) Cornell, (5) Yale, (6) Princeton, (7) Johns Hopkins, (8) University of California, (9) University of Michigan, (10) University of Pennsylvania.

Raymond M. Hughes, *A Study of the Graduate Schools of America* (Oxford, OH: Miami University, 1925), 26. See appendix B for information on hiring data.

34. "Charles Augustus Baylis—2G," box 4, 'Sheldon Fellowships 1926–1927' Sheldon Fellowships 1926–1927, Sheldon Fund Records.

35. W. E. Hocking to Alban Widgery, January 18, 1937, box 2, folder Do–Dy, HPD10.

36. Alward Brown to David Prall, February 2, 1939, box 2, folder "Brown, AE," HPD10.

37. Alward Brown to James Woods, August 22, 1930, box 2, folder "Brown, AE," HPD10.

38. James Woods to Alward Brown, August 29, 1930, box 2, folder "Brown, AE," HPD10; James Woods to Alward Brown, June 11, 1931, box 2, folder "Brown, AE," HPD10.

39. Brown to James Woods, March 8, 1934, box 2, folder "Brown, AE," HPD10; Alward Brown to R. B. Perry, November 16, 1934, box 2, folder "Brown, AE," HPD10; Brown to David Prall, February 2, 1939, box 2, folder "Brown, AE," HPD10.

40. Alward Brown to W. E. Hocking, October 21, 1935, box 2, folder "Brown, AE," HPD10.

41. Hocking to Alban Widgery, January 18, 1937, box 2, folder Do–Dy, HPD10.

42. R. B. Perry to Kenneth Murdock, December 6, 1933, box 4, folder "Philosophy and Psychology," Dean of FAS Records.

43. William T. Parry, "V. Jerauld Mcgill (1897–1977)," *Philosophy and Phenomenological Research* 38, no. 2 (1977): 283–86.

44. Ibid.; Richard T. Hull, ed., *Presidential Addresses of the American Philosophical Association, 1941–1950*, vol. 5, American Philosophical Association Centennial Series (Amherst, NY: Prometheus Books, 2005), 5:347–48; Winthrop Pickard Bell to R. B. Perry, May 23, 1927, box 6, folder B, R. B. Perry Correspondence; Embree and Barber, "The Golden Age of Phenomenology," 99; "Trayhern, Robert John," http://rbscp.lib.rochester.edu/4787.

45. Ralph Tyler Flewelling to Edmund Husserl, October 26, 1933, box 4, folder "Visiting Professor," USC School of Philosophy Records.

46. Edmund Husserl to Ralph Tyler Flewelling (Trans. by Dr. Von Koerber), November 23, 1933, box 4, folder "Visiting Professor," USC School of Philosophy Records.

47. Ralph Tyler Flewelling to Edmund Husserl, January 13, 1934, box 4, folder "Visiting Professor," USC School of Philosophy Records.

48. Edmund Husserl to Ralph Tyler Flewelling (trans. Dr. Von Koerber), March 11, 1934, box 4, folder "Visiting Professor," USC School of Philosophy Records; Ralph Tyler Flewelling to Edmund Husserl, April 4, 1934, box 4, folder "Visiting Professor," USC School of Philosophy Records.

49. Bell to R. B. Perry, May 23, 1927, box 6, folder B, R. B. Perry Correspondence.

50. Embree and Barber, "The Golden Age of Phenomenology," 103; Richard Zaner, "The Role of Dorion Cairns in the Reception of Phenomenology in North America: The First 'Born American' Phenomenologist," in *The Reception of Husserlian Phenomenology in North America*, ed. Michela Beatrice Ferri (New York: Springer, 2019), 132–35.

51. Claus-Dieter Krohn, *Intellectuals in Exile: Refugee Scholars and the New School for Social Research* (Amherst: University of Massachusetts Press, 1993), 27–29.

52. Fritz Kaufmann to Marvin Farber, September 24, 1939, box 11, folder "Kaufmann, Fritz, 1937–39," Marvin Farber Papers.

53. Betty Drury to Stephen Duggan, February 13, 1936, box 32, folder "Herbert Spiegelberg (1 of 2)," Emergency Committee Records; Krohn, *Intellectuals in Exile*, 15–16.

54. Krohn, *Intellectuals in Exile*, 25, 86–89.

55. Kenneth Murdock to R. B. Perry, August 7, 1933, box 3, folder "Philosophy and Psychology," Dean of FAS Records.

56. Brand Blanshard to Gustavus Watts Cunningham, November 9, 1941, box 20, folder "Sage School of Philosophy, 1935–1946, A–J," Cornell Dept. of Philosophy Records.

57. Paul Anderson to Laurens Hickok Seelye, March 11, 1941, box 32, folder "Herbert Spiegelberg (2 of 2)," Emergency Committee Records.

58. Geiger to MacCracken, November 5, 1933, box 11, folder "Geiger, Moritz (1 of 2)," Emergency Committee Records.

59. Hanna Hafkesbrints to Felix Warburg, September 28, 1933, box 11, folder "Geiger, Moritz (1 of 2)," Emergency Committee Records; Hanna Hafkesbrints to Felix Warburg, October 3, 1933, box 11, folder "Geiger, Moritz (1 of 2)," Emergency Committee Records; Edward Murrow to Henry Stuart, January 15, 1934, box 11, folder "Geiger, Moritz (1 of 2)," Emergency Committee Records; "Status of the Moritz Geiger Case," October 14, 1933, box 11, folder "Geiger, Moritz (1 of 2)," Emergency Committee Records.

60. Geiger to MacCracken, November 5, 1933, box 11, folder "Geiger, Moritz (1 of 2)," Emergency Committee Records.

61. Moritz Geiger to Mary Waite, May 26, 1934, box 11, folder "Geiger, Moritz (1 of 2)," Emergency Committee Records.

62. Henry MacCracken to Stephen Duggan, July 16, 1937, box 11, folder "Geiger, Moritz (2 of 2)," Emergency Committee Records.

63. Henry MacCracken to Stephen Duggan, January 3, 1943, box 14, folder "Fritz Kaufmann (1 of 3)," Emergency Committee Records.

64. Aron Gurwitsch to Betty Drury, September 12, 1943, box 13, folder "Gurwitsch, Aron," Emergency Committee Records.

65. Aron Gurwitsch to Betty Drury, January 9, 1941, box 13, folder "Gurwitsch, Aron," Emergency Committee Records.

66. Grathoff, *Philosophers in Exile*, 15 (April 5, 1940).

67. Ibid., 18 (August 23, 1940).

68. Leo Spitzer to Alfred Schütz, April 21, 1942, box 13, folder "Gurwitsch, Aron," Emergency Committee Records.

69. Grathoff, *Philosophers in Exile*, 41 (October 9, 1941).

70. Ibid., 58 (July 11, 1942).

71. Ibid., 63–64 (November 3, 1942).

72. Gurwitsch to Betty Drury, January 9, 1941, box 13, folder "Gurwitsch, Aron," Emergency Committee Records.

73. Frederick Beutel to W. E. Hocking, February 19, 1936, box 4, folder La–Ly, HPD10.

74. Krohn, *Intellectuals in Exile*, 24.

75. Maurice Picard to Gustavus Watts Cunningham, February 8, 1940, box 22, folder "Sage School of Philosophy Correspondence + Recommendations on Teaching Positions, 1935–1952, D–I," Cornell Dept. of Philosophy Records.

76. Fritz Kaufmann to Marvin Farber, September 14, 1937, box 11, folder "Kaufmann, Fritz, 1937–39," Marvin Farber Papers.

77. "General Information: Fritz Kaufmann," n.d., box 14, folder "Kaufmann, Fritz (1 of 3)," Emergency Committee Records; Fritz Kaufmann to Bernard Flexner, July 8, 1940, box 14, folder "Kaufmann, Fritz (2 of 3)," Emergency Committee Records.

78. Esther Simpson to John Whyte, May 18, 1936, box 14, folder "Kaufmann, Fritz (1 of 3)," Emergency Committee Records.

79. Gilbert Ryle to March 11, 1936, box 14, folder "Kaufmann, Fritz (1 of 3)," Emergency Committee Records; R.G. Collingwood to Walter Adams, March 12, 1936, box 14, folder "Kaufmann, Fritz (1 of 3)," Emergency Committee Records.

80. Dalton Howard to Betty Drury, April 13, 1938, box 14, folder "Kaufmann, Fritz (1 of 3)," Emergency Committee Records.

81. Herbert Spiegelberg to Committee in Aid of German Displaced Scholars, August 5, 1934, box 32, folder "Spiegelberg, Herbert (1 of 2)," Emergency Committee Records; "Further References," n.d., box 32, folder "Spiegelberg, Herbert (1 of 2)," Emergency Committee Records; "General Information," n.d., box 32, folder "Spiegelberg, Herbert (1 of 2)," Emergency Committee Records.

82. Herbert Spiegelberg to the president of Vassar College, December 12, 1937, box 32, folder "Spiegelberg, Herbert (1 of 2)," Emergency Committee Records; Herbert Spiegelberg to John Whyte, December 29, 1937, box 32, folder "Spiegelberg, Herbert (1 of 2)," Emergency Committee Records.

83. "Interview Memorandum," February 23, 1938, box 32, folder "Spiegelberg, Herbert (1 of 2)," Emergency Committee Records.

84. Betty Drury to Bernard Flexner, March 28, 1939, box 32, folder "Spiegelberg, Herbert (1 of 2)," Emergency Committee Records.

85. Herbert Spiegelberg to Frank Aydelotte, September 8, 1939, box 32, folder "Spiegelberg, Herbert (1 of 2)," Emergency Committee Records.

86. "Application for Renewal," May 22, 1940, box 32, folder "Spiegelberg, Herbert (2 of 2)," Emergency Committee Records; Herbert Spiegelberg to Betty Drury, May 9, 1940, box 32, folder "Spiegelberg, Herbert (2 of 2)," Emergency Committee Records.

87. Frank Aydelotte to Stephen Duggan, May 21, 1940, box 32, folder "Spiegelberg, Herbert (2 of 2)," Emergency Committee Records.

88. Thomas Barrows to Laurens Hickok Seelye, March 13, 1941, box 32, folder "Spiegelberg, Herbert (2 of 2)," Emergency Committee Records.

89. Herbert Spiegelberg to Laurence H. Seelye, June 21, 1942, box 32, folder "Spiegelberg, Herbert (2 of 2)," Emergency Committee Records.

90. George Psathas, "Introduction: In Memory of Herbert Spiegelberg, 1904–1990," *Human Studies* 15, no. 4 (1992): 363.

91. Alfred Schütz, "Felix Kaufmann: 1895–1949," *Social Research* 17, no. 1 (1950): 1–4.

92. "Excerpted from Confidential Memorandum (Concerning Austrian Scholars) Submitted to the Emergency Committee with Letter of May 5 from Malcom W. Davis," n.d., box 14, folder "Kaufmann, Felix," Emergency Committee Records.

93. Alvin Johnson to Stephen Duggan, May 24, 1938, box 13, folder "Kaufmann, Felix," Emergency Committee Records.

94. F. Kaufmann, *The Infinite in Mathematics*, 199.

95. Ibid., ix–xv, 188–201.

96. Krohn, *Intellectuals in Exile*, 59–73; Lewis A. Coser, *Refugee Scholars in America: Their Impact and Their Experiences* (New Haven, CT: Yale University Press, 1984), 104.

97. Coser, *Refugee Scholars in America*, 102–6; Krohn, *Intellectuals in Exile*, 70–71.

98. "Suggestions of the Coordinating Committee to the Graduate Faculty," January 20, 1941, folder "Graduate Faculty Minutes Sept. 1933–June 1945," box 1, New School Archives.

99. W. E. Hocking to Kinley Mather, January 29, 1936, folder "Gutkind, Dr. Eric," box 3, HPD10.

100. Kinley Mather to W. E. Hocking, January 30, 1936, folder "Gutkind, Dr. Eric," box 3, HPD10.

101. Malvine Husserl to Marvin Farber, February 17, 1936, box 9, folder "Husserl, Edmund and Mrs.," Marvin Farber Papers; Edmund Husserl to Marvin Farber,

February 18, 1936, box 9, folder "Husserl, Edmund and Mrs.," Marvin Farber Papers.

102. Edmund Husserl to Marvin Farber, November 20, 1936, box 9, folder "Husserl, Edmund and Mrs.," Marvin Farber Papers; Kah Kyung Cho, "Phenomenology as Cooperative Task: Husserl–Farber Correspondence during 1936–37," *Philosophy and Phenomenological Research* 50 (1990): 30.

103. Spiegelberg, *The Context of the Phenomenological Movement*, 242–46.

104. H. L. Van Breda and Thomas Vongehr, *Geschichte Des Husserl-Archivs* (Dordrecht: Springer, 2007), 39–62.

105. Fritz Kaufmann to Marvin Farber, May 21, 1937, box 11, folder "Kaufman, Fritz 1937–39," Marvin Farber Papers.

106. Fritz Kaufmann to Marvin Farber, September 23, 1938, box 11, folder "Kaufmann, Fritz 1937–39," Marvin Farber Papers.

107. Eugen Fink to Marvin Farber, October 31, 1938, box 6, folder "Fink, Eugen," Marvin Farber Papers; Marvin Farber to Eugen Fink, December 26, 1938, box 6, folder "Fink, Eugen," Marvin Farber Papers.

108. Eugen Fink to Marvin Farber, September 25, 1939, box 6, folder "Fink, Eugen," Marvin Farber Papers.

109. See Edmund Husserl, "Grundlegende Untersuschungen Zum Phänomeologischen Urpsrung Der Räumlichkeit Der Natur," in *Philosophical Essays in Memory of Edmund Husserl*, ed. Marvin Farber (Cambridge, MA: Harvard University Press, 1940).

110. See Marvin Farber, ed., *Philosophical Essays in Memory of Edmund Husserl* (Cambridge, MA: Published for the University of Buffalo by the Harvard University Press, 1940).

111. Fritz Kaufmann to Marvin Farber, February 11, 1939, box 11, folder "Kaufmann, Fritz, 1937–39," Marvin Farber Papers; Marvin Farber to Fritz Kaufmann, February 18, 1939, box 11, folder "Kaufmann, Fritz, 1937–39," Marvin Farber Papers.

112. Fritz Kaufmann to Marvin Farber, October 14, 1939, box 11, folder "Kaufmann, Fritz, 1937–39," Marvin Farber Papers; Fritz Kaufmann to Marvin Farber, October 15, 1939, box 11, folder "Kaufmann, Fritz, 1937–39," Marvin Farber Papers. See also Charles Hartshorne, "The Social Structure of Immediacy," in *Philosophical Essays in Memory of Edmund Husserl*, ed. Marvin Farber (Cambridge, MA: Published for the University of Buffalo by the Harvard University Press, 1940), 223–24.

113. Marvin Farber to Fritz Kaufmann, October 18, 1939, box 11, folder "Kaufmann, Fritz, 1937–39," Marvin Farber Papers.

114. Kaufmann to Marvin Farber, October 14, 1939, box 11, folder "Kaufmann, Fritz, 1937–39," Marvin Farber Papers.

115. Marvin Farber to Fritz Kaufmann, October 24, 1939, box 11, folder "Kaufmann, Fritz, 1937–39," Marvin Farber Papers.

116. Marvin Farber to Fritz Kaufmann, July 29, 1939, box 11, folder "Kaufmann, Fritz, 1937–39," Marvin Farber Papers.

117. Helmut Wagner, "Marvin Farber's Contribution to the Phenomenological Movement: An International Perspective," in *Philosophy and Science in Phenomenological Perspective*, ed. Kah Kyung Cho (Dordrecht: Martinus Nijhoff, 1984), 212; Marvin Farber to Gerhart Husserl, December 7, 1939, box 9, folder "Husserl, Gerhart, 1936–47," Marvin Farber Papers.

118. "New Science Unit Centers in Buffalo," *New York Times*, December 15, 1940.

119. Marvin Farber to Eugen Fink, April 10, 1940, box 6, folder "Fink, Eugen," Marvin Farber Papers.

120. Marvin Farber to Samuel Capen, April 3, 1946, box 3, folder "Capen, Samuel P., 1945–50," Marvin Farber Papers.

121. "International Phenomenological Society Statement of Cash Receipts and Expenses, February 1, 1942 to October 10, 1940," n.d., box 27, folder "International Phenomenological Society, Accounting Reports, 1942, 1946," Alfred Schütz Papers; "February 26, 1942," box 1, folder "Department of Philosophy Minutes, 1939–40–1949–50," HPD1; "June 8, 1944," box 1, folder "Department of Philosophy Minutes, 1939–40–1949–50," HPD1; "May 14, 1946," box 1, folder "Department of Philosophy Minutes, 1939–40–1949–50," HPD1; "May 25, 1943," box 1, folder "Department of Philosophy Minutes, 1939–40–1949–50," HPD1; "April 24, 1947," box 1, folder "Department of Philosophy Minutes, 1939–40–1949–50," HPD1.

122. George Boas to Marvin Farber, August 8, 1963, box 1, folder B, Marvin Farber Papers; Marvin Farber to Dorion Cairns, June 5, 1947, box 3, folder "Cairns, Dorian," Marvin Farber Papers; Alexander Galt to Richard Hays Williams, October 5, 1940, box 42, folder "International Phen. Society, D–K," *PPR* Papers.

123. "Journal of Philosophy and Phenomenological Research," n.d., box 24, folder "Marvin Farber Correspondence (1 of 14)," Alfred Schütz Papers.

124. Marvin Farber to Fritz Kaufmann, November 20, 1939, box 11, folder "Kaufmann, Fritz, 1937–39," Marvin Farber Papers; Marvin Farber to Fritz Kaufmann, October 15, 1939, box 11, folder "Kaufmann, Fritz, 1937–39," Marvin Farber Papers.

125. Marvin Farber to Eugen Fink, October 5, 1939, box 6, folder "Fink, Eugen," Marvin Farber Papers.

126. Marvin Farber to Alfred Schütz, July 17, 1940, box 24, folder "Farber, Marvin (1 of 14)," Alfred Schütz Papers.

127. Marvin Farber to Fritz Kaufmann, September 25, 1939, box 11, folder "Kaufmann, Fritz, 1937–39," Marvin Farber Papers.

128. Farber to Fritz Kaufmann, October 15, 1939, box 11, folder "Kaufmann, Fritz, 1937–39," Marvin Farber Papers; Marvin Farber to Fritz Kaufmann, Novem-

ber 25, 1939, box 11, folder "Kaufmann, Fritz, 1937–39," Marvin Farber Papers; Wagner, "Marvin Farber's Contribution," 212–13.

129. Marvin Farber to Fritz Kaufmann, August 30, 1939, box 11, folder "Kaufmann, Fritz, 1937–39," Marvin Farber Papers.

130. "Notes," *Philosophy and Phenomenological Research* 1, no. 1 (1940): 126.

131. Edmund Husserl, "Notizen Zur Raumkonstitution," *Philosophy and Phenomenological Research* 1, no. 1 (1940): 21–22.

132. Malvine Husserl's letter is not found in Farber's correspondence, but is discussed in a note to Alfred Schutz. The phrase "the enemy of the world" is placed in quotes. Marvin Farber to Alfred Schütz, July 13, 1940, box 24, folder "Farber, Marvin (1 of 14)," Alfred Schütz Papers.

133. Fritz Kaufmann to Marvin Farber, May 18, 1940, box 11, folder "Kaufmann, Fritz, 1940," Marvin Farber Papers.

134. Marvin Farber to Alfred Schütz, September 30, 1940, box 24, folder "Farber, Marvin (1 of 14)," Alfred Schütz Papers.

135. See Edmund Husserl, "Phänomenologie Und Anthropologie," *Philosophy and Phenomenological Research* 2, no. 1 (1941): 1–14.

136. "Notes," 126.

137. Marvin Farber to Alfred Schütz, August 20, 1939, box 20, folder "Schütz, Alfred, 1937–39," Marvin Farber Papers.

138. Eugen Fink to Marvin Farber, December 1, 1939, box 6, folder "Fink, Eugen," Marvin Farber Papers.

139. John Wild, quoted in Marvin Farber to Gerhart Husserl, October 5, 1940, box 9, folder "Husserl, Gerhart, 1936–47," Marvin Farber Papers.

140. See Ernest Nagel, "Symposium on Meaning and Truth, Part III: Discussion: Truth and Knowledge of the Truth," *Philosophy and Phenomenological Research* 5, no. 1 (1944): 50–68; Richard Brandt, "The Significance of Differences of Ethical Opinion for Ethical Rationalism," *Philosophy and Phenomenological Research* 4, no. 4 (1944), 469–95; Roy Wood Sellars, "The Meaning of True and False," *Philosophy and Phenomenological Research* 5, no. 1 (1944): 98–103; H. R. Smart, "What Is Deduction?," *Philosophy and Phenomenological Research* 5, no. 1 (1944): 37–49; Alfred Tarski, "The Semantic Conception of Truth: And the Foundations of Semantics," *Philosophy and Phenomenological Research* 4, no. 3 (1944): 341–76; Rudolf Carnap, "The Two Concepts of Probability: The Problem of Probability," *Philosophy and Phenomenological Research* 5, no. 4 (1945): 513–32; and Hans Reichenbach, "Reply to Donald C. Williams' Criticism of the Frequency Theory of Probability," *Philosophy and Phenomenological Research* 5, no. 4 (1945): 508–12.

141. Horace Kallen to Marvin Farber, May 28, 1945, box 10, folder "Kallen, Horace," Marvin Farber Papers.

142. W. V. O. Quine to Marvin Farber, November 12, 1945, box 17, folder "Quine, Willard V.," Marvin Farber Papers.

CHAPTER B

1. Later, Schütz helped facilitate Mises's immigration to the United States. Michael D. Barber, *The Participating Citizen: A Biography of Alfred Schutz* (Albany: State University of New York Press, 2004), 14–16, 19.

2. Alfred Schütz, *The Phenomenology of the Social World*, Northwestern University Studies in Phenomenology & Existential Philosophy (Evanston, IL: Northwestern University Press, 1967), 5–8.

3. Max Weber, quoted in ibid., 15.

4. Ibid., 16–17.

5. Ibid., 6.

6. Max Weber and Edward Shils, *Max Weber on the Methodology of the Social Sciences* (Glencoe, IL: Free Press, 1949), 90–93.

7. Schütz, *Phenomenology of the Social World*, 27–28.

8. Ibid., 17.

9. Ibid., xxxi.

10. Ibid., 18–19, 42.

11. Barber, *Participating Citizen*, 32.

12. Edmund Husserl, *The Phenomenology of Internal Time-Consciousness*, trans. James Churchill (Bloomington: Indiana University Press, 1964), 44–54, 63–70, 117–21.

13. Ibid., 110–11.

14. Helmut R. Wagner, *Alfred Schutz: An Intellectual Biography*, Heritage of Sociology (Chicago: University of Chicago Press, 1983), 36–37.

15. Barber, *Participating Citizen*, 41–42; Wagner, *Alfred Schutz: An Intellectual Biography*, 11–12.

16. Wagner, *Alfred Schutz: An Intellectual Biography*, 41–42.

17. Barber, *Participating Citizen*, 42–43; Wagner, *Alfred Schutz: An Intellectual Biography*, 46–47.

18. Schütz, *Phenomenology of the Social World*, 20–27.

19. Ibid., 26–31.

20. Ibid., 39–40.

21. Husserl, *Logical Investigations*, 1:191–200.

22. Schütz, *Phenomenology of the Social World*, 35–36, 75–78.

23. Ibid., 50–52.

24. Ibid., 91–96.

25. Ibid., 57–61, 144.

26. Ibid., 97–98.

27. Ibid., 22, 106–7.

28. Ibid., 101.

29. Ibid., 113–18.

30. Ibid., 163–67.

31. Ibid., 101–3.

32. Ibid., 172.

33. Ibid., 142–43.

34. Max Weber, quoted in ibid., 147.

35. Ibid., 151.

36. Ibid., 146–48.

37. Ibid., 169, 77–80.

38. Ibid., 180–84.

39. Ibid., 188–89.

40. Ibid., 189.

41. Ibid., 190–91.

42. Ibid., 195–99.

43. Ibid., 200.

44. Ibid., 200–201.

45. Ibid., 241–42.

46. Barber, *Participating Citizen*, 73–79; Wagner, *Alfred Schutz: An Intellectual Biography*, 64.

47. Barber, *Participating Citizen*, 80–84; Wagner, *Alfred Schutz: An Intellectual Biography*, 69–70.

48. Barber, *Participating Citizen*, 68–72.

49. Alfred Schütz, "June 30, 1945," in *A Friendship That Lasted a Lifetime: The Correspondence between Alfred Schütz and Eric Voegelin*, ed. Gerhard Wagner and Gilbert Weiss, trans. William Petropulos (Columbia: University of Missouri Press, 2011), 85.

50. Barber, *Participating Citizen*, 85–86.

51. Ibid., 131.

52. Ibid., 87–88, 131.

53. Alfred Schütz, quoted in ibid., 114.

54. Grathoff, *Philosophers in Exile*, 26 (November 9, 1940).

55. Ibid., 37 (April 26, 1941).

56. Barber, *Participating Citizen*, 88–91.

57. Ibid., 90–93.

58. Ibid., 97–99; Albert Salomon to Alfred Schütz, September 30, 1942, box 30, folder "Salomon, Albert," Alfred Schütz Papers.

59. Alfred Schütz, "The Scope and Function of a Department of Philosophy within the Graduate Faculty," May 22, 1953, box 4, folder "Memorandum on the Scope & Function of a Dept. of Philosophy in the Graduate Faculty," New School Graduate Faculty Collection., 2–3.

60. Alfred Schütz, "Other Minds: The Problem of Intersubjectivity in Contemporary Philosophy," 1957, box 16, folder "Other Minds, Spring Term 1957 (1 of 9)," Alfred Schütz Papers.

61. Alfred Schütz, "Sign and Symbol: Reading List," n.d., box 17, folder "Sign and Symbol I (4 of 4)," Alfred Schütz Papers.

62. Schütz's manuscripts were reconstructed and expanded upon by his student Thomas Luckmann. The resulting monograph was published in two volumes as *The Structures of The Life-World*. Barber, *Participating Citizen*, 219–23; Alfred Schütz and Thomas Luckmann, *The Structures of the Life-World*, 2 vols., Northwestern University Studies in Phenomenology & Existential Philosophy (Evanston, IL: Northwestern University Press, 1973).

63. Hans Jonas, "Alfred Schutz, 1899–1959," *Social Research* 26, no. 4 (1959): 471.

64. William James, quoted in Alfred Schütz, "On Multiple Realities," *Philosophy and Phenomenological Research* 5, no. 4 (1945): 533.

65. Ibid., 552.

66. Ibid., 564–71.

67. See Alfred Schütz, "The Well-Informed Citizen: An Essay on the Social Distribution of Knowledge," *Social Research* 13, no. 4 (1946): 463–78; and Alfred Schütz, "Making Music Together: A Study in Social Relationship," *Social Research* 18, no. 1 (1951): 97.

68. Michael D. Barber, "Schutz and the New School," in *The Golden Age of Phenomenology at the New School for Social Research, 1954–1973*, ed. Lester Embree (Athens: Ohio University Press, 2017), 43.

69. Barber, *Participating Citizen*, 217.

70. Jonas, "Alfred Schutz, 1899–1959," 474.

CHAPTER FOUR

Epigraphs: Raphael Demos, "Philosophical Aspects of the Recent Harvard Report on Education," *Philosophy and Phenomenological Research* 7, no. 2 (1946): 188; Edwin Boring to C. H. Moore, January 29, 1930, box 4, folder "Philosophy and Psychology (2)," Dean of FAS Records.

1. Thomas Lask, "Philosophical Group's Dominant View Is Criticized," *New York Times*, December 30, 1979.

2. Neil Gross, *Richard Rorty: The Making of an American Philosopher* (Chicago: University of Chicago Press, 2008), 223–25.

3. Edward B. Fiske, "Education 'Analysts' Win Battle in War of Philosophy," *New York Times*, January 6, 1981.

4. Richard Rorty, "Philosophy in America Today," *American Scholar* 51, no. 2 (1982): 183–200.

5. APA circular, quoted in Bruce Wilshire, *Fashionable Nihilism: A Critique of Analytic Philosophy* (Albany: State University of New York Press, 2002), 78.

6. Fiske, "Education 'Analysts' Win Battle."

7. John McDermott, quoted in ibid.

8. Rorty, "Philosophy in America Today," 187.

9. Ibid., 189.

10. W. S. Ferguson to W. E. Hocking, December 13, 1941, box 2, folder "Dean Ferguson, Sept. 1, 1941–Jan. 31, 1942," HPD11.

11. W. E. Hocking to W. S. Ferguson, December 20, 1941, box 2, folder "Dean Ferguson, Sept. 1, 1941–Jan. 31, 1942," HPD11.

12. See Harvard University, *Official Register of Harvard University: Announcement of the Courses of Instruction Offered by the Faculty of Arts and Sciences, 1942–43* (Cambridge, MA: Harvard University, 1942), 254–56; Harvard University, *Official Register of Harvard University: Announcement of the Courses of Instruction Offered by the Faculty of Arts and Sciences, 1943–44* (Cambridge, MA: Harvard University, 1943), 194–95; Harvard University, *Official Register of Harvard University: Announcement of the Courses of Instruction Offered by the Faculty of Arts and Sciences, 1944–45* (Cambridge, MA: Harvard University, 1944), 195–96.

13. Harvard University, *Official Register of Harvard University: Announcement of the Courses of Instruction Offered by the Faculty of Arts and Sciences, 1934–35* (Cambridge, MA: Harvard University, 1934), 325–28; and Harvard University, *Official Register of Harvard University: Announcement of the Courses of Instruction Offered by the Faculty of Arts and Sciences, 1936–37*, 197–98.

14. "Report to the President," August 15, 1942, box 3, folder "Dean's Report to the President, 1942," Records of the Dean, Addison Hibbard, 1935–1946, Northwestern University Archives, Evanston, IL.

15. Brand Blanshard, "Annual Report of the Department of Philosophy, 1945–46," July 2, 1946, box 343, folder "Reports to the President, Pharmacology–Physics, 1945," Yale Secretary's Office Records, 1899–1953.

16. Charles Hendel, "The Annual Report of the Department of Philosophy, 1952–53," July 7, 1953, box 348, folder "Reports to the President, Obstetrics and Gynecology–Physical Education, 1952–53," Yale Secretary's Office Records, 1899–1953.

17. Richard Norton Smith, *The Harvard Century: The Making of a University to a Nation* (New York: Simon and Schuster, 1986), 160–62.

18. James Conant, "Memorandum to the Committee on Objectives of a General Education," December 6, 1942, box 245, folder "General Education, Committee on Objectives of, 1943–1944," Records of the President of Harvard University, James Bryant Conant, Harvard University Archives, Cambridge, MA.

19. Harvard University Committee on the Objectives of a General Education in a Free Society, *General Education in a Free Society: Report of the Harvard Committee* (Cambridge, MA: Harvard University Press, 1945), vi.

20. Ibid., 195–98.

21. Robert A. McCaughey, *Stand, Columbia: A History of Columbia University in the City of New York, 1754–2004* (New York: Columbia University Press, 2003), 290.

22. Ibid., 290–93.

23. "Philosophy," 1927, box 1, folder "Mining and Metallurgy to Romance Languages," Reports of the Academic Departments to President N. M. Butler, Columbia University Archives, New York, NY.

24. Grayson Kirk, "Confidential Letter to the Members of the Philosophy Department," November 17, 1960, box 437, folder "Friess, Horace Leland," Columbia University Central Files, 1890–1984; Robert Cumming to Ernest Nagel, March 1, 1960, box 1, folder "Robert Cumming," Ernest Nagel Papers.

25. Ernest Nagel to Robert Cumming, March 2, 1960, box 1, folder "Robert Cumming," Ernest Nagel Papers.

26. Ernest Nagel to Robert Cumming, April 11, 1960, box 1, folder "Robert Cumming," Ernest Nagel Papers.

27. Marjorie Nicolson, "Committee Report," November 17, 1960, box 437, folder "Friess, Horace Leland," Columbia University Central Files, 1890–1984.

28. Ibid. The examples cited here are somewhat perplexing. Michigan's Philosophy Department was overwhelmingly dedicated to an analytic approach. At Yale, as will be discussed later, philosophical diversity was held as a value, but also a growing source of acrimonious conflict.

29. Horace Friess to Grayson Kirk, November 21, 1960, box 437, folder "Friess, Horace Leland," Columbia University Central Files, 1890–1984.

30. Ernest Nagel to Robert Cumming, April 5, 1960, box 1, folder "Robert Cumming," Ernest Nagel Papers.

31. Nicolson, "Committee Report," November 17, 1960, box 437, folder "Friess, Horace Leland," Columbia University Central Files, 1890–1984.

32. Robert Cumming to Ernest Nagel, May 16, 1960, box 1, folder "Robert Cumming," Ernest Nagel Papers.

33. Ernest Nagel to Robert Cumming, May 21, 1960, box 1, folder "Robert Cumming," Ernest Nagel Papers.

34. Robert Cumming to Ernest Nagel, June 14, 1960, box 1, folder "Robert Cumming," Ernest Nagel Papers. See also Gilbert Allardyce, "The Rise and Fall of the Western Civilization Course," *American Historical Review* 87, no. 3 (1982): 716.

35. Cumming to Ernest Nagel, June 14, 1960, box 1, folder "Robert Cumming," Ernest Nagel Papers.

36. Perry, *A Defense of Philosophy*, 17.

37. C. I. Lewis to B. F. Wright, May 31, 1946, box 9, folder "Philosophy," Dean of FAS Records.

38. Morton White, *A Philosopher's Story* (University Park: Pennsylvania State University Press, 1999), 126–28.

39. Henry Aiken, *Predicament of the University* (Bloomington: Indiana University Press, 1971), 8.

40. Ibid., 34.

41. Ibid., 25–27.

42. Ibid., 21.

43. Lewis to Buck, May 31, 1946, box 9, folder "Philosophy," Dean of FAS Records.

44. D. C. Williams to Paul Buck, March 6, 1950, box 5, folder "Provost Paul H. Buck, 1949–50," HPD11.

45. D. C. Williams to Paul Buck, September 30, 1949, box 5, folder "Provost Paul H. Buck, 1949–50," HPD11.

46. Ibid.

47. David Owen to D. C. Williams, March 1, 1950, box 7, folder O, HPD11; "Faculty Suggestions for New Second-Group Courses in General Education," November 2, 1946, folder "General Education Suggestions for Courses, 1947," Faculty Suggestions for New Courses in General Education, Harvard University Archives, Cambridge, MA.

48. D. C. Williams to R. B. Perry, March 23, 1949, box 7, folder "R. B. Perry," HPD11.

49. See Harvard University, *Official Register of Harvard University: Courses in General Education, 1948–1949*, vol. XLV, no. 10 (Cambridge, MA: Harvard University Press, 1948), 19, 21.

50. Kenneth Murdock to McGeorge Bundy, May 29, 1958, box 13, folder "Dean McGeorge Bundy, 1957–1958," HPD11; see also Harvard University, *Official*

Register of Harvard University: Courses in General Education, 1952–1953, vol. XLIX, no. 21 (Cambridge, MA: Harvard University, 1952), 20; Harvard University, *Official Register of Harvard University: Courses in General Education 1953–1954*, vol. L, no. 20 (Cambridge, MA: Harvard University Press, 1953), 20; and Harvard University, *Official Register of Harvard University: Courses in General Education 1954–1955*, vol. LI, no. 20 (Cambridge, MA: Harvard University, 1954).

51. White, *A Philosopher's Story*, 128–29.

52. Ibid., 129.

53. D. C. Williams to D. W. Gotshalk, November 12, 1959, box 14, folder G, HPD11.

54. Ibid.

55. D. C. Williams to Crane Brinton, March 16, 1951, box 9, folder B, HPD11.

56. D. C. Williams to David Owen, March 11, 1950, box 7, folder O, HPD11.

57. Williams to Gotshalk, November 12, 1959, box 14, folder G, HPD11.

58. D. C. Williams to David Owen, August 11, 1949, box 7, folder O, HPD11.

59. D. C. Williams to McGeorge Bundy, October 1, 1953, box 9, folder "Dean McGeorge Bundy, 1953–54," HPD11.

60. Kenneth Murdock to McGeorge Bundy, May 14, 1958, box 13, folder "Dean McGeorge Bundy, 1957–1958," HPD11.

61. "Revolving Appointment Fund," Revolving Appointment Fund, October 1939, Harvard University Archives, Cambridge, MA; Roderick Firth to Charles Parsons, March 9, 1962, box 18, folder P, HPD11.

62. Bruce Kuklick, "Philosophy at Yale in the Century after Darwin," *History of Philosophy Quarterly* 21, no. 3 (2004): 320, 325–26.

63. Charles Hendel, quoted in ibid., 324.

64. "Philosophy at Yale," *Yale Alumni Magazine*, June 1956, 13–14.

65. Brand Blanshard, "Report to the President by the Chairman, Department of Philosophy, June 1948," June 24, 1948, box 344, folder "Reports to the President, Naval Science–Physical Chemistry, 1947–48," Yale Secretary's Office Records, 1899–1953; Hayward Keniston, *Graduate Study and Research in the Arts and Sciences at the University of Pennsylvania*, Reports of the Educational Survey (Philadelphia: University of Pennsylvania Press, 1959).

66. Blanshard, "Report to the President, June 1948," June 24, 1948, box 344, folder "Reports to the President, Naval Science–Physical Chemistry, 1947–48," Yale Secretary's Office Records, 1899–1953.

67. Hendel, "The Annual Report of the Department of Philosophy, 1952–53," July 7, 1953, box 348, folder "Reports to the President, Obstetrics and Gynecology–Physical Education, 1952–53," Yale Secretary's Office Records, 1899–1953.

68. Brand Blanshard, "Report to the President by the Chairman, Department of Philosophy, June 1947," June 1947, box 343, folder "Reports to the President,

Metallurgy–Physics, 1946–47," Yale Secretary's Office Records, 1899–1953; Blanshard, "Report to the President by the Chairman, Department of Philosophy, June 1948," June 24, 1948, box 344, folder "Reports to the President, Naval Science–Physical Chemistry, 1947–48," Yale Secretary's Office Records, 1899–1953.

69. Blanshard, "Report to the President, June 1947," June 1947, box 343, folder "Reports to the President, Metallurgy–Physics, 1946–47," Yale Secretary's Office Records, 1899–1953.

70. Thomas Mendenhall, quoted in Justin Zaremby, *Directed Studies and the Evolution of American General Education* (New Haven, CT: Whitney Humanities Center, Yale University, 2006), http://directedstudies.yale.edu/sites/default/files/files/DIRECTED_STUDIES_HISTORY.pdf. 35.

71. Ibid., 32–41.

72. Blanshard, "Report to the President, June 1947," June 1947, box 343, folder "Reports to the President, Metallurgy–Physics, 1946–47," Yale Secretary's Office Records, 1899–1953.

73. Charles Hendel, "The Annual Report of the Department of Philosophy, 1951–52," 1952, box 347, folder "Reports to the President, Pediatrics–Physics, 1951–52," Yale Secretary's Office Records, 1899–1953.

74. Richard Bernstein, interview by Jonathan Strassfeld, October 23, 2017, New School for Social Research.

75. "Philosophy at Yale," 11.

76. Clark Kerr, *The Uses of the University*, 5th ed. (Cambridge, MA: Harvard University Press, 2001), 39–43.

77. Rebecca Lowen, *Creating the Cold War University: The Transformation of Stanford* (Berkeley: University of California Press, 1997), 110, 48–63; Joel Isaac, "Donald Davidson and the Analytic Revolution in American Philosophy, 1940–1970," *Historical Journal* 56, no. 3 (2013): 770–72.

78. Hubert L. Dreyfus, "Standing Up to Analytic Philosophy and Artificial Intelligence at MIT in the Sixties," *Proceedings and Addresses of the American Philosophical Association* 87 (2013): 84–85.

79. "Proceedings of the American Philosophical Association, 1938: Twelfth Annual Report," 187–89.

80. Roderick Firth to J. P. Elder, January 24, 1958, box 14, folder G–O, HPD11; John Ladd to D. C. Williams, April 27, 1949, box 6, folder "John Ladd," HPD11; "1928 January 17," box 1, folder "Minutes of the Division of Philosophy and Department of Philosophy and Psychology 1924–1929," HPD1; "1941 November 13," box 1, folder "Department of Philosophy Minutes, 1939–40–1949–50," HPD1; "1952 June 2," box 2, folder "Department of Philosophy Minutes, 1950–51–1959–60," HPD1.

81. See the appendix for information on sources. The criteria for selecting these departments will be discussed later in the text. However, the list comports with

contemporary peer evaluations of departments. Nine of the eleven departments are in the top eleven as ranked by a 1925 study (Stanford and UCLA are not ranked; Johns Hopkins [8] and Wisconsin [11] instead place in the top eleven). Nine of the eleven departments also appear in the top eleven of a 1957 study (Stanford is not ranked, and Pennsylvania is ranked twelfth; instead Minnesota (9) and Illinois (10) appear). Finally, ten of the eleven appear in the top eleven of a 1964 ACE study (Pennsylvania is ranked seventeenth; instead Pittsburgh [8] appears). Hughes, *Study of the Graduate Schools of America*; Keniston, *Graduate Study at the University of Pennsylvania*; Allan Murray Cartter, *An Assessment of Quality in Graduate Education* (Washington, DC: American Council on Education, 1966).

82. All statistics are drawn from the data I have collected, and include only assistant, associate, and full professors unless otherwise noted.

83. This list includes faculty with a primary appointment in philosophy and those with secondary appointments who performed significant work, including graduate education, within the philosophy department. Visiting faculty are not included. Biographical information for most American faculty was retrievable through the ProQuest Dissertation & Theses database. Other sources included the *Directory of American Scholars*, obituaries and memorials, faculty webpages, and direct emails to faculty.

84. Robert Paul Wolff, *A Life in the Academy*, 264, https://app.box.com/shared /n72u3p7pyj, Total Memoir in One File.docx.

85. C. I. Lewis to Payson Wild, November 8, 1946, box 8, folder "Dean P. S. Wild— Miss Priest, Secy., 1946–7 (GSAS)," HPD11.

86. Herbert Spiegelberg, "Apologia Pro Bibliographia Mea," in *Phenomenological Perspectives: Historical and Systematic Essays in Honor of Herbert Spiegelberg*, ed. Philip Bossert (The Hague: Martinus Nijhoff, 1975), 268–70; Carlo Ierna, "Herbert Spiegelberg: From Munich to North America," in *The Reception of Husserlian Phenomenology in North America*, ed. Michela Beatrice Ferri (New York: Springer, 2019), 153–55.

87. Wolff, *A Life in the Academy*, 264.

88. C. I. Lewis to C. H. Moore, November 15, 1927, box 4, folder "Philosophy (and Psychology) (2)," HPD10.

89. Curt Ducasse to James Woods, November 24, 1930, box 2, folder Do–Dy, HPD10.

90. These classifications were made by examining a philosopher's writings and, when available, discussions of their work. Such classifications are disputable by their nature. Therefore, I took the additional step of posting my initial results on the philosophy blog *Leiter Reports* to solicit corrections and suggestions. See Brian Leiter, "Philosophy Faculty at the Leading American Programs, 1930–1979: Feedback Sought," *Leiter Reports* (blog), May 12, 2016, http:// leiterreports.typepad.com/blog/2016/05/philosophy-faculty-at-the-leading -american-programs-1930-1979-feedback-sought.html.

91. Raphael Morris Cohen, William Frankena, Cooper Harold Langford, C. I. Lewis, W. V. O. Quine, Henry Sheffer, and Charles Leslie Stevenson.

92. Hans Reichenbach, Rudolf Carnap, and Ralph W. Church.

93. Paul Marhenke, Charles W. Morris, Ernest Nagel, Harold R. Smart, A. Cornelius Benjamin, and Frederic Brenton Fitch.

94. Chicago: A. Cornelius Benjamin, Raphael Morris Cohen, Charles W. Morris, and Rudolf Carnap. Michigan: William Frankena and Cooper Harold Langford. Yale: Frederic Brenton Fitch and Charles Leslie Stevenson. Cornell: Ralph W. Church and Harold R. Smart.

95. "Philosophy at Yale," 14.

96. C. I. Lewis to Paul Buck, November 24, 1944, box 1, folder "Dean Buck, 1944–45," HPD11.

97. "The Philosophy Department of the Graduate Faculty of Political and Social Science at the New School for Social Research: A Documentation," page 236, February 1979, box 6, folder "Philosophy Department Struggle in 1958–59, 1979," New School Graduate Faculty Collection: Robert Paul Wolff to John Everett, February 5, 1979, box 6, folder "Philosophy Department Struggle in 1958–59, 1979," New School Graduate Faculty Collection.

CHAPTER C

Epigraph: Hubert L. Dreyfus, *What Computers Can't Do: The Limits of Artificial Intelligence*, rev. ed. (New York: Harper & Row, 1979), 280.

1. Yasmin Anwar, "Hubert Dreyfus, Preeminent Philosopher and Ai Critic, Dies at 87," http://news.berkeley.edu/2017/04/24/hubert-dreyfus/; Sean Kelly, "In Memoriam: Hubert L. Dreyfus (1929–2017)," https://philosophy.fas.harvard .edu/news/memoriam-hubert-l-dreyfus-1929-2017.

2. See Hubert L. Dreyfus and Sean Kelly, *All Things Shining: Reading the Western Classics to Find Meaning in a Secular Age* (New York: Free Press, 2011).

3. Hubert L. Dreyfus, "Curriculum Vitae," http://blogi.lu.lv/broks/files/2012/11 /Hubert-Dreyfus-CV-24.01.2011.pdf.

4. W. V. O. Quine to Paul Buck, January 29, 1953, box 9, folder "Provost Paul Buck, 1952–53," HPD11.

5. Dreyfus, "Standing Up to Analytic Philosophy," 78–79.

6. Lester Embree, "Biographical Sketch of Aron Gurwitsch," http://www.gur witsch.net/biography.htm.

7. Harold Garfinkel and Anne Warfield Rawls, *Ethnomethodology's Program: Working Out Durkeim's Aphorism*, Legacies of Social Thought (Lanham, MD: Rowman & Littlefield Publishers, 2002), 84, 257–58; Richard Zaner, "Gurwitsch at the New School," in *The Golden Age of Phenomenology at the New School for Social Research, 1954–1973*, ed. Lester Embree (Athens: Ohio University Press, 2017), 124–25; John Schwenkler, "A Life of Being-in-the-World: Hubert Dreyfus, 1929–2017," *First Things* (May 1, 2017), https://www .firstthings.com/web-exclusives/2017/05/a-life-of-being-in-the-world; Hubert L.

Dreyfus, foreword to *Body and World*, ed. Samuel Todes (Cambridge, MA: MIT Press, 2001).

8. Dreyfus, "Curriculum Vitae."

9. Dreyfus, "Standing Up to Analytic Philosophy," 84.

10. Dreyfus, *Being-in-the-World*, 46–59.

11. Several companions to *Being and Time* were written prior to Dreyfus's *Being-in-the-World*: Michael Gelven, *A Commentary on Heidegger's "Being and Time"; a Section-by-Section Interpretation*, Harper Torchbooks (New York: Harper & Row, 1970); Walter Eisenbeis, *The Key Ideas of Martin Heidegger's Treatise "Being and Time"* (Washington, DC: University Press of America, 1983); Joseph Kockelmans, *A Companion to Martin Heidegger's "Being and Time"*, Current Continental Research (Washington, DC: Center for Advanced Research in Phenomenology and University Press of America, 1986); and Eugene Francis Kaelin, *Heidegger's "Being and Time": A Reading for Readers* (Tallahassee: University Presses of Florida / Florida State University Press, 1988).

12. Mark Okrent, review of *Being-in-the-World: A Commentary on Heidegger's "Being and Time", Division I*, by Hubert L. Dreyfus, *Philosophical Review* 102, no. 2 (1993): 290.

13. Woessner, *Heidegger in America*, 207–8.

14. Herbert Simon, quoted in Dreyfus, *What Computers Can't Do*, 81–82.

15. Ibid., 80.

16. Ibid., 83–84.

17. Ibid., 100.

18. Ibid., 129.

19. Ibid., 67–69, 176–77.

20. Ibid., 72.

21. Ibid., 156, 78–79.

22. Michael Rescorla, "The Computational Theory of Mind," in *The Stanford Encyclopedia of Philosophy*, Spring 2017 ed., ed. Edward N. Zalta, https://plato.stanford.edu/archives/spr2017/entries/computational-mind/.

23. Dreyfus, *What Computers Can't Do*, 163–67.

24. Merleau-Ponty, *Phenomenology of Perception*, xiv.

25. Dreyfus, *What Computers Can't Do*, 154.

26. Ibid., 177–78.

27. Ibid., 183–87.

28. Ibid., 189–91.

29. Ibid., 197–200.

30. Ibid., 200–202.

31. Ibid., 206.

32. Ibid., 210–13.

33. Ibid., 208.

34. Ibid., 210.

35. Ibid., 213–14.

36. Ibid., 221.

37. Heidegger, *Being and Time*, 95–98.

38. Ibid., 236.

39. Dreyfus, *What Computers Can't Do*, 261–62.

40. Ibid., 233.

41. William Earle, "Executive's Datebook, 1964," box 2, folder "Appointment Books, 1961–1965," William Earle Papers.

42. Ibid.

43. Dreyfus, *What Computers Can't Do*, 3.

44. Ibid., 102–3.

45. Ibid., 238–41.

46. Ibid., 239–42.

47. Ibid., 242.

48. Ibid., 244–45.

49. Ibid., 248–50, 76–77.

50. Dreyfus, "Standing Up to Analytic Philosophy," 89.

51. Hubert L. Dreyfus, Stuart E. Dreyfus, and Tom Athanasiou, *Mind over Machine: The Power of Human Intuition and Expertise in the Era of the Computer* (New York: Free Press, 1986), 90–93.

52. On the response to Dreyfus by AI researchers, see Pamela McCorduck, *Machines Who Think: A Personal Inquiry into the History and Prospects of Artificial Intelligence* (San Francisco: W. H. Freeman, 1979), 193–205.

53. Edward Feigenbaum, quoted in ibid., 197.

54. Dreyfus, *What Computers Can't Do*, 232–33.

CHAPTER FIVE

Epigraphs: Giovanna Borradori, *The American Philosopher: Conversations with Quine, Davidson, Putnam, Nozick, Danto, Rorty, Cavell, Macintyre, and Kuhn* (Chicago: University of Chicago Press, 1994), 57; Brand Blanshard et al., *Philosophy in American Education, Its Tasks and Opportunities* (New York: Harper & Brothers, 1945), 34.

1. Walter Brogan and James Risser, *American Continental Philosophy: A Reader*, Studies in Continental Thought (Bloomington: Indiana University Press, 2000), back cover.

2. Justin Leiber, "Linguistic Analysis and Existentialism," *Philosophy and Phenomenological Research* 32, no. 1 (1971): 48.

3. Stanley Cavell, "Existentialism and Analytical Philosophy," *Daedalus* 93, no. 3 (1964): 947.

4. Neil Levy, "Analytic and Continental Philosophy: Explaining the Differences," *Metaphilosophy* 34, no. 3 (2003): 284.

5. Maurice Mandelbaum to Alfred Schütz, April 29, 1940, box 28, folder "American Philosophical Association," Alfred Schütz Papers.

6. Marvin Farber to Fritz Kaufmann, January 2, 1941, box 11, folder "Kaufmann, Fritz, 1941–42," Marvin Farber Papers; Marvin Farber to Alfred Schütz, January 4, 1940, box 20, folder "Schütz, Alfred, 1940," Marvin Farber Papers.

7. Roberto Walton, "Spain and Latin America," in *Encyclopedia of Phenomenology*, ed. Lester Embree et al. (Boston: Kluwer Academic, 1997), 675–79.

8. See Eduardo Nicol, "La psicología de las situaciones vitales y el problema antropologico," *Philosophy and Phenomenological Research* 4, no. 2 (1943): 229.

9. See Marvin Farber, "The Significance of Phenomenology for the Americas," *Philosophy and Phenomenological Research* 4, no. 2 (1943): 209–10.

10. Richard Hays Williams to N. Sharkey, June 5, 1941, box 42, folder "Canada," *PPR* Papers.

11. Fritz Kaufmann to Marvin Farber, August 21, 1940, box 11, folder "Kaufmann, Fritz, 1940," Marvin Farber Papers.

12. "A Symposium on Meaning and Truth, Part I," *Philosophy and Phenomenological Research* 4, no. 2 (1943): 236–84; "A Symposium on Meaning and Truth, Part II," *Philosophy and Phenomenological Research* 4, no. 3 (1944): 317–410.

13. "A Symposium on Probability: Part I," *Philosophy and Phenomenological Research* 5, no. 4 (1945): 449–532; "A Symposium on Probability: Part II," *Philosophy and Phenomenological Research* 6, no. 1 (1945): 11–86.

14. "A Symposium on Educational Philosophy," *Philosophy and Phenomenological Research* 7, no. 2 (1946).

15. "A First Symposium on Russian Philosophy and Psychology," *Philosophy and Phenomenological Research* 5, no. 2 (1944): 157–254.

16. Cornelius Kruse to Helmut Kuhn, January 8, 1948, box 12, folder "Kruse, Cornelius, 1939–40," Marvin Farber Papers.

17. Helmut Wagner, "Chapter 14: Scholarly Acceptance," February 14, 1977, box 24, folder "Wagner, Helmut mss. Re Alfred Schutz, 1977 (Changes)," Marvin

Farber Papers, 49–50; Helmut Kuhn to Marvin Farber, December 23, 1947, box 24, folder "Farber, Marvin (8 of 14)," Alfred Schütz Papers.

18. Marvin Farber to Alfred Schütz, January 3, 1947, box 24, folder "Farber, Marvin (8 of 14)," Alfred Schütz Papers.

19. Marvin Farber to members of the editorial staff of *PPR*, February 15, 1947, box 24, folder "Farber, Marvin (8 of 14)," Alfred Schütz Papers.

20. Marvin Farber to members of the editorial staff of *PPR*, March 19, 1947, box 24, folder "Farber, Marvin (8 of 14)," Alfred Schütz Papers.

21. Alfred Schütz to Marvin Farber, February 19, 1947, box 20, folder "Schütz, Alfred, 1947," Marvin Farber Papers.

22. Fritz Kaufmann to Marvin Farber, August 10, 1940, box 11, folder "Kaufmann, Fritz, 1940," Marvin Farber Papers.

23. Alice Kaufmann, quoted in Fritz Kaufmann to Marvin Farber, July 31, 1940, box 11, folder "Kaufmann, Fritz, 1940," Marvin Farber Papers. Translation by Jonathan Strassfeld.

24. Alice Kaufmann, quoted in Fritz Kaufmann to Farber, July 31, 1940.

25. Wolin, *Heidegger Controversy*, 3.

26. Karl Jaspers, "Letter to the Freiburg University Denazification Committee (December 22, 1945)," in *The Heidegger Controversy: A Critical Reader*, ed. Richard Wolin (New York: Columbia University Press, 1991), 148–49.

27. Wolin, *Heidegger Controversy*, 167.

28. Marvin Farber, "Remarks about the Phenomenological Program," *Philosophy and Phenomenological Research* 6, no. 1 (1945): 3–4.

29. Ibid., 3.

30. Ibid., 4.

31. Marvin Farber to Alfred Schütz, March 11, 1947, box 24, folder "Farber, Marvin (8 of 14)," Alfred Schütz Papers.

32. Marvin Farber to Hugo Bergmann, March 23, 1946, box 2, folder "Bergmann, Hugo," Marvin Farber Papers.

33. Edmund Husserl, "Die Welt Der Lebendigen Gegenwart Und Die Konstitution Der Ausserleiblichen Umwelt," *Philosophy and Phenomenological Research* 6, no. 3 (1946): 323–43; Marvin Farber to Hugo Bergmann, October 21, 1946, box 2, folder "Bergmann, Hugo," Marvin Farber Papers.

34. Fritz Kaufmann to Marvin Farber, October 5, 1945, box 11, folder "Kaufmann, Fritz, 1945," Marvin Farber Papers; Alfred Schütz to Marvin Farber, November 6, 1946, box 20, folder "Schütz, Alfred, 1946," Marvin Farber Papers; Marvin Farber to Eugen Fink, November 2, 1946, box 6, folder "Fink, Eugen," Marvin Farber Papers; Wagner, "Marvin Farber's Contribution," 228–30.

35. Alfred Schütz to Marvin Farber, January 10, 1948, box 20, folder "Schütz, Alfred, 1948," Marvin Farber Papers; see also Edmund Husserl, "Persönliche

Aufzeichnungen," *Philosophy and Phenomenological Research* 16, no. 3 (1956): 293–302.

36. Wagner, "Marvin Farber's Contribution," n228; Lester Embree et al., "United States of America," in *Encyclopedia of Phenomenology*, ed. Lester Embree, et al. (Boston: Kluwer Academic, 1997), 720; "Husserliana," http://ophen.org /series-506; "Phaenomenologica," Husserl Archives Leuven, https://hiw .kuleuven.be/hua/editionspublications/phaenomenologica.

37. Wagner, "Marvin Farber's Contribution," 231–35.

38. John Wild to Marvin Farber, September 4, 1940, box 25, folder "Wild, John, 1938–1942," Marvin Farber Papers.

39. Marvin Farber to Alfred Schütz, June 1, 1945, box 24, folder "Farber, Marvin (6 of 14)," Alfred Schütz Papers.

40. Wild, *The Radical Empiricism of James*, 365.

41. John Wild, *The Challenge of Existentialism* (Bloomington: Indiana University Press, 1955), 3.

42. Wild, *The Radical Empiricism of James*, 358.

43. Wild, *The Challenge of Existentialism*, 9–22.

44. "1942," box 1, folder "Department of Philosophy Minutes, 1939–40–1949–50," HPD1. See also chapter 3.

45. John Wild to Marvin Farber, November 10, 1941, box 25, folder "Wild, John, 1938–1942," Marvin Farber Papers.

46. John Wild to Marvin Farber, July 8, 1941, box 25, folder "Wild, John, 1938–1942," Marvin Farber Papers.

47. John Wild to Marvin Farber, September 5, 1941, box 25, folder "Wild, John, 1938–1942," Marvin Farber Papers.

48. Marvin Farber to Alfred Schütz, March 14, 1942, box 24, folder "Farber, Marvin (3 of 14)," Alfred Schütz Papers.

49. John Wild to Marvin Farber, October 31, 1940, box 25, folder "Wild, John, 1938–1942," Marvin Farber Papers; John Wild to Marvin Farber, November 5, 1940, box 25, folder "Wild, John, 1938–1942," Marvin Farber Papers.

50. Wild to Farber, November 5, 1940, box 25, folder "Wild, John, 1938–1942," Marvin Farber Papers.

51. John Wild to Marvin Farber, February 23, 1947, box 25, folder "Wild, John, 1938–1942," Marvin Farber Papers.

52. Marvin Farber to John Wild, March 14, 1947, box 25, folder "Wild, John, 1938–1942," Marvin Farber Papers.

53. Marvin Farber to John Wild, February 24, 1942, box 25, folder "Wild, John, 1938–1942," Marvin Farber Papers.

54. Marvin Farber, "Experience and Subjectivism," in *Philosophy for the Future: The Quest of Modern Materialism*, ed. Roy Wood Sellars, V. J. McGill, and Marvin Farber (New York: Macmillan, 1949), 610–11.

55. Ibid., 612.

56. Gabriel Ricci, "Importing Phenomenology: The Early Editorial Life of Philosophy and Phenomenological Research," *History of European Ideas* 42, no. 3 (2016): 408–9; Marvin Farber to Edmund Husserl, March 26, 1937, box 9, folder "Husserl, Edmund and Mrs.," Marvin Farber Papers.

57. Farber, "Experience and Subjectivism," 591–94.

58. Ibid., 592.

59. Ibid., 626.

60. Wagner, "Marvin Farber's Contribution," 220–21.

61. Marvin Farber to Aron Gurwitsch, October 22, 1951, box 24, folder "Gurwitsch, Aron (4 of 8)," Alfred Schütz Papers.

62. Wagner, "Marvin Farber's Contribution," 220–21.

63. Marvin Farber to Paul Henle, June 23, 1950, box 15, folder "Henle, Paul," *PPR* Papers; Paul Henle to Marvin Farber, July 3, 1950, box 15, folder "Henle, Paul," *PPR* Papers.

64. Wagner, "Marvin Farber's Contribution," 213–14.

65. Forrest Williams to William Earle, December 12, 1950, box 7, folder "Correspondence, 1950," William Earle Papers.

66. Eric Unger, "Logical Positivism and the Moral Problem," *Nineteenth Century and After*, July–December 1948, 76.

67. Frederick C. Copleston, "The Human Person in Contemporary Philosophy," *Philosophy* 25, no. 92 (1950): 17.

68. Harvard University, *Official Register of Harvard University: Announcement of the Courses of Instruction Offered by the Faculty of Arts and Sciences, 1949–50* (Cambridge, MA: Harvard University, 1949), 220; Radcliffe College, *Official Register of Radcliffe College: Courses of Instruction Offered in Fall and Spring Terms, 1949–50* (Cambridge, MA: Radcliffe College, 1949), 220.

69. Radcliffe College, *Official Register of Radcliffe College: Courses of Instruction Offered in Fall and Spring Terms, 1950–51* (Cambridge, MA: Radcliffe College, 1950), 203. The course was not given because Ladd look a position at Brown.

70. Michael Friedman, "A Turning Point in Philosophy: Carnap-Cassirer-Heidegger," in *Logical Empiricism: Historical & Contemporary Perspectives*, ed. Paolo Parrini, Wesley C. Salmon, and Merrilee H. Salmon (Pittsburgh: University of Pittsburgh Press, 2003), 14; Friedman, *A Parting of the Ways*, 156–57.

71. See Carnap, "Überwindung der Metaphysik." See also A. J. Ayer, "The Genesis of Metaphysics," *Analysis* 1, no. 4 (1934): 56; Marjorie Glicksman, "A Note on

the Philosophy of Heidegger," *Journal of Philosophy* 35, no. 4 (1938): 93–104; Paul Marhenke, "The Criterion of Significance," *Proceedings and Addresses of the American Philosophical Association* 23 (1949): 1–21; Robert Evans, "Existentialism in Greene's *The Quiet American*," *Modern Fiction Studies* 3, no. 3 (1957).

72. Eric Schliesser, "The Nothing Noths," Digressions & Impressions, October 30, 2017, http://digressionsnimpressions.typepad.com/digressionsimpressions/2017/10/the-nothing-noths.html.

73. Carl Hamburg, "A Cassirer-Heidegger Seminar," *Philosophy and Phenomenological Research* 25, no. 2 (1964): 208.

74. Max Rieser, "Remarks on the Eleventh International Congress of Philosophy," *Journal of Philosophy* 51, no. 3 (1954): 99; Richard Sanders, "Walter Cerf, 1907–2001," *Proceedings and Addresses of the American Philosophical Association* 77, no. 5 (2004): 161.

75. As Edward Said has explained: "Orientalism is a style of thought based upon an ontological and epistemological distinction made between 'the Orient' and (most of the time) 'the Occident.'" This framework is enacted as a means of managing the Orient by "making statements about it, authorizing views of it, describing it, teaching it, settling it, ruling over it." It is the job of the Orientalist scholar "to piece together a portrait, a restored picture as it were, of the Orient of the Oriental; fragments . . . supply the material, but the narrative shape, continuity, and figures are constructed by the scholar for whom scholarship consists of circumventing the unruly (un-Occidental) nonhistory of the Orient with orderly chronicle, portraits, and plots." Through this process, Oriental knowledge is "domesticated . . . to the West, [by] filtering it through regulatory codes, classifications, specimen cases, periodical reviews, dictionaries, grammars, commentaries, editions, translations, all of which together formed a simulacrum of the Orient and reproduced it materially in the West, for the West." Edward Said, *Orientalism* (New York: Vintage, 2003), 3–4, 151, 66.

76. Rieser, "Remarks on the Eleventh International Congress of Philosophy," 100, 105.

77. Ibid., 100.

78. Ibid., 101.

79. Ibid.

80. Ibid., 104.

81. Walter Cerf, "The Eleventh International Congress of Philosophy," *Philosophical Review* 64, no. 2 (1955): 280.

82. Ibid., 281.

83. Ibid., 297, 98.

84. Ibid., 299.

85. Walter Cerf, "Value Decisions," *Philosophy of Science* 18, no. 1 (1951): 26.

86. Walter Cerf, "An Approach to Heidegger's Ontology," *Philosophy and Phenomenological Research* 1, no. 2 (1940): 78.

87. Walter Cerf, "Logical Positivism and Existentialism," *Philosophy of Science* 18, no. 4 (1951): 327.

88. Walter Cerf, "Existentialist Mannerism and Education," *Journal of Philosophy* 52, no. 6 (1955): 141, 151.

89. Ludwig Landgrebe, "The Study of Philosophy in Germany: A Reply to Walter Cerf," *Journal of Philosophy* 54, no. 5 (1957): 128.

90. W. E. Hocking to Henry Bugbee, February 27, 1954, box 4, folder "Henry Bugbee (1 of 2)," W. E. Hocking Correspondence.

91. Henry Bugbee to W. E. Hocking, March 2, 1954, box 4, folder "Henry Bugbee (1 of 2)," W. E. Hocking Correspondence.

92. Richard McKeon, "Experience and Metaphysics," *Proceedings of the XIth International Congress of Philosophy* 4 (1953): 86–87.

93. Cotkin, *Existential America*, 92–95.

94. Woessner, *Heidegger in America*, 103–11.

95. Calvin Schrag, "アメリカにおける現象学的哲学の諸段階," 理想 5, no. 468 (1972): 6. A translation of the article was provided by its author.

96. D. C. Williams to Paul Buck, September 29, 1950, box 9, folder "Provost Buck, 1950–51," HPD11.

97. Roderick Firth to Hiram McLendon, February 3, 1959, box 14, folder Mc, HPD11.

98. Brand Blanshard to D. C. Williams, January 30, 1960, box 19, folder X/Y/Z, HPD11.

99. D. C. Williams to Brand Blanshard, February 5, 1960, box 19, folder X/Y/Z, HPD11.

100. D. C. Williams to Paul Wienpahl, December 21, 1959, box 15, folder S, HPD11.

101. Fulton, *Apostles of Sartre*, 22–23.

102. Asher Moore to William Earle, April 24, 1961, box 9, folder "Correspondence, 1961," William Earle Papers.

103. William Barrett, *What Is Existentialism?* (New York: Partisan Review, 1947); D. C. Williams to William Barrett, November 6, 1947, box 5, folder B, HPD11.

104. See Grene, *Dreadful Freedom*; Ralph Harper, *Existentialism, a Theory of Man* (Cambridge, MA: Harvard University Press, 1948); Helmut Kuhn, *Encounter with Nothingness: An Essay on Existentialism*, Humanist Library (Hinsdale, IL: H. Regnery, 1949); Jean André Wahl, *A Short History of Existentialism* (New York: Philosophical Library, 1949); and Walter Arnold Kaufmann, *Existentialism from Dostoevsky to Sartre* (New York: Meridian, 1956).

105. See Andrew D. Osborn, "The Philosophy of Edmund Husserl in Its Development from His Mathematical Interests to His First Conception of Phenomenology in *Logical Investigations*" (PhD, Columbia University, 1934); Farber, *Philosophical Essays in Memory of Husserl*; E. Parl Welch, *The Philosophy of Edmund Husserl: The Origin and Development of His Phenomenology* (New York: Columbia University Press, 1941); and Marvin Farber, *The Foundation of Phenomenology: Edmund Husserl and the Quest for a Rigorous Science of Philosophy* (Cambridge, MA: Harvard University Press, 1943).

106. See Husserl, *Ideas*.

107. Jean-Paul Sartre, *Existentialism*, trans. Bernard Frechtman (New York: Philosophical Library, 1947); Jean-Paul Sartre, *Existentialism and Humanism*, trans. Philip Mairet (London: Methuen, 1948); Jean-Paul Sartre, *The Emotions: Outline of a Theory*, trans. Bernard Frechtman (New York: Philosophical Library, 1948); Jean-Paul Sartre, *The Psychology of Imagination*, trans. Bernard Frechtman (New York: Philosophical Library, 1948); Jean-Paul Sartre, *Anti-Semite and Jew*, trans. George Joseph Becker (New York: Schocken, 1948); Jean-Paul Sartre, *What Is Literature?*, trans. Bernard Frechtman (London: Methuen, 1950).

108. Martin Heidegger, *Existence and Being* (Chicago: H. Regnery, 1949).

109. Karl Jaspers, *Existentialism and Humanism, Three Essays*, trans. E. B. Ashton (New York: R. F. Moore, 1952).

110. See Merleau-Ponty, *Phenomenology of Perception*.

111. Samuel Capen to Marvin Farber, February 7, 1947, box 11, folder "Kaufmann, Fritz, 1946–52," Marvin Farber Papers.

112. "Philosophy Department of the Graduate Faculty at the New School: A Documentation," pages 70–71, February 1979, box 6, folder "Philosophy Department Struggle in 1958–59," New School Graduate Faculty Collection; Michela Beatrice Ferri, "The History of the Husserl Archives Established in Memory of Alfred Schutz at the New School for Social Research," in *The Reception of Husserlian Phenomenology in North America*, ed. Michela Beatrice Ferri (New York: Springer, 2019), 232–35.

113. Osborne P. Wiggins, "My Years at the New School," in *The Golden Age of Phenomenology at the New School for Social Research, 1954–1973*, ed. Lester Embree (Athens: Ohio University Press, 2017), 353.

114. Richard Zaner, "My Path to the New School," in *The Golden Age of Phenomenology at the New School for Social Research, 1954–1973*, ed. Lester Embree (Athens: Ohio University Press, 2017), 271.

115. See Lester Embree and Michael D. Barber, *The Golden Age of Phenomenology at the New School for Social Research, 1954–1973*, Series in Continental Thought (Athens: Ohio University Press, 2017), 174–384.

116. Thomas Nenon, "A History of the Center for Advanced Research in Phenomenology, Inc.," in *The Reception of Husserlian Phenomenology in North America*, ed. Michela Beatrice Ferri (New York: Springer, 2019), 283–87.

117. Alfred Schütz, "William James' Concept of the Stream of Thought Phenomenologically Interpreted," *Philosophy and Phenomenological Research* 1, no. 4 (1941): 443–44, 452.

118. Aron Gurwitsch, *The Field of Consciousness: Theme, Thematic Field, and Margin*, ed. Richard M. Zaner, Collected Works of Aron Gurwitsch (1901–1973) (New York: Springer, 2010), 2–4, 19–21.

119. Ibid., 49–52, 88, 112.

120. Ibid., 310–12.

121. William Earle to Elsie Earle, February 6, 1948, box 6, folder "Correspondence 1948, January–July," William Earle Papers.

122. Northwestern University, *Announcement of Courses in the College of Liberal Arts for the Academic Year 1957–58* (Chicago: Northwestern University, 1957).

123. William Earle to Elsie Earle, December 1, 1951, box 7, folder "Correspondence, 1951," William Earle Papers; Cecil Hemley to William Earle, December 9, 1957, box 8, folder "Correspondence, 1957, May–Dec.," William Earle Papers; Robin Hemley, *Nola: A Memoir of Faith, Art, and Madness* (St. Paul, MN: Graywolf, 1998), 85–87.

124. See Karl Jaspers, *Reason and Existenz; Five Lectures*, trans. William Earle (New York: Noonday Press, 1955); Karl Jaspers and Rudolf Bultmann, *Myth and Christianity: An Inquiry into the Possibility of Religion without Myth*, trans. Norbert Guterman (New York: Noonday Press, 1958); Jean-Paul Sartre, *The Transcendence of the Ego: An Existentialist Theory of Consciousness* (New York: Noonday Press, 1957).

125. William Earle to Karl Popper, January 28, 1964, box 4, folder 9, Northwestern Philosophy Department Administrative Records.

126. "Present State and Future Plans of the Philosophy Department," 1980, box 8, folder 22, Northwestern Philosophy Department Administrative Records.

127. Robert Browning, "Northwestern University Department of Philosophy Annual Commentary to the Dean of the College, August 1966," July 28, 1966, box 9, folder "Chairmen's Reports, 1965–1966," Records of Dean Simeon Leland.

128. Lowen, *Creating the Cold War University*, 148–63.

129. Robert Browning, "Department of Philosophy Report, 1959–60," 1960, box 8, folder "Chairmen's Reports, 1959–60," Records of Dean Simeon Leland.

130. John Wild to Simeon Leland, June 4, 1962, box 8, folder "Chairmen's Reports, 1961–62," Records of Dean Simeon Leland.

131. "Maurice Merleau-Ponty—in Praise of Philosophy," box 83, folder "Wild, John and Eddie, James (tr.); In Praise of Philosophy, by Maurice Merleau-Ponty; 1963," Records of the Northwestern University Press, Northwestern University Archives, Evanston, IL.

132. See Husserl, *Crisis of European Sciences*; Husserl and Landgrebe, *Experience and Judgment*; Maurice Merleau-Ponty, *Sense and Non-sense*, trans. Hubert Dreyfus and Patricia Allen Dreyfus, Northwestern University Studies in Phenomenology & Existential Philosophy (Evanston, IL: Northwestern University Press, 1964); Paul Ricoeur, *History and Truth*, trans. Charles A. Kelbley, Northwestern University Studies in Phenomenology & Existential Philosophy (Evanston, IL: Northwestern University Press, 1965); and Schütz and Luckmann, *Structures of the Life-World*.

133. "Register of the Officers and Faculty of the University of North Carolina, 1795–1945, Compiled by the Staff of the North Carolina Collection," https://docsouth.unc.edu/true/faculty/faculty.html.

134. Theodore Kisiel, "Heidegger Circle: History," http://heidegger-circle.org/history.html.

135. Baring, *Converts to the Real*, 14.

136. For further information on the faculties of Catholic philosophy departments, including areas of specialization, see Daniel O. Dahlstrom, "The Reception of Phenomenology and Existentialism by American Catholic Philosophers: Some Facts and Some Reasons," in *The Catholic Reception of Continental Philosophy in North America*, ed. Gregory P. Floyd and Stephanie Rumpza (Toronto: University of Toronto Press, 2020).

137. Bruce Kuklick, "Philosophy and Inclusion in the United States," in *The Humanities and the Dynamics of Inclusion since World War II*, ed. David A. Hollinger (Baltimore: Johns Hopkins University Press, 2006), 161–62.

138. James Chappel, *Catholic Modern: The Challenge of Totalitarianism and the Remaking of the Church* (Cambridge, MA: Harvard University Press, 2018), 116–17.

139. Joseph W. Koterski and John J. Drummond, "W. Norris Clarke, S.J., 1915–2008," *Proceedings and Addresses of the American Philosophical Association* 82, no. 5 (2009): 202–3.

140. Daniel J. Martino, "Stephen Strasser's Philosophical Legacy and Duquesne University's Simon Silverman Phenomenology Center," in *Phenomenology of Life—from the Animal Soul to the Human Mind: Book I*, vol. XCIII, ed. Anna-Teresa Tymieniecka, Analecta Husserliana (Dordrecht: Springer, 2007), xxvi–xxvii; Anna-Teresa Tymieniecka, "The Theme: The History of American Phenomenology-in-Progress," in *American Phenomenology: Origins and Developments*, vol. XXVI, ed. Eugene Francis Kaelin and Calvin O. Schrag, Analecta Husserliana (Boston: Kluwer Academic, 1989), xiv–xv.

141. Scott D. Churchill and Frederick J. Wertz, "An Introduction to Phenomenological Research in Psychology: Historical, Conceptual, and Methodological Foundations," in *The Handbook of Humanistic Psychology: Theory, Research, and Practice*, ed. Kirk J. Schneider, J. Fraser Pierson, and James F. T. Bugental (Los Angeles: Sage Publications, 2015), 277–78; Thomas F. Cloonan, "The Early History of Phenomenological Psychological Research in America," *Journal of*

Phenomenological Psychology 26, no. 1 (1995): 109; Tymieniecka, "The Theme," xiv–xv.

142. Dahlstrom, "Reception of Phenomenology and Existentialism," 32–35.

143. John Wild et al., "Sein Und Zeit: An Informal English Paraphrase of Sections 1–53," Cambridge, MA: Andover–Harvard Theological Seminary, 1957.

144. Ibid.; Radcliffe College, *Courses of Instruction Offered by the Faculty of Arts and Sciences, 1956–57* (Cambridge, MA: Radcliffe College, 1956); Radcliffe College, *Courses of Instruction Offered by the Faculty of Arts and Sciences, 1957–58* (Cambridge, MA: Radcliffe College, 1957); Bob Kirkpatrick to William Earle, April 13, 1955, box 8, folder "Correspondence, 1955," William Earle Papers.

145. Richard Rorty, foreword to *Heidegger, Authenticity, and Modernity: Essays in Honor of Hubert L Dreyfus*, vol. 1, ed. Mark A. Wrathall and Jeff Malpas (Cambridge, MA: MIT Press, 2000), ix–x.

146. Roderick Firth to McGeorge Bundy, January 21, 1958, box 13, folder "Dean McGeorge Bundy, 1957–1958," HPD11; Roderick Firth to McGeorge Bundy, March 19, 1958, box 13, folder "Dean McGeorge Bundy, 1957–1958," HPD11.

147. William Earle, "1958 Diary," box 2, folder "Appointment Books, 1952–1960," William Earle Papers; William Earle, "Harvard Cooperative Society Appointment Book," box 2, folder "Appointment Books, 1952–1960," William Earle Papers.

148. Henry Aiken et al. to John Wild, April 14, 1960, box 15, folder W, HPD11.

149. Bugbee to W. E. Hocking, March 2, 1954, box 4, folder "Henry Bugbee (1 of 2)," W. E. Hocking Correspondence.

150. McGeorge Bundy to Nathan Pusey, April 22, 1960, box 13, folder "Dean McGeorge Bundy, 1959–1960," HPD11.

151. Kuklick, "Philosophy at Yale after Darwin," 320–23.

152. Robert Fogelin to President and Fellows of Yale University, August 1, 1970, box 13, folder "Department of Philosophy, 1969–1970," Office of the President, Yale University, Annual and Special Reports, Yale University Archives, New Haven, CT.

153. Fritz Kaufmann to Marvin Farber, March 11, 1944, box 11, folder "Kaufmann, Fritz, 1944," Marvin Farber Papers.

154. Douglas Morgan, "Philosophy Annual Report," July 20, 1959, box 8, folder "Chairmen's Reports, 1958–1959," Records of Dean Simeon Leland.

155. Browning, "Northwestern Department of Philosophy Annual Commentary, August 1966," July 28, 1966, box 9, folder "Chairmen's Reports, 1965–1966," Records of Dean Simeon Leland.

156. "Present State and Future Plans," 1980, box 8, folder 22, Northwestern Philosophy Department Administrative Records.

157. D. C. Williams to Brand Blanshard, January 15, 1960, box 13, folder B, HPD11; D. C. Williams to William Frankena, February 12, 1960, box 17, folder M, HPD11; Roderick Firth to Stanley Cavell, November 1, 1961, box 16, folder C, HPD11; Stanley Cavell to Roderick Firth, December 30, 1961, box 16, folder C, HPD11.

158. See Roderick Firth to Maurice Mandelbaum, October 24, 1961, box 17, folder J, HPD11; Maurice Mandelbaum to Roderick Firth, October 31, 1961, box 17, folder J, HPD11; and Roderick Firth to Richard Brandt, October 31, 1961, box 19, folder S(2), HPD11; Richard Brandt to Roderick Firth, November 3, 1961, box 19, folder S(2), HPD11.

159. Ledger Wood to D. C. Williams, January 29, 1960, box 18, folder P, HPD11.

160. D. C. Williams to Ledger Wood, February 5, 1960, box 18, folder P, HPD11.

161. Williams to Frankena, February 12, 1960, box 17, folder M, HPD11; D. C. Williams to Romane Clark, February 5, 1960, box 16, folder D, HPD11. "Spiritual types" referred to a description of existentialists from earlier in the letter.

162. Dagfinn Føllesdal, "Husserl's Notion of Noema," *Journal of Philosophy* 66, no. 20 (1969): 686. See also Frege, "Sense and Reference," 211.

163. See Ronald McIntyre and David Woodruff Smith, "Husserl's Identification of Meaning and Noema," *Monist* 59, no. 1 (1975): 115–32.

164. Jeffrey Yoshimi, Clinton Tolley, and David Woodruff Smith, "California Phenomenology," in *The Reception of Husserlian Phenomenology in North America*, ed. Michela Beatrice Ferri (New York: Springer, 2019), 368.

165. Dagfinn Føllesdal, "Statement of Plans," box 12, folder "Føllesdal, Dagfinn (1 of 4)," W. V. O. Quine Papers.

166. Morton White to Roderick Firth, n.d., box 18, folder "G. E. L. Owen—1960–1965," HPD11.

167. Cotkin, *Existential America*, 1, 147–49.

168. Gilbert Harman to Robert Goheen, February 9, 1970, box 2, folder "Chairs—Philosophy, 1962–1972," President Robert Goheen Papers.

169. Ledger Wood to Robert Goheen, February 23, 1970, box 2, folder "Chairs—Philosophy, 1962–1972," President Robert Goheen Papers.

170. Richard Rorty to Robert Goheen, October 22, 1971, box 2, folder "Chairs—Philosophy, 1962–1972," President Robert Goheen Papers.

171. Richard Rorty to Robert Goheen, November 10, 1970, box 2, folder "Chairs—Philosophy, 1962–1972," President Robert Goheen Papers.

172. Dreyfus, "Standing Up to Analytic Philosophy," 84.

173. Hocking to Henry Bugbee, February 27, 1954, box 4, folder "Henry Bugbee (1 of 2)," W. E. Hocking Correspondence.

174. Ibid.

175. D. W. Gotshalk to Roderick Firth, May 6, 1959, box 14, folder I, HPD11; Morgan, "Philosophy Annual Report," July 20, 1959, box 8, folder "Chairmen's Reports, 1958–1959," Records of Dean Simeon Leland; Robert Browning, "Philosophy Departmental Report," July 30, 1957, box 8, folder "Chairmen's Reports, 1956–1957," Records of Dean Simeon Leland; Roderick Firth to Carl Hempel, November 14, 1961, box 18, folder N, HPD11; Franklin Ford to Nathan Pusey, October 30, 1962, box 273, folder "Philosophy, 1962–63," Records of the President of Harvard University, Nathan Marsh Pusey, Harvard University Archives, Cambridge, MA.

176. Kingsley Price and Stephen Barker, "Jobs in Philosophy by Areas—1970–79," *Proceedings and Addresses of the American Philosophical Association* 53, no. 5 (1980): 609.

177. Woessner, *Heidegger in America*, 173–75. See also Martin Heidegger, *German Existentialism*, trans. Dagobert D. Runes (New York: Wisdom Library, 1965).

178. Borradori, *American Philosopher*, 57.

179. Rieser, "Remarks on the Eleventh International Congress of Philosophy," 101.

180. See Paul E. Johnson, *A Shopkeeper's Millennium: Society and Revivals in Rochester, New York, 1815–1837*, 1st rev. ed. (New York: Hill and Wang, 2004), 140.

181. Rogers Albritton to Kurt Fischer, February 13, 1964, box 16, folder F, HPD11; Kurt Fischer to Rogers Albritton, February 18, 1964, box 16, folder F, HPD11.

182. Lester Embree, introduction to *The Golden Age of Phenomenology at the New School for Social Research, 1954–1973*, ed. Lester Embree (Athens: Ohio University Press, 2017), 9.

CHAPTER D

1. Iris Marion Young, "House and Home: Feminist Variations on a Theme," in *Motherhood and Space: Configurations of the Maternal through Politics, Home, and the Body*, ed. Sarah Boykin Hardy and Caroline Alice Wiedmer (New York: Palgrave Macmillan, 2005), 125–27; Neus Torbisco Casals, Idil Boran, and Iris Marion Young, "Interview with Iris Marion Young," *Hypatia* 23, no. 3 (2008): 176.

2. Young, "House and Home," 125–28.

3. Meena Dhanda, "Theorising with a Practical Intent: Gender, Political Philosophy and Communication, an Interview with Iris Marion Young," *Women's Philosophy Review*, no. 26 (2000): 6–7.

4. See Iris Marion Young, "From Anonymity to Speech: A Reading of Wittgenstein's Later Writing" (PhD diss., Pennsylvania State University, 1974).

5. Patchen Markell, "Iris Marion Young, 1949–2006," *Proceedings and Addresses of the American Philosophical Association* 80, no. 5 (2007): 184–85; Danielle Allen et al. "Iris Marion Young," *PS: Political Science and Politics* 40, no. 1 (2007): 168.

6. Ann Ferguson and Mechthild Nagel, introduction to *Dancing with Iris: The Philosophy of Iris Marion Young*, ed. Ann Ferguson and Mechthild Nagel (Oxford: Oxford University Press, 2009).

7. Mechthild Nagel, "Iris M. Young, 1949–2006," Solidarity, 2007, https://solidarity-us.org/atc/128/p540/.

8. Casals, Boran, and Young, "Interview with Iris Marion Young," 174–75.

9. Ferguson and Nagel, introduction to *Dancing with Iris*, 4.

10. Iris Marion Young, "Beyond the Unhappy Marriage: A Critique of the Dual Systems Theory," in *Women and Revolution : A Discussion of the Unhappy Marriage of Marxism and Feminism*, ed. Lydia Sargent (Boston: South End Press, 1981), 44–50.

11. Ibid., 51–52.

12. Ibid., 55.

13. Iris Marion Young, *Justice and the Politics of Difference* (Princeton, NJ: Princeton University Press, 2011), 13.

14. Iris Marion Young, "Gender as Seriality: Thinking about Women as a Social Collective," *Signs* 19, no. 3 (1994): 715–16.

15. Ibid., 717.

16. Ibid., 718–19.

17. Ibid., 723–24.

18. Ibid., 726.

19. Ibid., 726–30.

20. Ibid., 731.

21. Iris Marion Young, "Humanism, Gynocentrism, and Feminist Politics," in *Throwing Like a Girl and Other Essays in Feminist Philosophy and Social Theory* (Bloomington: Indiana University Press, 1990), 73–77.

22. Ibid., 85.

23. Iris Marion Young, introduction to *On Female Body Experience: "Throwing Like a Girl" and Other Essays* (New York: Oxford University Press, 2005), 1.

24. Ibid., 3–4.

25. Iris Marion Young, "Lived Body vs Gender: Reflections on Social Structure and Subjectivity," *Ratio* 15, no. 4 (2002): 415–17.

26. Ibid., 417–18.

27. Iris Marion Young, "Throwing Like a Girl: A Phenomenology of Feminine Body Comportment Motility and Spatiality," *Human Studies* 3, no. 2 (1980): 137–38, 142.

28. Ibid., 139–41.

29. Ibid., 145.

30. Ibid., 144.

31. Ibid., 148.

32. Ibid., 145–46.

33. Iris Marion Young, "Menstrual Meditations," in *On Female Body Experience: "Throwing Like a Girl" and Other Essays* (New York: Oxford University Press, 2005), 97.

34. Iris Marion Young, "Breasted Experience: The Look and the Feeling," in *On Female Body Experience: "Throwing Like a Girl" and Other Essays* (New York: Oxford University Press, 2005), 80–81.

35. Iris Marion Young, "Pregnant Embodiment: Subjectivity and Alienation," in *On Female Body Experience: "Throwing Like a Girl" and Other Essays* (New York: Oxford University Press, 2005), 47–49.

36. Ibid., 50–51.

37. Ibid., 51–52.

38. Ibid., 57.

39. Young, "House and Home," 115–16.

40. Ibid., 117–18.

41. Ibid., 133–34.

42. Ibid., 136–37.

43. John Rawls, *A Theory of Justice* (Cambridge, MA: Belknap Press of Harvard University Press, 1971); Amadae, *Rationalizing Capitalist Democracy*, 149–52, 258–73.

44. John Gray quipped that Rawls's *Theory of Justice* was "a transcendental deduction of the Labour Party in 1963." Quoted in Corey Robin, *The Reactionary Mind: Conservatism from Edmund Burke to Sarah Palin* (New York: Oxford University Press, 2011), 114.

45. Young, *Justice and the Politics of Difference*, 5.

46. Ibid., 149.

47. Ibid., 10.

48. Ibid., 18.

49. Ibid., 3, 25.

50. Ibid., 25.

51. Ibid., 23.

52. Ibid., 25, 31, 38.

53. Ibid., 20–21.

54. Ibid., 24–27.

55. Ibid., 9, 43–44, 61–62.

56. Ibid., 43–47.

57. Ibid., 166.

58. Ibid., 227–29, 37.

59. Ibid., 9.

60. Ibid., 184–85.

CHAPTER SIX

Epigraph: Grene, "Reception of Continental Philosophy in America," 24.

1. I do not say that SPEP's founders organized *as* Continental philosophers, because I find no evidence that members of the organization embraced the term until significantly later. However, the idea of Continental philosophy and the organization of SPEP were reactions to the same institutional situation.

2. John Wild, Richard Ira Sugarman, and Roger B. Duncan, *The Promise of Phenomenology: Posthumous Papers of John Wild* (Lanham, MD: Lexington Books, 2006), xxviii.

3. Daniel Marcelle, "The Great Gurwitsch–Føllesdal Debate Concerning the Noema," in *Phenomenology 2010*, vol. 3, ed. Dermot Moran and Hans-Rainer Sepp (Bucharest: Zeta Books, 2011), 243–44.

4. Yoshimi, Tolley, and Smith, "California Phenomenology," in *The Reception of Husserlian Phenomenology in North America*, 376.

5. Searle has denied that Husserl influenced his own theory of intentionality. However, both Føllesdal and Hubert Dreyfus provided comments on his manuscript, evidencing at least a secondhand Husserlian influence. John Searle, *Intentionality: An Essay in the Philosophy of Mind* (Cambridge: Cambridge University Press, 1983).

6. Michael Dummett, *Origins of Analytical Philosophy* (Cambridge, MA: Harvard University Press, 1993), 26–27, 73–75.

7. There are some examples of phenomenologists from outside the "West Coast" and Harvard lineages, such as J. N. Mohanty, whose work foregrounded phenomenological engagement with analytic philosophy. However, they are exceptions to a strong general trend.

8. I am grateful to the Society for Phenomenology and Existential Philosophy and the presenters at its fiftieth-anniversary conference for providing the materials for this account of its early history. See Calvin Schrag, "Celebrating Fifty Years of the Society for Phenomenology and Existential Philosophy," *Journal of Speculative Philosophy,* 26, no. 2 (2012): 87–88.

9. Ibid., 88.

10. Robert Scharff, email interview with Jonathan Strassfeld, November 8, 2018.

11. Ibid.

12. Edward Casey, "Random Reflections of a Founding Witness," *Journal of Speculative Philosophy* 26, no. 2 (2012): 96.

13. Ibid., 94–95.

14. Robert Scharff, "American Continental Philosophy in the Making: The Society for Phenomenology and Existential Philosophy's Early Days," *Journal of Speculative Philosophy* 26, no. 2 (2012): 109, 111; Robert Scharff, "John Wild, Lifeworld Experience, and the Founding of SPEP," *Continental Philosophy Review* 44, no. 3 (2004): 290.

15. David Carr, "A Philosophical History of the Society for Phenomenology and Existential Philosophy?," *Journal of Speculative Philosophy* 26, no. 2 (2012): 104–5, 107.

16. Casey, "Random Reflections of a Founding Witness," 98.

17. Nancy Fraser, "Tales from the Trenches: On Women Philosophers, Feminist Philosophy, and the Society for Phenomenology and Existential Philosophy," *Journal of Speculative Philosophy* 26, no. 2 (2012): 182.

18. Debra Bergoffen, "The Society for Phenomenology and Existential Philosophy, Feminism, and the Epoché," *Journal of Speculative Philosophy* 26, no. 2 (2012): 279.

19. Fraser, "Tales from the Trenches," 182.

20. Bergoffen, "Society for Phenomenology and Existential Philosophy," 279.

21. Fraser, "Tales from the Trenches," 182–83.

22. Nancy Holland, "Thoughts on Thirty Years in the Society for Phenomenology and Existential Philosophy," *Journal of Speculative Philosophy* 26, no. 2 (2012): 185–86.

23. George Psathas, "A Brief History," http://www.sphs.info/; Scharff, email interview with Strassfeld, November 8, 2018.

24. George Psathas, "In Memory of Herbert Spiegelberg and the Phenomenological Workshops," *Human Studies* 15, no. 4 (1992): 400–410.

25. Waltraut Stein, "Sym-philosophizing in an Ethics Class," in *Phenomenological Perspectives: Historical and Systematic Essays in Honor of Herbert Spiegelberg*, ed. Philip Bossert (The Hague: Martinus Nijhoff, 1975), 229.

26. Richard D. Chessick, "The Phenomenology of Erwin Straus and the Epistemology of Psychoanalysis," *American Journal of Psychotherapy* 53, no. 1 (1999): 91–92.

27. Algis Mickunas and Burt C. Hopkins, "History of the Husserl Circle," in *The Reception of Husserlian Phenomenology in North America*, ed. Michela Beatrice Ferri (New York: Springer, 2019), 261–63; Daniel Marcelle, "The Impact of North American Phenomenological Organizations: The Chronicle Revisited,"

in *The Reception of Husserlian Phenomenology in North America*, ed. Michela Beatrice Ferri (New York: Springer, 2019), 243–44.

28. Statistics based on analysis of hiring and promotion (see appendix B). My primary data source is the online Yale University Register. However, the Philosophy Department's annual reports provided additional information on tenure decisions. "Yale University Historical Register Online," http://avideo.library .yale.edu/hro/index.php.

29. Robert Fogelin to Kingman Brewster, January 21, 1972, box 306, folder "Philosophy, 1969–1970," President Kingman Brewster Records.

30. Howard Lamar to Kingman Brewster, May 10, 1972, box 306, folder "Philosophy, 1969–1970," President Kingman Brewster Records.

31. Victor Chen, "Students Begin 3-Day Vigil: The Book on Richard J. Bernstein," *Yale Daily News*, March 2, 1965; James Adams, "30 on Midnight Picket Line Protest Bernstein Case," *Yale Daily News*, March 2, 1965.

32. John Delvin, "Yale Pickets Win Tenure Review," *New York Times*, March 3, 1965.

33. Victor Chen, "Department Votes Down Bernstein," *Yale Daily News*, March 8, 1965; Michael Winger, "Brumbaugh: Shift on Bernstein Forced," *Yale Daily News*, March 9, 1965.

34. Carr, "Philosophical History of the Society for Phenomenology," 104.

35. Robert Fogelin to President and Fellows of Yale University, January 1, 1972, box 13, folder "Department of Philosophy, 1971–1972," Office of the President, Yale University, Annual and Special Reports, Yale University Archives, New Haven, CT; John Smith to President and Fellows of Yale University, August 1, 1972, box 13, folder "Department of Philosophy, 1971–1972," Office of the President, Yale University, Annual and Special Reports, Yale University Archives, New Haven, CT.

36. Fogelin to President and Fellows of Yale, August 1, 1970, box 13, folder "Department of Philosophy, 1969–1970," Office of the President, Yale University, Annual and Special Reports, Yale University Archives, New Haven, CT.

37. Bruce Kuklick, email interview with Jonathan Strassfeld, October 31, 2018.

38. Ruth Barcan Marcus, "Statement to Joint Board Re. David Carr," October 3, 1974, box 306, folder "Philosophy, 1969–1970," President Kingman Brewster Records.

39. Gary Herrmann, "Carr Denied Tenure in 'Unusual' Action," *Yale Daily News*, October 7, 1974.

40. Marcus, "Statement to Joint Board Re. Carr," October 3, 1974, box 306, folder "Philosophy, 1969–1970," President Kingman Brewster Records.

41. John Smith to Horace Taft, October 7, 1974, box 306, folder "Philosophy, 1969–1970," President Kingman Brewster Records.

42. Marcus, "Statement to Joint Board Re. Carr," October 3, 1974, box 306, folder "Philosophy, 1969–1970," President Kingman Brewster Records.

43. Ruth Barcan Marcus to Kingman Brewster, April 21, 1974, box 306, folder "Philosophy, 1969–1970," President Kingman Brewster Records; Ruth Barcan Marcus to the Executive Committee and Howard Lamar May 16, 1974, box 306, folder "Philosophy, 1969–1970," President Kingman Brewster Records.

44. Smith to Taft, October 7, 1974, box 306, folder "Philosophy, 1969–1970," President Kingman Brewster Records.

45. Howard Lamar to Horace Taft, January 7, 1974, box 306, folder "Philosophy, 1969–1970," President Kingman Brewster Records.

46. Karsten Harries to Howard Lamar, January 10, 1974, box 306, folder "Philosophy, 1969–1970," President Kingman Brewster Records.

47. Kingman Brewster to Karsten Harries, February 24, 1975, box 350, folder "Philosophy, 1973–1975," President Kingman Brewster Records.

48. "Summary of Annual Report, 1975–76, Department of Philosophy," 1976, box 350, folder "Philosophy, 1975–76," President Kingman Brewster Records.

49. Ruth Barcan Marcus to Karsten Harries, May 7, 1975, box 350, folder "Philosophy, 1973–1975," President Kingman Brewster Records.

50. "Philosophy," 1976, box 350, folder "Philosophy, 1975–76," President Kingman Brewster Records.

51. Ruth Barcan Marcus to Junior Appointments Committee, February 10, 1977, box 350, folder "Philosophy, 1976–77," President Kingman Brewster Records.

52. Jeremy Weinberg, "Turmoil Threatens Philosophy Department," *Yale Daily News*, September 20, 1990; "Philosophy's Comeback Kids," *Yale Daily News*, November 8, 2013.

53. Joseph Greenbaum to Philosophy Department, November 23, 1976, box 10, folder "Philosophy Dept. Evaluation, 1977: Repts., Responses, Correspondence," New School Graduate Faculty Collection.

54. "Philosophy Department of the Graduate Faculty at the New School: A Documentation," page 14, February 1979, box 6, folder "Philosophy Department Struggle in 1958–59," New School Graduate Faculty Collection; Albert Hofstadter, "State of the Philosophy Department," June 1978, box 6, folder "Philosophy Department Struggle in 1958–59, 1979," New School Graduate Faculty Collection.

55. Richard Rorty, quoted in Gross, *Richard Rorty*, 218.

56. This phenomenon is well documented in the field of history; see Robert B. Townsend, "Precedents: The Job Crisis of the 1970s," *Perspectives on History*, April 1997, https://www.historians.org/publications-and-directories/perspectives-on-history/april-1997/precedents-the-job-crisis-of-the-1970s.

57. "Documentation," February 1979, box 6, folder "Philosophy Department Struggle in 1958–59, 1979," New School Graduate Faculty Collection. 188.

58. "Program Chart #1," April 1, 1976, box 10, folder "Philosophy Dept. Evaluation, 1977: Repts., Responses, Correspondence," New School Graduate Faculty Collection; "Documentation," February 1979, box 6, folder "Philosophy Department Struggle in 1958–59, 1979," New School Graduate Faculty Collection. 38.

59. "Documentation," February 1979, box 6, folder "Philosophy Department Struggle in 1958–59, ,1979," New School Graduate Faculty Collection. 82; "Philosophy Rating Committee: New School for Social Research," box 10, folder "Philosophy Dept. Evaluation, 1977: Repts., Responses, Correspondence," New School Graduate Faculty Collection, 1.

60. Allen Austill, "Appendix A: Report on the Status of the Graduate Faculty of Political and Social Science," page 8, March 29, 1979, box 2, folder "Reports: Self-Study (Middle States), 1981 Feb. (7 of 10)," New School Graduate Faculty Collection.

61. John Everett to Dorothy Harrison, May 9, 1977, box 10, folder "Philosophy Dept. Evaluation, 1977: Repts., Responses, Correspondence," New School Graduate Faculty Collection.

62. Wilshire, *Fashionable Nihilism*, 52–54.

63. "Draft Report: Sociology Rating Committee," box 10, folder "Sociology Dept. Response to N.Y. State Evaluation," New School Graduate Faculty Collection.

64. "Research," box 10, folder "Philosophy Dept. Evaluation, 1977: Repts., Responses, Correspondence," New School Graduate Faculty Collection, 2–3.

65. Richard Rorty to Joseph Greenbaum, June 10, 1977, box 10, folder "Philosophy Dept. Evaluation, 1977: Repts., Responses, Correspondence," New School Graduate Faculty Collection.

66. "Documentation," February 1979, box 6, folder "Philosophy Department Struggle in 1958–59, 1979," New School Graduate Faculty Collection, 30–31.

67. "Suggestions of the Coordinating Committee to the Graduate Faculty," January 20, 1941, box 1, folder "Graduate Faculty Minutes, Sept. 1933–June 1945," New School Graduate Faculty Collection.

68. Kurt Riezler, quoted in "1945: Discussion for Proposals for Changes in Requirements for Degrees Executive Faculty Meeting April 25," April 25, 1945, box 1, folder "Graduate Faculty Minutes, Sept. 1933–June 1945," New School Graduate Faculty Collection.

69. John Everett to The Members of the Faculty, December 20, 1979, box 10, folder IVa: "Responses to CRISIS: 1978–79," New School Graduate Faculty Collection.

70. Austill, "Appendix A," pages 22–25, March 29, 1979, box 2, folder "Reports: Self-Study (Middle States), 1981 Feb. (7 of 10)," New School Graduate Faculty Collection.

71. Arthur Vidich to Executive Faculty members, April 3, 1979, box 10, folder IIIb: "Responses to NY State Review," New School Graduate Faculty Collection.

72. See Alan Donagan to John Everett, February 2, 1979, box 6, folder "Philosophy Department Struggle in 1958–59, 1979," New School Graduate Faculty Collection; Alasdair MacIntyre to John Everett, February 21, 1979, box 6, folder "Philosophy Department Struggle in 1958–59, 1979," New School Graduate Faculty Collection; Paul Ricoeur to John Everett, April 5, 1979, box 6, folder "Philosophy Department Struggle in 1958–59, 1979," New School Graduate Faculty Collection; and Jürgen Habermas to John Everett, February 2, 1979, box 6, folder "Philosophy Department Struggle in 1958–59, 1979," New School Graduate Faculty Collection.

73. W. V. O. Quine to John Everett, February 2, 1979, box 6, folder "Philosophy Department Struggle in 1958–59, 1979," New School Graduate Faculty Collection.

74. Members of the executive faculty to the trustees, May 22, 1979, box 10, folder IVa: "Responses to CRISIS: 1978–79," New School Graduate Faculty Collection.

75. "Statement of Purpose and Resolution by the Board of Trustees of New School for Social Research," September 19, 1979, box 10, folder IVb: "Responses to CRISIS: 1978–79," New School Graduate Faculty Collection.

76. F. Champion Ward et al., "A Distinctive Future for the Graduate Faculty of Political and Social Science," May 1980, box 10, folder IVb: "Responses to CRISIS: 1978–79," New School Graduate Faculty Collection.

77. John Everett to the board of trustees, June 3, 1980, box 10, folder IVb: "Responses to CRISIS: 1978–79," New School Graduate Faculty Collection.

78. Judith Friedlander, *A Light in Dark Times: The New School for Social Research and Its University in Exile* (New York: Columbia University Press, 2018), 316.

79. Herbert Spiegelberg, "Memories of My American Life for My American Children and Children's Children," *Human Studies* 15, no. 4 (1992): 375–77.

80. Ierna, "Herbert Spiegelberg," 162–63.

81. William McBride, "Phenomenology's History Revisited," review of *The Phenomenological Movement: A Historical Introduction*, by Herbert Spiegelberg, *Human Studies* 7, no. 3/4 (1984): 372; Karl Schuhmann, "Markers on the Road to the Conception of the Phenomenological Movement: Appendix to Spiegelberg's Paper," *Philosophy and Phenomenological Research* 43, no. 3 (1983): 306.

82. Samuel Hart, review of *The Phenomenological Movement: A Historical Introduction*, by Herbert Spiegelberg, *Philosophical Review* 73, no. 1 (1964): 114.

83. Peter M. Simons, review of *The Context of the Phenomenological Movement*, by Herbert Spiegelberg, *Philosophy and Phenomenological Research* 44, no. 3 (1984): 426.

84. Herbert Schneider, quoted in Spiegelberg, *Phenomenological Movement*, 1:xxi.

85. Daniela Verducci, "A.-T. Tymieniecka: A Phenomenologist in the United States. The Adventures of a Polish-Born American," in *The Reception of*

Husserlian Phenomenology in North America, ed. Michela Beatrice Ferri (New York: Springer, 2019), 207–8.

86. Anna-Teresa Tymieniecka, *Phenomenology and Science in Contemporary European Thought* (New York: Farrar, 1962), xvii–xix.

87. Ibid., 19–21, 60.

88. Ibid., 19.

89. Verducci, "A.-T. Tymieniecka," 208; Tymieniecka, *Phenomenology and Science in Contemporary European Thought*, 176.

90. Vidich to Executive Faculty, April 3, 1979, box 10, folder IIIb: "Responses to NY State Review," New School Graduate Faculty Collection.

91. Joseph Kockelmans, "Phenomenological Psychology in the United States: A Critical Analysis of the Actual Situation," *Journal of Phenomenological Psychology* 1, no. 2 (1971): 139–42.

92. Cloonan, "Early History of Phenomenological Psychological Research," 103–8.

93. Amedeo Giorgi, "Psychology: A Human Science," *Social Research* 36, no. 3 (1969): 414; Amedeo Giorgi, quoted in Cloonan, "Early History of Phenomenological Psychological Research," 112, 14.

94. "Books of the XX Century," https://www.isa-sociology.org/en/about-isa /history-of-isa/books-of-the-xx-century/.

95. Peter L. Berger and Thomas Luckmann, *The Social Construction of Reality: A Treatise in the Sociology of Knowledge* (London: Penguin, 1967), 13–15.

96. Ibid., 33–34.

97. Ibid., 219.

98. Ibid., 70–85, 208–11.

99. Garfinkel and Rawls, *Ethnomethodology's Program*, xx–xxi; Zaner, "Gurwitsch at the New School," 124; Gurwitsch, *The Field of Consciousness: Theme, Thematic Field, and Margin*, 49–52.

100. Garfinkel and Rawls, *Ethnomethodology's Program*, 66, 84, 167.

101. Ibid., 114–20.

102. Desjarlais and Throop, "Phenomenological Approaches in Anthropology," 88–89.

103. Ibid., 89–90.

104. See, for example, Yi-Fu Tuan, "Humanistic Geography," *Annals of the Association of American Geographers* 66, no. 2 (1976): 266.

105. Anne Buttimer, "Grasping the Dynamism of Lifeworld," *Annals of the Association of American Geographers* 66, no. 2 (1976): 283–85.

106. Jorge Otero-Pailos, *Architecture's Historical Turn: Phenomenology and the Rise of the Postmodern* (Minneapolis: University of Minnesota Press, 2010), 108.

107. Marc Redfield, *Theory at Yale: The Strange Case of Deconstruction in America* (New York: Fordham University Press, 2016), 29–30.

108. Ibid., 6.

109. Barry Smith, "Derrida Degree a Question of Honor," *Times*, May 9, 1992.

110. Allan Bloom, *The Closing of the American Mind: How Higher Education Has Failed Democracy and Impoverished the Souls of Today's Students* (New York: Simon and Schuster, 1987), 152.

111. See Roger Kimball, *Tenured Radicals: How Politics Has Corrupted Our Higher Education* (New York: Harper & Row, 1990); and Keith Windschuttle, *The Killing of History: How a Discipline Is Being Murdered by Literary Critics and Social Theorists* (Paddington, Australia: Macleay, 1994).

112. "Yale Scholar Wrote for Pro-Nazi Newspaper," *New York Times*, December 1, 1987; David Lehman, "The (De) Man Who Put the Con in Deconstruction," *Los Angeles Times*, March 13, 1988.

113. Redfield, *Theory at Yale*, 38.

114. Thomas G. Pavel, "The Heidegger Affair," *MLN* 103, no. 4 (1988): 887–88, 894–95.

115. Paul L. Montgomery, "Scholar Breaks with Heidegger," *New York Times*, April 11, 1964; Woessner, *Heidegger in America*, 112–19.

116. Robert B. Westbrook, *John Dewey and American Democracy* (Ithaca, NY: Cornell University Press, 1991), 198–200.

117. Thomas L. Akehurst, "The Nazi Tradition: The Analytic Critique of Continental Philosophy in Mid-century Britain," *History of European Ideas* 34, no. 4 (2008): 550–54.

118. Joyce Appleby, Lynn Hunt, and Margaret C. Jacob, *Telling the Truth about History* (New York: Norton, 1994), 206–7.

119. David H. Hirsch, "After Alien Gods," *Sewanee Review* 96, no. 4 (1988): 717.

120. David H. Hirsch, "Paul de Man and the Politics of Deconstruction," *Sewanee Review* 96, no. 2 (1988): 337–38.

121. Clark Glymour, "In Light of Some Recent Discussion over at New Apps, I Bring You Clark Glymour's Manifesto . . . ," Choice & Inference, December 23, 2011.

CONCLUSION

1. Rorty, "Philosophy in America Today," 196.

2. Ibid., 190.

3. Ibid., 197.

4. On the sociological underpinnings of Rorty's disciplinary migration and insightful analysis of his reception by political theorists, see Loren Goldman, "Notes on Richard Rorty, Homo Academicus Politicus," *Analyse und Kritik* 41, no. 1 (2019).

5. Kuklick, *The Rise of American Philosophy*, 9.

6. Rorty, "Philosophy in America Today," 198.

7. Ibid., 198–99.

8. See ibid., 198.

9. Richard Rorty, *Philosophy and the Mirror of Nature* (Princeton, NJ: Princeton University Press, 1979), 318.

10. Ibid., 324.

11. Rorty, "Philosophy in America Today," 196.

12. Theodore W. Schick, "Rorty and Davidson on Alternate Conceptual Schemes," *Journal of Speculative Philosophy* 1, no. 4 (1987): 291.

13. Thomas Kuhn, *The Structure of Scientific Revolutions*, 3rd ed. (Chicago: University of Chicago Press, 1996), 324–26.

14. Peter Galison, *Image and Logic: A Material Culture of Microphysics* (Chicago: University of Chicago Press, 1997), 51.

15. T. Kuhn, *Structure of Scientific Revolutions*, 46.

16. Ibid., 47.

17. Galison, *Image and Logic*, 783.

18. Ibid., 47.

19. Ibid., 46, 52.

20. Ibid., 803.

21. Marcus to The Executive Committee and Howard Lamar May 16, 1974, box 306, folder "Philosophy, 1969–1970," President Kingman Brewster Records.

22. White, *A Philosopher's Story*, 33–34.

23. Grene, *The Knower and the Known*, 246.

24. Alfred North Whitehead, *Process and Reality: An Essay in Cosmology* (New York: Macmillan, 1929), 137.

25. Ibid., 139.

26. Ibid., 140.

APPENDIX

1. "Philosophy: Faculty History Project," https://www.lib.umich.edu/faculty-history/philosophy; "Chairs and Faculty since 1949: Department of Philosophy," https://philosophy.princeton.edu/about/faculty-1949; "Yale University Historical Register Online."

2. Leiter, "Philosophy Faculty at the Leading American Programs."

Bibliography

ARCHIVAL SOURCES AND INTERVIEWS

Alfred Schütz Papers, Beinecke Rare Book and Manuscript Library, New Haven, CT.

Bernstein, Richard. Interview by Jonathan Strassfeld. October 23, 2017, New School for Social Research.

Burton Dreben Papers (unorganized), private collection of Warren Goldfarb, Cambridge, MA.

Central Files, 1890–1984, Columbia University Archives, New York, NY.

Dept. of Philosophy records, 1892–1952, Division of Rare and Manuscript Collections, Cornell University Library, Ithaca, NY.

Emergency Committee in Aid of Displaced Foreign Scholars Records, Manuscripts and Archives Division, The New York Public Library, New York, NY.

Ernest Nagel Papers, Columbia University Archives, New York, NY.

Faculty Suggestions for New Courses in General Education: UAIII 10.199.35, Harvard University Archives, Cambridge, MA.

Graduate Faculty of the New School for Social Research Collection, New School Archives, New York, NY.

Graduate Student Folders, Pre-1917, Harvard University Archives, Cambridge, MA.

Harvard University Department of Philosophy Records (1906–1979): Dept. of Philosophy and Psychology & Dept. of Philosophy: Minutes of Departmental Meetings and Correspondence Files, 1924–1960 (UAV 687.1), Harvard University Archives, Cambridge, MA.

Harvard University Department of Philosophy Records (1906–1979): Dept. of Philosophy & Dept. of Philosophy and Psychology: outgoing correspondence, 1910–1915 (UAV 687.2), Harvard University Archives, Cambridge, MA.

Harvard University Department of Philosophy Records (1906–1979): Dept. of Philosophy and Psychology; the Dept. of Psychology; and the Division of Philosophy and Psychology: correspondence and other records, ca. 1927–1938 (UAV 687.10), Harvard University Archives, Cambridge, MA.

Harvard University Department of Philosophy Records (1906–1979): Division of Philosophy and Psychology & Dept. of Psychology: General Correspondence, 1938–1965 (UAV 687.11), Harvard University Archives, Cambridge, MA.

Harvard University Department of Philosophy Records (1906–1979): Dept. of Philosophy; Dept. of Philosophy and Psychology; Division of Philosophy and Psychology; and Dept. of Psychology: Administrative Records, including Correspondence, Memos, Reports and Other Material Relating to Departmental Issues (UAV 687.15), Harvard University Archives, Cambridge, MA.

Kingman Brewster Jr., President of Yale University, Records, Yale University Archives, New Haven, CT.

Kuklick, Bruce, email interview by Jonathan Strassfeld, October 31, 2018.

Marvin Farber Papers, University Archives: State University of New York at Buffalo, Buffalo, NY.

Marvin Farber *PPR* Papers, University Archives: State University of New York at Buffalo, Buffalo, NY.

Office of the President: Robert F. Goheen, Princeton University Archives, Princeton, NJ.

Office of the President, Yale University, Annual and Special Reports, Yale University Archives, New Haven, CT.

Philosophy Department General Administrative Records, Northwestern University Archives, Evanston, IL.

Ralph Barton Perry Correspondence, Harvard University Archives, Cambridge, MA.

Records from the Committee on General Scholarships and the Sheldon Fund, Harvard University Archives, Cambridge, MA.

Records from the Committee on the William H. Milton Fund and the Joseph R. Clark Bequest, Harvard University Archives, Cambridge, MA.

Records of the Dean of Faculty of Arts and Sciences, Harvard University Archives, Cambridge, MA.

Records of the Dean, Addison Hibbard, 1935–1946, Northwestern University Archives, Evanston, IL.

Records of the Dean, Simeon E. Leland, Northwestern University Archives, Evanston, IL.

Records of the Northwestern University Press, Northwestern University Archives, Evanston, IL.

Records of the President of Harvard University, James Bryant Conant, Harvard University Archives, Cambridge, MA.

Records of the President of Harvard University, Nathan Marsh Pusey, Harvard University Archives, Cambridge, MA.

Reports of the Academic Departments to President N. M. Butler, Columbia University Archives, New York, NY.

Revolving Appointment Fund, 1939 October, Harvard University Archives, Cambridge, MA.

Scharff, Robert, email interview by Jonathan Strassfeld, November 8, 2018.

Secretary's Office Records, 1899–1953, Yale University Archives, New Haven, CT.

University of Southern California School of Philosophy Records, USC Libraries Special Collections, Los Angeles, CA.

William A. Earle Papers, Northwestern University Archives, Evanston, IL.

William Ernest Hocking correspondence, 1860–1979, Houghton Library, Cambridge, MA.

Winthrop Pickard Bell Fonds, Mount Allison University Archives, Sackville, New Brunswick.

W. V. O. Quine Papers, Houghton Library, Cambridge, MA.

PUBLISHED SOURCES

Adams, James. "30 on Midnight Picket Line Protest Bernstein Case." *Yale Daily News*, March 2, 1965.

Aiken, Henry. *Predicament of the University*. Bloomington: Indiana University Press, 1971.

Akehurst, Thomas L. "The Nazi Tradition: The Analytic Critique of Continental Philosophy in Mid-century Britain." *History of European Ideas* 34, no. 4 (2008): 548–57.

Allardyce, Gilbert. "The Rise and Fall of the Western Civilization Course." *American Historical Review* 87, no. 3 (1982): 695–725.

Althusser, Louis. *On Ideology*. Translated by Ben Brewster. New York: Verso, 2008.

Amadae, S. M. *Rationalizing Capitalist Democracy: The Cold War Origins of Rational Choice Liberalism*. Chicago: University of Chicago Press, 2003.

Anwar, Yasmin. "Hubert Dreyfus, Preeminent Philosopher and AI Critic, Dies at 87." http://news.berkeley.edu/2017/04/24/hubert-dreyfus/.

Appleby, Joyce, Lynn Hunt, and Margaret C. Jacob. *Telling the Truth about History*. New York: Norton, 1994.

Ayer, A. J. "The Genesis of Metaphysics." *Analysis* 1, no. 4 (1934): 55–58.

Barber, Michael D. *The Participating Citizen: A Biography of Alfred Schutz*. Albany: State University of New York Press, 2004.

———. "Schutz and the New School." In *The Golden Age of Phenomenology at the New School for Social Research, 1954–1973*, edited by Lester Embree. Athens: Ohio University Press, 2017.

Baring, Edward. *Converts to the Real: Catholicism and the Making of Continental Philosophy*. Cambridge, MA: Harvard University Press, 2019.

Barrett, William. *What Is Existentialism?* New York: Partisan Review, 1947.

Bell, Jason. "Phenomenology's Inauguration in English and in the North American Curriculum: Winthrop Bell's 1927 Harvard Course." In *The Reception of Husserlian Phenomenology in North America*, edited by Michela Beatrice Ferri. New York: Springer, 2019.

Berger, Peter L., and Thomas Luckmann. *The Social Construction of Reality: A Treatise in the Sociology of Knowledge*. London: Penguin, 1967.

Bergoffen, Debra. "The Society for Phenomenology and Existential Philosophy, Feminism, and the Epoché." *Journal of Speculative Philosophy* 26, no. 2 (2012): 278–90.

"Biography of Dr. Winthrop Pickard Bell." http://www.mta.ca/wpbell/bio.htm.

Blanshard, Brand, Curt John Ducasse, Charles William Hendel, Arthur Edward Murphy, and Max Carl Otto. *Philosophy in American Education, Its Tasks and Opportunities*. New York: Harper & Brothers, 1945.

Bloom, Allan. *The Closing of the American Mind: How Higher Education Has Failed Democracy and Impoverished the Souls of Today's Students*. New York: Simon and Schuster, 1987.

Borradori, Giovanna. *The American Philosopher: Conversations with Quine, Davidson, Putnam, Nozick, Danto, Rorty, Cavell, Macintyre, and Kuhn*. Chicago: University of Chicago Press, 1994.

Brandt, Richard. "The Significance of Differences of Ethical Opinion for Ethical Rationalism." *Philosophy and Phenomenological Research* 4, no. 4 (1944): 469–95.

Brogan, Walter, and James Risser. *American Continental Philosophy: A Reader*. Studies in Continental Thought. Bloomington: Indiana University Press, 2000.

Buttimer, Anne. "Grasping the Dynamism of Lifeworld." *Annals of the Association of American Geographers* 66, no. 2 (1976): 277–92.

Cairns, Dorion. "My Own Life." http://thenewschoolhistory.org/wp-content/uploads/2014/07/cairns_myownlife-web.pdf.

———. "The Philosophy of Edmund Husserl." PhD diss., Harvard University, 1933.

Cairns, Dorion, Lester Embree, and John Wild. "A Letter to John Wild About Husserl." *Research in Phenomenology* 5 (1975): 155–81.

Carnap, Rudolf. "The Two Concepts of Probability: The Problem of Probability." *Philosophy and Phenomenological Research* 5, no. 4 (1945): 513–32.

———. "Überwindung der Metaphysik durch logische Analyse der Sprache." *Erkenntnis* 2 (1931): 219–41.

Carr, David. "A Philosophical History of the Society for Phenomenology and Existential Philosophy?" *Journal of Speculative Philosophy* 26, no. 2 (2012): 102–7.

Cartter, Allan Murray. *An Assessment of Quality in Graduate Education.* Washington, DC: American Council on Education, 1966.

Casals, Neus Torbisco, Idil Boran, and Iris Marion Young. "Interview with Iris Marion Young." *Hypatia* 23, no. 3 (2008): 173–81.

Casey, Edward. "Random Reflections of a Founding Witness." *Journal of Speculative Philosophy,* 26, no. 2 (2012): 93–101.

Cavell, Stanley. "Existentialism and Analytical Philosophy." *Daedalus* 93, no. 3 (1964): 946–74.

Cerf, Walter. "An Approach to Heidegger's Ontology." *Philosophy and Phenomenological Research* 1, no. 2 (1940): 177–90.

———. "The Eleventh International Congress of Philosophy." *Philosophical Review* 64, no. 2 (1955): 280–99.

———. "Existentialist Mannerism and Education." *Journal of Philosophy* 52, no. 6 (1955): 141–52.

———. "Logical Positivism and Existentialism." *Philosophy of Science* 18, no. 4 (1951): 327–38.

———. "Value Decisions." *Philosophy of Science* 18, no. 1 (1951): 26–34.

"Chairs and Faculty since 1949: Department of Philosophy." https://philosophy.princeton.edu/about/faculty-1949.

Chandler, Albert. "Plato's Theory of Ideas Studied in the Light of Husserl's Theory of Universals." PhD diss., Harvard University, 1913.

Chappel, James. *Catholic Modern: The Challenge of Totalitarianism and the Remaking of the Church.* Cambridge, MA: Harvard University Press, 2018.

Chen, Victor. "Department Votes Down Bernstein." *Yale Daily News,* March 8, 1965.

———. "Students Begin 3-Day Vigil: The Book on Richard J. Bernstein." *Yale Daily News,* March 2, 1965

Chessick, Richard D. "The Phenomenology of Erwin Straus and the Epistemology of Psychoanalysis." *American Journal of Psychotherapy* 53, no. 1 (1999): 82–95.

Cho, Kah Kyung. "Phenomenology as Cooperative Task: Husserl–Farber Correspondence during 1936–37." *Philosophy and Phenomenological Research* 50 (1990): 27–43.

Churchill, Scott D., and Frederick J. Wertz. "An Introduction to Phenomenological Research in Psychology: Historical, Conceptual, and Methodological Foundations." In *The Handbook of Humanistic Psychology: Theory, Research, and Practice*, edited by Kirk J. Schneider, J. Fraser Pierson, and James F. T. Bugental. Los Angeles: Sage Publications, 2015.

Cloonan, Thomas F. "The Early History of Phenomenological Psychological Research in America." *Journal of Phenomenological Psychology* 26, no. 1 (1995): 46–126.

Cohen, Benjamin. "An Interview with Marjorie Grene." *Believer*, no. 22 (March 1, 2005). https://believermag.com/an-interview-with-marjore-grene/.

Copleston, Frederick C. "The Human Person in Contemporary Philosophy." *Philosophy* 25, no. 92 (1950): 3–19.

Coser, Lewis A. *Refugee Scholars in America: Their Impact and Their Experiences*. New Haven, CT: Yale University Press, 1984.

Costello, Harry Todd, and Grover Smith. *Josiah Royce's Seminar, 1913–1914: As Recorded in the Notebooks of Harry T. Costello*. New Brunswick, NJ: Rutgers University Press, 1963.

Cotkin, George. *Existential America*. Baltimore: Johns Hopkins University Press, 2003.

Dahlstrom, Daniel O. *The Heidegger Dictionary*. New York: Bloomsbury, 2013.

———. "The Reception of Phenomenology and Existentialism by American Catholic Philosophers: Some Facts and Some Reasons." In *The Catholic Reception of Continental Philosophy in North America*, edited by Gregory P. Floyd and Stephanie Rumpza. Toronto: University of Toronto Press, 2020.

de Beauvoir, Simone. *The Prime of Life*. Translated by Peter Green. London: Andre Deutsch and Weidenfeld & Nicolson, 1962.

Delvin, John. "Yale Pickets Win Tenure Review." *New York Times*, March 3, 1965.

Demos, Raphael. "Philosophical Aspects of the Recent Harvard Report on Education." *Philosophy and Phenomenological Research* 7, no. 2 (1946): 187–213.

Desjarlais, Robert, and C. Jason Throop. "Phenomenological Approaches in Anthropology." *Annual Review of Anthropology* 40 (2011): 87–102.

Dhanda, Meena. "Theorising with a Practical Intent: Gender, Political Philosophy and Communication, an Interview with Iris Marion Young." *Women's Philosophy Review*, no. 26 (2000): 6–27.

Dougherty, Jude P. "Paul Weiss, 1901–2002." *Proceedings and Addresses of the American Philosophical Association* 77, no. 5 (2004): 174–75.

Dreyfus, Hubert L. *Being-in-the-World: A Commentary on Heidegger's Being and Time, Division I*. Cambridge, MA: MIT Press, 1991.

———. "Curriculum Vitae." http://blogi.lu.lv/broks/files/2012/11/Hubert -Dreyfus-CV-24.01.2011.pdf.

———. Foreword to *Body and World*, edited by Samuel Todes. Cambridge, MA: MIT Press, 2001.

———. "Standing Up to Analytic Philosophy and Artificial Intelligence at MIT in the Sixties." *Proceedings and Addresses of the American Philosophical Association* 87 (2013): 78–92.

———. *What Computers Can't Do: The Limits of Artificial Intelligence*. Rev. ed. New York: Harper & Row, 1979.

Dreyfus, Hubert L., Stuart E. Dreyfus, and Tom Athanasiou. *Mind over Machine: The Power of Human Intuition and Expertise in the Era of the Computer*. New York: Free Press, 1986.

Dreyfus, Hubert L., and Sean Kelly. *All Things Shining: Reading the Western Classics to Find Meaning in a Secular Age*. New York: Free Press, 2011.

Dummett, Michael. *Origins of Analytical Philosophy*. Cambridge, MA: Harvard University Press, 1993.

Eaton, Ralph Monroe. *General Logic*. New York: C. Scribner's Sons, 1931.

Eisenbeis, Walter. *The Key Ideas of Martin Heidegger's Treatise "Being and Time"*. Washington, DC: University Press of America, 1983.

Embree, Lester. "Biographical Sketch of Aron Gurwitsch." http://www.gur witsch.net/biography.htm.

———. "Editorial Foreword." In *The Philosophy of Edmund Husserl, by Dorion Cairns*, edited by Lester Embree. Dordrecht: Springer, 2013.

———. Introduction to *The Golden Age of Phenomenology at the New School for Social Research, 1954–1973*, edited by Lester Embree. Athens: Ohio University Press, 2017.

———. "The Legacy of Dorion Cairns and Aron Gurwitsch." In *American Phenomenology: Origins and Developments*, vol. XXVI, edited by Eugene Francis Kaelin and Calvin O. Schrag. Analecta Husserliana. Boston: Kluwer Academic, 1989.

Embree, Lester, and Michael D. Barber. "The Golden Age of Phenomenology: At the New School for Social Research, 1954–1973." In *The Reception of Husserlian Phenomenology in North America*, edited by Michela Beatrice Ferri. New York: Springer, 2019.

———. *The Golden Age of Phenomenology at the New School for Social Research, 1954–1973*. Series in Continental Thought. Athens: Ohio University Press, 2017.

Embree, Lester, James M. Edie, Don Ihde, Joseph J. Kockelmans, and Calvin O. Schrag. "United States of America." In *Encyclopedia of Phenomenology*, edited by Lester Embree, Elizabeth Behnke, David Carr, J. Claude Evans, Jose Huertas-Jourda, Joseph J. Cockelmans, William R. McKenna, et al. Boston: Kluwer Academic, 1997.

Evans, Robert. "Existentialism in Greene's *The Quiet American*." *Modern Fiction Studies* 3, no. 3 (1957): 241–48.

Ewald, Oscar. "Contemporary Philosophy in Germany (1906)." *Philosophical Review* 16, no. 3 (1907): 237–65.

———. "German Philosophy in 1907." *Philosophical Review* 17, no. 4 (1908): 400–26.

———. "German Philosophy in 1908." *Philosophical Review* 18, no. 5 (1909): 514–35.

———. "German Philosophy in 1913." *Philosophical Review* 23, no. 6 (1914): 615–33.

Farber, Marvin. "Experience and Subjectivism." In *Philosophy for the Future: The Quest of Modern Materialism*, edited by Roy Wood Sellars, V. J. McGill, and Marvin Farber. New York: Macmillan, 1949.

———. *The Foundation of Phenomenology: Edmund Husserl and the Quest for a Rigorous Science of Philosophy*. Cambridge, MA: Harvard University Press, 1943.

———. *Phenomenology as a Method and as a Philosophical Discipline*. Buffalo, NY: University of Buffalo, 1928.

———. "Remarks about the Phenomenological Program." *Philosophy and Phenomenological Research* 6, no. 1 (1945): 1–10.

———. "The Significance of Phenomenology for the Americas." *Philosophy and Phenomenological Research* 4, no. 2 (1943): 208–16.

Farber, Marvin, ed. *Philosophical Essays in Memory of Edmund Husserl*. Cambridge, MA: Published for the University of Buffalo by the Harvard University Press, 1940.

Feigl, Herbert. "The Wiener Kreis in America." In *The Intellectual Migration: Europe and America, 1930–1960*, edited by Donald Fleming and Bernard Bailyn. Cambridge, MA: Belknap Press of Harvard University Press, 1969.

Ferguson, Ann, and Mechthild Nagel. Introduction to *Dancing with Iris: The Philosophy of Iris Marion Young*, edited by Ann Ferguson and Mechthild Nagel. Oxford: Oxford University Press, 2009.

Ferri, Michela Beatrice. "The History of the Husserl Archives Established in Memory of Alfred Schutz at the New School for Social Research." In *The Reception of Husserlian Phenomenology in North America*, edited by Michela Beatrice Ferri. New York: Springer, 2019.

"A First Symposium on Russian Philosophy and Psychology." *Philosophy and Phenomenological Research* 5, no. 2 (1944): 157–254.

Fisher, H. H. "Henry Lanz." *American Slavic and East European Review* 5, no. 1/2 (1946): 222.

Fiske, Edward B. "Education 'Analysts' Win Battle in War of Philosophy." *New York Times*, January 6, 1981.

Føllesdal, Dagfinn. "Husserl's Notion of Noema." *Journal of Philosophy* 66, no. 20 (1969): 680–87.

Fraser, Nancy. "Tales from the Trenches: On Women Philosophers, Feminist Philosophy, and the Society for Phenomenology and Existential Philosophy." *Journal of Speculative Philosophy* 26, no. 2 (2012): 175–84.

Frege, Gottlob. "Sense and Reference." *Philosophical Review* 57, no. 3 (1948): 209–30.

Friedlander, Judith. *A Light in Dark Times: The New School for Social Research and Its University in Exile*. New York: Columbia University Press, 2018.

Friedman, Michael. *A Parting of the Ways: Carnap, Cassirer, and Heidegger*. Chicago: Open Court, 2000.

———. "A Turning Point in Philosophy: Carnap-Cassirer-Heidegger." In *Logical Empiricism: Historical & Contemporary Perspectives*, edited by Paolo Parrini, Wesley C. Salmon, and Merrilee H. Salmon. Pittsburgh: University of Pittsburgh Press, 2003.

Frost-Arnold, Greg. "When Did 'Analytic Philosophy' Become an Actor's Category?" *Obscure and Confused Ideas*, May 2011. http://obscureandconfused .blogspot.com/2011/05/when-did-analytic-philosophy-become.html.

Fulton, Ann. *Apostles of Sartre: Existentialism in America, 1945–1963*. Evanston, IL: Northwestern University Press, 1999.

"Further Education." http://www.mta.ca/wpbell/fureduc.htm.

Galison, Peter. *Image and Logic: A Material Culture of Microphysics*. Chicago: University of Chicago Press, 1997.

Garfinkel, Harold, and Anne Warfield Rawls. *Ethnomethodology's Program: Working Out Durkeim's Aphorism*. Legacies of Social Thought. Lanham, MD: Rowman & Littlefield Publishers, 2002.

Gelven, Michael. *A Commentary on Heidegger's 'Being and Time'; a Section-by-Section Interpretation*. Harper Torchbooks. New York: Harper & Row, 1970.

Gibson, W. R. Boyce, and Herbert Spiegelberg. "From Husserl to Heidegger: Excerpts from a 1928 Freiburg Diary by W.R. Boyce Gibson." *Journal of the British Society for Phenomenology* 2 (1971): 58–83.

Giorgi, Amedeo. "Psychology: A Human Science." *Social Research* 36, no. 3 (1969): 412–32.

Glicksman, Marjorie. "A Note on the Philosophy of Heidegger." *Journal of Philosophy* 35, no. 4 (1938): 93–104.

Glymour, Clark. "In Light of Some Recent Discussion over at New Apps, I Bring You Clark Glymour's Manifesto . . . ," Choice & Inference, December 23, 2011. http://choiceandinference.com/2011/12/23/in-light-of-some-recent-discussion-over-at-new-apps-i-bring-you-clark-glymours-manifesto/.

Goldman, Loren. "Notes on Richard Rorty, Homo Academicus Politicus." *Analyse und Kritik* 41, no. 1 (2019): 31–70.

Gordon, Peter Eli. *Continental Divide: Heidegger, Cassirer, Davos.* Cambridge, MA: Harvard University Press, 2010.

Grathoff, Richard, ed. *Philosophers in Exile: The Correspondence of Alfred Schutz and Aron Gurwitsch, 1939–1959.* Translated by J. Claude Evans. Bloomington: Indiana University Press, 1989.

Greer, William R. "Susanne K. Langer, Philosopher, Is Dead at 89." *New York Times,* July 19, 1985.

Grene, Marjorie. "The Concept of 'Existenz' in Contemporary German Philosophy." PhD diss., Radcliffe College, 1935.

———. *Dreadful Freedom: A Critique of Existentialism.* Chicago: University of Chicago Press, 1948.

———. "In and On Friendship." In *Human Nature and Natural Knowledge: Essays Presented to Marjorie Grene on the Occasion of Her Seventy-Fifth Birthday,* edited by Alan Donagan, Anthony N. Perovich, and Michael V. Wedin. Boston: D. Reidel, 1986.

———. "Intellectual Autobiography." In *The Philosophy of Marjorie Grene,* edited by Randall E. Auxier and Lewis Edwin Hahn. Chicago: Open Court 2002.

———. "Kierkegaard: The Philosophy." *Kenyon Review* 9, no. 1 (1947): 48–69.

———. *The Knower and the Known.* Berkeley: University of California Press, 1974.

———. *Martin Heidegger.* New York: Hillary House, 1957.

———. "A Note on the Philosophy of Heidegger: Confessions of a Young Positivist." In *Philosophy in and out of Europe,* edited by Marjorie Grene. Berkeley: University of California Press, 1976.

———. "On Some Distinctions between Men and Brutes." *Ethics* 57, no. 2 (1947): 121–27.

———. *A Philosophical Testament*. Chicago: Open Court, 1995.

———. "Philosophy of Medicine: Prolegomena to a Philosophy of Science." *PSA: Proceedings of the Biennial Meeting of the Philosophy of Science Association, 1976*, 77–93.

———. "The Reception of Continental Philosophy in America." In *Philosophy in and out of Europe*, edited by Marjorie Grene. Berkeley: University of California Press, 1976.

———. "Reply to Charles M. Sherover." In *The Philosophy of Marjorie Grene*, edited by Randall E. Auxier and Lewis Edwin Hahn. Chicago: Open Court, 2002.

———. "Reply to Phillip R. Sloan." In *The Philosophy of Marjorie Grene*, edited by Randall E. Auxier and Lewis Edwin Hahn. Chicago: Open Court, 2002.

———. *The Understanding of Nature: Essays in the Philosophy of Biology*. Boston: D. Reidel, 1974.

Gross, Neil. *Richard Rorty: The Making of an American Philosopher*. Chicago: University of Chicago Press, 2008.

Gura, Philip F. *American Transcendentalism: A History*. New York: Hill and Wang, 2007.

Gurwitsch, Aron. *The Field of Consciousness: Theme, Thematic Field, and Margin*. Collected Works of Aron Gurwitsch (1901–1973). Edited by Richard M. Zaner. New York: Springer, 2010.

Hamburg, Carl. "A Cassirer-Heidegger Seminar." *Philosophy and Phenomenological Research* 25, no. 2 (1964): 208–22.

Harper, Ralph. *Existentialism, a Theory of Man*. Cambridge, MA: Harvard University Press, 1948.

Hart, Samuel. Review of *The Phenomenological Movement: A Historical Introduction*, by Herbert Spiegelberg. *Philosophical Review* 73, no. 1 (1964): 113–16.

Hartshorne, Charles. Review of *Jahrbuch für Philosophie und Phänomenologische Forschung*, by Edmund Husserl. *Philosophical Review* 38, no. 3 (1929): 284–93.

———. "The Social Structure of Immediacy." In *Philosophical Essays in Memory of Edmund Husserl*, edited by Marvin Farber. Cambridge, MA: Published for the University of Buffalo by the Harvard University Press, 1940.

Harvard University. *Harvard University Catalogue: 1915–16*. Cambridge, MA: Harvard University, 1916.

———. *Harvard University Catalogue: 1917–18*. Cambridge, MA: Harvard University, 1917.

———. *Official Register of Harvard University: Announcement of the Courses of Instruction Offered by the Faculty of Arts and Sciences, 1924–25*. Vol. XXI, no. 37, Cambridge, MA: Harvard University, 1924.

———. *Official Register of Harvard University: Announcement of the Courses of Instruction Offered by the Faculty of Arts and Sciences, 1926–27*. Vol. XIII, no. 36, Cambridge, MA: Harvard University, 1926.

———. *Official Register of Harvard University: Announcement of the Courses of Instruction Offered by the Faculty of Arts and Sciences, 1934–35*. Cambridge, MA: Harvard University, 1934.

———. *Official Register of Harvard University: Announcement of the Courses of Instruction Offered by the Faculty of Arts and Sciences, 1935–36*. Cambridge, MA: Harvard University, 1935.

———. *Official Register of Harvard University: Announcement of the Courses of Instruction Offered by the Faculty of Arts and Sciences, 1936–37*. Cambridge, MA: Harvard University, 1936.

———. *Official Register of Harvard University: Announcement of the Courses of Instruction Offered by the Faculty of Arts and Sciences, 1942–43*. Cambridge, MA: Harvard University, 1942.

———. *Official Register of Harvard University: Announcement of the Courses of Instruction Offered by the Faculty of Arts and Sciences, 1943–44*. Cambridge, MA: Harvard University, 1943.

———. *Official Register of Harvard University: Announcement of the Courses of Instruction Offered by the Faculty of Arts and Sciences, 1944–45*. Cambridge, MA: Harvard University, 1944.

———. *Official Register of Harvard University: Announcement of the Courses of Instruction Offered by the Faculty of Arts and Sciences, 1949–50*. Cambridge, MA: Harvard University, 1949.

———. *Official Register of Harvard University: Courses in General Education, 1948–1949*. Vol. XLV, no. 10, Cambridge, MA: Harvard University, 1948.

———. *Official Register of Harvard University: Courses in General Education, 1952–1953*. Vol. XLIX, no. 21, Cambridge, MA: Harvard University, 1952.

———. *Official Register of Harvard University: Courses in General Education, 1953–1954*. Vol. L, no. 20, Cambridge, MA: Harvard University, 1953.

———. *Official Register of Harvard University: Courses in General Education, 1954–1955*. Vol. LI, no. 20, Cambridge, MA: Harvard University, 1954.

———. *Reports of the President and Treasurer of Harvard College, 1908–09*. Cambridge, MA: Harvard University, 1910.

———. *Reports of the President and Treasurer of Harvard College, 1911–12*. Cambridge, MA: Harvard University Press, 1913.

Harvard University Committee on the Objectives of a General Education in a Free Society. *General Education in a Free Society: Report of the Harvard Committee*. Cambridge, MA: Harvard University Press, 1945.

Heidegger, Martin. *Being and Time*. Translated by John Macquarrie and Edward Robinson. New York: Harper, 1962.

———. *Existence and Being*. Edited by Werner Brock. Chicago: H. Regnery, 1949.

———. *German Existentialism*. Translated by Dagobert D. Runes. New York: Wisdom Library, 1965.

———. *History of the Concept of Time*. Studies in Phenomenology and Existential Philosophy. Bloomington: Indiana University Press, 1985.

———. "Letter on Humanism." Translated by Frank A. Capuzzi and J. Glenn Gray. In *Basic Writings*, edited by David Farrell Krell. San Francisco: Harper, 1993.

———. *Ontology: The Hermeneutics of Facticity*. Translated by John van Buren. Studies in Continental Thought. Bloomington: Indiana University Press, 1999.

Hemley, Robin. *Nola: A Memoir of Faith, Art, and Madness*. St. Paul, MN: Graywolf Press, 1998.

Herrmann, Gary. "Carr Denied Tenure in 'Unusual' Action." *Yale Daily News*, October 7, 1974.

Hirsch, David H. "After Alien Gods." *Sewanee Review* 96, no. 4 (1988): 714–24.

———. "Paul de Man and the Politics of Deconstruction." *Sewanee Review* 96, no. 2 (1988): 330–38.

Hocking, W. E. "From the Early Days of the 'Logische Untersuchungen'." In *Edmund Husserl, 1859–1959*, edited by the editorial committee of Phaenomenologica. The Hague: M. Nijhoff, 1959.

———. "What Does Philosophy Say?" *Philosophical Review* 37, no. 2 (1928): 133–55.

Holland, Nancy. "Thoughts on Thirty Years in the Society for Phenomenology and Existential Philosophy." *Journal of Speculative Philosophy* 26, no. 2 (2012): 185–88.

Holt, Edwin, Walter Marvin, W. P. Montague, R. B. Perry, Walter Pitkin, and Edward Gleason Spaulding. "The Program and First Platform of Six Realists." *Journal of Philosophy, Psychology and Scientific Methods* 7, no. 15 (1910): 393–401.

Hughes, Raymond M. *A Study of the Graduate Schools of America*. Oxford, OH: Miami University, 1925.

Hull, Richard T., ed. *Presidential Addresses of the American Philosophical Association, 1941–1950*. American Philosophical Association Centennial Series, Vol. 5. Amherst, NY: Prometheus Books, 2005.

Huntress, Erminie Greene. "The Phenomenology of Conscience." PhD diss., Radcliffe College, 1937.

Husserl, Edmund. *Cartesian Meditations*. Translated by Dorion Cairns. The Hague: M. Nijhoff, 1965.

———. *The Crisis of European Sciences and Transcendental Phenomenology: An Introduction to Phenomenological Philosophy*. Translated by David Carr. Northwestern University Studies in Phenomenology & Existential Philosophy. Evanston, IL: Northwestern University Press, 1970.

———. "Die Welt Der Lebendigen Gegenwart Und Die Konstitution Der Ausserleiblichen Umwelt." *Philosophy and Phenomenological Research* 6, no. 3 (1946): 323–43.

———. "Grundlegende Untersuschungen Zum Phänomeologischen Urpsrung Der Räumlichkeit Der Natur." In *Philosophical Essays in Memory of Edmund Husserl*, edited by Marvin Farber. Cambridge, MA: Harvard University Press, 1940.

———. *Ideas: General Introduction to Pure Phenomenology*. Translated by William Ralph Boyce Gibson. New York Routledge, 2013.

———. *Logical Investigations*. Translated by J. N. Findlay. International Library of Philosophy and Scientific Method. 2 vols. New York: Humanities Press, 1970.

———. *Logical Investigations*. Translated by Dermot Moran. Vol. 1. New York: Routledge, 2001.

———. "Notizen Zur Raumkonstitution." *Philosophy and Phenomenological Research* 1, no. 1 (1940): 21–37.

———. "Persönliche Aufzeichnungen." *Philosophy and Phenomenological Research* 16, no. 3 (1956): 293–302.

———. "Phänomenologie Und Anthropologie." *Philosophy and Phenomenological Research* 2, no. 1 (1941): 1–14.

———. *The Phenomenology of Internal Time-Consciousness*. Translated by James S. Churchill. Bloomington: Indiana University Press, 1964.

Husserl, Edmund, and Ludwig Landgrebe. *Experience and Judgment: Investigations in a Genealogy of Logic*. Translated by James S. Churchill and Karl Ameriks. Evanston, IL: Northwestern University Press, 1973.

"Husserliana." http://ophen.org/series-506.

Ierna, Carlo. "Herbert Spiegelberg: From Munich to North America." In *The Reception of Husserlian Phenomenology in North America*, edited by Michela Beatrice Ferri. New York: Springer, 2019.

Isaac, Joel. "Donald Davidson and the Analytic Revolution in American Philosophy, 1940–1970." *Historical Journal* 56, no. 3 (2013): 757–79.

James, William. *The Correspondence of William James*. Vol. 10. Charlottesville: University Press of Virginia, 1992.

Jaspers, Karl. *Existentialism and Humanism, Three Essays*. Translated by E. B. Ashton. New York: R. F. Moore, 1952.

———. "Letter to the Freiburg University Denazification Committee (December 22, 1945)." In *The Heidegger Controversy: A Critical Reader*, edited by Richard Wolin. New York: Columbia University Press, 1991.

———. *Reason and Existenz; Five Lectures*. Translated by William Earle. New York: Noonday Press, 1955.

Jaspers, Karl, and Rudolf Bultmann. *Myth and Christianity: An Inquiry into the Possibility of Religion without Myth*. Translated by Norbert Guterman. New York: Noonday Press, 1958.

"John Daniel Wild." http://www.gf.org/fellows/all-fellows/john-daniel-wild/.

Johnson, Paul E. *A Shopkeeper's Millennium: Society and Revivals in Rochester, New York, 1815–1837*. 1st rev. ed. New York: Hill and Wang, 2004.

Jonas, Hans. "Alfred Schutz, 1899–1959." *Social Research* 26, no. 4 (1959): 471–74.

Kaelin, Eugene Francis. *Heidegger's Being and Time: A Reading for Readers*. Tallahassee: University Presses of Florida / Florida State University Press, 1988.

Kaufmann, Felix, *The Infinite in Mathematics: Logico-mathematical Writings*, edited by Brian McGuinness. Vienna Circle Collection. Boston: D. Reidel, 1978.

Kaufmann, Walter Arnold. *Existentialism from Dostoevsky to Sartre*. New York: Meridian, 1956.

Kelly, Sean. "In Memoriam: Hubert L. Dreyfus (1929–2017)." https://philosophy.fas.harvard.edu/news/memoriam-hubert-l-dreyfus-1929-2017.

Keniston, Hayward. *Graduate Study and Research in the Arts and Sciences at the University of Pennsylvania*. Reports of the Educational Survey. Philadelphia: University of Pennsylvania Press, 1959.

Kerr, Clark. *The Uses of the University*. 5th ed. Cambridge, MA: Harvard University Press, 2001.

Kimball, Roger. *Tenured Radicals: How Politics Has Corrupted Our Higher Education*. New York: Harper & Row, 1990.

Kisiel, Theodore. "Heidegger Circle: History." http://heidegger-circle.org/history.html.

Kloppenberg, James T. *Uncertain Victory: Social Democracy and Progressivism in European and American Thought, 1870–1920*. New York: Oxford University Press, 1986.

Kockelmans, Joseph. *A Companion to Martin Heidegger's "Being and Time"*. Current Continental Research. Washington, DC.: Center for Advanced Research in Phenomenology and University Press of America, 1986.

――――. "Phenomenological Psychology in the United States: A Critical Analysis of the Actual Situation." *Journal of Phenomenological Psychology* 1, no. 2 (1971): 139–72.

Koterski, Joseph W., and John J. Drummond. "W. Norris Clarke, S.J., 1915–2008." *Proceedings and Addresses of the American Philosophical Association* 82, no. 5 (2009): 202–3.

Krohn, Claus-Dieter. *Intellectuals in Exile: Refugee Scholars and the New School for Social Research.* Amherst: University of Massachusetts Press, 1993.

Kuhn, Helmut. *Encounter with Nothingness: An Essay on Existentialism.* Hinsdale, IL: H. Regnery, 1949.

Kuhn, Thomas. *The Structure of Scientific Revolutions.* 3rd ed. Chicago: University of Chicago Press, 1996.

Kuklick, Bruce. *A History of Philosophy in America, 1720–2000.* New York: Clarendon Press, 2001.

――――. "Philosophy and Inclusion in the United States." In *The Humanities and the Dynamics of Inclusion since World War II*, edited by David A. Hollinger. Baltimore: Johns Hopkins University Press, 2006.

――――. "Philosophy at Yale in the Century after Darwin." *History of Philosophy Quarterly* 21, no. 3 (2004): 313–36.

――――. *The Rise of American Philosophy, Cambridge, Massachusetts, 1860–1930.* New Haven, CT: Yale University Press, 1977.

Landgrebe, Ludwig. "The Study of Philosophy in Germany: A Reply to Walter Cerf." *Journal of Philosophy* 54, no. 5 (1957): 127–31.

Lask, Thomas. "Philosophical Group's Dominant View Is Criticized." *New York Times*, December 30, 1979.

Lehman, David. "The (De) Man Who Put the Con in Deconstruction." *Los Angeles Times*, March 13, 1988.

Leiber, Justin. "Linguistic Analysis and Existentialism." *Philosophy and Phenomenological Research* 32, no. 1 (1971): 47–56.

Leiter, Brian, "Philosophy Faculty at the Leading American Programs, 1930–1979: Feedback Sought," Leiter Reports, May 12, 2016, http://leiterreports.typepad.com/blog/2016/05/philosophy-faculty-at-the-leading-american-programs-1930-1979-feedback-sought.html.

Levy, Neil. "Analytic and Continental Philosophy: Explaining the Differences." *Metaphilosophy* 34, no. 3 (2003): 284–304.

Lovejoy, Arthur. "On Some Conditions of Progress in Philosophical Inquiry." *Philosophical Review* 26, no. 2 (1917): 123–63.

Lowen, Rebecca. *Creating the Cold War University: The Transformation of Stanford.* Berkeley: University of California Press, 1997.

Malik, Charles. "The Metaphysics of Time in the Philosophies of A. N. White-head and M. Heidegger." PhD diss., Harvard University, 1937.

Mancosu, Paolo. *The Adventure of Reason: Interplay between Philosophy of Mathematics and Mathematical Logic, 1900–1940.* Oxford: Oxford University Press, 2010.

Marcelle, Daniel. "The Great Gurwitsch–Føllesdal Debate Concerning the Noema." In *Phenomenology 2010*, vol. 3, edited by Dermot Moran and Hans-Rainer Sepp. Bucharest: Zeta Books, 2011.

———. "The Impact of North American Phenomenological Organizations: The Chronicle Revisited." In *The Reception of Husserlian Phenomenology in North America*, ed. Michela Beatrice Ferri. New York: Springer, 2019.

Marhenke, Paul. "The Criterion of Significance." *Proceedings and Addresses of the American Philosophical Association* 23 (1949): 1–21.

"Marjorie Glicksman Grene: Curriculum Vitae." https://www.phil.vt.edu/people/MGreneCV.pdf.

Markell, Patchen. "Iris Marion Young, 1949–2006." *Proceedings and Addresses of the American Philosophical Association* 80, no. 5 (2007): 184–85.

Martino, Daniel J. "Stephen Strasser's Philosophical Legacy and Duquesne University's Simon Silverman Phenomenology Center." In *Phenomenology of Life—from the Animal Soul to the Human Mind: Book I*, edited by Anna-Teresa Tymieniecka. Analecta Husserliana. Dordrecht: Springer, 2007.

Marx, Karl. *Capital: A Critique of Political Economy.* Edited by Friedrich Engels and Ernest Untermann. Translated by Samuel Moore and Edward B. Aveling. New York: The Modern Library, 1936.

McBride, William. "Phenomenology's History Revisited." Review of *The Phenomenological Movement: A Historical Introduction*, by Herbert Spiegelberg. *Human Studies* 7, no. 3/4 (1984): 363–73.

McCaughey, Robert A. *Stand, Columbia: A History of Columbia University in the City of New York, 1754–2004.* New York: Columbia University Press, 2003.

McCorduck, Pamela. *Machines Who Think: A Personal Inquiry into the History and Prospects of Artificial Intelligence.* San Francisco: W. H. Freeman, 1979.

McIntyre, Ronald, and David Woodruff Smith. "Husserl's Identification of Meaning and Noema." *Monist* 59, no. 1 (1975): 115–32.

McKeon, Richard. "Experience and Metaphysics." *Proceedings of the XIth International Congress of Philosophy* 4 (1953): 83–89.

Merleau-Ponty, Maurice. *Phenomenology of Perception.* Translated by Donald A. Landes. New York: Routledge, 2012.

———. *Sense and Non-sense.* Translated by Hubert L. Dreyfus and Patricia Allen Dreyfus. Northwestern University Studies in Phenomenology & Existential Philosophy. Evanston, IL: Northwestern University Press, 1964.

Mickunas, Algis, and Burt C. Hopkins. "History of the Husserl Circle." In *The Reception of Husserlian Phenomenology in North America*, edited by Michela Beatrice Ferri. New York: Springer, 2019.

Montgomery, Paul L. "Scholar Breaks with Heidegger." *New York Times*, April 11, 1964.

Murray, E. "Summaries of Articles: 'Psychologische Prinzipienfragen,' by H. Cornelius." *Philosophical Review* 16, no. 1 (1907): 101–12.

Nagel, Ernest. "Impressions and Appraisals of Analytic Philosophy in Europe. I." *Journal of Philosophy* 33, no. 1 (1936): 5–24.

———. "Symposium on Meaning and Truth, Part III: Discussion: Truth and Knowledge of the Truth." *Philosophy and Phenomenological Research* 5, no. 1 (1944): 50–68.

Nagel, Mechthild. "Iris M. Young, 1949–2006," Solidarity, 2007, https://solidarity-us.org/atc/128/p540/.

Nenon, Thomas. "A History of the Center for Advanced Research in Phenomenology, Inc." In *The Reception of Husserlian Phenomenology in North America*, edited by Michela Beatrice Ferri. New York: Springer, 2019.

"New Science Unit Centers in Buffalo." *New York Times*, December 15, 1940.

Nicol, Eduardo. "La psicología de las situaciones vitales y el problema antropologico." *Philosophy and Phenomenological Research* 4, no. 2 (1943): 227–32.

Northwestern University. *Announcement of Courses in the College of Liberal Arts for the Academic Year 1957–58*. Chicago: Northwestern University, 1957.

"Notes." *Philosophy and Phenomenological Research* 1, no. 1 (1940): 126–26.

Okrent, Mark. Review of *Being-in-the-World: A Commentary on Heidegger's "Being and Time", Division I*, by Hubert L. Dreyfus. *Philosophical Review* 102, no. 2 (1993): 290–93.

Osborn, Andrew D. *Edmund Husserl and His Logical Investigations*. New York: Garland, 1980.

———. "The Philosophy of Edmund Husserl in Its Development from His Mathematical Interests to His First Conception of Phenomenology in *Logical Investigations*." PhD diss, Columbia University, 1934.

Otero-Pailos, Jorge. *Architecture's Historical Turn: Phenomenology and the Rise of the Postmodern*. Minneapolis: University of Minnesota Press, 2010.

Palmer, George Herbert, and Ralph Barton Perry. "Philosophy, 1870–1929." In *The Development of Harvard University since the Inauguration of President Eliot, 1869–1929*. Cambridge, MA: Harvard University Press, 1930.

Parry, William T. "V. Jerauld Mcgill (1897–1977)." *Philosophy and Phenomenological Research* 38, no. 2 (1977): 283–86.

Pavel, Thomas G. "The Heidegger Affair." *MLN* 103, no. 4 (1988): 887–901.

Perry, R. B. *A Defense of Philosophy.* Cambridge, MA: Harvard University Press, 1931.

"Phaenomenologica." Husserl Archives Leuven, https://hiw.kuleuven.be /hua/editionspublications/phaenomenologica.

"Philosophy at Yale." *Yale Alumni Magazine,* June 1956.

"Philosophy: Faculty History Project." https://www.lib.umich.edu/faculty -history/philosophy.

"Philosophy's Comeback Kids." *Yale Daily News,* November 8, 2013.

Pitkin, Walter. "Is Agreement Desirable?" *Journal of Philosophy, Psychology and Scientific Methods* 9, no. 26 (1912): 711–15.

———. *On My Own.* New York: C. Scribner's Sons, 1944.

Price, Kingsley, and Stephen Barker. "Jobs in Philosophy by Areas—1970–79." *Proceedings and Addresses of the American Philosophical Association* 53, no. 5 (1980): 609–12.

"Proceedings of the American Philosophical Association, 1931." *Philosophical Review* 41, no. 2 (1932): 180–209.

"Proceedings of the American Philosophical Association, 1938: Twelfth Annual Report of the Board of Officers." *Philosophical Review* 48, no. 2 (1939): 177–95.

Psathas, George. "A Brief History." http://www.sphs.info/.

———. "In Memory of Herbert Spiegelberg and the Phenomenological Work-shops." *Human Studies* 15, no. 4 (1992): 399–409.

———. "Introduction: In Memory of Herbert Spiegelberg, 1904–1990." *Human Studies* 15, no. 4 (1992): 362–63.

Radcliffe College. *Courses of Instruction Offered by the Faculty of Arts and Sci-ences, 1956–57.* Cambridge, MA: Radcliffe College, 1956.

———. *Courses of Instruction Offered by the Faculty of Arts and Sciences, 1957–58.* Cambridge, MA: Radcliffe College, 1957.

———. *Official Register of Radcliffe College: Courses of Instruction Offered in Fall and Spring Terms, 1949–50.* Cambridge, MA: Radcliffe College, 1949.

———. *Official Register of Radcliffe College: Courses of Instruction Offered in Fall and Spring Terms, 1950–51.* Cambridge, MA: Radcliffe College, 1950.

"Ralph Monroe Eaton." http://www.gf.org/fellows/all-fellows/ralph-mon roe-eaton/.

Rawls, John. *A Theory of Justice.* Cambridge, MA: Belknap Press of Harvard University Press, 1971.

Redfield, Marc. *Theory at Yale: The Strange Case of Deconstruction in America.* New York: Fordham University Press, 2016.

"Register of the Officers and Faculty of the University of North Carolina, 1795–1945, Compiled by the Staff of the North Carolina Collection." https://docsouth.unc.edu/true/faculty/faculty.html.

Reichenbach, Hans. "Reply to Donald C. Williams' Criticism of the Frequency Theory of Probability." *Philosophy and Phenomenological Research* 5, no. 4 (1945): 508–12.

Rescorla, Michael. "The Computational Theory of Mind." In *The Stanford Encyclopedia of Philosophy*, Spring 2017 ed., edited by Edward N. Zalta. https://plato.stanford.edu/archives/spr2017/entries/computational-mind/.

Ricci, Gabriel. "Importing Phenomenology: The Early Editorial Life of Philosophy and Phenomenological Research." *History of European Ideas* 42, no. 3 (2016): 399–411.

Ricoeur, Paul. *History and Truth.* Translated by Charles A. Kelbley. Northwestern University Studies in Phenomenology & Existential Philosophy. Evanston, IL: Northwestern University Press, 1965.

Rieser, Max. "Remarks on the Eleventh International Congress of Philosophy." *Journal of Philosophy* 51, no. 3 (1954): 99–105.

Robin, Corey. *The Reactionary Mind: Conservatism from Edmund Burke to Sarah Palin.* New York: Oxford University Press, 2011.

Rorty, Richard. Foreword to *Heidegger, Authenticity, and Modernity: Essays in Honor of Hubert L. Dreyfus.* Vol. 1, edited by Mark A. Wrathall and Jeff Malpas. Cambridge, MA: MIT Press, 2000.

———. *Philosophy and the Mirror of Nature.* Princeton, NJ: Princeton University Press, 1979.

———. "Philosophy in America Today." *American Scholar* 51, no. 2 (1982): 183–200.

Royce, Josiah. "Recent Logical Inquiries and Their Psychological Bearings." *Psychological Review* 9, no. 2 (1902): 105–33.

Russell, Bertrand. "On Denoting." *Mind* 114, no. 456 (2005): 873–87.

Said, Edward. *Orientalism.* New York: Vintage, 2003.

Sanders, Richard. "Walter Cerf, 1907–2001." *Proceedings and Addresses of the American Philosophical Association* 77, no. 5 (2004): 161–62.

Sartre, Jean-Paul. *Anti-Semite and Jew.* Translated by George Joseph Becker. New York: Schocken Books, 1948.

———. *Being and Nothingness: An Essay on Phenomenological Ontology.* Translated by Hazel E. Barnes. New York: Washington Square Press, 1992.

———. *The Emotions: Outline of a Theory.* Translated by Bernard Frechtman. New York: Philosophical Library, 1948.

———. *Existentialism.* Translated by Bernard Frechtman. New York: Philosophical Library, 1947.

———. *Existentialism and Humanism.* Translated by Philip Mairet. London: Methuen, 1948.

———. *Existentialism Is a Humanism.* Translated by Carol Macomber. New Haven, CT: Yale University Press, 2007.

———. *The Psychology of Imagination.* Translated by Bernard Frechtman. New York: Philosophical Library, 1948.

———. *The Transcendence of the Ego: An Existentialist Theory of Consciousness.* New York: Noonday Press, 1957.

———. *The Transcendence of the Ego: An Existentialist Theory of Consciousness.* Translated by Forrest Williams and Robert Kirkpatrick. New York: Hill and Wang, 1991.

———. *What Is Literature?* Translated by Bernard Frechtman. London: Methuen, 1950.

Scharff, Robert. "American Continental Philosophy in the Making: The Society for Phenomenology and Existential Philosophy's Early Days." *Journal of Speculative Philosophy* 26, no. 2 (2012): 108–17.

———. "John Wild, Lifeworld Experience, and the Founding of SPEP." *Continental Philosophy Review* 44, no. 3 (2004): 285–90.

Schick, Theodore W. "Rorty and Davidson on Alternate Conceptual Schemes." *Journal of Speculative Philosophy* 1, no. 4 (1987): 291–303.

Schliesser, Eric. "Nagel's Philosophic Prophecy . . . Or How Analytic Philosophy as We Know It Was Invented . . ." *New APPS: Art, Politics, Philosophy, Science,* October 2011, https://www.newappsblog.com/2011/10/nagels-philosophic -prophecyor-how-analytic-philosophy-as-we-know-it-was-invented.html.

———. "The Nothing Noths." Digressions & Impressions, October 30, 2017, http://digressionsnimpressions.typepad.com/digressionsimpressions/2017 /10/the-nothing-noths.html.

———. "On the Invention of Analytic Philosophy by Ernest Nagel (II)." *New APPS: Art, Politics, Philosophy, Science.* http://www.newappsblog. com/2011/10/on-the-invention-of-analytic-philosophy-by-ernest-nagel-ii .html.

Schrag, Calvin. "Celebrating Fifty Years of the Society for Phenomenology and Existential Philosophy." *Journal of Speculative Philosophy,* 26, no. 2 (2012): 86–92.

———. "アメリカにおける現像学的哲学の諸段階." 理想 5, no. 468 (1972): 71–78.

Schuhmann, Karl. *Husserl-Chronik: Denk- Und Lebensweg Edmund Husserls.* Den Haag: Martinus Nijhoff, 1977.

———. "Markers on the Road to the Conception of the Phenomenological Movement: Appendix to Spiegelberg's Paper." *Philosophy and Phenomenological Research* 43, no. 3 (1983): 299–306.

Schütz, Alfred. "Felix Kaufmann: 1895–1949." *Social Research* 17, no. 1 (1950): 1–7.

———. "Making Music Together: A Study in Social Relationship." *Social Research* 18, no. 1 (1951): 76–97.

———. "On Multiple Realities." *Philosophy and Phenomenological Research* 5, no. 4 (1945): 533–76.

———. *The Phenomenology of the Social World*. Northwestern University Studies in Phenomenology & Existential Philosophy. Evanston, IL: Northwestern University Press, 1967.

———. "The Well-Informed Citizen: An Essay on the Social Distribution of Knowledge." *Social Research* 13, no. 4 (1946): 463–78.

———. "William James' Concept of the Stream of Thought Phenomenologically Interpreted." *Philosophy and Phenomenological Research* 1, no. 4 (1941): 442–52.

Schütz, Alfred, and Thomas Luckmann. *The Structures of the Life-World*. Northwestern University Studies in Phenomenology & Existential Philosophy. 2 vols. Evanston, IL: Northwestern University Press, 1973.

Schütz, Alfred, and Eric Voegelin. *A Friendship That Lasted a Lifetime: The Correspondence between Alfred Schütz and Eric Voegelin*, edited by Gerhard Wagner and Gilbert Weiss. Columbia: University of Missouri Press, 2011.

Schwenkler, John. "A Life of Being-in-the-World: Hubert Dreyfus, 1929–2017." *First Things*, May 1, 2017. https://www.firstthings.com/web-exclusives/2017/05/a-life-of-being-in-the-world.

Searle, John. *Intentionality: An Essay in the Philosophy of Mind*. Cambridge: Cambridge University Press, 1983.

Sellars, Roy Wood. "The Meaning of True and False." *Philosophy and Phenomenological Research* 5, no. 1 (1944): 98–103.

———. "Reflections on the Career of Marvin Farber." In *Phenomenology and Natural Existence: Essays in Honor of Marvin Farber*, edited by Dale Maurice Riepe. Albany: State University of New York Press, 1973.

Shpet, Gustav. *Appearance and Sense: Phenomenology as the Fundamental Science and Its Problems*. Phaenomenologica. Boston: Kluwer Academic, 1991.

Simons, Peter M. Review of *The Context of the Phenomenological Movement*, by Herbert Spiegelberg. *Philosophy and Phenomenological Research* 44, no. 3 (1984): 426–28.

Smart, H. R. "What Is Deduction?" *Philosophy and Phenomenological Research* 5, no. 1 (1944): 37–49.

Smith, Barry. "Derrida Degree a Question of Honor." *Times*, May 9, 1992.

Smith, Barry, and David Woodruff Smith. *The Cambridge Companion to Husserl*. Cambridge: Cambridge University Press, 1995.

Smith, Richard Norton. *The Harvard Century: The Making of a University to a Nation.* New York: Simon and Schuster, 1986.

Soames, Scott. *Philosophical Analysis in the Twentieth Century.* Vol. 1. Princeton, NJ: Princeton University Press, 2003.

Spiegelberg, Herbert. "Apologia Pro Bibliographia Mea." In *Phenomenological Perspectives: Historical and Systematic Essays in Honor of Herbert Spiegelberg,* edited by Philip Bossert. The Hague: Martinus Nijhoff, 1975.

———. *The Context of the Phenomenological Movement.* The Hague: Martinus Nijhoff, 1981.

———. "Memories of My American Life for My American Children and Children's Children." *Human Studies* 15, no. 4 (1992): 364–77.

———. *The Phenomenological Movement: A Historical Introduction.* Phaenomenologica, 2nd ed. Vol. 1, The Hague: M. Nijhoff, 1965.

———. *The Phenomenological Movement: A Historical Introduction.* Phaenomenologica, 2nd ed. Vol. 2, The Hague: M. Nijhoff, 1965.

———. *The Phenomenological Movement: A Historical Introduction.* Edited by Karl Schuhmann. 3rd rev. and enl. ed. Boston: Martinus Nijhoff, 1982.

"A Statement of Policy." *Analysis* 1, no. 1 (1933): 1–2.

Stein, Waltraut. "Sym-philosophizing in an Ethics Class." In *Phenomenological Perspectives: Historical and Systematic Essays in Honor of Herbert Spiegelberg.* The Hague: Martinus Nijhoff, 1975.

"A Symposium on Educational Philosophy." *Philosophy and Phenomenological Research* 7, no. 2 (1946): 187–292.

"A Symposium on Meaning and Truth, Part I." *Philosophy and Phenomenological Research* 4, no. 2 (1943): 236–84.

"A Symposium on Meaning and Truth, Part II." *Philosophy and Phenomenological Research* 4, no. 3 (1944): 317–410.

"A Symposium on Probability: Part I." *Philosophy and Phenomenological Research* 5, no. 4 (1945): 449–532.

"A Symposium on Probability: Part II." *Philosophy and Phenomenological Research* 6, no. 1 (1945): 11–86.

Tarski, Alfred. "The Semantic Conception of Truth: And the Foundations of Semantics." *Philosophy and Phenomenological Research* 4, no. 3 (1944): 341–76.

Thompson, E. P. *The Making of the English Working Class.* New York: Vintage, 1966.

Townsend, Robert B. "Precedents: The Job Crisis of the 1970s." *Perspectives on History,* no. April 1997. https://www.historians.org/publications-and-directories/perspectives-on-history/april-1997/precedents-the-job-crisis-of-the-1970s.

"Trayhern, Robert John." http://rbscp.lib.rochester.edu/4787.

Tuan, Yi-Fu. "Humanistic Geography." *Annals of the Association of American Geographers* 66, no. 2 (1976): 266–76.

Tuttle, J. R. "Summaries of Articles: 'Philosophie Als Strenge Wissenschaft,' by Edmund Husserl." *Philosophical Review* 20, no. 5 (1911): 573–85.

Tymieniecka, Anna-Teresa. *Phenomenology and Science in Contemporary European Thought.* New York: Farrar, 1962.

———. "The Theme: The History of American Phenomenology-in-Progress." In *American Phenomenology: Origins and Developments,* edited by Eugene Francis Kaelin and Calvin O. Schrag. Boston: Kluwer Academic, 1989.

Unger, Eric. "Logical Positivism and the Moral Problem." *Nineteenth Century and After,* July–December 1948.

Van Breda, H. L., and Thomas Vongehr. *Geschichte Des Husserl-Archivs.* Dordrecht: Springer, 2007.

Verducci, Daniela. "A.-T. Tymieniecka: A Phenomenologist in the United States. The Adventures of a Polish-Born American." In *The Reception of Husserlian Phenomenology in North America,* edited by Michela Beatrice Ferri. New York: Springer, 2019.

Veysey, Laurence R. *The Emergence of the American University.* Chicago: University of Chicago Press, 1965.

Wagner, Helmut R. *Alfred Schutz: An Intellectual Biography.* Chicago: University of Chicago Press, 1983.

———. "Marvin Farber's Contribution to the Phenomenological Movement: An International Perspective." In *Philosophy and Science in Phenomenological Perspective,* edited by Kah Kyung Cho. Dordrecht: Martinus Nijhoff, 1984.

Wahl, Jean André. *A Short History of Existentialism.* New York: Philosophical Library, 1949.

Walton, Roberto. "Spain and Latin America." In *Encyclopedia of Phenomenology,* edited by Lester Embree, Elizabeth Behnke, David Carr, J. Claude Evans, Jose Huertas-Jourda, Joseph J. Cockelmans, William R. McKenna, et al. Boston: Kluwer Academic, 1997.

Weber, Max, and Edward Shils. *Max Weber on the Methodology of the Social Sciences.* Glencoe, IL: Free Press, 1949.

Weinberg, Jeremy. "Turmoil Threatens Philosophy Department." *Yale Daily News,* September 20, 1990.

Welch, E. Parl. *The Philosophy of Edmund Husserl: The Origin and Development of His Phenomenology.* New York: Columbia University Press, 1941.

Westbrook, Robert B. *John Dewey and American Democracy.* Ithaca, NY: Cornell University Press, 1991.

White, Morton. *A Philosopher's Story*. University Park: Pennsylvania State University Press, 1999.

Whitehead, Alfred North. *Process and Reality: An Essay in Cosmology*. New York: Macmillan, 1929.

Wiggins, Osborne P. "My Years at the New School." In *The Golden Age of Phenomenology at the New School for Social Research, 1954–1973*, edited by Lester Embree. Athens: Ohio University Press, 2017.

Wild, John. *The Challenge of Existentialism*. Bloomington: Indiana University Press, 1955.

———. *The Radical Empiricism of William James*. Westport, CT: Greenwood, 1980.

Wild, John, Richard Ira Sugarman, and Roger B. Duncan. *The Promise of Phenomenology: Posthumous Papers of John Wild*. Lanham, MD: Lexington Books, 2006.

Wild, John, Robert J. Trayhern, Bert Dreyfus, and C. de Deugd. "Sein Und Zeit: An Informal English Paraphrase of Sections 1–53." Cambridge, MA: Andover–Harvard Theological Seminary, 1957.

Wilshire, Bruce. *Fashionable Nihilism: A Critique of Analytic Philosophy*. Albany: State University of New York Press, 2002.

Windschuttle, Keith. *The Killing of History: How a Discipline Is Being Murdered by Literary Critics and Social Theorists*. Paddington, Australia: Macleay, 1994.

Winger, Michael. "Brumbaugh: Shift on Bernstein Forced." *Yale Daily News*, March 9, 1965.

Woessner, Martin. *Heidegger in America*. Cambridge: Cambridge University Press, 2011.

Wolff, Robert Paul. *A Life in the Academy*. https://app.box.com/shared /n72u3p7pyj, Total Memoir in One File.docx.

Wolin, Richard, ed. *The Heidegger Controversy: A Critical Reader*. New York: Columbia University Press, 1991.

Woo, Elaine. "Marjorie Grene Dies at 98; Historian of Philosophy Known as Independent Thinker." *Los Angeles Times*, March 22, 2009.

Wood, Gordon. "Intellectual History and the Social Sciences." In *New Directions in American Intellectual History*, edited by John Higham and Paul Keith Conkin. Baltimore: Johns Hopkins University Press, 1979.

"Yale Scholar Wrote for Pro-Nazi Newspaper." *New York Times*, December 1, 1987.

"Yale University Historical Register Online." http://avideo.library.yale.edu /hro/index.php.

Yoshimi, Jeffrey, Clinton Tolley, and David Woodruff Smith. "California Phenomenology." In *The Reception of Husserlian Phenomenology in North America*, edited by Michela Beatrice Ferri. New York: Springer, 2019.

Young, Iris Marion. "Beyond the Unhappy Marriage: A Critique of the Dual Systems Theory." In *Women and Revolution: A Discussion of the Unhappy Marriage of Marxism and Feminism*, edited by Lydia Sargent. Boston: South End Press, 1981.

———. "Breasted Experience: The Look and the Feeling." In *On Female Body Experience: "Throwing Like a Girl" and Other Essays*. New York: Oxford University Press, 2005.

———. "From Anonymity to Speech: A Reading of Wittgenstein's Later Writing," PhD diss. Pennsylvania State University, 1974.

———. "Gender as Seriality: Thinking about Women as a Social Collective." *Signs* 19, no. 3 (1994): 713–38.

———. "House and Home: Feminist Variations on a Theme." In *Motherhood and Space: Configurations of the Maternal through Politics, Home, and the Body*, edited by Sarah Boykin Hardy and Caroline Alice Wiedmer. New York: Palgrave Macmillan, 2005.

———. "Humanism, Gynocentrism, and Feminist Politics." In *Throwing Like a Girl and Other Essays in Feminist Philosophy and Social Theory*. Bloomington: Indiana University Press, 1990.

———. Introduction to *On Female Body Experience: "Throwing Like a Girl" and Other Essays*. New York: Oxford University Press, 2005.

———. *Justice and the Politics of Difference*. Princeton, NJ: Princeton University Press, 2011.

———. "Lived Body vs Gender: Reflections on Social Structure and Subjectivity." *Ratio* 15, no. 4 (2002): 410–28.

———. "Menstrual Meditations." In *On Female Body Experience: "Throwing Like a Girl" and Other Essays*. New York: Oxford University Press, 2005.

———. "Pregnant Embodiment: Subjectivity and Alienation." In *On Female Body Experience: "Throwing Like a Girl" and Other Essays*. New York: Oxford University Press, 2005.

———. "Throwing Like a Girl: A Phenomenology of Feminine Body Comportment Motility and Spatiality." *Human Studies* 3, no. 2 (1980): 137–56.

Zaner, Richard. "Gurwitsch at the New School." In *The Golden Age of Phenomenology at the New School for Social Research, 1954–1973*, edited by Lester Embree. Athens: Ohio University Press, 2017.

———. "My Path to the New School." In *The Golden Age of Phenomenology at the New School for Social Research, 1954–1973*, edited by Lester Embree. Athens: Ohio University Press, 2017.

———. "The Role of Dorion Cairns in the Reception of Phenomenology in North America: The First 'Born American' Phenomenologist." In *The Reception of Husserlian Phenomenology in North America*, edited by Michela Beatrice Ferri. New York: Springer, 2019.

Zaremby, Justin. *Directed Studies and the Evolution of American General Education*. New Haven, CT: Whitney Humanities Center, Yale University, 2006. http://directedstudies.yale.edu/sites/default/files/files/DIRECTED_STUDIES_HISTORY.pdf.

Index

Belnap, Nuel, 227
Berger, Gaston, 182
Berger, Peter, 113, 240
Bergman, Gustav, 162
Bergmann, Hugo, 165
Bergson, Henri, 48, 63, 101
Berkeley, George, 48
Bernstein, Richard, 132, 189, 226
"Beyond the Unhappy Marriage" (Young),
 203–4
Bidez, Joseph, 75
Binswanger, Ludwig, 238
biology, 65–68
Black, Max, 112
Blanshard, Brand, 83, 88, 130–31, 178
Bloom, Allan, 244
bodies, 202–17. *See also* embodied phenom-
 enology; feminism; gender
Boelen, Bernard, 187
Boole, George, 70
Boston College, 186
bracketing, 12–13, 64–65
Brandeis University, 126, 145
Brandt, Richard, 98, 192
"Breasted Experience" (Young), 209
Brewster, Kingman, 226, 229–30
Broad, C. D., 45
Brock, Werner, 180
Brown, Alward Embury, 47, 78
Brown, William Adams, 35
Brown University, 139
Bryn Mawr, 79
Buck, Dean Paul, 127
Bugbee, Henry, 125, 176, 188, 197
Bundy, McGeorge, 188
Butler, Judith, 204, 223
Buttimer, Anne, 242

Cairns, Dorion, 44–49, 79–82, 89–95, 102, 161,
 163, 168, 180–81
Camus, Albert, 177
Caputo, John, 239
Carnap, Rudolf, 57, 59, 70, 75–76, 81, 98, 112,
 162, 172–73, 195, 250
CARP (Center for Advanced Research in
 Phenomenology), 181, 198
Carr, David, 189, 222, 227–31, 239
Cartesianism. *See* Descartes, René
Cartesian Meditations (Husserl), 82
Casey, Edward, 189, 222, 239
Cassirer, Ernst, 112, 173
Catholic Church, 3
Catholic universities, 184–86, 190, 308n136.

See also Dusquene University; University
 of Louvain; *and specific universities*
Catholic University of America, 186–87
"Causality and Quantum Theory" (Dreyfus),
 145
Cavell, Stanley, 160, 171, 220
Cerf, Walter, 163, 173–75, 197
Challenge of Existentialism, The (Wild), 179
Chandler, Albert, 37
Chapman, Harmon, 187
Chappell, Vere, 231
Chisholm, Roderick, 127
Cho, Kah Kyung, 91, 239
Chronicle of Higher Education, 231
Claremont Graduate University, 187
clarity, as philosophy's goal, 1–2, 70–75, 147,
 176, 242–43. *See also* analytic philosophy
Clarke, W. Norris, 186
Closing of the American Mind, The (Bloom),
 244–45
Cohen, Arthur, 183
Cohen, Morris Raphael, 87
Cohen, Stephen Marshall, 129
Collingwood, R. G., 87
Columbia University, 32–34, 79, 122–24, 128,
 139–42, 250, 254–55
Committee for Pluralism in Philosophy, 115–16,
 232–33
Committee on the Status of Women (SPEP), 223
commodity fetishism, 6
community studies, 5–6
Comte, Auguste, 100
Conant, James Bryant, 121
"Confessions of a Young Positivist" (Grene),
 55, 59
"Conflict of Ideals in Modern Civilization,
 The" (course), 126
consciousness, 11–15, 17–19, 21–23, 25, 27, 102–
 7. *See also* intentionality; transcendental
 phenomenology
"Contemporary Continental and Analytic
 Philosophy" (course), 198
"Contemporary Philosophy" (course), 48
Continental Divide (Gordon), 3
Continental philosophy: American university
 course offerings in, 4–5, 187–95; anachro-
 nism's dangers and, 31–32, 42; as analytic
 philosophy's other, 1–4, 7, 171–77, 195–99,
 221, 236–38, 249–50, 252–56; Artificial
 Intelligence researchers' antipathy toward,
 157–58; definitions of, 1; as erasing earlier
 American engagement with Europe, 171,
 177; esotericism of, 195–99; existentialism's

Hunt, Lynn, 245
Hunter College, 79
Huntress, Erminie, 49
Husserl, Edmund: American graduate
    students and, 32–33, 37–48, 74, 81–82; ana-
    lytic philosophy and, 220–21, 238; Carr's
    tenure case and, 228–29; as Continental
    philosopher, 1, 180; death of, 91–92; Frege
    and, 192–93, 220–21; Heidegger and,
    16–19, 21, 163–64, 246; Merleau-Ponty
    and, 24–25, 27; *Nachlaß* of, 92–93, 96–97,
    146, 165, 180–81, 185; phenomenologi-
    cal movement and, 7, 9–12, 21–22, 31–32,
    36–37, 84–87, 101, 154–55, 165–66, 182, 196,
    220, 236–38, 240; USC's recruitment of, 81.
    See also University of Louvain; Van Breda,
    Herman Leo
Husserl, Gerhart, 86, 93, 95, 163
Husserl, Malvine, 91–92, 96, 163, 287n131
Husserl Circle, 225
Husserliana (series), 165
"Husserl's Notion of Noema" (Føllesdal), 192
Huxley, Aldous, 153–54

idealism, 11–15, 25, 27, 166–70, 245. *See also*
    Husserl, Edmund
ideal types, 107–8
"Ideas of Man and the World in Western
    Thought" (course), 127
Ideen (Husserl), 11, 14–15, 39, 47–48, 102, 169,
    180
identity relations, 71–72, 204, 212–17, 279n2
Ihde, Don, 239
illusions, 27–29
immanence, 12–13, 101
"Impression and Appraisals of Analytic Phi-
    losophy in Europe" (Nagel), 73
incommensurability thesis, 250–51
Ingarden, Roman, 238
In Praise of Philosophy (Merleau-Ponty), 184
Institute of International Education, 82
intentional arc, 27–29, 208
intentionality, 13–15, 17–22, 28–29, 101–9, 146–
    47, 192–93. *See also* Artificial Intelligence
    (AI)
interdisciplinarity, 90, 99–100, 111–12, 118–21,
    131, 134, 224, 232. *See also* "theory"
International Congress of Philosophy (1953),
    173–76
International Phenomenological Society
    (IPS), 94–95, 161–62, 165
interpretive sociology, 100, 102–6
intersubjectivity, 14–15, 224

intuitions, 12–13, 71
Irigaray, Luce, 223
"Is Agreement Desirable?" (Pitkin), 36

Jacob, Margaret, 245
Jahrbuch für Philosophie und phänomenologis-
    che Forschung, 95, 161, 170–71
James, Patricia Ann, 58, 84
James, William, 33, 35, 61, 113, 117, 143, 166,
    181–82, 250, 269n7
Jaspers, Karl, 56, 146, 164, 172, 180, 183
"Jew and Contemporary Literature, The" (de
    Man), 245
Johns Hopkins University, 84–85, 192
Johnson, Alvin, 90, 112
Johnson, Paul, 5, 198
Joint Board of Permanent Officers of the Fac-
    ulty of Arts and Sciences (Yale), 228
Jonas, Hans, 112–14, 232, 245
Journal of Phenomenological Psychology, 186
Journal of Philosophy, 77, 161, 173, 175
justice, 212–17
Justice and the Politics of Difference (Young),
    212

Kallen, Horace, 98, 162
Kant, Immanuel, 63, 65, 149
Kaufmann, Alice, 163–64
Kaufmann, Felix, 71, 86, 89, 93, 95, 97, 100,
    102, 162–63, 168
Kaufmann, Fritz, 11–12, 82, 86–87, 92–97, 161,
    163, 180, 182, 246
Kaufmann, Walter, 179, 183, 190, 194–95
Kelsen, Hans, 99–100
Kerr, Clark, 133
Killing of History, The (Windschuttle), 245
Kimball, Roger, 245
Kirk, Grayson, 122
Kloppenburg, James, 61
Knower and the Known, The (Grene), 65
Kockelmans, Joseph, 184
Koren, Henry, 186
Koyré, Alexandre, 11, 89
Kristeva, Julia, 223
Kubrick, Stanley, 148
Kuhn, Helmut, 162, 168, 179, 184
Kuhn, Thomas, 250–52
Kuklick, Bruce, 3, 129, 227, 248
Kung, Guido, 186

Lacan, Jacques, 243
Ladd, John, 172
Lamar, Howard, 226, 229

Phénoménologie de la perception (Merleau-Ponty), 25, 64, 156, 169

phenomenology: AI critiques and, 147–58; alternative communities devoted to, 4–5, 219–35; American philosophy departments and, 1–2, 7, 32–35, 37–42, 119–40, 183–99; computer science and, 145–58; definitions of, 1–2, 10–11; as first philosophy, 40–41, 165–66, 169–71, 196, 234; gender and, 54–68, 194–95, 201–17, 223, 239, 241–42; immigration dynamics and, 2, 7, 79–90, 99–100, 109–14, 137–38, 171–77, 181–82, 184; intuitionism and, 71; in Latin America, 161–62; linguistic analysis and, 192–93; marginalization of, 4–5, 7–8, 58–59; methodologies of, 9–15; Orientalism and, 171–77, 196–99, 254, 304n75; postwar associations with Nazism and, 163–65; pragmatism and, 33, 39–40, 181–82; reproductive capacity and, 140–43; as "theory" in other disciplines, 4, 212, 239–46; transcendental, 9, 36–37, 40–41; US existentialism fad and, 177–87. *See also* West Coast phenomenology; *and specific scholars and works*

"Phenomenology and Existentialism" (course), 187

Phenomenology and Science in Contemporary European Thought (Tymieniecka), 237–38

Phenomenology and the Problem of History (Carr), 228

Phenomenology as a Method and as a Philosophical Discipline (Farber), 39, 169

Phenomenology of Perception (Merleau-Ponty), 64

Phenomenology of the Social World, The (Schütz), 102

Philosophical Essays in Memory of Edmund Husserl (Farber), 93

Philosophical Review, 44, 147, 161, 173, 237

philosophy (discipline of): alternative institutions supporting, 4–5, 219–35; American universities and, 1–3, 32–35, 74–79, 119–40, 171–77, 195–99, 225–31, 244–46, 248–56, 279n2, 280n33, 295n81; Continental designation's formation in, 159–60; gender and, 54–68, 201–17, 223, 241–42; Great Depression's hiring freezes and, 58, 74–79, 133–34; humanism and, 125–26, 129–32, 134; Jewish immigration and, 79–90, 99–100, 137–38, 171–77, 181–84; literary art and, 179–87; as mediator between regimes of knowledge, 8, 35–36, 40–41, 77–79, 122, 125, 128, 130–31, 133–34, 248; methodological pluralism

and, 33–40, 93, 115–19, 141–42, 169, 183, 187–90, 225–31, 247–50, 280n20; Second World War and, 119–20; social relations' reproduction and, 6, 58–68, 118–19, 183–95, 254–56. *See also* analytic philosophy; Continental philosophy; Harvard University; New School for Social Research; "theory"; Yale University

Philosophy and the Mirror of Nature (Rorty), 247

"Philosophy in America Today" (Rorty), 247–49

"Philosophy of Art" (course), 126

"Philosophy of Conscience, The" (Huntress), 49

"Philosophy of Edmund Husserl, The" (Cairns), 46, 49

"Philosophy of Medicine" (Grene), 59

"Philosophy of the State" (course), 126

Pitkin, Walter, 32–33, 36, 269n7

Plato, 149

Plessner, Helmuth, 65, 68

pluralism (departmental), 33–36, 49, 93, 115–19, 141–42, 169, 183–90, 225–31, 247–50, 280n20

Pohl, Frederik, 148

Polany, Michael, 64–66

Popper, Karl, 183, 245

Portmann, Adolf, 68

positivism, 168, 172–73, 202, 212, 246. *See also* empiricism; logical positivism

postmodernism, 244

postphenomenology, 242, 244

poststructuralism, 4, 242–43

PPR (Philosophy and Phenomenological Research), 94–99, 111, 161–71, 180, 221

pragmatism, 8, 33, 39–40, 53, 56–57, 61, 166, 181–82, 226

praktognosia, 27

Prall, David, 56

pregnancy, 209–10

preservation, 211

Price, H. H., 245

Princeton University, 136, 139–40, 194, 227, 232; Calvinist roots of, 33

Principia Mathematica (Russell and Whitehead), 70

process philosophy, 56–57, 255

"Program and First Platform of Six Realists, The" (Perry, Pitkin, et al.), 36

Psathas, George, 207–8, 224

psychiatry, 224–25

psychologism, 10–11, 113, 240

xenophobia, 79–86
Xirau, Joaquín, 161

Yale Alumni Magazine, 129–30, 141–42
Yale Daily News, 226, 228, 230

Yale University, 33, 120, 123, 129, 134, 140–42, 179, 184, 189–94, 225–31, 316n28
Young, Iris Marion, 7, 201–17, 223, 239, 252

Zaner, Richard, 114, 181, 239